Post-Global Aesthetics

Latin American Literatures in the World

Literaturas Latinoamericanas en el Mundo

Edited by / Editado por
Gesine Müller

Editorial Board
Ana Gallego (Granada)
Gustavo Guerrero (Paris)
Héctor Hoyos (Stanford)
Ignacio Sánchez Prado (St. Louis)
Mariano Siskind (Harvard)
Patricia Trujillo (Bogotá)

Volume 14 / Volumen 14

Post-Global Aesthetics

21st Century Latin American Literatures and Cultures

Edited by
Gesine Müller and Benjamin Loy

DE GRUYTER

This project has received funding from the European Research Council (ERC) under the European Union's Horizon 2020 Research and Innovation programme – Grant Agreement Number 646714

European Research Council
Established by the European Commission

ISBN 978-3-11-153058-1
e-ISBN (PDF) 978-3-11-076214-3
e-ISBN (EPUB) 978-3-11-076221-1
ISSN 2513-0757
DOI https://doi.org/10.1515/9783110762143

This work is licensed under the Creative Commons Attribution-NonCommercial-NoDerivatives 4.0 International License. For details go to https://creativecommons.org/licenses/by-nc-nd/4.0/.

Creative Commons license terms for re-use do not apply to any content (such as graphs, figures, photos, excerpts, etc.) not original to the Open Access publication and further permission may be required from the rights holder. The obligation to research and clear permission lies solely with the party re-using the material.

Library of Congress Control Number: 2022940838

Bibliographic information published by the Deutsche Nationalbibliothek
The Deutsche Nationalbibliothek lists this publication in the Deutsche Nationalbibliografie; detailed bibliographic data are available on the Internet at http://dnb.dnb.de.

© 2024 the author(s), published by Walter de Gruyter GmbH, Berlin/Boston
This volume is text- and page-identical with the hardback published in 2023.
The book is published open access at www.degruyter.com.

Typesetting: Integra Software Services Pvt.

www.degruyter.com

Contents

Benjamin Loy (University of Vienna) and Gesine Müller (University of Cologne)
Towards a Post-Global Age: Introductory Notes about the End(s) of Globalization and World Literature —— 1

1 Approaching the Post-Global (from Latin American Perspectives)

Gesine Müller (University of Cologne)
The Post-Global Challenge in the Debate over World Literature: Latin American Perspectives —— 11

Alexis Radisoglou (Durham University)
Ethnoplanetarity as Post-Globality: Four Theses and a Postscript on a Contemporary Decolonial Constellation —— 29

Jorge J. Locane (University of Oslo)
Sobre el mundo, sobre el imperio: notas conjeturales para pensar el tono apocalíptico de ciertas humanidades actuales —— 45

Romina Wainberg (Stanford University)
Writing about Writing Amidst the End of Worlds: An Invitation —— 61

2 Anthropocene Narratives I: Geo-Poetics

Ursula K. Heise (University of California, Los Angeles)
The Vanishing Metropolis: Environmental Justice and Urban Narrative in Latin America —— 77

Jobst Welge (University of Leipzig)
Post-Natural Histories: Mimicry and Deep Time in Pola Oloixarac's *Las Constelaciones Oscuras* and Carlos Fonseca's *Museo Animal* —— 95

Jenny Haase (University of Halle-Wittenberg)
"Para contarte de la isla": entrelazamientos corporales, ecológicos y económicos en la poesía de Rosabetty Muñoz —— 115

3 Anthropocene Narratives II: Exhausted Resources

Nicolás Campisi (Georgetown University)
Documentary Mines: Archives of Ecohorror in the Anthropocene —— 131

Azucena Castro (Stockholm University/University of Buenos Aires) and Luis I. Prádanos (Miami University)
Retos estéticos del postdesarrollo: imaginarios no extractivos y futuros postfósiles en medios culturales andinos —— 149

Jan Knobloch (University of Cologne)
Globalization Reversed: Reading Scales of Collapse in Pedro Mairal's *El año del desierto* —— 169

4 Digital Worlds: Trends and Traps

Carolina Gainza C. (Universidad Diego Portales/Santiago de Chile)
Pensar la condición digital desde la literatura digital latinoamericana: apropiaciones, decolonización y tecnodiversidad —— 191

Carolina Ferrer (Université du Québec à Montréal)
Convergencias y divergencias de la globalización y las humanidades digitales: constitución, circulación y desaparición de tendencias conceptuales —— 209

Benjamin Loy (University of Vienna)
La novela (post-)global como trampa: *Kentukis* (2018) de Samanta Schweblin —— 223

5 New Narratives of Migration and Displacement

Gustavo Guerrero (Université Paris-Seine)
Perder el mundo: la poesía venezolana ante la experiencia de la migración —— 249

Ignacio M. Sánchez Prado (Washington University, St. Louis)
México, Estados Unidos y la era post-global: De la cultura fronteriza a la nueva cuestión binacional —— 259

Benjamin Loy and Gesine Müller
Towards a Post-Global Age
Introductory Notes about the End(s) of Globalization and World Literature

Thinking about how to approach the question, "What comes after globalization?" shaped early deliberations around this book project in early 2020. Ideas about what a post-global world might look like departed from the increasing indications of a fundamental historical shift: after thirty years of shaping the world, the current phase of accelerated globalization appeared to be coming to an end. However, if at that moment our reflections focused on phenomena such as climate change, global migrations and inequality, and the surge of neonationalism across the globe, nobody could presage how the soon to follow events of the Covid-19 pandemic and the war in Ukraine would intensify this notion of finding ourselves at a historical threshold, where the exhaustion of the globalist project becomes evident once and for all.

From 1989 onwards, the historical present has undoubtedly been dominated by optimistic and progressive discourses of all-embracing global integration, borne by the ideals of economic and social liberalization (King 2017). It has also been steeped in optimism, both in terms of the philosophy of history (Fukuyama 1992) and in terms of technology, as promoted by the digital revolution. However, since at least the turn of the millennium, the dark sides and asymmetries of what Ulrich Beck has termed the "world risk society" (Beck 1999) – with its globally networked societies, economies, and cultures – have also grown more and more apparent (Stiglitz 2002, Appadurai 2006, Hirst et al. 2009, Turek 2017, Diamond 2018, Hüther et al. 2019). Today, there are unmistakable, fundamental cracks in the formerly hegemonic manner in which the world has been ordered and perceived from a Western perspective. Over the past fifteen years, wide-ranging developments have debunked the optimistic paradigm of globalism – whose manifold inequalities and dead ends certainly have been glaringly visible for most of the world's population since 1989. It is telling that only with the accelerated succession of global crisis also affecting the Western centers of this globalist optimism – financial crises, epidemics, military conflicts, and new waves of both migration and displacement – a new process of reflection on the past decades has been triggered.

Benjamin Loy, University of Vienna
Gesine Müller, University of Cologne

∂ Open Access. © 2023 the author(s), published by De Gruyter. [cc) BY-NC-ND] This work is licensed under the Creative Commons Attribution-NonCommercial-NoDerivatives 4.0 International License.
https://doi.org/10.1515/9783110762143-001

All of these recent trends have led to a manifest exhaustion of said globalization paradigm – yet they have not dismantled related forms of global connectedness (O'Sullivan 2019). Hence, when we invoke the advent of a post-global era, this makes no claim that worldwide phenomena of networking and integration have been discounted or discarded. Rather, this emerging concept is considered an attempt at a critical discursive and epistemological response to the production, consequences, and asymmetries of globality itself. The term of "post-globality" has been little used until now (Flew 2020). However, we consider it a useful framework to discuss the complex implications of the mentioned process of exhaustion of the globalization-paradigm, as it allows for subsuming and critically discussing other approaches to these phenomena, while not losing sight of new constellations of global relatedness.

Contrary to concepts such as "deglobalization" (Bello 2005, James 2018), which are fixated on world trade and economic policy dimensions, our notion of post-globality not only aims to integrate the philosophical and aesthetic dimensions of the problematic economic, ecological, social, and technological dimensions of exhaustion, but to understand them as fundamentally dialectic. The prevailing notions of a "[n]egative globality" as "the underside of the great narrative of global modernization" (Moreiras 2001: 51) and the loss and exhaustion of a determinate kind of world (Siskind 2019) are accompanied by the creation of new perceptions and inventions of alternative (post-)global forms of life.

Doubtlessly, much has been said in recent years in the debates for and against the legitimacy of "global" perspectives in the fields of literary and cultural studies, particularly within the paradigm of World Literature mirroring these sort of philosophical and political discussions (Apter 2013, Moser/Simonis 2014, Cheah 2016, Mufti 2016, Müller/Siskind 2019). In some cases, the terms of "world" or "globality" have been dismissed and supplemented by alternative concepts such as "planetarity" (Spivak 1999), "other globes" (Ferdinand et al. 2019), or "earth literature" (Stockhammer 2018). This is not the place to recall or to examine these concepts in detail. Rather, we would like to highlight the shared assumption of these works regarding the potential of fiction and narrative as a place of world-making and of (self-)reflexivity about perceptions of living in a world shaped by processes of globalization. "Globalization" is a phenomenon that – due to its complexity and abstractness – can only be grasped in the form of (ever-competing) imaginaries (Pratt 2018) and narrative(s) – as recent publications in the field of political sciences, law, and economy have also underlined (Roberts/Lamp 2021). For what the contributions in this book aspire to is less an intervention into ongoing conceptual debates, even if some of the articles do address this aspect, but more an investigation of concrete examples – texts, films, works of art – to show how processes of transforming notions of globality are represented and reflected in specific artistic practices.

Approaching the post-global in contemporary works of art (and particularly in literary texts) raises the question of how these works draw on discourses and images of globality on a thematic scale but also on the level of form. Numerous studies on world literature have posited the existence of a specific form of "global novel" (Hoyos 2015, Ganguly 2016) or of a so-called "plot of globalization" describing "the use by contemporary authors of the traditional literary device of *entrelacement*, or 'multi-strand narration,' as a means of representing the intricate and problematic ties that bind us together in the age of globalized capitalism" (Beecroft 2016: 195). However, if we assume that "literatures operating in certain cultural environments are prone to employ specific formal features adapted to the specific contexts in which they find themselves" (Beecroft 2016: 195), the crucial question would be how post-global aesthetics with their increased conscience of the dialectical character of globalization reflect this in their creation of artistic forms, using for example dialectical continua such as connection/exclusion or entanglement/disentanglement. Metaphor and allegory as preferred forms of representation of globality come into play, as well as genre and narratives forms, such as dystopian narratives or archival fictions. Further, we assume that all kinds of post-global aesthetics are crucially influenced by a questioning of the epistemological conditions and implications of changing notions of the world and the question of what practical, normative dimensions contribute to processes of "world-making" in the current period of diverse and rapid upheavals in global systems of order. The incorporation of non-Western epistemologies (Santos 2008), such as indigenous cosmologies and post-anthropocentric approaches, as well as literary traditions of the post-colonial Global South (Cheah 2016, Burns 2019) represent an important dimension of most of the contributions in this book.

With its focus on these sorts of transformations on the level of aesthetic form, this book equally opts for a shift of perspective regarding the fact that a predominant strain of research within world literature studies over the past decade has focused on material exchange processes of a globalized market (Müller 2022). With this volume we seek to move away from questions of the spatial widening of material circulation in order to focus in on the artistic exploration of the post-global in Latin American literatures and cultures. However critically the institution of literature and the status of this medium may be considered in the present, we insist on its role as a privileged space for enacting discrepancies of perception, as Jacques Rancière postulates, pointing to its ability to intervene in the "relationship between practices and forms of visibility and modes of saying that carves up one or more common worlds" (Rancière 2011: 4). Especially in regard to the ambivalence of globalization processes, whose perception and assessment are characterized by divergent perspectives, we can take up Rancière's contention that literary works are able to depict this "distribution and [. . .] redistribution of space and time, place and identity, speech and noise, the visible and the invisible" as a paradigmatic illustration of the "distribution of the perceptible" (Rancière 2011: 4).

The example of Latin America serves as an observational microcosm of the ambivalences posed by the globalized experience of the world over the past decades. The past three decades of intensified global interconnectedness have neither solved nor prevented a myriad of problems in the region: ongoing massive social inequality, economic instability, the continued destruction of ecosystems, the persistence of endemic violence, new surges of political and social polarization, waves of migration, and failures of the state in some countries of the region, most notably Venezuela. In fact, one might hypothesize that many of the listed phenomena, especially in the economic and ecological realms, have been exacerbated, if not caused by the negative side effects of globalization processes, which have disproportionately impacted Latin America (García Canclini 2014). All of these effects have been navigated and enacted in many works of 21st-century Latin American literature. Especially since the late 2000s, as the contributions in this book aim to show, numerous distinct aesthetics emerged, aesthetics that squarely address the experience of "world exhaustion" outlined above.

These questions are discussed in the five chapters of this book, the first of them being dedicated to theoretical approaches to the problem of the post-global from Latin American perspectives. The next four chapters are organized around thematic focuses, each of which represents a different symptom of today's globalization phase which lends itself to the exploration of post-global aesthetics. The contributions of chapters two and three focus on problems subsumed under the concept of Anthropocene narratives (Dürbeck/Hüpkes 2020). Within globalized economic and social relationships, the ambivalences of world exhaustion processes and asymmetries are perhaps most readily visible in the global flows of resources and merchandise and their attendant ecological consequences. Over the past thirty years, with the liberalization and expansion of world trade; the addition of enormous new consumer markets, especially in Asia; and the march of technological progress, the exploitation of Latin American resources has escalated to an unprecedented scale. The global asymmetries of these processes are made visible by differing local perspectives. Products which get sold in the supermarkets or processed in the factories of Europe, North America, and Asia are often sourced from Latin America, where they are extracted using processes with deeply problematic ecological and social implications. The destructive interconnections of global production chains across the region range from clearcut logging in the Brazilian Amazon, to soybean monoculture in Argentina for cattle feed, to the extraction of Chilean lithium deposits for electric car batteries. Consequently, these issues increasing appear in contemporary Latin American literature (and other art forms) (Hoyos 2019). At the same time, these writings and media draw on an immense corpus of imaginaries and fictions that look back on Latin America's long history as an arena of (post)colonial resource extraction and the corresponding elimination of ecosystems complete with their human, zoological, and botanical diversity (Beckman 2013). It is against this backdrop that the post-global literatures of Latin America portray the problematic ecological and social repercussions of the region's involvement in the contemporary and historical dimensions of global economic cycles. Apart from this, in the context of discussions around defining the Anthropocene as the latest geohistorical era, Latin American perspectives (Ulloa 2017) have increasingly tackled the collapse of traditional epistemological borders between humans and nature (Latour 1999) as a subject for aesthetic reflection.

As the contributions to chapter four show, a further point of interest when taking a post-global aesthetics perspective on Latin American literatures and cultures is the revolutionary potential of the digital transformation that has already had a radical impact on Latin American societies. Over the past twenty years, this key aspect of a post-global writing practice has drawn increasing attention from both scholarship and publishing (Gainza 2018). Experiences of digitality are invariably marked by how forcefully it penetrates virtually every aspect of human life. They are also shaped fundamentally by its ambiguous utility, which pairs productive world creation with new phenomena of affective alienation and exploitation (Staab 2019, Nassehi 2019). Although the egalitarian promise of the world wide web was initially at the core of works engaging with the onward march of digitalization, more recently the focus has been placed on global asymmetries (Chan 2014), stemming from the West's technological head start, and on regional opportunities. Here, literature exposes the tensions between world creation, in the sense of new ways of enacting contemporary life in the digital realm, and phenomena of large-scale world exhaustion extending as far as the breakdown of mental health caused by media consumption, which must always also be inextricably considered "world consumption" in the context of a global audience.

The final chapter of this book addresses the dimensions of migration and displacement representing an ongoing challenge – though tragedy might be a more suitable term – for the post-global world and for Latin America in particular. Even after the age of 'classic' exile and migration literature from Latin America, which came out of the politically repressive regimes of the 1970s and 1980s, issues of forced displacement and migration remain a central aesthetic subject. Latin American literatures especially draw on new phenomena of world creation and exploration, as Siskind (2019) describes with regard to "end of the world" experiences. The hope that the prosperity pledged by globalization would also offer Latin American societies an exit from past social, political, and economic polarizations and instabilities has proved illusory. In many cases, links to new transnational phenomena have had their own grievous repercussions in specific national contexts. For example, Mexico's decision to sign the NAFTA free trade agreement with the United States and Canada did not bring newfound economic and social stability. Quite the contrary, the arrangement caused serious domestic economic upheaval and an unprecedented wave of violence, accompanied by ever-clearer indications that the state was failing. Similarly, the example of Argentina's national declaration of bankruptcy in 2001 gave early evidence that individual countries' dependency on international legal and financial regimes, such as those of the IMF or WTO, could, in some cases, wreak havoc on their societies. Even in places such as Venezuela or Bolivia, where political projects were launched within alternative transnational ideological and economic alliances in the early 2000s, their political and social horizons two decades later are dominated by civil war-like conflicts and massive waves of displacement and migration. Those same trends continue to affect the chronically unstable countries of Central America as well as Haiti in the Caribbean. Especially given ever-tightening US immigration policies, more and more of these countries' nationals emigrate to other Latin American countries, establishing new patterns of intra-regional migration and producing new forms of migration narratives as well.

This book is the outcome of a conference entitled "Post-Global Aesthetics: 21st Century Latin American Literatures and Cultures" that took place in June 2021. It was the closing conference of the European Research Council Consolidator Grant project, "Reading Global. Constructions of World Literature and Latin America", realized at University of Cologne between 2015 and 2021. The shift in perspective from the project's focus on material dimensions of the global book market to post-global aesthetics of contemporary Latin American literatures allowed for looking back on the achievements and the limits of this project whose realization would not have been possible without the generous funding by the European Research Council, the commitment of its team members, and the exchange with numerous colleagues from all over the world. We would like to thank to all of them, as well as to Valeska Díaz, Ceylan Küfner, and Jordan Lee Schnee for their valuable work in realizing the conference and editing this book's manuscript.

Works Cited

Appadurai, Arjun (2006): *Fear of Small Numbers: An Essay on the Geography of Anger.* Durham, NC: Duke University Press.
Apter, Emily (2013): *Against World Literature: On the Politics of Untranslatability.* London: Verso.
Beck, Ulrich (1999): *World Risk Society.* Cambridge, UK: Polity Press.
Beckman, Ericka (2013): *Capital Fictions: The Literature of Latin America's Export Age.* Minneapolis, MN: University of Minneapolis Press.
Beecroft, Alexander (2016): "On the Tropes of Literary Ecology: The Plot of Globalization". In: Habjan, Jernej/Imlinger, Fabienne (eds.): *Globalizing Literary Genres: Literature, History, Modernity.* London: Routledge, pp. 195–212.
Bello, Walden (2005): *Deglobalization: Ideas for a New World Economy.* London: Zed Books.
Burns, Lorna (2019): *Postcolonialism After World Literature: Relation, Equality, Dissent.* London: Bloomsbury.
Chan, Anita Say (2014): *Networking Peripheries: Technological Futures and the Myth of Digital Universalism.* Cambridge, MA: MIT Press.
Cheah, Pheng (2016): *What is a World? On Postcolonial Literature as World Literature.* Durham, NC: Duke University Press.
Diamond, Patrick (ed.) (2018): *The Crisis of Globalization: Democracy, Capitalism and Inequality in the Twenty-First Century.* London: I.B. Tauris.
Dürbeck, Gabriele/Hüpkes, Philip (2020) (eds.): *The Anthropocenic Turn. The Interplay Between Disciplinary and Interdisciplinary Responses to a New Age.* New York: Routledge.
Ferdinand, Simon et al. (ed.) (2019): *Other Globes: Past and Peripheral Imaginations of Globalization.* London: Palgrave Macmillan.
Flew, Terry (2020): "Globalization, Neo-Globalization and Post-Globalization: The Challenge of Populism and the Return of the National". In: *Global Media and Communication*, vol. 16, no. 1, pp. 19–39.
Fukuyama, Francis (1992): *The End of History and the Last Man.* New York: Free Press.
Gainza, Carolina (2018): *Narrativas y poéticas digitales en América Latina: Producción literaria en el capitalismo informacional.* Santiago de Chile: Cuarto propio.
Ganguly, Debjani (2016): *This Thing Called the World: The Contemporary Novel as Global Form.* Durham, NC: Duke University Press.
García Canclini, Néstor (2014): *Imagined Globalization.* Transl. George Yúdice. Durham, NC: Duke University Press.
Hirst, Paul et al. (2009): *Globalization in Question.* Cambridge, UK: Polity Press.
Hoyos, Héctor (2019): *Things with a History: Transcultural Materialism and the Literatures of Extraction in Contemporary Latin America.* New York: Columbia University Press.
—— (2015): *Beyond Bolaño. The Global Latin American Novel.* New York: Columbia University Press.
Hüther, Michael/Diermeier, Matthias/Goecke, Henry (2019): *Die erschöpfte Globalisierung. Zwischen transatlantischer Orientierung und chinesischem Weg.* Berlin/Heidelberg: Springer.
James, Harold (2018): "Deglobalization: The Rise of Disembedded Unilateralism". In: *Annual Review of Financial Economics*, vol. 10, pp. 219–237.

King, Stephen D. (2017): *Grave New World: The End of Globalization, the Return of History*. New Haven, CT: Yale University Press.
Latour, Bruno (1999): *Politiques de la nature: comment faire entrer les sciences en démocratie*. Paris: La Découverte.
Moreiras, Alberto (2001): *The Exhaustion of Difference. The Politics of Latin American Cultural Studies*. Durham, NC: Duke University Press.
Mufti, Aamir R. (2016): *Forget English! Orientalisms and World Literatures*. Cambridge, MA: Harvard University Press.
Moser, Christian/Simonis, Linda (eds.) (2014): *Figuren des Globalen. Weltbezug und Welterzeugung in Literatur, Kunst und Medien*. Göttingen: V&R Unipress.
Müller, Gesine (2022): *How is World Literature Made? Global Circulations of Latin American Literatures*. Berlin/Boston: De Gruyter.
Müller, Gesine/Siskind, Mariano (eds.) (2019): *World Literature, Cosmopolitanism, Globality: Beyond, Against, Post, Otherwise*. Berlin/Boston: De Gruyter.
Nassehi, Armin (2019): *Muster: Theorie der digitalen Gesellschaft*. Munich: Beck.
O'Sullivan, Michael (2019): *The Levelling: What's Next After Globalization*. New York: Public Affairs.
Pratt, Mary Louise (2018): *Los imaginarios planetarios*. Madrid: Aluvión.
Rancière, Jacques (2011): *Politics of Literature*. Transl. Julie Rose. Cambridge, UK: Polity Press.
Roberts, Anna/Lamp, Nicolas (2021): *Six Faces of Globalization. Who Wins, Who Loses, and Why It Matters*. Cambridge, MA: Harvard University Press.
Santos, Boaventura de Sousa (ed.) (2008): *Another Knowledge is Possible: Beyond Northern Epistemologies*. London: Verso.
Siskind, Mariano (2019): "Towards a Cosmopolitanism of Loss: An Essay About the End of the World". In: Müller, Gesine/Siskind, Mariano (eds.): *World Literature, Cosmopolitanism, Globality: Beyond, Against, Post, Otherwise*. Berlin/Boston: De Gruyter, pp. 205–235.
Spivak, Gayatri Chakravorty (1999): *Imperative zur Neuerfindung des Planeten / Imperatives to Re-Imagine the Planet*. Goetschel, Willi (ed.). Transl. Bernard Schweizer. Vienna: Passagen.
Staab, Philipp (2019): *Digitaler Kapitalismus – Markt und Herrschaft in der Ökonomie der Unknappheit*. Berlin: Suhrkamp.
Stiglitz, Joseph E. (2002): *Globalization and Its Discontents*. New York: W. W. Norton.
Stockhammer, Robert (2018): "World Literature or Earth Literature? Remarks on a Distinction". In: Müller, Gesine et al. (eds.): *Re-Mapping World Literature: Writing, Book Markets and Epistemologies between Latin America and the Global South*. Berlin/Boston: De Gruyter, pp. 211–224.
Turek, Jürgen (2017): *Globalisierung im Zwiespalt: Die postglobale Misere und Wege, sie zu bewältigen*. Bielefeld: Transcript.
Ulloa, Astrid (2017): "Dinámicas ambientales y extractivas en el siglo XXI: ¿Es la época del Antropoceno o del Capitaloceno en Latinoamérica?". In: *Desacatos*, no. 54, pp. 58–73.

1 Approaching the Post-Global (from Latin American Perspectives)

Gesine Müller
The Post-Global Challenge in the Debate over World Literature
Latin American Perspectives

During the post-global period of the past decade, the optimistic paradigm of globality, which had found its cultural-theory counterpart in new universalist and cosmopolitan discourses, was superseded once and for all. We have seen a growing exhaustion of the global project, compounded by experiences of multidimensional crises (Siskind 2019). Epidemics and pandemics, armed conflicts, and new waves of refugees and migration have all contributed to this, as have global phenomena of alienation and the ecological repercussions of human life and economic activity – repercussions that can no longer be ignored. The latest voices in the debate are now tackling these problems and asking whether the concept of world literature has in fact been overly complicit in globalization's political and economic dynamics. If so, these scholars argue, the concept itself is a dead end.

This essay will consider literary portrayals in order to show how the exhaustion of the global project has been reflected in Latin American literary production from the post-global period of the past decade. What notions of globality, and especially of exhaustion and new creation, have been developing within it? How can these trends be viewed in the context of the ongoing debate around world literature? I would like to address these questions in reference to four literary examples: the novel *La transmigración de los cuerpos* (2013) by the Mexican writer Yuri Herrera (translated into English as *The Transmigration of Bodies*, 2016); the short story *El jardinero nocturno* from the collection *Un verdor terrible* (2020a) by the Chilean Benjamín Labatut (translated into English as *When We Cease to Understand the World*, 2020b); the novel *Las constelaciones oscuras* (2015) by the Argentine author Pola Oloixarac (translated into English as *Dark Constellations*, 2019); and the novel *Los cuerpos del verano* (2019) by Martín Felipe Castagnet, also from Argentina, (translated into English as *Bodies of Summer*, 2017). All these works explore the theme of world creation/exhaustion by proceeding from narrative premises that involve epidemic experiences and/or dynamics of creation and exhaustion in increasingly digitalized worlds.

This ties into questions of how today's Latin American literatures are canonized as world literature (Müller 2020; Guerrero et al. 2020; Sánchez Prado 2021).

Gesine Müller, University of Cologne

However, I will not take this occasion to discuss market-oriented approaches or the market metaphor that has been inscribed in the debate around world literature. Rather, I will draw on processes of "worlding", a perspective Pheng Cheah (2016) introduced to this discussion. Especially during periods when political parties and decision-makers are rather bewildered by worldwide developments – as we have observed at various junctures of the global COVID-19 pandemic – and when capitalist structures and processes of globalization have been the targets of mounting criticism, while global asymmetries are ever more visible and glaring, there is substantial interest in literary texts that present new options for "world" creation. The current upheavals of 2020–21 have offered a fresh context for framing literary writing as an ethical-political force in a world to be created anew.

World Exhaustion/Creation

Against the backdrop of this debate over world literature and the conceptual problems it raises, this essay locates the notion of "world creation/exhaustion" through the viewpoint of Latin American studies. This notion holds three distinct layers of meaning:

1. In one sense, it denotes the exhaustion of globalization practices and the ways they are addressed in contemporary literary texts. Although the current phenomena of exhaustion and disillusionment can be traced further back, the 2008 financial and economic crisis can be seen as the turning point of an "exhausted globalization": the crisis "was interpreted simultaneously as a disaster of society and a distension of the political possibilities because its cause lay in an economic system that, molded by globalization, had fallen out of step with the standards of humanity" (Hüther et al. 2019: 8). Seen through the lenses of economics and the social sciences, the notion of an exhaustion of the current phase of globalization provides a unique entry point for envisioning a future form of globalization that is truly inclusive. Within cultural studies, we can liken the concept of exhaustion to the exhaustion of globalization postulated by economists (Hüther et al. 2019): a dynamic within which to identify central sets of intersecting questions. This also implies that even with a (nearly) unabated outward velocity, or even in the absence of structural changes, processes of growth and/or entanglement can "run out". This "vacancy", which will require more precise elaboration, increasingly serves in literature and film as a void in which new (world) creations emerge in an era lacking grand narratives.

Ultimately, the impression that the trends are changing course partly results from a sense that the various narratives about the increasingly overt global problems and asymmetries can no longer be strung together into a consistent story or systemic narrative (Tally 2019).
2. In a second, meta-linguistic sense, the concept of world creation/exhaustion also encompasses the exhaustion of theory about global processes, an exhaustion that goes hand in hand with real-world practices. The interplay between global development and theoretical production has developed to a point at which the notion of "world" is increasingly exhausted, although processes of "worlding" in literature are still being assigned meaning. Cheah (2016) reframes world literature on two levels. On one level, he argues that the very model of a capitalist market that girdles the whole globe yet obstructs worldwide community is countered by a model of the world derived from the narrative literature of the post-colonial South. On another level, he famously asserts that literature should be understood as a world-making activity.
3. The third dimension of the exhaustion concept pertains to the exhaustion of the earth's resources, which conversely exposes the problems with the "world" concept, as regions are unevenly responsible for and affected by it. The Latin American region is prototypical of this starkly apparent asymmetry. That is especially true of the concept of "exhaustion", which could scarcely have been deployed in any non-negative sense given modernity's logics of acceleration and growth (Rosa 2013). And this is precisely an area where current trends in Latin American literary production come into play, as they envision alternative imaginaries of the global beyond an acceleration dogma that is no longer economically, ecologically, or socially sustainable. Meanwhile, recent reactionary anti-globalist currents have provoked the question of how else such alternative perceptions of the world can be characterized, instead, using a dialectic of exhaustion and new creation that might also be politically progressive.

In that sense, the concept of world creation/exhaustion is deliberately framed as ambivalent. Invariably, the dynamic of exhaustion is also countered by a trend of creatively harnessing world creation processes; their potential to imagine new worlds that move between global and local spheres plays out particularly in literary and cultural production. Along these lines, Anna Katharina Schaffner points to the inherent link between creation and exhaustion in her genealogical study *Exhaustion: A History* (2016), which focuses on individual and collective states of human exhaustion. She stresses the importance of fictionalized exhaustion scenarios to help us grasp the phenomenon while also highlighting literature's power to create anew: "Fictions [dealing with exhaustion] also form culture – they do not just mirror certain historical dynamics, values, and medical paradigms but also help to create, to complicate, and to question them" (Schaffner 2016: 14). She also introduces a further aspect that, in my view, is another core prerequisite for any analysis of the concept of exhaustion: the transdisciplinary perspective. Schaffner is principally referring to the socio-historical, medical, and aesthetic meanings whose effects intersect here[1]. My own broader definition of world creation/exhaustion, which I alluded to earlier, also incorporates dimensions of economics, ecology, technology, and cultural theory.

Digitalization/Pandemic

In the context of current phenomena of world creation/exhaustion, I would like to single out two aspects and illuminate them – separately and in their entanglements – via the examples of post-global Latin American literature listed above: digitalization and pandemics. After all, the question of how digital revolution is connected to post-global ideas of the world took on a fresh urgency and topicality during the world coronavirus shutdown, when personal, social, and professional activities were relegated to digital spaces to an unprecedented degree, further blurring the lines between disparate realms of human life under the umbrella of digital ubiquity. Experiences of digitality are invariably and fundamentally shaped by the force with which the digital penetrates virtually every aspect of human life, as well as by its ambiguous utility, which combines productive world creation with new phenomena of affective alienation and exploitation (Staab 2019; Nassehi 2019). The possibilities of endless connection and new community are juxtaposed against experiences of emotional exhaustion and overload. Yet at the same time, globalized experiences of contamination present a crisis for imaginaries of an infinitely extensible world that can be limitlessly connected. Latin America, past and present, serves once again as a paradigmatic space of experience and observation in reference to epidemics, as portrayed by numerous texts of post-global literature since 2008. These epidemic fictions are not always based on factual history, although the AIDS pandemic did inspire an entire genre of such "viral" writings (Meruane 2014).

---

1 "In order properly to understand the many historical transformations of the idea of exhaustion, an interdisciplinary view that considers medical, sociohistorical, and aesthetic developments as interconnected process is essential" (Schaffner 2016: 14).

Rather, epidemics frequently function as allegorical pretexts for portraying experiences of world exhaustion. In terms of genre, these same experiences of utter insecurity caused by contaminated existence have sparked a renaissance of utopian, dystopian, and science fiction.

These writings invariably also address the violation of established borders of humanness in the domains of trans and post-humanism as they inspect the opacity and transgressive tendencies of new biological and technological phenomena on a narrative level. Here, literature exposes the tension between world creation, in the sense of new ways of enacting contemporary life in the digital realm, and phenomena of large-scale world exhaustion, extending as far as the breakdown of mental health through media consumption, which must always also be inextricably considered "world consumption" in the context of a global public. Along the way, literature itself has been transformed by medial changes. Simultaneously, it serves as a medium for reflecting on these transformation processes. This is especially true in Latin America, where literature "over the last decade [. . .] has sought to reveal the modes through which Latin American society participates in the spread of ubiquitous technological flows, confronting and sometimes overcoming the social barriers that technology establishes" (Gentic/Bush 2016: 12–13). The depth and breadth of these creative responses will be visible as we consider four literary examples of very recent Latin American literatures that deal with world creation/exhaustion in epidemic and/or digital contexts.

Yuri Herrera, *La transmigración de los cuerpos* (2013)

Herrera's *La transmigración de los cuerpos* (2013) confronts us with experiences of world exhaustion, as we encounter a seemingly post-apocalyptic world in which the residents of an outwardly desolate metropolis are all quarantined at home due to an epidemic. The novel's setting is marked by violence and prostitution and can be read as a staging of the capitalist market in its problematic legal and illegal dimensions. Various interpreters of the novel, such as Betina Keizman (2019) and Eduardo Becerra (2016), have pointed to the problematic production and power mechanisms of a neoliberal economic system that characterizes the exhausted society in the novel. Becerra asserts that in contemporary Latin American literature, this system is often portrayed in terms of the tensions between surplus and scarcity. In Herrera's book, infection and disease present the critical points of departure for the plot, which navigates questions of control over life and death, body and immunity, and state and para-state control structures (Keizman 2019: 171–72). The novel opens with a concrete experience of deficiency and exhaustion on the part of the main character, El Alfaqueque:

> A scurvy thirst awoke him and he got up to get a glass of water, but the tap was dry and all that trickled out was a thin stream of dank air. Eyeing the third of mezcal on the table with venom, he got the feeling it was going to be an awful day. He had no way of knowing it already was, had been for hours, truly awful, much more awful than the private little inferno he'd built himself on booze. (Herrera 2016: Ch. 1)

And so the novel begins. Soon, after El Alfaqueque goes out into the street on that ungodly day, the narrator states:

> What worried him most was not knowing what to fear; he was used to fending off the unexpected, but even the unexpected had its limits; you could trust that when you opened the door every morning the world wouldn't be emptied of people. This, though, was like falling asleep in an elevator and waking up with the doors open on a floor you never knew existed. (Herrera 2016: Ch. 1)

This new space the novel introduces is one of world creation/exhaustion: a hollowed-out world dominated by violence and death, as demonstrated by the subplot of Herrera's main character arranging an exchange of two corpses. Through the epidemic that shapes his narrative space, Herrera creates a moment of stagnation in the unnamed Mexican metropolis, which is otherwise a loud and lively underworld. His narrative is set in an atmosphere of deathly silence: the populace is frightened, and the streets have grown vacant ever since the news spread of a virus that causes the infected to cough blood before meeting a swift death. Because the pathogen can be transmitted not only from human to human, but also via a specific insect vector, many residents have stopped leaving home entirely. Only at the end of the novel is a treatment announced that renders the virus survivable, and people begin to relax again. During the course of the novel, however, Herrera's protagonist is one of the few people still moving around the city: whether to arrange his business and negotiate "deals" between various criminal parties, such as the titular exchange of dead bodies, or to hunt for an open pharmacy where he can buy condoms and pursue a love affair with his neighbor La Tres Veces Rubia.

The city's nightmarish atmosphere often verges on the surreal (Herrera 2013: 9, 96); terror casts real experience in an even starker light. However, humorous elements too continually color the epidemic's portrayal. In the end, El Alfaqueque only gains the affections of his love interest, La Tres Veces Rubia, who had previously paid him no attention, due to the unusual circumstances of her self-isolation.

As both the love story and Alfaqueque's business dealings progress, the unique silence pervades the city (Herrera 2013: 10, 38, 82). There is not even the slightest breeze, and only near the end of the narrative, with the conclusion of the (temporary) state of emergency, does a storm arrive. The silence is so utter and so eschatological that even the soapbox preacher at the nearby park, who normally proclaims the end of the world, is struck speechless:

> There were a few people out and about, but more like ephemeral grubs than lords of the land. A few in cars with the windows rolled up. In a park three blocks away, the man who used to predict the end of days, now alone, in silence, thrown off. A guy in a white robe crossing the street with quick steps. And pharmacies, two-bit pharmacies, open. (Herrera 2016: Ch. 2)

Nevertheless, the motif of the epidemic is used to depict not only ubiquitous death, fear, and silence, but also a special intensity of life that can only develop in such an emergency. A prime example is the love affair with La Tres Veces Rubia, "a burning miracle of flesh" (Herrera 2016: Ch. 4), which occurs during this stagnant period. Another is the protagonist's encounter with a group of men at a strip club. In violation of the usually fixed, unspoken hierarchy between paying johns and female sex workers, many men are now sleeping on or under the tables ("like really sleeping, not booze-induced sleeping", Herrera 2016: Ch. 4), while others are just chatting with the prostitutes, leaving out the usual condescending sexualized gestures: "They haven't been out for days, he heard Óscar say behind him. Claim it's too dangerous but if you ask me, this is their chance of a lifetime" (Herrera 2016: Ch. 4).

The government barely plays any role anymore under these circumstances in which life is exhausted and created anew. At one point, an official announcement arrives about the general situation, which it claims will soon normalize ("everything would be back to normal any minute now, that it was essential to exercise extreme caution but not to panic", Herrera 2016: Ch. 2), a message that seems almost grotesque considering the novel's plot. Life in this post-apocalyptic place strikes readers as anything but normal. El Alfaqueque takes the message as "a reassuring little pat on the head to say Any silence is purely coincidental" (Herrera 2016: Ch. 2). Meanwhile, Soifer (2019: 38) interprets this message as the state's concession that it lacks solutions. The government cannot combat the emergency with anything beyond that "pat on the head", as it has lost control of the situation. The only appearance by representatives of the state, Soifer points out, is when the protagonist encounters a soldier who is enforcing the quarantine rules. Overall, the state clearly can no longer guarantee its citizens' safety and, following neoliberal principals, is now only protecting the workings of the market and entrusting all other domains to its logic.

In terms of this narrative space beyond the scope of state structures, *La transmigración de los cuerpos* (2013) is in line with Herreras's earlier novels, especially *Trabajos del reino* (2004) and *Señales que precederán al fin del mundo* (2009) (Soifer 2019: 34). All three works are connected by the guiding metaphor of *transmigración*, which in Spanish can refer to both human migration and the transmigration of souls. In *Trabajos del reino*, Keizman (2019: 172) identifies the protagonist's *transmigración* to become an artist and poet in the framework of a drug cartel while in *Señales que precederán al fin del mundo*, the *transmigración* represents an explicit exchange of bodies and identities. In *La transmigración de los cuerpos*, bodies become commodities and death creates work in an omnipresent fight for survival, as the life-threatening ramifications of modern post-global society become tangible.

Overall, we can observe that Herrera's novel portrays the neoliberal and post-global society as the root cause of an exhausted world in the realms of the professional, the social community, and the sovereignty of citizens, placing a particular emphasis on the debasement of humanity and the human body. At the same time – and this is equally central to dynamics of exhaustion and new creation – the novel also makes reference to new spaces and dynamics that only emerge as a result of the emergency and that particularly shape the characters' sexual and emotional experiences. The text can be interpreted as a global Latin American novel – fully in line with Hoyos's (2015) definition – that depicts Mexican themes of violence and death in the context of governmental and paragovernmental power structures and then expands these structures beyond local contexts to symbolize the exhausting experience of the post-global period. Literary scholars (including Becerra 2016) have read Herrera's novel as an example of the rise of apocalyptic dystopias in Latin America, whose skepticism they attribute to the manifold socio-cultural and economic crisis of post-global society.

Benjamín Labatut, "El jardinero nocturno" (2020)

In "El jardinero nocturno", the Chilean[2] author Benjamín Labatut also employs dystopian elements within a setting that otherwise resembles real-world experiences and also contains nonfictional episodes from the history of science. The text is set in a Chilean mountain village, which is left unnamed. The opening of

---

[2] Labatut was born in Rotterdam in 1980 as the son of a diplomat and grew up in various places (The Hague, Buenos Aires, and Lima); he has lived permanently in Chile since 1994.

this text, which concludes his book *El verdor terrible* (published in 2020), likewise confronts the reader with a menacing situation:

> It is a vegetable plague, spreading from tree to tree. Unstoppable, invisible, a hidden rot, unseeing, unseen by the eyes of the world. Was it born of the deep dark earth? Was it brought to the surface by the mouths of the tiniest creatures? A fungus, perhaps? No, it travels faster than spores, it breeds inside tree roots, buried in their wooden hearts. An ancient, crawling evil. Kill it. Kill it with fire. Light it up and watch it burn, torch all those sickly beeches, firs and giant oaks that have stood the test of time, douse their trunks wounded from a thousand insect bites. Dying now, diseased and dying, dead as they stand. Let it burn and watch the flames reach up to the sky, for left alone it will consume the world, feeding on the death of others, nurtured by all the green grass turned grey. Quiet now, listen. Listen to it grow. (Labatut 2020b: Part I)

Labatut presents an apocalyptic scenario: an unknown blight has been attacking tree roots and spreading rapidly. Centuries-old trees fall victim to it, and their trunks are eaten by pests. A voice sounds an appeal to stop the plague by fire in order to prevent "an ancient, crawling evil" from destroying the larger world, but foremost what is left of natural vegetation. The same text, which is divided into isolated episodes revolving around the narrator's encounters with the "night gardener", later mentions a fire that has almost entirely burned down an old-growth forest near the village. A connection is implied between the opening sequence and this fire, but it is left vague.

Given the ambiguity of portrayals of world exhaustion/creation – vacillating between destruction and new creation – Labatut's text ought to be read in the context of the larger volume in which it appears[3]. As a book, *El verdor terrible* (2020a) is formally difficult to classify. Some critics have called it a "novel", others a collection of standalone short stories, some of which have essayistic aspects. Labatut combines lucid scientific history with mellifluous yet precise language and fictional elements in a successful aesthetic response to the question of the knowledge's limits. Here, literature contextualizes the boundaries and ambiguities of scientific knowledge in order, ultimately, to convey the incomprehensible, destructive, and sometimes even bizarre facets of scientific progress. With examples spanning from the chemist Fritz Haber to the mathematician Alexander Grothendieck to Heisenberg and Schrödinger, Labatut shows how scientists push thought to the very edge. The novel is suffused with the idea that there is no such thing as purely beneficial progress, and that even the most magnificent inventions hold the potential to harm humanity. "El jardinero nocturno" exhibits

---

[3] Adrian Nathan West's English translation, titled *When We Cease to Understand the World*, was shortlisted for the International Booker Prize 2021, which dramatically increased the text's circulation.

that same ambivalent dynamic. The preceding chapters in the volume include detailed, factual accounts of the research of various scientists whom the night gardener then mentions to the narrator. Some important background behind the events of "El jardinero nocturno" can be found in the third chapter of the volume, "El corazón del corazón", which describes some of the context around Alexander Grothendieck's withdrawal from mathematics. This chapter discusses the ecological catastrophe that Grothendieck predicted for humanity alongside his idea that some outside creature, which he called *le rêveur* and eventually equated with God, spoke to him in his dreams. Some readers might hear echoes of this in the enigmatic voice that warns of global destruction in the opening of "El jardinero nocturno".

On an evening walk with his dog in the remote Chilean mountain village, which is only inhabited in summertime, the narrator meets the title character, a man who only gardens at night out of consideration for the plants, which are sleeping then – as though anesthetized – and therefore cannot feel their transplantation. Labatut's narrative centers on brief, individual episodes surrounding the narrator's acquaintanceship with the night gardener and the latter's stories of clashes between nature and science. For example, during a walk in the woods, the narrator and his seven-year-old daughter stumble upon two dead dogs. All signs point to poisoning as their cause of death: "there are many deadly chemicals used for gardening, and there are many wonderful gardens in this place" (Labatut 2020b: Part III). The lushness of the many beautiful, well-kept gardens is inextricably linked with this lethal substance, an ambivalent episode straddling creation and destruction that typifies Labatut's perspective.

Frustrated with the poor growth in his garden, the narrator reaches out to the night gardener, who previously told him the history of fertilizer during one of their encounters. The German chemist Fritz Haber, the inventor of modern nitrogen fertilizer, was also the first person to invent a weapon of mass destruction, chlorine gas, which was deployed in the First World War. Paradoxically, his fertilizer – which the press called "Bread from the Air" because it harnessed airborne nitrogen – also saved hundreds of millions of people from starvation. The side effect of which, in turn, is today's overpopulation and the risk of exhausting the earth's resources.

In the final episode, the night gardener tells his own story. Formerly a mathematician, he was beginning a promising career when he learned about fellow mathematician Alexander Grothendieck. Grothendieck had revolutionized geometry in the 1960s, but at age 40, at the height of his international success, he abruptly quit mathematics for a life of solitude in the Pyrenees. The night gardener followed in Grothendieck's footsteps, reacting to family and health problems but also to the insight that mathematics – not the atom bomb, computers, biological warfare, or climate change – would change the world forever. Indeed, he believed that mathematical insights would transform the planet "to the point where, in a couple of decades at most, we would simply not be able to grasp what being human really meant" (Labatut 2020b: Part VI). He gives the example of quantum mechanics, which has vastly reshaped contemporary human life through the experience of accelerating digitalization (the internet, mobile phones, computers with artificial intelligence). Yet already there was no human left, he said, who truly understood quantum mechanics or could fully explain its workings (Labatut 2020a: 209). According to the narrator, these pessimistic visions of the future led the night gardener to devote himself to his garden and abandon science.

Labatut takes this characterization of modern science, according to which the proliferation of mathematical knowledge has surpassed human comprehension and ultimately defied it – even inverted it to a certain degree – and juxtaposes a parallel description of a natural phenomenon in which exuberant fertility foreshadows death. As the two men look at the oldest tree in the narrator's garden, a lemon tree, the night gardener tells him about lemon trees' brilliant, wasteful, and tragic fates:

> When they come to the end of their life cycle, they put out a final, massive crop of lemons. In their last spring their flowers bud and blossom in enormous bunches and fill the air with a smell so sweet that it stings your nostrils from two blocks away; then their fruits ripen all at once, whole limbs break off due to their excessive weight, and after a few weeks the ground is covered with rotting lemons. It is a strange sight, he said, to see such exuberance before death. (Labatut 2020b: Part VI)

Here, fruitfulness takes on a monstrous quality; vitality and bounty constitute nothing but the excess that precedes death. However, there is no accurate way to identify that moment of self-destruction. In this case, someone would have to bring themselves to chop down the lemon tree and determine its age by the rings of its trunk. Because neither the narrator nor the night gardener is prepared to do so, the timing of the tree's imminent exhaustion remains uncertain.

Pola Oloixarac, *Las constelaciones oscuras* (2015)

Pola Oloixarac's novel *Las constelaciones oscuras* (2015) portrays the dynamics of creation and exhaustion in a fictional digitalized world that is being reshaped by at least three major pioneering projects: efforts to process data inside living tissue; the development of an artificial immune system for the entire earth's surface, intended to prevent the spread of epidemics; and an endeavor to process and manipulate huge quantities of data about humanities' genetic material[4]. Bieke Willem has asserted that the rise and fall of the "Stromatolithon project"[5] in the novel, a gigantic archive of digital and genetic data, should be read as "archival fiction" as laid out in Roberto González Echevarría's *Myth and Archive* (1990): "The novel not only confers a central place to the archive in its plot but also calls attention to the power relations inherent in the process of collecting and accessing data" (Willem 2020: 132). From that perspective, creation in the novel should always be viewed in the context of these power relations. That former employees of the project, Cassio and Piera, hack the archive at the end of the novel to make it publicly accessible is also central to this reading. The novel takes place in three different, interwoven temporal layers, and alternately describes the late nineteenth century research expeditions of the botanist Niklas Bruun, who is obsessed with hybrid life forms, and the coming-of-age story of the hacker Cassio from his birth in 1982 to his earliest hacking attempts to his final public hack in 2024, mentioned above, in which he is assisted by the ambitious young biologist Piera.

As dynamics of creation and exhaustion in fictionalized digital worlds go, *Las constelaciones oscuras* is very condensed: on a multitude of levels here, creation is inconceivable without exhaustion and vice versa. For example, the subject of the exhaustion of scientific paradigms has led to radical new creations in the Anthropocene. As early as the late nineteenth century, Niklas Bruun thought the days of Darwin's evolutionary theory were numbered and advocated a new understanding of evolution based on species' mutual contamination and hybridization:

> He was sure that evolution *à la Darwinienne* was on its last legs, and in the new classification system that he was designing, certain species fit inside others; they invaded one another, arriving at a matrix of forms that couldn't be reduced to the issue of mere survival, much less that of generations (an idea he found repugnant). Evolutionary change, he believed, happened much more quickly – within the lifespan of a single individual. Rather than waiting for reproductive cycles to silently select useful features, it occurred via mimesis, and as the result of unexpected contact. (Oloixarac 2019: "Cassio")

In 2024, when this evolutionary step indeed occurs in Oloixarac's fiction, as a result of the merger of technology and biology – the author invokes the "apocalyptic trajectory of the Anthropocene" (2019, "Cassio") – the event is twofold. First, the Stromatolithon project has the ability to process unlimited amounts of

---

[4] In regard to Oloixarac's novel, see also Jobst Welge's chapter in this volume, which analyzes how the novel stages the blurring of the traditional division between human and natural history.
[5] This has a historical precursor in the project to regionally reorganize the genetic data of the Latin American continent (LATAM), which had originated around the end of the military dictatorship in Argentina.

data thanks to quantum computing, and it pairs this ability with total digital access to information from human DNA samples. Second, this evolutionary step happens within the person of Cassio, who deliberately infects himself with a computer virus and becomes a hybrid life form. Oloixarac emphasizes this double manifestation of fundamental upheavals in several passages of the novel: "One movement works as the surface, where visible change occurs; the other movement is the structure, hidden beneath the flow of mortal life" (Oloixarac 2019: "Cassio"). On the concrete level in which Cassio himself transgresses the boundary to post-humanness, the concept of virus is central as an intersection between biology and digitality. The experiment at the end of the novel is Piera's first time working with a computer virus, and simultaneously it deploys the first biological virus Cassio has ever programmed. Upon being injected with the virus, Cassio ceases to be human and his inner workings merge with a machine. For the first time, the programmer Cassio is not only a virus's creator but also its vector. After the injection, Cassio loses consciousness. This can be read as another aspect of an exhaustion that pervades all creative impulses and projects in the novel and is indeed inescapably inscribed in them.

Within the Stromatolithon project, it is a matter of changing the deep structure of human forms of existence, or, as Oloixarac describes them elsewhere in the original Spanish edition, *sintáctica del orden futuro* (literally "syntax of the future order", Oloixarac 2015: 88). This project amounts to no less than a new world vision represented by the enormous continent of data, which can be manipulated by both biological knowledge and the knowledge of data processing. The objective is "to geolocalize the specificity of their persons, to re-create their vital trajectories on the world's newly unfolded map" (Oloixarac 2019: "Piera"). The result is a sort of digital doubling of reality. By combining digitally documented and genetic biographies, the "cloud of information" becomes "the densest possible definition of inhabited territory" (Oloixarac 2019: "Piera"). With his hack at the end of the novel, Cassio destroys the nearly absurd concentration of power and the astronomical monetary value generated by such all-encompassing access to information and replaces it with a decentralized digital knowledge structure.

The subjects of the plague and the excess preceding death, discussed earlier in reference to Labatut, are also present in Pola Oloixarac's work, albeit in quite a different guise. One day, Cassio meets the "Resistance": two young women named Noelia and Ailín who believe that the earth is increasingly defending itself against humans' behavior and will cast them off sooner or later. They give the example of a mountain climber who got lost and was devoured by rats, part of a growing plague. Both women paint their faces with black-and-white stripes to evade the facial recognition of the omnipresent cameras in public space. Cassio dismisses these measures, believing that the only way to escape surveillance is to transform into another species.

He goes to the mountains himself, where he can hear the rats squeaking in the dark. Every twenty-five years, the massive blossoms of a native species of bamboo (*Chusquea culeou*) attract swarms of rats, on which the plant has an aphrodisiac effect. In a stone hut on a peak, the other members of the Stromatolithon project are already awaiting Cassio. They spread "bit codes" around the hut as bait and then activate them. When the rats ingest the codes, the fluid enters their bodies, causing the animals first to lose their sense of direction and then to turn bluish-green, like stellar nebulae, and finally die.

It is in reference to these stellar images that Max, the director of the Stromatolithon project – who is wearing the black-and-white face paint of the Resistance on this special occasion – invokes the title's *constelaciones oscuras*:

> We have to understand these things as dark constellations – that's what the Incas called them. They organized the sky in terms of the dark regions between stars, the interior shapes with bright perimeters. But what creates space for meaning isn't the bright dots or the presence of light – for dark constellations, the light is the noise. What matters is the darkness. (Oloixarac 2019: "Piera")

This passage calls to mind Giorgio Agamben's definition of the contemporary, which itself makes repeated references to the night sky and emphasizes the dark areas over the bright stars, before concluding:

> The contemporary is he who firmly holds his gaze on his own time so as to perceive not its light, but rather its darkness. All eras, for those who experience contemporariness, are obscure. The contemporary is precisely the person who knows how to see this obscurity, who is able to write by dipping his pen in the obscurity of the present. (Agamben 2009: 44)

As the second attribute of the contemporary, Agamben stresses the bravery it takes to behold the darkness, a bravery that Cassio also shows within this fiction when he uses his own body as a scientific experiment, initiating the creation of a new hybrid species.

Martín Castagnet, *Los cuerpos del verano* (2016)

Martín Castagnet's novel *Los cuerpos del verano*, which is also deeply preoccupied with digital worlds, can be read as a laconic sci-fi vision of the endgame of exhaustion. What if human consciousness could be posthumously uploaded to the internet, where it would either continue living alongside other human souls or else be "burned" onto a new body like a rewritable CD?

In this exploration of the transcendence of human mortality in a digital world, the book plays with the ambivalence of world creation/exhaustion in a temporally unspecified future and an unnamed city. That the people who are thus living on in new bodies require a permanently connected battery can be interpreted as a metaphor for the ambivalence always embedded in such fantasies of creation and exhaustion. The novel describes how the character of Ramiro Olivaires, known as Rama, returns to a body and re-integrates into society and the real world:

> It's good to have a body again, even if it's the body of a fat woman that no one else wanted. It's nice to be able to stroll down the sidewalk and feel the texture of the world. I like to cough until I'm hoarse and inhale the smell of the used clothes in my bedroom. (Castagnet 2017: Part 1.1)

That is the opening of Castagnet's novel. Since his death, his narrator Rama has spent almost a century living only in digital form – as a mutable human soul. He has returned to his old house and to daily life with his original family, but not to his previous body: instead, he has been reborn as an older, short, and heavyset woman plugged into a battery. Our narrator character is trying to get his bearings and often mentions how different things were "in his time", a time that stretches far beyond readers' own experiential horizons in terms of digital capabilities.

In his own time, Rama was one of the first in his country who could choose an afterlife on the internet, an option that was not yet available when his parents died. Whereas earlier generations once viewed the printing press and medicine as game-changing boons to humanity, the corresponding innovations in the novel's era are the "state of flotation" ("estado de flotación") on the internet and the ability to recycle a body after a person's death. Death still exists but no longer concludes a human life. Instead, it is possible to go on existing afterwards in digital or analog form, and thus to prolong human life – if not always in the real world, then at least in the digital one. To enter this state, an individual's brain activity first needs to be stored in digital form so that it can be preserved. After death, the human soul can be transferred to another human body, akin to "burning" a CD (*quemar un cuerpo*). When the protagonist died, he was put in the digital "state of flotation"; "migrating" to another body was not yet possible at that time.

The digital state of flotation – a reference to a genre of Japanese art whose name means "pictures of the floating world" – has its own temporal framework. Time is no longer measured in hours or days but in online messages, a flood of data and communications in which the dead float. Not only can they spent time with relatives, friends, and colleagues in digital places called "nodes", and even meet new people there, but their relatives in the physical world can now stay in contact with the "dead". For example, after returning to the real world, the protagonist communicates with his daughter Vera, who has already died, on an almost daily basis.

In the present day of the novel, most people prefer to switch bodies after death. Those who opt merely for an internet-based afterlife are in the minority. Another even smaller minority keeps their old bodies and does not replace them after death; this group is scorned by most of society and labeled "pachamas", a word derived from the Indian caste system.

In the novel, Castagnet finds metaphors for contemporary lived experience, an approach that he would take in another direction in his next novel, *Los mantras modernos* (2017). Therein, facing the total exhaustion of the world, humanity has delegated all the work of communication and prediction to technology. Meanwhile, some have gained a new ability: to disappear voluntarily (*desaparecer voluntariamente*), in other words, to radically withdraw from everyday life. This is an exhausted world in which people cultivate new capabilities but are permanently searching for one another.

Conclusion

The literary portrayals of exhaustion and new creation demonstrate a profound understanding of what we term (post-)global lived experience, particularly in terms of ambivalently shown pandemic/epidemic and digital worlds. In grappling with the current realities of the post-global period, the four authors discussed here pursued four distinct paths for investigating the relationship between reality and fiction in their texts and for reflecting upon the contemporary experience of world creation in an imaginary space. The transdisciplinary dimension of the notion of exhaustion lies at the core of analyzing all these texts. In addition to medical, aesthetic, and technological meanings, my analysis of Herrera's and Labatut's works has particularly shown the relevance of complex dimensions pertaining to economics, ecology, and the history of science.

Whereas Herrera makes particular use of dystopian plot points – such as the specific circumstances of the epidemic that have emptied out his fictional city – the impression of dystopia, of an unsalvageable future peering back at us, is also evident in Labatut's use of language and especially rhythm. "El jardinero nocturno" takes a step away from the factual, scientific realm to show the ambivalence of the history of science in images that are at once horrifying and poetic, and thus all the more tangible.

The fiction of Oloixarac and finally Castagnet likewise re-examines the relationship between reality and fiction by reflecting intensified contemporary realities in their fictional worlds. Over the course of the novel, Oloixarac's narrative extends into a future that transcends the readers' temporal horizons, raising questions about humanity's future and about digital opportunities and threats. In Castagnet's book, we find an even farther-reaching detachment from the actual strictures of our contemporary life. A particularly memorable image is that of a person who, having cheated death, must always carry around a battery to persist in the increasingly digitized experiential realms of life, learning, and work.

All these different portrayals of the ambivalence of exhaustion and creation should be treated as methods for keeping alive "the worlding force", to quote Pheng Cheah's "Working Hypotheses for Interpreting Postcolonial World Literature" (2016: 210). Fiction opens up ambivalent, dynamic, and complex spaces that also always involve aspects of contemporary vacancy, stagnation, or imminent exhaustion.

In these portrayals of globality, exhaustion, and fresh creation in the literatures of the post-global period, and with a view to the ongoing debate over world literature, we can observe a highly productive artistic confrontation with pandemic and digital realities in imagined spaces. This can also serve as a model outside of Latin America, renewing our perspective on the possibilities of "world literature" in the post-global period beyond asymmetrical constellations of power. Especially given current reactionary anti-globalist trends, such alternative perceptions of the world are enormously valuable. We are seeing a new potential for multipolar dynamics by which the literary work appears as a paradoxical representation of worlds that are exhausted and yet in the midst of renewal.

Works Cited

Agamben, Giorgio (2009): "What Is the Contemporary?". In: *"What Is an Apparatus?" and Other Essays*. Transl. David Kishik and Stefan Pedatella. Stanford: Stanford University Press, pp. 39–54.

Becerra, Eduardo (2016): "De la abundancia a la escasez. Distopías latinoamericanas del siglo XXI". In: *Cuadernos de Literatura*, 20, pp. 250–263.

Gentic, Tania/Bush, Matthew (2016): "Introduction: Mediatized Sensibilities in a Globalized Era". In: Bush, Matthew/Gentic, Tania (eds.): *Technology, Literature, and Digital Culture in Latin America: Mediatized Sensibilities in a Globalized Era*. New York: Routledge, pp. 1–22.

Castagnet, Martín Felipe (2017): *Bodies of Summer*. Transl. Frances Riddle. Victoria: Dalkey Archive Press.

— (2016): *Los cuerpos del verano*. Buenos Aires: Sigilo.

Cheah, Pheng (2016): *What Is a World? Postcolonial Literature as World Literature*. Durham: Duke University Press.

Ferdinand, Simon/Villaescusa-Illán, Irene/Peeren, Esther (eds.) (2019): *Other Globes: Past and Peripheral Imaginations of Globalization*. Cham: Palgrave Macmillan.
González Echevarría, Roberto (1990): *Myth and Archive. A Theory of Latin American Narrative*. Cambridge: Cambridge University Press.
Guerrero, Gustavo et al. (eds.) (2020): *Literatura latinoamericana mundial. Dispositivos y disidencias*. Berlin/Boston: De Gruyter.
Herrera, Yuri (2016): *The Transmigration of Bodies*. Transl. Lisa Dillman. High Wycombe/Los Angeles: & Other Stories.
— (2013): *La transmigración de los cuerpos*. Cáceres: Periférica.
Hoyos, Héctor (2015): *Beyond Bolaño. The Global Latin American Novel*. New York: Columbia University Press.
Hüther, Michael/Diermeier, Matthias/Goecke, Henry (2019): *Die erschöpfte Globalisierung. Zwischen transatlantischer Orientierung und chinesischem Weg*. Berlin/Heidelberg: Springer.
Keizman, Betina (2019): "Transmigraciones y desaparición del trabajo en dos novelas latinoamericanas recientes". In: *A Contracorriente*, 16, 3, pp. 161–183.
Labatut, Benjamín (2020a). "El jardinero nocturno". In: *Un verdor terrible*. Barcelona: Anagrama, pp. 81–87.
Labatut, Benjamín (2020b). "The Night Gardener". In: *When We Cease to Understand the World*. Transl. Adrian Nathan West. London: Pushkin Press.
Meruane, Lina (2014): *Viral Voyages: Tracing AIDS in Latin America*. New York: Palgrave Macmillan.
Müller, Gesine (2022): *How is World Literature Made? Global Circulations of Latin American Literatures*. Transl. Marie Deer. Berlin/Boston: De Gruyter.
Nassehi, Armin (2019): *Muster. Theorie der digitalen Gesellschaft*. Munich: C.H. Beck.
Oloixarac, Pola (2019). *Dark Constellations*. Transl. Roy Kesey. New York: Soho Press.
— (2015): *Las constelaciones oscuras*. Buenos Aires: Random House.
Rosa, Hartmut (2013): *Social Acceleration. A New Theory of Modernity*. Transl. Jonathan Trejo-Mathys. New York: Columbia University Press.
Sánchez Prado, Ignacio (2021): *Mexican Literature as World Literature*. London/New York: Bloomsbury Academic.
Schaffner, Anna K. (2016): *Exhaustion: A History*. New York: Columbia University Press.
Siskind, Mariano (2019): "Towards a cosmopolitanism of loss: an essay about the end of the world". In: Müller, Gesine/Siskind, Mariano (eds.): *World Literature, Cosmopolitanism, Globality: Beyond, Against, Post, Otherwise*. Berlin/Boston: De Gruyter, pp. 205–235.
Soifer, Alejandro (2019): "Una economía de la crueldad. Estado, organizaciones sociales marginales y necromercado en 'Trabajos del reino' y 'La transmigración de los cuerpos' de Yuri Herrera". In: *Latin American Literary Review*, 46, pp. 34–43.
Staab, Philipp (2019): *Digitaler Kapitalismus – Markt und Herrschaft in der Ökonomie der Unknappheit*. Berlin: Suhrkamp.
Tally, Robert T. (2019): "The End-of-the-World as World System". In: Ferdinand, Simon/Villaescusa-Illán, Irene/Peeren, Esther (eds.): *Other Globes: Past and Peripheral Imaginations of Globalization*. Cham: Palgrave Macmillan, pp. 267–283.
Willem, Bieke (2020): "A 'New Continent of Data': Pola Oloixarac's *Dark Constellations* and the Latin American Jungle Novel". In: *Lit: Literature Interpretation Theory*, 31, 2, pp. 129–145.

Alexis Radisoglou
Ethnoplanetarity as Post-Globality
Four Theses and a Postscript on a Contemporary Decolonial Constellation

If one of the imperatives of thinking post-globally is to extricate us from the "one-becoming pulsion" of the globe (Elias/Moraru 2015: xi–xii), then surely post-globality will have to come in many forms and different permutations. One such variant of an emerging post-global paradigm, I first suggested in an article in 2019, is a peculiar cultural constellation to which I gave the name of "ethnoplanetarity" (Radisoglou 2019). What this notion sought to encapsulate, in brief, was what I identified as a notable tendency in works of art of the 21st century, namely the close conjunction of a *national* thematics or field of representation with a *planetary* perspective that extends itself to the vast spatiotemporalities of terrestrial life in the *long durée* of cosmological history. If the article – a close analysis of Patricio Guzmán's films *Nostalgia de la luz* (2010) and *El botón de nácar* (2015) – was rather tentative or even speculative in its delineation of the term, I would like to take the opportunity of the present essay to bring into sharper relief what I mean by ethnoplanetarity, and how I conceive of the conceptual and epistemological gains the term offers as well as the political valences it entails. I will be concerned here, then, not so much with a close reading of individual works as with a programmatic outline of the ways in which ethnoplanetarity can help instantiate a properly "post-global aesthetics"[1]. My contention is, as the following four theses and a postscript demonstrate, that ethnoplanetarity is *here*; that it is a *post-global*, *contemporary*, and *decolonial* constellation; and that it forms part of the broader domain of *epistemologies of the South*.

Thesis One: Ethnoplanetarity is here

One need only look to contemporary cultural production from Chile to conclude that ethnoplanetarity is, indeed, a thing. Guzmán's two films, along with 2019's

---
[1] In my reflections on the post-global, I will also be drawing here on my introduction, with Christoph Schaub, to a special issue of The Germanic Review [journal name in italics] on 'Post-Global Perspectives on German Literature'. See Radisoglou/Schaub 2022.

Alexis Radisoglou, Durham University

La cordillera de los sueños, form part of a cinematic triptych that articulates the dictatorial and colonial histories of the Chilean nation with contemplations of the origins of the cosmos, the role of the element of water on "blue planet" Earth, and the geo-history of the Andean Mountains. In a body of work that strongly resonates with that of Guzmán and that includes the poetic documentary *Kon Kon* (2010), the poet, artist and filmmaker Cecilia Vicuña constellates the violence of the Pinochet regime and the forceful marginalization of Chile's indigenous populations within a wider reflection on the fragility of planetary life under conditions of neoliberal hegemony and ecological crisis[2]. The Berlin-based visual artist Michelle-Marie Letelier, finally, time and again situates her projects in the Atacama Desert, which also served Guzmán as the setting of *Nostalgia de la luz*, exploring the complex imbrication of planetary materialities and geological formations with the political, economic and environmental histories of Chile in the global context of an extractivist economy[3].

On a first level, then, ethnoplanetarity operates as a *descriptive* category. To say that it is here is to give a name to a conspicuously prominent feature of contemporary cultural production, and to ask scholars in various fields and areas to keep an eye for and engage with it. In this sense – and this is an important caveat to make here at the very outset – my mobilization of the prefix *ethno-* has nothing to do with a valorization of this term on a normative level; nor, more crucially still, is it meant to suggest anything like the culturalism, biologism, or outright racism that a term like "ethno-nationalism" would imply. While *ethno-* in this latter sense – and rightly so – has profoundly negative connotations, my use of it seeks, perhaps somewhat infelicitously, to denote no more than *something pertaining to a nation state* – an attendance, that is, to the contingent but particular historical formation (and analytic category) of a political entity like "Chile". It is entirely consistent, in this respect, that the national, in works like Guzmán's, Vicuña's, and Letelier's, appears almost exclusively as trauma.

Thesis Two: Ethnoplanetarity is Post-Global

What interests me about the works of Guzmán, Vicuña, and Letelier is not simply their articulation of a national with a planetary level. More crucial to me is

---

[2] For an analysis of *Kon Kon* explicitly within the framework of "planetarity", see Amich (2013).
[3] A comprehensive overview of Letelier's work can be found on her website (http://michellemarieletelier.net). For a detailed discussion of some of her recent projects, see Page (2021).

that what seems to be at stake in this conjunction is, in fact, a third dimension: that of the *global*. In each of these artistic projects – less explicitly in Guzmán, more pronouncedly in Vicuña and Letelier – an ethnoplanetary perspective effectuates an interrogation of the condition of globality. Or, more emphatically still: Ethnoplanetarity seeks to supplant the discourse of the global. How to conceive, then, of the entanglements and tensions between the national, the global, and the planetary? Why this double lever of *ethno-* and planetarity to unhinge the order of the global? And what to make of the recurrence of the national if it is to be more than atavism or regression? Is ethnoplanetarity a matter of dialectics, a constellation akin to that of the "glocal" – only that glocality's suspension or bracketing of the national (a moment proper to the era of globalization) is replaced here, or indeed sublated into, ethnoplanetarity's bracketing or suspension of the global (the moment proper to an emerging *post*-global paradigm)?

The critical discourse of planetarity has, of course, for a considerable period of time now been one of the main contenders for the instantiation of such a post-global paradigm. In its contemporary form, one can trace it from essays by Gayatri Chakravorty Spivak and Masao Miyoshi to more recent work by scholars such as Emily Apter, Susan Stanford Friedman, Amy Elias, Christian Moraru, and Dipesh Chakrabarty, with Elias and Moraru having gone as far as positing a wholesale "planetary turn" in the humanities (Spivak 1999; Miyoshi 2001; Apter 2013; Elias/Moraru 2015; Moraru 2017; Chakrabarty 2021). Different accentuations notwithstanding, what unites such work is its promotion of the planet as a politico-epistemological counter-figure to the globe – a shared endeavor, in Spivak's influential phrase, for planetarity to "overwrite the globe" (Spivak 1999: 44). While the globe, thereby, appears as a figure of one-ness – of systemic integration, cultural and economic homogenization, and frictionless flows and movements in standardized time – the planet, as "concurrently symbiotic and oppositional" to the globe, comes imbued with an altogether different "form of relationality" (Elias/Moraru 2015: xiii; vii). Moraru, in a programmatic essay that also cites the work of Apter, has spoken of globality's "fashioning [of] the polymorphic world into a sphere-like totality whose 'smooth surface allow[s] the unimpeded flow of capital, information[,] and language'" (Moraru 2017: 126) – a material and discursive operation that finds its radical counterpart in Elias and Moraru's sense of planetarity as "a multicentric and pluralizing [. . .] structure of relatedness critically keyed to non-totalist, non-homogenizing, and anti-hegemonic operations typically and polemically subtended by an eco-logic" (Elias/Moraru 2015: xiii). What is at stake, in other words, in this turn to planetarity, is a shift "from *globe* as financial-technocratic system toward *planet* as world-ecology" (Elias/Moraru 2015: xvi).

Planetarity, then, is post-global. Its *post*-ness, however, is not to be understood in the sense of a temporal succession, but as a radical interrogation and performative reinscription of a given framework, namely the historically contingent formation of neoliberal globality. This is precisely one of the nuances of Spivak's term: To have the planet "overwrite" the globe is a process of *worlding otherwise*. It is predicated on a "new episteme" that is, however, "heuristic rather than deterministic", and "cautiously exploratory" (Elias/Moraru: xxv). It is a fitting conjuncture, in this context, that the very etymology of the word "planet" – from Ancient Greek πλανάω (to wander, to roam, to err) – eschews the instrumental and fully circumscribed trajectories of global integration.

The planetary apertures in works like Guzmán's, Vicuña's and Letelier's, I contend, must be seen as an aesthetic instantiation of such a post-global imaginary. What characterizes each of these works is a capaciousness in form and content that seeks to do justice to the multiple, and multiply differentiated, modes of *being-in-time-and-space* of which earthly belonging is comprised. Crucial to this is what I have called a form of "heteroscalarity" (Radisoglou 2019: 196–200) – a kaleidoscopic shifting between or interweaving of various temporal and spatial layers which is achieved, in each case, through specific aesthetic and articulatory practices. My sense of heteroscalarity here resonates profoundly with Susan Stanford Friedman's programmatic statement, in her *Planetary Modernisms*, that

> we need a fluid approach to spatio/temporal scale, one that can move flexibly back and forth between large and small, between large-scale structural patterns that distance helps us see and the small-scale particularities that nearness brings into visibility. Fluid, moving scales create bird's-eye and ground-level views that can inform and complement each other (Friedman 2015: 94).

For Friedman, thereby, "[scalar] thinking [. . .] in both temporal and spatial terms allows for the flexibility to zoom in, zoom out – back and forth from big to small, from the *longue durée* across the globe, to the particularities of distinctive periods and places, to the variations within localized periods, and to the 'worlds' created in forms of expressive/symbolic culture" (Friedman 2015: 96). Guzmán and Letelier's multi-perspectival approaches to the Atacama – at once a geological formation, a center of cosmological research, a site of extractivist activity, a trade route, home to indigenous peoples, location of a political prison, and burial site of Chile's murdered *desaparecidos* – are paradigmatic cases for a form of "scalar literacy" (Clark 2019: 38–56) that eschews the one-dimensionality and temporal myopia of the global. The coastal landscape of Concón in Vicuña's near-eponymous film similarly, as Candice Amich has demonstrated, is "a site where economics, history, ecology, bodies, art and memory converge through a formal engagement with place" (Amich 2013: 135). And so, importantly for my argument here, each of these works also mediate between – or refract through each other – artistic individuality, collective experience, national history, global interconnections, and the history of the cosmos.

But why, then, *ethno*-? It is through this dimension, I contend, that planetarity gains contour as a properly post-global paradigm. Two aspects, in my view, are at play here: Firstly, there is the risk of planetarity's devolving into a form of cosmological a-politicism or mere aesthetic transcendence. This would bring with it a dissolution of the particularities and differential parameters of earthly existence – even an evacuation of historicity as such – that would threaten to undermine the political force and transformative potential of planetarity as a specifically post-global paradigm. Nothing is gained, politically or epistemologically, if the master narrative of the globe-as-one is supplanted by a revelling in the even grander still sublimity of cosmic belonging. Bluntly put, if *Nostalgia de la luz*, for instance, were only about the awe-inspiring galaxies brought close by the gigantic telescopes stationed in the Atacama, the film would amount to little more than elevated kitsch.

Ethnoplanetarity, then, on this first level, is about the persistence of the national as a "really existing" container for political processes, collective experience, and memorial practices. If Friedman calls for a new paradigm that is "cosmic and grounded at the same time" (Friedman 2015: 8), then the national in ethnoplanetarity also performs that task of *grounding*. The ground, however, must not be mistaken for a foundation or a root. Ethnoplanetarity is not, as I emphasized at the very outset of this essay, about a return to or an affirmation of the national as a positive and regulating principle of being-in-the-world. On the contrary, what is at stake here is an insistence on the pains and traumas inflicted through the framework of the nation – a reminder that the *concrete*, grounded histories and memories of this still-virulent formation cannot simply be overcome through the terrifugal motions of a cosmological imaginary. If the nation is no answer to the problematic of the globe, post-globality will still have to reckon with its legacies.

This brings me to a second, perhaps more salient point, which will also bring into sharper relief why the domain of the national has a stake in a specifically *post-global* project of ethnoplanetarity. It is an established argument today in the field of Latin American Studies that an inextricable nexus exists between the continent's military dictatorships of the mid and late 20th century and the full transition of several of its countries to the conditions of a global market under neoliberal hegemony. Idelber Avelar, in his influential study *The Untimely Present*, has spoken of a "new present ushered in by the military regimes: a global market in which every corner of social life has been commodified" (Avelar 1999:

1). Referring, variously, to a "global market", a "market logic", "neoliberalism", "the free market", and "global capital", Avelar argues that the very "raison d'être" of these dictatorships "was the physical and symbolic elimination of all resistance to the implementation" of such a regime of neoliberal globality (Avelar 1999: 1; 2; 13).

Guzmán, Vicuña and Letelier's Chile is, of course, a – perhaps *the* – paradigmatic case for this kind of process. And so the close attendance in their works to the brutal legacies of Chile's recent national history must also be read as an antidote to a form of historical obsolescence on which the country's very insertion into the condition of globality is predicated in the first place. Avelar has argued that "the neoliberalism implemented in the aftermath of the dictatorships is founded upon the passive forgetting of its barbaric origin", that the "free market established by the [. . .] dictatorships", indeed, "must [. . .] impose forgetting not only because it needs to erase the reminiscence of its barbaric origins but also because it is proper to the market to live in a perpetual present" (Avelar 1999: 2). Juan Poblete, similarly, speaks of "the implementation of [a] neoliberal memory apparatus" specifically in Chile, emphasizing "the difficulty of national collective memory under current global conditions", and the "forgetfulness and presentism" inherent in a "predatory capitalism whose only horizon is the short-term" (Poblete 2015: 92; 93; 98; 99). Crucially, thereby, for Poblete "under neoliberal globalization, the *national* becomes, to a significant degree, [. . .] a memory counterpoint" (Poblete 2015: 94; my emphasis)[4]. It is in this sense precisely that the national in ethnoplanetarity comes to function to post-global effect. And so, yes, post-globality will ultimately have to follow a planetary trajectory, but to reach this novel plane, it will also have to pass through the dimension of the national. This is the *ethno-* of ethnoplanetarity: not stable root, nor foundation or even a firm ground, but a stepping-stone towards something new[5] – the paradigm of post-globality.

Thesis Three: Ethnoplanetarity is Contemporary

To say that ethnoplanetarity is contemporary is more than to assert the fact that it inhabits, temporally, the now of the formation of globality. While

---

[4] On the question of *Memory Art in the Contemporary World* in the specific context of the Global South, see Andreas Huyssen's eponymous recent monograph (Huyssen 2022).

[5] One is reminded here, perhaps, of Édouard Glissant's notion, in his outline of a "poetics of relation", of a "root [that] begins to act like a rhizome" (Glissant 1997: 21).

ethnoplanetarity's contemporaneity does comprise this more conventional understanding – the contemporary as an alignment or synchronicity with the today – my own use of the term is animated by its composite or hyphenated nature[6]. What interests me, in other words, is the heterochronicity of ethnoplanetarity – its refraction or dispersal into a series of differentiated *co-temporalities*. The "con-temporaneity" of works like Guzmán's, Vicuña's, and Letelier's, then, resides in pitting the homogenizing temporal regime of neoliberal globality against a variety of other temporal orders, including those of cosmological time, geological processes, national memory, and, importantly, indigenous cosmogonies and world-ecologies. As a result, time itself is brought into a critical constellation.

In his much-cited essay "What is the Contemporary?", Giorgio Agamben advances a similar understanding of what it means to be contemporary. "Contemporariness", he writes, is

> a singular relationship with one's own time, which adheres to it and, at the same time, keeps a distance from it. More precisely, it is *that relationship with time that adheres to it through a disjunction and an anachronism*. Those who coincide too well with the epoch, those who are perfectly tied to it in every respect, are not contemporaries, precisely because they do not manage to see it; they are not able to firmly hold their gaze onto it (Agamben 2009: 41; emphasis in the original).

Contemporaneity, then, for Agamben is also a matter of *un*-timeliness, of "disconnection and out-of-jointness": "Those who are truly contemporary", he argues, "who truly belong to their time, are those who neither perfectly coincide with it nor adjust themselves to its demands. [. . .] But precisely because of this condition, precisely through this disconnection and this anachronism, they are more capable than others of perceiving and grasping their own time" (Agamben 2009: 40).

A *con-temporary* constellation in precisely this sense, ethnoplanetarity stands in what I have previously called a relationship of "disjunctive affiliation" with the hegemonic temporality of neoliberal globality (Radisoglou 2019: 201). What is at stake here is what Jonathan Crary has described as globality's "time without time" (Crary 2013: 29), the flat presentism of digital instantaneity, ceaseless consumption, and techno-capitalistic mass synchronization. The "24/7" logic of such a temporal regime, as Crary has argued in his eponymous book, "in its peremptory reductiveness, [. . .] celebrates a hallucination of presence, of an unalterable permanence composed of incessant, frictionless operations. It belongs to the aftermath of a common life made into the object of technics" (Crary

---

[6] In what follows, I draw heavily on the section on "Contemporaneity" in my previous essay on ethnoplanetarity (Radisoglou 2019: 200–207).

2013: 29). As such, it is also predicated on a form of historical erasure: In a suggestive passage that powerfully resonates with works such as Guzmán's, Vicuña's and Letelier's, Crary notes that

> [a] 24/7 world is a disenchanted one in its eradication of shadows and obscurity and of alternative temporalities. It is a world identical to itself, a world with the shallowest of pasts, and thus in principle without specters. But the homogeneity of the present is an effect of the fraudulent brightness that presumes to extend everywhere [. . .]. A 24/7 world produces an apparent equivalence between what is immediately available, accessible, or utilizable and what exists. The spectral is, in some way, the intrusion or disruption of the present by something out of time and by the ghosts of what has not been deleted by modernity, of victims who will not be forgotten, of unfulfilled emancipation (Crary 2013: 19–20).

The (un)timelines, or (a)synchronicity, inherent in ethnoplanetarity's contemporaneity, I would argue, constitutes precisely such an intrusion or disruption of the selfsameness of global time. The "dissensual" (Rancière 2010) effect of the time of ethnoplanetarity, thereby, has its roots in the artistic production of an *ästhetische Eigenzeit*, or the differential specificity of a peculiarly aesthetic temporality. The very *form* of such an aesthetic temporality – to draw here on an Adornian register – can, in turn, be understood as a determinate negation of the social-historical content of global time[7]. This explains, incidentally, why ethnoplanetarity is legible as a post-global constellation even if, as in the case of Guzmán, the question of globality is not explicitly part of the content of a work of art.

Equally crucially, however, it is once again the articulation of the planetary with the national that brings the contours of post-globality into sharper relief. For what distinguishes the temporal heteroscalarity peculiar to ethnoplanetarity – a temporality both "cosmic and grounded" (Friedman 2015: 8) – is that it eschews at once the narrow parameters of homogenous global time *and* the historical forgetting which the latter is predicated on. In other words: Ethnoplanetarity both extends itself to *other* times beyond the global *and* critically attends to the national histories that are constitutively part of globality's very genealogy. It encompasses, that is, both the planetarians' attention to scales that render the planet "in the species of alterity" (Spivak 1999: 44) – including the time of cosmic history, non-human life, and inorganic matter – and what Poblete calls the "memory counterpoint" of the national or indeed "the national as memory" itself (Poblete 2015: 94; 93) – a "memory value", in Avelar's formulation, that transcends the all-pervasive logic of exchange which structures the system of

---

[7] For the notion of determinate negation, or *bestimmte Negation*, as deployed here, see Adorno (2013) and Menke (1999).

neoliberal globality (Avelar 1999: 5). The champion of ethnoplanetarity, then, must be a figure closely akin to that of Agamben's contemporary, "the one who, dividing and interpolating time, is capable of transforming it and putting it in relation with other times [. . .] able to read history in unforeseen ways" (Agamben 2009: 53) – to read it, as one may venture to say here, in ways that are *post-global*.

Thesis Four: Ethnoplanetarity is Decolonial

To read history *in unforeseen ways* means both to unveil the logic that governs dominant conceptions of historical events and time, and to instantiate new modes of historicizing and of historicity as such. To conceive of ethnoplanetarity in such a way is to suggest that what is at stake here is a critical analysis, interrogation, and – importantly – performative constitution of *epistemes* of being-in-the-world. It is in this sense precisely that ethnoplanetarity can also be subsumed under the larger project of decoloniality. Ethnoplanetarity's politico-epistemological investment, I contend, lies simultaneously with an unravelling of what Catherine E. Walsh and Walter Mignolo, in their programmatic work *On Decoloniality*, have called "the colonial matrix of power", and with the delineation and instantiation of Walsh and Mignolo's "*otherwise* that is the decolonial *for*" (Walsh/Mignolo 2018: 4; 10). Once again, thereby, it is the articulation of the national with the planetary that plays a crucial role in bringing about this form of twofold criticality.

The discourse of planetarity, of course, has from its very outset been directed not simply against the figure of the globe-as-one but also against the very epistemologies underwriting this globalizing thrust – a Western rationality, that is, whose "darker side" (Walsh/Mignolo 2018: 112), whether dialectically conceived or not, has always been complicit in grasping the world as something to be measured, totalized, and mastered. Planetarity, in contrast, is imbued with a different form of relationality which, in disjoining itself from the universality to which the colonial matrix of power lays claim, seeks to attend to the *pluriversality* of earthly belonging. Walsh and Mignolo, much in the same vein, speak of the decolonial project's "creating and illuminating pluriversal [. . .] paths that disturb the totality from which the universal and the global are most often perceived" (Walsh/Mignolo 2018: 2). And so the strong insistence by the champions of a planetary paradigm on relationality and "being-in-relation", on a "thickening [. . .] web of relations" (Elias/Moraru 2015: xxi; xii), and "our common bonds to the planet" (Miyoshi 2001: 296); on planetarity as "bioconnective" and "eco-cosmological";

and on "stewardship", an "ethics of care", and the relatedness of "[the] human [. . .] the nonhuman, the organic, and the inorganic in all of their richness" (Elias/Moraru 2015: xxiv; xvi; xxiii; xxiv; xiii) is also strikingly concordant with what Walsh and Mignolo refer to as *vincularidad*. Invoking the work of indigenous thinkers such as Nina Pacari, Fernando Huanacuni Mamani, and Félix Patzi Paco, they define *vincularidad* – an alternative term, precisely, for "relationality" – as "the awareness of the integral relation and interdependence amongst all living organisms (in which humans are only a part) with territory or land and the cosmos. It is a relation and interdependence in search of balance and harmony of life in the planet" (Walsh/Mignolo 2018: 1).

What I have called above the planetary apertures in Guzmán, Vicuña, and Letelier constitute elements precisely of such *vincularidad* or relationality. The macroscopic projections into cosmic time and space are as much part of this as is the microscopic attention to organic and inorganic matter. It encompasses the interest in the elements as well as the engagement with the textures of the sea, the mountains, and the desert. And it entails, of course, the strong ecological – indeed: ecocritical – dimension that animates the work of Vicuña and Letelier in particular. What manifests itself here is a radical rejoinder not only of the homogenizing trajectory of global integration but also, and more fundamentally, of the subjection of the world to instrumental rationality, extractivist activity, the will to mastery, and the violent taxonomies of Eurocentric modes of thought.

Crucially, thereby, this planetary or decolonial *vincularidad* is closely tied, in the works of all three artists mentioned here, to forms of a specifically indigenous world-ecology. This is evident, for instance, in Guzmán's careful attention to the ways of living and the language of the Selk'nam and Kawésqar; in Vicuña's documentation of the indigenous fishermen's *bailes chinos* in the coastal landscape of Concón[8]; and in Letelier's exploration of the figure of the Giant of Tarapacá, a massive anthropomorphic geoglyph in the Atacama Desert whose origins date back to pre-Columbian times. The dialogue with indigenous cultures, then, is significant in two ways in the broader context of an emergent post-global aesthetics: For what manifests itself here is, firstly, an attendance to the connection between coloniality and globality and, secondly, an invocation of the altogether different nexus between indigeneity, decoloniality and post-

---

8 The *baile chino* is etymologically linked not to the Spanish term denoting ethnicity or race but to the Quechua word for "to serve". As Amich writes: "'Chino' is a Quechua word that means 'to serve' and thus is a label that designates function – as in 'to serve' the sea – and not ethnicity; the majority of chino fishermen in central Chile today are most likely of Diaguita or Mapuche background" (Amich 2013: 135).

globality. In other words: These works are cognizant of the fact that the political and epistemological colonization of Latin America is of constitutive – indeed originary – importance for both the unfolding of the process of capitalist globalization and the parallel institution of the colonial matrix of power. If, however, as Anibal Quijano has argued, "the model of power that is globally hegemonic today presupposes an element of coloniality" (Quijano 2000: 533), then it is precisely – so Guzmán, Vicuña and Letelier seem to suggest – in an indigenous decoloniality, or decolonial indigeneity, that the possibility of unlocking a post-global order resides[9]. To say this, importantly, is also to stress that such invocations of indigenous life have nothing to do with a "return" to a primordial harmony or the redemption of a past innocence, but belong with a futural order. Amich, in her discussion of *Kon Kon*, speaks of "the way in which indigenous epistemology harnesses 'claims to a different historicity' that makes it efficacious in the face of neoliberal assaults" (Amich 2013: 145). Channeling the work of Arif Dirlik, she suggests that "the potential of an indigenous alternative relies on 'indigenous ideals as they have been reworked by a contemporary consciousness, where indigenism appears not merely as a reproduction of the past, but as a project to be realized'" (Amich 2013: 145). In my own terms, then, post-globality, what I have called above a particular form of con-temporaneity, and decoloniality are inextricably intertwined here. Amich concludes by saying that

> [in] her negation of the epistemic violence done to colonized peoples, Vicuña's intimations of planetarity unleash both new and old relationships to time, history, and place. It follows that two requirements of a poetics of planetarity are, first, that it register the sensory violence of globalization, and, second, that it retreat from the desire to dominate time and space and embrace instead the alterity of the planet (Amich 2013: 149).

It is in this sense precisely that Vicuña's work – like Guzmán's and Letelier's, too – becomes a paradigmatic case for a post-global cultural production that seeks at once to offer a critique of the colonial matrix of power and to instantiate a decolonial *otherwise*.

What, then, of ethnoplanetarity? If planetarity as such already has a decolonial kernel, it is perhaps not intuitively obvious why one would want to stress

---

[9] One interesting question in this context, in fact, is that about ethnoplanetarity as a potential force in the arena of contemporary Latin American nationhood. To what extent, that is, can recent attempts, in countries such as Ecuador or Bolivia, to include elements of an indigenous world-ecology in the official constitution of the nation be considered an effort at instituting a form of ethnoplanetarity in the properly political sphere? In the Chilean context, the ongoing work by the Constitutional Convention that has been tasked with drafting a new constitution for the country will be of interest in this framework too, as will be the policies of the newly sworn-in president Gabriel Boric.

here its conjunction with the national – a conceptual domain, after all, that arguably is itself deeply entrenched in the *episteme* of colonial modernity[10]. And yet, not least *because of* this entrenchment, I insist here on the usefulness – the possible epistemological gains – of such a constellation. Three aspects, to me, stand out here, each one of them related to the role of the nation as a contingent, imaginary, but nevertheless "really existing" institution that has historically functioned as a contested terrain in (de)colonial struggles and as a testing ground for (post-)global trajectories.

The first aspect has to do, in a more general way, with what I have stated above about the national as a form of *grounding* of the planetary – not in the sense of a root or a foundation, but as a counterpoise to what I called the "terrifugal" intimations of a planetary imaginary. Crucially, this has nothing to do with the regressive valorization of the nation or *ethnos* as an antidote – to echo Marx here – to globality's supposed logic of *all that is solid melting into air* (Marx/Engels 2008). Though they are coeval as elements of a symptomatology of globalization and its discontents, the anti-global and the post-global come with radically opposite political valences. What is at stake here, rather, is a sort of referral of planetarity to what Elias and Moraru call an "anthropologically pertinent scalarity" (Elias/Moraru 2015: xvii). It is not desirable, I have argued in my previous essay, to "resolve the historical particularities" that have occurred in the framework of specific national situations – including "political conflict, violence and trauma" – in a "new master narrative of cosmic belonging that, instead of departing from the false homogeneity of the global, would simply reiterate it on an even grander scale". In other words: Political history cannot be "subsumed [. . .] under, or absorbed by, a natural history that transcends – or, indeed, is alien to – the modes and vicissitudes of human praxis" (Radisoglou 2019: 205). The persistence of the national in works such as Guzmán's, Vicuña's and Letelier's – one that manifests itself predominantly in the form of a memory of the military dictatorship – can, accordingly, also be read as a reminder of what I have called "the irrefutable weight attached to that which cannot simply be alleviated in a cosmological re-scaling" (Radisoglou 2019: 205). In this sense, then, my insistence here on the national – not in itself, but as a relational element in the heteroscalar constellation of ethnoplanetarity – also resonates with Walsh and Mignolo's imperative for any decolonial project "to interrupt the idea of dislocated, disembodied, and disengaged abstraction" (Walsh/Mignolo 2018: 3).

---

10 On the constitution and functioning of the nation state in a specifically Latin American context, see Quijano (2000).

This brings me to a second aspect: In the context of Walsh and Mignolo's call for an engagement with concrete and specific histories, the interrogation of the legacies of the Pinochet regime – something particularly pronounced in the work of Guzmán – takes on an important role. If the national situation of Chile during that period also represented, as David Harvey has argued, the "first experiment with neoliberal state formation" (Harvey 2005: 7), then the dictatorship marked both the transition to Chile's insertion into the orbit of neoliberal globality and the violent erasure of previous paths and possible alternative trajectories. Poblete argues that in the course of this momentous shift towards what he calls the "postsocial"[11] world of global neoliberal hegemony, "the social becomes [. . .] the object of national memory" (Poblete 2015: 97) – or, in the suggestive phrase of the title of his essay, of "The Memory of the National and the National as Memory". It is this conception of the nation as a "time/space for which memory processes are fundamental and constitutive, even in the midst of the neoliberal postsocial tabula rasa" (Poblete 2015: 104) that resonates with my employment of the national for the paradigm of ethnoplanetarity. But while for Poblete, the "social national" (Poblete 2015: 101) has to do, primarily, with certain forms of collectivity and the structures of a welfare state, I conceive of this sphere in a more performative sense as a field of contestation and contingent historical struggles. And so the memory of the dictatorship, as a particular instance of the memory of the national, is also a memory, in Avelar's register, "of everything that was left unaccomplished and mournful in the past" (Avelar 1999: 2) – a memory, that is, of the regime's brutal vanquishing of a historical movement that was not in thrall with neoliberal globality, and that arguably was also propelled by a decolonial undercurrent.

Most importantly, however – and this is the third aspect of the national's significance for a decolonial undertaking – ethnoplanetarity is able to bring into relief the constitutive role of the national itself in the perpetuation of colonial violence against indigenous populations. Quijano has argued that "[after] independence, the dominants in the countries of the Southern Cone [. . .] considered the conquest of the territories that the indigenous peoples populated, as well as the extermination of these inhabitants, necessary as an expeditious form of homogenizing the national population and facilitating the process of

---

11 Poblete defines the postsocial as "a social configuration that results from the transformation of the welfare state, with the end of its ethos of the social as a solidarity-based commitment administered by the state and its replacement by a competitive state whose rationality derives from the neoliberal version of the economy and whose ethos, instead of socializing and distributing risk in solidarity, individualizes and privatizes it. Obviously, the postsocial does not imply the disappearance of society, but it does involve its radical restructuring" (Poblete 2015: 97).

constituting a modern nation-state 'a la europea'" (Quijano 2000: 562). Amich, similarly, in the more specific context of the dictatorship in Chile, contends that "the neoliberal nation signifies the erasure of an alternative indigenous ethos that spans the Andean region" (Amich 2013: 147). Her insistence, thereby, on "ecological damage and political violence as the twin offspring of neoliberal state formation" (Amich 2013: 137) – an argument powerfully present in both Vicuña's and Letelier's work in particular – underlines the inextricable entwinement of the national in a colonial-global nexus from which indigenous populations have suffered most harshly. Ethnoplanetarity as a decolonial constellation both acknowledges and seeks to extricate itself from this very nexus.

Postscript: Ethnoplanetarity is an Epistemology of the South

I want to conclude here, by way of a postscript, with a fifth and final thesis, one that emerges quite naturally from – and indeed suffuses – each of the previous four. That I opened this essay with the invocation of the "hereness" of ethnoplanetarity in a specific place – the Chile of Guzmán's, Vicuña's and Letelier's artistic work – is no coincidence. Nor is the fact that Chilean cultural production then became emblematic of what one could call a broader *topicality* that comprises other places, an expansive now-time, and the pressing issue of decolonial inquiry. It is precisely this amalgamation of specific spatiotemporalities with more expansive trajectories of transformation that also characterizes the critical project of *epistemologies of the South*. Boaventura de Sousa Santos, in his programmatic text on *The Coming Age of the Epistemologies of the South*, has argued that the geographical signifier here is modified into "an epistemological, nongeographical South, composed of many epistemological souths having in common the fact that they are all knowledges born in struggles" against what I have called above the colonial-global nexus (Santos 2018: 1). What is at stake in such epistemologies, for Santos, is an "alternative thinking of alternatives" (Santos 2018: 6). "Dominant politics", he writes, "becomes epistemological when it is able to make a credible claim that the only valid knowledge available is the one that ratifies its own dominance (Santos 2018: 6). In such an epochal *Zeitgeist*, it seems to me that the way out of this impasse is premised upon the emergence of a new epistemology that is explicitly political" (Santos 2018: vii). This notion is echoed in Russell West-Pavlov's more searching question whether the concept of the "Global South" is "a term whose polyvalence offers a multitude of possible frameworks for posing new questions and searching for new answers – in other words, for the production of innovative knowledge based in a non-Euro-Atlantic epistemological matrix (or better, network of matrices)" (West-Pavlov 2018: 3). West-Pavlov conjectures that the South denoted here is a "relational sign" or a "shifter not merely because it is a mobile term with variously inflected meanings but because it works like a deictic marker, linking discourses, places, and speakers in such a way as to generate new subject positions, fields of agency, and possibilities of action" that keep "multiplying without homogenizing or totalizing the relationships which they sketch out" (West-Pavlov 2018: 2; 11).

What is at play here, once again, is the very *vincularidad* or relationality that also marks the constellation of ethnoplanetarity. And indeed, the affinities between the forms the latter takes – culturally, aesthetically – and the range of meanings carried by the notion of epistemologies of the South are striking. They fully coincide not only in their relational trajectories and broader politico-epistemological directionality, but also in specific aspects such as the insistence on "pluriversality" rather than "abstract universality", the critique of the "coloniality of knowledge (as of power)" (Santos 2018: 8), the foregrounding of indigenous experience, and the promotion of what Santos calls an "ecology of knowledges, that is, the recognition of the copresence of different ways of knowing and the need to study the affinities, divergences, complementarities, and contradictions among them in order to maximize the effectiveness of the struggles of resistance against oppression" (Santos 2018: 8). It is not, of course, a tautology to say that ethnoplanetarity is an epistemology of the South – not all epistemologies of the South are ethnoplanetary – but in each of the parameters I have sketched out in the preceding theses, it is without a doubt a paradigmatic cultural expression of such an epistemology of the South. What remains is the question about the scope and efficacy of ethnoplanetarity – the role it has to play in the encounter not only with the global North but also, as a cultural constellation or indeed *aesthetics*, with the dominant *national philologies* of Western Europe. It is perhaps in this encounter that the true measure of ethnoplanetarity's post-*global* force will fully be determined.

Works cited

Adorno, Theodor W. (2013): *Aesthetic Theory*. Transl. Robert Hullot-Kentor. London: Bloomsbury.
Agamben, Giorgio (2009): *"What is an Apparatus?" and Other Essays*. Transl. David Kishik and Stefan Pedatella. Stanford: Stanford University Press.
Amich, Candice (2013): "From Precarity to Planetarity". In: *The Global South*, Vol. 7, No. 2, pp. 134–152.

Apter, Emily (2013): *Against World Literature: On the Politics of Untranslatability*. London: Verso.
Avelar, Idelber (1999): *The Untimely Present: Postdictatorial Latin American Fiction and the Task of Mourning*. Durham, NC: Duke University Press.
Chakrabarty, Dipesh (2021): *The Climate of History in a Planetary Age*. Chicago: The University of Chicago Press.
Clark, Timothy (2019): *The Value of Ecocriticism*. Cambridge: Cambridge University Press.
Crary, Jonathan (2013): *24/7: Late Capitalism and the Ends of Sleep*. London: Verso.
Elias, Amy J./Moraru, Christian (2015): "Introduction: The Planetary Condition". In: Elias, Amy J./Moraru, Christian (eds.): *The Planetary Turn: Relationality and Geoaesthetics in the Twenty-First Century*. Evanston, IL: Northwestern University Press, pp. xi–xxxvii.
Friedman, Susan Stanford (2015): *Planetary Modernisms: Provocations on Modernity Across Time*. New York: Columbia University Press.
Glissant, Édouard (1997): *Poetics of Relation*. Transl. Betsy Wing. Ann Arbor: Michigan University Press.
Harvey, David (2005): *A Brief History of Neoliberalism*. Oxford: Oxford University Press.
Huyssen, Andreas (2022): *Memory Art in the Contemporary World: Confronting Violence in the Global South*. London: Lund Humphries.
Marx, Karl/Engels, Friedrich (2008): *The Communist Manifesto*. Oxford: Oxford University Press.
Menke, Christoph (1999): *The Sovereignty of Art: Aesthetic Negativity in Adorno and Derrida*. Cambridge, MA: MIT Press.
Moraru, Christian (2017): "'World', 'Globe', 'Planet': Comparative Literature, Planetary Studies, and Cultural Debt After the Global Turn". In: Heise, Ursula et al. (eds.): *Futures of Comparative Literature: ACLA State of the Discipline Report*. New York: Routledge, pp. 124–133.
Miyoshi, Masao (2001): "Turn to the Planet: Literature, Diversity, and Totality". In: *Comparative Literature*, Vol. 53, No. 4, pp. 283–297.
Page, Joanna (2021): *Decolonizing Science in Latin American Art*. London: UCL Press.
Poblete, Juan (2015): "The Memory of the National and the National as Memory". In: *Latin American Perspectives*, Vol. 42, No. 3, pp. 92–106.
Quijano, Anibal (2000): "Coloniality of Power, Eurocentrism, and Latin America". In: *Nepantla: Views from the South*, Vol. 1, No. 3, pp. 533–580.
Rancière, Jacques (2010): *Dissensus: On Politics and Aesthetics*. Transl. Steven Corcoran. London: Bloomsbury.
Radisoglou, Alexis (2019): "Ethnoplanetarity: Contemporaneity and Scale in Patricio Guzman's *Nostalgia de la luz* and *El botón de nácar*". In: Ferdinand, Simon/Villaescusa-Illán, Irene/Pereen, Esther (eds.): *Other Globes: Past and Peripheral Imaginations of Globalization*. Cham: Palgrave Macmillan, pp. 195–211.
Radisoglou, Alexis/Schaub, Christoph (2022): "Introduction: Figuring the Planet: Post-Global Perspectives on German Literature". In: *The Germanic Review*, Vol. 97, No. 2, pp. 125–133.
Santos, Boaventura de Sousa (2018): *The End of the Cognitive Empire: The Coming of Age of Epistemologies of the South*. Durham, NC: Duke University Press.
Spivak, Gayatri Chakravorty (1999): *Imperative zur Neuerfindung des Planeten/Imperatives to Re-imagine the Planet*. Ed. Willi Goetschel. Transl. Bernard Schweizer. Vienna: Passagen.
Walsh, Catherine E./Mignolo, Walter (2018): *On Decoloniality: Concepts, Analytics, Praxis*. Durham, NC: Duke University Press.
West-Pavlov, Russell (2018): "Toward the Global South". In: West-Pavlov, Russell (ed.): *The Global South and Literature*. Cambridge: Cambridge University Press, pp. 1–20.

Jorge J. Locane
Sobre el mundo, sobre el imperio
notas conjeturales para pensar el tono apocalíptico
de ciertas humanidades actuales

> Una sola vez en mi vida he tenido ocasión de examinar los quince mil dodecasílabos del *Polyolbion*, esa epopeya topográfica en la que Michael Drayton registró la fauna, la flora, la hidrografía, la orografía, la historia militar y monástica de Inglaterra; estoy seguro de que ese producto considerable, pero limitado, es menos tedioso que la vasta empresa congénere de Carlos Argentino. Éste se proponía versificar toda la redondez del planeta.
> Jorge Luis Borges, "El Aleph"

1 Perspectiva

Mundo, globalización, estéticas posglobales. Son categorías, por naturaleza, ambiciosas, difusas o desbordantes. Esta contribución responde a una convocatoria concebida para reflexionar sobre el estado aparentemente decepcionante del mundo en el contexto más reciente de la actual fase de la globalización. Las migraciones masivas —y muchas veces fatales— en el tren de aterrizaje de aviones, el timón de un barco o en el lomo de un tren apodado la Bestia; el generalizado colapso ambiental y la insultante concentración económica serían síntomas manifiestos de que el proyecto globalizador iniciado con la Caída del Muro habría fracasado. La pandemia y la toma del Estado por parte de ideologías conservadoras, populistas, nacionalistas o neoproteccionistas (dependiendo de la óptica con que se las quiera —o pueda— abordar) serían elementos agravantes de una coyuntura definida por el desengaño, la decadencia y el pesimismo en relación con una época previa de entonación festiva y triunfalista.

La lectura de los fenómenos, sin embargo, varía de acuerdo con el lugar desde donde se los examine. Una perspectiva poshumanista, por ejemplo, podría ver en el otoño del antropoceno razones de celebración para las muchas especies amenazadas por la agencia humana: la extinción del ser humano, o el de su hegemonía, puede implicar la emancipación de agentes no-humanos. La marcha de las multitudes hambrientas y desesperadas dispuestas a derribar los muros de

---

Jorge J. Locane, Universidad de Oslo

∂ Open Access. © 2023 the author(s), published by De Gruyter. [CC BY-NC-ND] This work is licensed under the Creative Commons Attribution-NonCommercial-NoDerivatives 4.0 International License.
https://doi.org/10.1515/9783110762143-004

contención que protegen el ilusorio bienestar del norte puede estar anunciando el quiebre de un orden excluyente perimido y la autoridad de una casta global. O, si la perspectiva se desplaza a Asia, se advertirían indicios de que la era del dominio americano ha comenzado a resquebrajarse y que el lugar rector pronto será asaltado por la todavía no abiertamente expansionista República Popular China. Los datos empíricos por sí mismos no estarían, pues, diciendo nada. Solo una vez que una voluntad analítica, siempre marcada por su posición en las estructuras de producción y subjetivación, los atraviesa, adquieren significados socialmente relevantes y también funcionales a determinados intereses. Toda modulación optimista o pesimista sería, por lo tanto, ideológica. Sería expresión de un anclaje de clase, de género, de preferencia sexual, de especie, étnico y también geocultural.

No se trata de predicar un relativismo radical; sino, más bien, de recurrir a esa provocación relativista como primera estrategia para poner en evidencia un lugar de enunciación y su nutriente ideológico. En las páginas que siguen, no obstante, voy a tratar de adoptar una mirada concreta —latinoamericanista y decolonial— para evaluar ciertas derivas discursivas globalizantes y ahora posglobalizantes. Con esto, hago visible el lugar de enunciación y la ideología científica —si es que aún se les da crédito a los postulados de Louis Althusser— desde los cuales pretendo hablar. Los planteos —menos definitorios que especulativos— van a girar en torno a dos ideas: 1. Que el mundo es una necesidad y una invención europea/occidental y que cualquier alegato en favor de tal categoría —autoritario o progresista— contiene una cuota de voluntarismo asertivo —si no colaboracionista— del programa imperial de expansión capitalista; y 2. Que las percepciones celebratorias o desencantadas de la "historia universal" (europea) están íntimamente ligadas a la distribución de posiciones —subalternas o dominantes— en las relaciones de poder. Si bien ambos serían susceptibles de ser discutidos, no me inquieta tanto el desengaño actual como el entusiasmo previo. Una intuición que motiva estas notas es que la literatura latinoamericana, en tanto expresión plebeya, formulada desde los bordes del sistema-mundo, se mostraría reticente a convalidar la existencia del mundo como una unidad continua, integrada y abarcable por una conciencia humana, y mucho menos a abonar la idea de que su constitución, y posterior reafirmación durante la fase inaugurada con la Caída del Muro, haya sido algo susceptible de ser considerado positivo. Por el contrario, su contribución habría sido disonante, no-confirmatoria, contrahegemónica; tendiente, en todo caso, a la incertidumbre y al fragmento. Habría sospechado, *por regla general*, de la representación armónica y continua del mundo y, por lo tanto, no mostraría *ahora* una entonación desencantada o condenatoria. Su vocación natural habría sido, en suma, la de afirmar la imposibilidad del mundo, al menos concebido como horizonte de acción ideal —explícito o implícito— de la violencia imperial.

2 Un recorrido por el mundo. De Sloterdijk a Rhodes, vía Kant y Schmitt

Sostiene Peter Sloterdijk que

> La hipótesis de que la Tierra sea representable adecuadamente en forma de esfera y, por ello, mediante un globo terráqueo con imágenes sobre él de superficies de continentes y mares, no ocupaba en la Edad Media, que se iba perdiendo a lo lejos, más que a un puñado de teólogos, cartógrafos y comerciantes estimulados por apetitos de lejanía. Para la amplia mayoría de los europeos, desde el siglo XVI hasta la declaración de independencia americana, significaba una especulación gratuita, sin repercusión digna de mención sobre la vida propia; y más, después de que los viajes de Colón, Vasco da Gama y Magallanes hubieran proporcionado un raro voto empírico en favor del supuesto precedente. (2010 [2005]: 191)

La idea de que el mundo es un objeto esférico que puede ser recorrido físicamente y abarcado intelectual o simbólicamente como una unidad es de factura reciente. La especulación teórica al respecto cuenta con algunos milenios de historia, pero su aceptación y popularización —el hecho de que se haya convertido en sentido común y *vox populi*, mucho más que un simple paradigma científico— son, en realidad, fenómenos jóvenes que hoy cuesta percibir como tales. ¿Cómo se explica esta evolución? ¿Cómo se logró tal consenso? ¿Qué factores contribuyeron a que el mundo tomara la forma material y simbólica que hoy todos creemos que tiene?

A estas preguntas intenta responder Sloterdijk desde su "esferología", en particular en el volumen II *Globos. Macroesferología* (2004 [1999]) y en el que complementa (y revisa) la trilogía *En el mundo interior del capital. Para una teoría filosófica de la globalización* (2010 [2005]). En estos volúmenes se propone refutar la noción de globalización como un fenómeno reciente, vinculado a la circulación acelerada de mercancías, capitales y personas, e incluso —frente a Immanuel Wallerstein— como un desarrollo inaugurado en 1492 con el proceso de expansión material de Europa. En su modelo, la globalización —el largo proceso mediante el cual el mundo adquiere una forma esférica, transitable y unificada— aparece segmentada en tres grandes fases: 1. la globalización metafísica —producto de la especulación filosófica del mundo (europeo) clásico—; 2. la globalización terrestre —definida por los viajes de circunvalación y conquista, desde la llegada de Cristóbal Colón a América hasta el fin de las ambiciones imperiales de Alemania en 1945—; y 3. la globalización electrónica —como el régimen de integración informática y comunicativa y la consecuente sincronización del mundo que generan las tecnologías desde 1945 hasta nuestros días—.

La narrativa de Sloterdijk es teleológica y, con sus importantes matices, se inscribe en una larga corriente discursiva interesada en dar cuenta del mundo, ya sea en su denominación antigua —el aristotélico *kósmos*— o en la actual —*Welt*/*world*/mundo—. A esta tradición, a la que ha colaborado de manera particularmente entusiasta el pensamiento alemán, propongo asignarle un carácter performativo. Enunciar el mundo sería al mismo tiempo afirmarlo en su materialidad. Sin esta línea de pensamiento, sus contornos serían más vagos, su superficie menos continua, su tangibilidad y abarcabilidad menos evidentes. En la medida que se lo describe —sin que importen los propósitos—, el mundo adquiere consistencia material: se lo hace inteligible, se lo objetiva y, así, se lo transforma en un artefacto sobre el cual es posible desplegar un proyecto militar, ideológico, político, económico, etc.

La tradición tiene una serie de puntales. Hacia fines del siglo XVIII, como expresión característica de la Ilustración, Immanuel Kant publica *Idea para una historia universal en clave cosmopolita* (2006 [1784]) y *Sobre la paz perpetua* (1998 [1795]) donde presenta argumentos en favor de una constitución republicana mundial que garantice los derechos fundamentales de todas las personas. Su programa es jurídico, normativo, no moral: propone una serie de pautas legales para regular las relaciones internacionales y la condición humana. El mundo adquiere, así, la fisonomía de un territorio uniforme amalgamado por una serie de principios legales, entre los cuales se incluye el derecho a la hospitalidad, esto es, a que nadie sea tratado *a priori* como enemigo al encontrarse en territorio extranjero. Es cierto que Kant censura el comportamiento de los conquistadores europeos en los territorios de ultramar como abuso del principio de hospitalidad. No obstante, su ideario —que hoy nutre la agenda cosmopolita de una parte del pensamiento progresista— no escapa a su época. Kant es expresión de una clase en ascenso y por aquel entonces revolucionaria, remite a la imaginación burguesa y a su utopía máxima: convertir al planeta en un lugar regido por *su* tutelaje moral y epistémico, por *sus* principios y valores, lo que, desde luego, incluye en un lugar prominente el de libre comercio. Ciudadanos, personas, y, por lo tanto, portadores legítimos de derechos, son, en primer término, quienes contribuyen al comercio sano y lo promueven. La paz perpetua, un mundo unificado por una serie de reglas compartidas, constituiría el terreno más fértil y deseable para que la burguesía se realice como clase hegemónica. No obstante, como hace notar Carl Schmitt, interferir en el libre comercio, para la conciencia burguesa y principalmente en los debates de la época, suponía una violación del derecho de gentes y una razón para desatar una guerra considerada justa:

Si los bárbaros se oponen al derecho a la hospitalidad, a la libre misión, al libre comercio y a la libre propaganda, violan los derechos de los españoles que existen según el Derecho de Gentes, y si en tal caso no sirve de nada la persuasión pacífica por parte de los españoles, éstos tienen un motivo para librar una guerra justa. La guerra justa, por otra parte, facilita el título, basado en el Derecho de Gentes, para la ocupación y anexión del suelo americano y el avasallamiento de pueblos americanos. A ello se añaden otras razones para una guerra justa de los españoles contra los americanos, razones que —en el lenguaje moderno— serían alegadas para "intervenciones típicamente humanitarias", y que conducen a derechos de ocupación e intervención de los españoles cuando éstos defienden a personas que son sometidas injustamente por los bárbaros en sus tierras. Este derecho de intervención de los españoles es válido, en especial, cuando éstos actúan a favor de aquellos indios que ya se han convertido al cristianismo. Sobre la base de tales frases comunes y argumentaciones posibles puede justificarse, desde luego, la Conquista española en su totalidad. (2003 [1950]: 96)

En su *El nomos de la Tierra en el Derecho de Gentes del "Jus publicum europaeum"* (2003 [1950]), Schmitt muestra cómo algunos posicionamientos relativos a la conquista de América que han sido considerados alegatos en favor de la soberanía de las poblaciones vernáculas, en realidad, deben ser entendidos como modos divergentes de justificar el dominio y la expansión europea. No se trataba —para plantearlo con una fórmula más amplia— de discutir la legitimidad de la conquista del mundo, sino de encontrar el mejor modo de justificarla. Desde frentes opuestos, y mediados por la filosofía de la historia y el espíritu de Friedrich Hegel, Kant y Schmitt coinciden en su teleología mundializadora orientada a hacer valer en toda la superficie de la Tierra —y, así, unificarla como mundo— un repertorio de principios de raigambre europea. La lectura en paralelo de Kant y Schmitt —que responderían a una perspectiva liberal-republicana y una conservadora-autoritaria, respectivamente— revela que el antiguo derecho de gentes y su evolución como derechos humanos pueden ser instrumentalizados para someter a sociedades a la univocidad, a las derivas subjetivas a una norma de alcance universal. El diseño de Kant —que opera como sustrato de cierta vertiente del idealismo progresista occidental— no deja, en este sentido, de ser totalitario, etnocéntrico y de clase ya que afirma la proyección mundial de una suma de valores y un ideario propios de un *único* grupo social: la burguesía europea.

Kant, Hegel, Schmitt, son, pues, puntales en una corriente de pensamiento que, desde ángulos divergentes y en función de diferentes proyectos, ha optado por abandonar el parroquialismo para poner en el centro de su especulación el objeto mundo. Este sería —renuncia a cualquier humildad mediante— su territorio natural, su campo de acción. Como en el caso de Alexander von Humboldt, con su *Kosmos – Entwurf einer physischen Weltbeschreibung* [Cosmos. Borrador de una descripción física del mundo] (1845–1862) o Luís de Camões con sus *Os Lusíadas* (1572) y ahora Wallerstein con su *world-system* y Sloterdijk con su *Esferas*, se trata de enfoques totalizadores que desbordan la realidad inmediata para postular enlaces —descriptivos o normativos— a escala mundial. Correspondería, en la medida que considera al mundo —y no a su comarca— como un lugar que puede ser representado por medio de *una* narrativa integradora, a una óptica cosmopolita. Es un pensamiento que se siente competente para dar cuenta de la totalidad, pero, desde el momento en que el mundo o el universo no se pueden "ver", esa competencia debe ser subordinada a la imaginación (Cheah 2008: 26). Al mismo tiempo que se lo narra, se lo describe, se lo aborda, el mundo adquiere estatus material, no antes. Primero se lo imagina desde narrativas teleológicas y totalizadoras, después existe como tal y, así, pasa a ser susceptible de ser unificado materialmente por medio de tecnologías como los mapas, los buques transatlánticos o los cables de fibra óptica que atraviesan los mares.

Independientemente de cuál sea la motivación y el trasfondo ideológico, todas estas fórmulas tienen en común que afirman la unidad y abarcabilidad del mundo: el mundo es uno y puede o debe ser pensado en su totalidad. Si se admite este criterio mínimo como denominador común, entonces, como parte del corpus, habría que contar el ideario de Cecil Rhodes quien en una de sus cartas de 1891 argumentaba en favor de que los británicos abandonaran su provincianismo para adoptar una mirada totalizante:

> Creo, con todo el entusiasmo que se cría en el alma de un inventor, que no es autoglorificación lo que deseo, sino el deseo de vivir para registrar mi patente en beneficio de aquellos que, creo, son el pueblo más grande que el mundo ha visto, pero cuya culpa es que no conocen su fuerza, su grandeza y su destino, y que están perdiendo el tiempo en sus asuntos locales menores, pero que estando dormidos no saben que a través de la invención del vapor y la electricidad, y en vista de su enorme aumento, deben ahora ser entrenados para ver el mundo como un todo, y no solo considerar las cuestiones sociales de las Islas Británicas. [la traducción es mía][1]

Este pasaje permite postular que la noción de mundo está íntimamente ligada a un lugar de enunciación definido por una conciencia de superioridad. Depende de una perspectiva abarcadora, trascendente, que supera las limitaciones de la percepción humana regular. El mundo sería, así, el resultado óptimo de una razón, como mínimo, totalizadora, pero rápidamente también mesiánica e imperial.

---

[1] "I believe, with all the enthusiasm bred in the soul of an inventor, it is not self-glorification I desire, but the wish to live to register my patent for the benefit of those who, I think, are the greatest people the world has ever seen, but whose fault is that they do not know their strength, their greatness, and their destiny, and who are wasting their time on their minor local matters, but being asleep do not know that through the invention of steam and electricity, and in view of their enormous increase, they must now be trained to view the world as a whole, and not only consider the social questions of the British Isles" (Rhodes 1902: 68).

Toda esta tradición así como los dispositivos discursivos y materiales que dinamizan las fases de Sloterdijk —el pensamiento griego, los viajes de conquista y colonización, las redes informáticas—[2] son occidentales/europeos. En este sentido, habría que considerar que el mundo es, en primer término, una invención que responde a necesidades del norte y más particularmente de la burguesía europea en tanto clase social que se autoatribuye la conducción del destino universal. El desmantelamiento del mundo bipolar y el considerado fin de la historia, a partir de 1990, habría representado la realización de la utopía burguesa de unificar materialmente el mundo como un mercado, sin mayores interferencias ideológicas y sin hostilidades. No es de extrañar, por lo tanto, que en las narrativas del norte se haya propagado un cierto entusiasmo afirmativo —cuyo mejor vocero fue por un momento Francis Fukuyama— de esa fase histórica que se ha popularizado como *la* globalización. Por fin, se había realizado la desiderata kantiana; por fin, el espíritu había alcanzado su forma más acabada; por fin, los límites del mundo coincidían con los de un gran mercado donde no es identificable un centro y la palabra clave es "libertad". La literatura del norte y para el norte habría adquirido, entonces, una entonación celebratoria. La economía material y simbólica se había sacado de encima el lastre de los Estados nacionales y eso se percibía como una conquista liberal y progresista.

Sin embargo, la actual debacle ambiental, las crisis migratorias, las reafirmaciones étnicas y el resurgimiento de la guerra arancelaria habrían puesto en evidencia que la concreción de la utopía había sido ilusoria y que el mundo tantas veces imaginado todavía es un proyecto o incluso un proyecto ya fracasado.

Esta percepción de la historia resulta, sin embargo, unilateral, ideológica y etnocentrada. Respondería al desengaño de una ideología liberal que, triunfante en la Guerra Fría, ahora se ve obligada a confrontar con sus propias contradicciones. Vista desde el sur, desde las periferias, y desde una razón subalterna, la globalización de los 90 no habría sido ninguna panacea, el mundo jamás habría tomado una apariencia continua y abarcable y la crisis generalizada actual —política, económica, ambiental, sanitaria— no sería un error de cálculos o atribuible

---

[2] En su modelo, la actual fase de la globalización habría dado lugar a un orden policéntrico y, como reacción a la tendencia homogeneizadora, también a un retorno defensivo al provincianismo. "La globalización" –escribe Sloterdijk– "está saturada en un sentido moral desde que todas partes del mundo las víctimas hacen saber a los culpables las consecuencias de sus crímenes: esto caracteriza el núcleo de la situación postunilateral, postimperial, poscolonial" (2010 [2005]: 28). Las tecnologías que unifican el mundo y lo sincronizan, fundamentalmente la www, están controladas, sin embargo, por los Estados y corporaciones occidentales hegemónicos.

a gestiones "ilegítimas" como la de Donald Trump sino la auténtica realización, la fase más desarrollada, del expansionismo capitalista europeo.

La pregunta que surge, entonces, es si, desde el sur, desde los territorios subyugados por el expansionismo, es posible imaginar el mundo como totalidad. Con "desde el sur" no me refiero a una perspectiva crítica, sino a un lugar de enunciación material, a un anclaje físico y a condiciones de producción específicas. ¿Es posible que una subjetividad marcada negativamente por las relaciones de poder geopolítico imagine un mundo integrado, continuo y transitable? ¿Que lo considere su patrimonio o terreno de acción natural? En todo caso, ¿de qué manera la condición subalterna permite desplegar una mirada totalizadora? Si se admite que el mundo es el horizonte de acción de una imaginación totalitaria o una conciencia que, como Rhodes, se autopercibe superior, ¿se lo puede pensar desde las periferias? Eventualmente, ¿qué forma toma? Y de manera más específica, ¿existió para la literatura del sur *un* mundo posterior a la Guerra Fría relativamente armónico?

3 En las provincias. De Constitución a Angosta, vía Lacandona

En su estudio sobre la sensibilidad cosmopolita latinoamericana, Mariano Siskind incluye un capítulo dedicado a contrastar la narrativa de Julio Verne y la de Eduardo Holmberg[3]. A modo de conclusión, arriba a la idea de que

> Las novelas de Verne producen imágenes eficaces del mundo como una totalidad liberal mediada por relaciones sociales modernas, porque están seguras del lugar que ocupan, como *novelas francesas*, en el proceso histórico de expansión mundial de las instituciones, las prácticas y los valores modernos burgueses. ¿Qué determina, entonces, la "diferencia situacional radical [latinoamericana de *Nic-Nac*] en la producción cultural de sentido" (Jameson, 1987: 26)? *Viaje maravilloso del señor Nic-Nac al planeta Marte* ni siquiera intenta afirmar un mundo, un universo unificado por la hegemonía de una clase social y sus aspiraciones globales. En cambio, la novela despliega un imaginario universalista alternativo que enseguida niega, como si sus condiciones marginales de producción de universalidades discursivas solo permitieran subrayar los límites de su imposibilidad. (2016 [2014]: 78)

La "diferencia situacional radical", la que, para el caso, va de Francia a Argentina en el siglo XIX, es determinante: mientras que la posición central permite y

---

[3] El texto se publicó en diferentes lenguas y versiones sensiblemente divergentes. Cito de la incluida en la traducción al español del libro *Cosmopolitan Desires* en tanto la más reciente y, por lo tanto, la que, por el momento, se puede considerar definitiva.

autoriza un despliegue totalizador, la periférica remarca los límites de semejante proyección e incluso la inconsistencia de la noción de mundo. Todas las narrativas comentadas arriba se inscriben de diferentes modos dentro de un régimen de producción comparable al de Verne y aparecen definidas por la certidumbre que otorga la hegemonía político-cultural. En el sur, y no solo en el siglo XIX, la perspectiva sería menos asertiva, más vacilante; el mundo ahí no sería tan evidente y sincrético. En todo caso, adquiriría un carácter forzado o fragmentario, atravesado por diferencias irreconciliables y por las determinaciones del desarrollo desigual y combinado.

Así como los relatos mundializadores —ya sea en la ficción o en la especulación teórica— abundan en el norte, en el sur resulta más difícil identificarlos. *Viaje maravilloso del señor Nic-Nac al planeta Marte* habría sido una suerte de ejercicio fallido del siglo XIX. "El Aleph" (1996 [1945]), de Jorge L. Borges, sí parece ser evidencia irrefutable de que el sur también puede producir despliegues totalizadores. Creo, no obstante, que el cuento de Borges con frecuencia ha sido instrumentalizado para propósitos que revierten su intención de poner en duda la abarcabilidad e inteligibilidad del mundo, o el universo, por parte de una conciencia humana. Todos los puntos del orbe, en "El Aleph", coinciden en un punto localizado en un sótano de una casa del barrio de Constitución en Buenos Aires. El fragmento local —y periférico—, sugiere, contiene el universo, pero el proyecto de representar esa totalidad trascedente, mediante el poema titulado "La Tierra" —"una descripción del planeta" (1996 [1945]: 619)— que compone Carlos Argentino Daneri, solo puede ser objeto de burla por parte de Borges. Semejante empresa, a los ojos del narrador, no puede resultar más que en un "pedantesco fárrago" (1996 [1945]: 621). Así, el cuento de Borges revela el carácter desmesurado y pretencioso de la voluntad totalizadora. El mundo, eventualmente, podrá ser representado por una conciencia segura de su posición hegemónica, pero no —de manera eficaz, al menos— por un personaje llamado "Argentino". De esta manera, la condición periférica inscripta en el fracaso del proyecto de Daneri sirve para marcar los límites de la apropiación simbólica del mundo en tanto desmesurada y pedante.

El *Canto general* (1950), de Pablo Neruda, es abarcador, pero antes afirmativo del fragmento que de la totalidad. En el marco de los procesos de construcción identitaria poscoloniales, demarca y subraya los límites de una región. De inspiración bíblica, el *Cántico cósmico* (1989), de Ernesto Cardenal, sí constituiría un caso puntual que pretende cubrir el todo, lo mismo tal vez que *Galáxias* (1984), de Haroldo de Campos.

La transición del siglo XX al XXI, sin embargo, habría sido especialmente prolífica en lo que refiere a imágenes (aprobatorias) de un mundo interconectado. En otro lugar (2016), sin embargo, traté de mostrar que la ficción producida *en* América Latina en el contexto de la actual fase de la globalización, antes que la integración del mundo y con ello la posibilidad de pensarlo como una unidad relativamente armónica y transitable, habría destacado el carácter desigual y excluyente del proceso de modernización global impulsado por el neoliberalismo. Lejos de cualquier entonación optimista, habría alertado sobre la proliferación de fronteras y la destrucción ambiental causada por el extractivismo y el consumismo. Para eso, se habría detenido no tanto en los espacios de tránsito y en los flujos —que es lo que las corrientes críticas liberales, selectivas, se apuraron a relevar— como en los dominios locales —subnacionales— y en los impactos de la modernización compulsiva en dicho nivel. Propongo retomar algunos argumentos expuestos en ese trabajo porque lo que acá me interesa en primer término es poner de relieve la idea de que el proyecto globalizador —el concepto (neo)liberal de mundo— no comenzó a fracasar recientemente sino que, examinado desde las periferias —a los ojos de las "víctimas" que menciona Sloterdijk—, siempre ha sido una empresa considerada destructiva, violenta e ilegítima y que, por lo tanto, las actuales alarmas del norte serían más bien una toma de conciencia ideológica y tardía de la zona progresista del liberalismo.

Los paisajes escatológicos, que dejan poco margen para cualquier optimismo, abundan en la literatura latinoamericana de las últimas tres o cuatro décadas. Pretender consignarlos en su totalidad sería un despropósito, y las lecturas de novelas como *Única mirando el mar* (1993), de Fernando Contreras Castro, *2010: Chile en llamas* (1998), de Darío Oses, *Plop* (2002), de Rafael Pinedo, o *El año del desierto* (2005), de Pedro Mairal, son concluyentes y no escasean. Desde una programática de denuncia con matices indigenistas, el trabajo de Homero Aridjis —a caballo entre la literatura y el activismo— se ha centrado en alertar sobre la devastación epistémica y ambiental impulsada por los procesos modernizadores. En 1985 convocó a cien intelectuales y artistas y formó el llamado Grupo de los cien para promover una toma de conciencia y alentar políticas ecologistas. En 1995, con el eco del levantamiento zapatista de fondo y la consecuente actualización de un repertorio de demandas que se remontan hasta 1492, dictó una conferencia titulada "Hacia el fin del milenio" donde hacía un balance y vaticinaba rasgos del siglo XXI. Sostenía que, entonces,

> Las historias nacionales buscarán confundirse con las historias universales. En esos recuentos totales, hechos en el Primer Mundo, y repetidos en el Tercero, América Latina (a cuyo territorio los europeos trajeron su religión, idioma y calendario) casi no existirá. Y si existe, será por sus desastres naturales, sus violaciones a los derechos humanos, sus conflictos sociales, y por la enorme inseguridad en sus calles y carreteras. La Amazonía puede convertirse en el próximo milenio en el desierto más grande del mundo. Algunas ciudades latinoamericanas, como la ciudad de México, sobrepobladas, contaminadas, devastados sus recursos naturales y sin agua, serán el escenario de frecuentes emergencias

ecológicas; otras, conformarán la geografía del crimen, la prostitución, la droga y el secuestro. A causa de la devaluación de nuestras gentes, causada por las crisis económicas, los latinoamericanos tendremos que luchas contra una nueva esclavitud. (1995: 4)

El pensamiento y la escritura latinoamericanos de la época están hiperpoblados de pasajes como este. El escenario general del fin de la historia, según se lo percibía desde los territorios del sur, era de creciente devastación. El levantamiento zapatista había anunciado que la violencia de la empresa colonial lejos estaba de haber sido erradicada, sino que más bien había mutado hacia una forma menos explícita, más sofisticada. El exterminio de la naturaleza que había impulsado la modernidad seguía en marcha e incluso se estaba acelerando: en pocos años acabaría con los reservorios que, como el Amazonas o Lacandona, todavía no habían sido arrasados del todo. La esclavitud se reactualizaría. Así, el mundo que hasta la Caída del Muro estaba compartimentado en dos grandes bloques no dejaba de estar dividido, sino que la gran brecha se reconstituía a partir de un eje horizontal: al norte, el capitalismo triunfante; al sur, el capitalismo en su expresión más salvaje y decadente. Las narrativas del sur, sin embargo, valen como provincianas. La narrativa del norte, hegemónica, tendería a la propagación y a imponerse como de validez universal. Cuando los enunciados del poder preconizaban prosperidad; los subalternos, marcados por la "diferencia situacional radical", advertían sobre el carácter eminentemente bárbaro de esa prosperidad, en realidad, ilusoria y reservada para pocos.

La distribución desigual de beneficios y costos, que es constitutiva de los procesos de globalización, refiere también al de la movilidad en tanto un bien de acceso restringido. Desde la descomposición del mundo comunista, la percepción que se propagó en el norte, tanto a través de los medios de comunicación como de ciertos aportes académicos, acentuaba la creciente permeabilidad de las fronteras. No solo se habían diluido los rígidos límites que separaban los territorios capitalistas de los comunistas sino que también vacilaban las delimitaciones nacionales. El progresismo liberal comenzaba, así, a vislumbrar un territorio continuo donde no solo circulaban libremente los bienes materiales y simbólicos, sino que también las diferencias étnicas y los celos de los nacionalismos pasaban a diluirse en una confraternización universal y superadora. Esta lectura estaba, naturalmente, marcada por una posición de enunciación. Era una verdad parcial, pero experimentada desde un lugar hegemónico y, por lo tanto, con capacidad de proyectarse e ingresar en otros sistemas de subjetivación. La literatura latinoamericana —otra vez: la signada por condiciones materiales de producción específicas— no era tan confirmatoria de esa verdad parcial. Narraba en muchos casos la verdad *otra*: la de los guetos de exclusión, la de las rígidas compartimentaciones urbanas, la de la contundente materialidad de los muros que intentan inmunizar el bienestar del norte.

Angosta (2007 [2003]), de Héctor Abad Faciolince, es uno de estos textos. Informa sobre la experiencia de un grupo de personajes que se aloja en el hotel La Comedia ubicado en la ciudad imaginaria Angosta. Esta ciudad ficcional, que, no obstante, presenta atributos referenciales que remiten a Bogotá y Medellín, está compartimentada en tres "sektores" estratificados verticalmente y correspondientes a Tierra Fría, Tierra Templada y Tierra Caliente. Cada uno de estos territorios conforma una economía material y simbólica diferenciada de las otras y corresponde a un grupo social que va de los aventajados que habitan Tierra Fría a los parias que se amontonan en Tierra Caliente. La circulación entre las tres zonas se encuentra altamente regulada y el acceso a la de confort, también conocida como Paradiso, reservado para muy pocos:

> el acceso al Sektor F está completamente restringido y, además de la muralla natural que levantan las montañas, Paradiso está aislado por un *obstacle zone*, o área de exclusión, que consiste en una barrera de mallas, alambrados, caminos de huellas, cables de alta tensión, sensores electrónicos y multitud de torres de vigilancia con soldados que pueden disparar sin previo aviso a los intrusos. Por tierra (bien sea en bus, en metro, en bicicleta o en automóvil) hay un único acceso a Paradiso, a través del Check Point, un búnker subterráneo que está manejado por una fuerza de intervención internacional. (24)

Así, el relato de Faciolince, con un anclaje en el sur, resalta la proliferación de inequidades sociales, pero también las restricciones al movimiento. Pone en evidencia que el desplazamiento así como se ha visto favorecido para algunos sectores y tal vez, acaso, en las regiones del norte global, para otros y en el sur muestra severas limitaciones. En perspectiva local, desde los territorios afectados negativamente por la globalización neoliberal, el mundo habría tomado, entonces, la apariencia de un lugar atravesado por fronteras infranqueables y por la incomunicación entre los compartimientos que lo conforman. El mundo, dado el caso, estaría compuesto por mundos reñidos entre sí y, si se considera que el único aeropuerto internacional de Angosta está ubicado en la zona de confort, en Tierra Fría, su transitabilidad no sería un bien universal sino exclusivo de una casta social.

Que textos como *Papeles falsos* (2010), de Valeria Luiselli, con personajes itinerantes, hayan sido afirmativos del carácter continuo, relativamente armónico y transitable del mundo no se impone sobre la evidencia incontestable que presentan numerosas fuentes redactas y puestas en circulación *en* América Latina donde el mismo adquiere una apariencia en el mejor de los casos fragmentaria y marcada por la violencia material y simbólica. Es cierto que *en* América Latina también se han escrito (algunos) textos que dan por supuesta la abarcabilidad del mundo y su consecuente carácter unitario, uno de ellos es *No será la Tierra* (2006), donde Jorge Volpi narra las grandes transformaciones históricas acaecidas durante las últimas décadas del siglo XX sin detenerse en fronteras nacionales o siquiera continentales. La recepción crítica en el sur, no obstante, no ha sido benévola y más bien ha remarcado el fracaso de semejante proyecto. En su reseña del libro, en una entonación general que recuerda a las observaciones de Borges al desmesurado plan de Argentino Daneri, Rafael Lemus anotó: "Lo intenta ahora [escribir una novela total], con mayor tesón y vanidad, como si antes hubiera fracasado apenas por falta de voluntad, en *No será la Tierra*. Pocas novelas menos pudorosas y más ambiciosas que esta última. Pocas, por lo mismo, más fallidas. Su intención: construir una novela-enciclopedia capaz de recorrer paso a paso los eventos centrales del siglo XX" (2006).

Creo que esta escritura, en cierta medida de raigambre latinoamericana, pero de "amplias miras", representa más bien casos puntuales y no —aunque la crítica del norte ha tendido a generalizarla— *la* literatura latinoamericana. Esta literatura suele no interpelar a la crítica vernácula no solo por sus excesos en términos de contenido o información. La crítica que se pronuncia *desde* América Latina la considera artificiosa y censurable también desde el punto de vista formal. Al respecto, el argumento de Lemus es que Volpi "[c]ree saludable escribir desde el vacío, sujeto apenas a las demandas del circuito editorial internacional" (2006). Su registro —sugiere Lemus— es plano, sin marcas culturales específicas, diseñado en función de la legibilidad y la traducción. De manera más amplia, lo que se podría sostener, entonces, es que la imaginación mundializante latinoamericana que cobró vida durante el último proceso globalizador responde, en realidad, a un horizonte de expectativas occidental y está orientada a los anaqueles del mercado internacional. Sería, así, un producto que intenta acomodarse a las necesidades de un supuesto consumidor sin identidad cultural, pero, antes que a eso, a una crítica académica o periodística que, desde el norte, le pide a la literatura latinoamericana evidencia de las hipótesis que ella misma pergeña.

La escritura producida al sur y en función de representaciones y expectativas localizadas sería menos solidaria con esas demandas y, por lo tanto, habría afirmado la inabarcabilidad del mundo o, dado el caso, la segmentación derivada de la violencia colonial y del desarrollo desigual y combinado. Las escrituras del sur —vale decir— habrían rebatido la integración conciliadora del mundo, a través de las tecnologías y los discursos, que el norte progresista se apuró a celebrar en los albores de nuestro proceso globalizador.

4 Líneas de fuga. El submundo y el supramundo

Escribo estas notas en agosto de 2021. Gracias a los programas de vacunación, la pandemia de Covid-19 parece estar en retroceso. Los indicadores fatales se curvan hacia abajo y otras noticias los reemplazan en las primeras planas. Una es la toma de Kabul por parte de los talibanes. Otra, una seguidilla de incursiones al espacio encabezadas por "excéntricos" millonarios. Ambas constituyen vectores discursivos que reactualizan la condición del objeto conocido como mundo.

La retirada de las tropas occidentales de Afganistán y el ágil avance de las milicias talibanes hasta llegar a la capital ponen punto final a una misión que se ha extendido más de lo conveniente. Veinte años de ocupación estadounidense y de influjo ideológico a través del gobierno de Ashraf Ghani no lograron corregir una deriva local disonante, hostil a una definición occidental y homogénea de mundo. No solo se ha perdido Afganistán como territorio controlado materialmente por Occidente, también han fracasado los principios de libre mercado, libertad de culto, democracia e igualdad de derechos para las mujeres de un modo que, por su celeridad y ausencia de obstáculos, bien puede extenderse a otros enclaves locales de la región. El sur, una vez más, reemerge, manifiesta su diferencia y hace evidente la inviabilidad constitutiva de un mundo forjado por las armas. Se trata de una reterritorialización que evidencia que las concepciones alternativas del mundo se encuentran subyugadas o en estado larvado en los enclaves periféricos. Muestra también que la Historia no ha detenido su marcha y que el mundo todavía no ha llegado a ser tal, que no puede, incluso, ser tal. En todo caso, que la eventual euforia occidental respondía a condiciones circunstanciales y evaluaciones apresuradas. Preocupado por la insurgencia revolucionaria que interfería la hegemonía occidental, hace cincuenta y cinco años Carl Schmitt se preguntaba: "¿Quién podrá impedir que, de manera análoga, pero mucho más intensa, surjan nuevas especies insospechadas de enemistad que provoquen por su parte apariencias y formas inesperadas de un nuevo partisanismo?" (1966: 130). Los talibanes reactualizan la pregunta de Schmitt en el siglo XXI. Son una manifestación partisana que —guste o no guste a las formas progresistas de pensamiento— señala uno de los límites del mundo.

Otro límite, en una dirección opuesta, lo señala la coalición de hombres millonarios blancos y de habla inglesa que últimamente se han lanzado, por iniciativa privada, a la conquista del espacio. Con emprendimientos individuales pero solidarios entre sí, Richard Branson, Jeff Bezos, en julio, y próximamente Elon Musk están dando los primeros pasos concretos hacia territorios que hasta el momento habían sido visitados ante todo por la ficción prospectiva. Caracterizados como "turismo espacial", estos viajes están logrando transportar a los pasajeros más allá de la atmósfera y no responderían más que al "espíritu aventurero" de los millonarios: durante los viajes, observan la curvatura de la Tierra y se mantienen ingrávidos por algunos minutos; después, vuelven a la superficie. Son, sin embargo, vuelos experimentales que prometen convertirse en regulares y de mayor alcance en breve tiempo. Llegar a la Luna y después a Marte no es algo que estos emprendedores descarten para sí mismos.

Se trata de una operación desterritorializadora que implica dos acciones complementarias: la ocupación de otros planetas y, potencialmente, el abandono del que habitamos. Estos viajes representan, en cierto modo, una nueva fase en el programa de expansión occidental: el horizonte ahora es el espacio exterior; anuncian que pronto habrá que inventar palabras para nombrarlo y mapas para unificarlo y hacerlo transitable. Pero también informan sobre el carácter autodestructivo del proyecto de mundo de las élites del norte. Así como el agotamiento de Europa durante el lento transcurrir de la Edad Media condujo a la nobleza a financiar los viajes exploratorios que llevaron a Colón a América, el agotamiento del mundo, el anunciado colapso ambiental, ahora estaría favoreciendo un nuevo plan de exploración y conquista. La modernidad habría, así, alcanzado su límite: habría devastado el planeta. Y, aunque todavía no sea constatable, las élites occidentales que han encabezado el proceso ya estarían abriendo una salida de emergencia y preparando condiciones para abandonarlo. Los viajes al espacio marcan, así, un límite por exceso: el norte produjo todo el mundo que pudo producir, hasta hacerlo colapsar.

Para cerrar, entonces, el sur de los talibanes estaría operando a nivel submundo y minando la integridad del mundo desde abajo. Negaría su consistencia y uniformidad. El norte de los Bezos y cía., por su parte, lo hace a nivel supramundo y lo da por acabado desde arriba, desde la demasía. Habría, acá, un exceso de mundo. En cualquier caso, ya sea que se piense y se observe el mundo desde el norte, o el no-mundo desde el sur, algo queda claro: el expansionismo conduce a una aporía. Si al mundo se lo conquista, se lo convierte en un territorio inhabitable y hostil, pero, si no se lo conquista, no puede ser más que un mosaico de mundos.

Bibliografía

Abad Faciolince, Héctor (2007 [2003]): *Angosta*. Bogotá: Planeta.
Aridjis, Homero (1995): "Hacia el fin del milenio". *Encuentros*, nr. 11. Centro cultural del BID.
Borges, Jorge L. (1996 [1945]): "El Aleph". *Obras completas I*. Buenos Aires: Emecé, pp. 617–627.

Cheah, Pheng (2008): "What Is a World? On World Literature as World-Making Activity". *Daedalus* 3, pp. 26–38, https://doi.org/10.1162/daed.2008.137.3.26.
Kant, Immanuel (2006 [1784]): *Idea para una historia universal en clave cosmopolita*. México DF: Universidad Nacional Autónoma de México.
— (1998 [1795]): *Sobre la paz perpetua*. Madrid: Tecnos.
Lemus, Rafael (2006): "No será la Tierra, de Jorge Volpi". *Letras libres*, 31 de diciembre, https://www.letraslibres.com/mexico/libros/no-sera-la-tierra-jorge-volpi.
Locane, Jorge J. (2016): *Miradas locales en tiempos globales. Intervenciones literarias sobre la ciudad latinoamericana*. Madrid/Frankfurt a.M.: Iberoamericana/Vervuert.
Schmitt, Carl (2003 [1950]): *El nomos de la Tierra en el Derecho de Gentes del "Jus publicum europaeum"*. Buenos Aires: Struhart & Cía.
— (1966 [1963]): *Teoría del partisano. Acotación al concepto de lo político*. Madrid: Instituto de Estudios Políticos.
Siskind, Mariano (2016 [2014]). *Deseos cosmopolitas. Modernidad global y literatura mundial en América Latina*. Buenos Aires: Fondo de Cultura Económica.
Sloterdijk, Peter (2010 [2005]): *En el mundo interior del capital. Para una teoría filosófica de la globalización*. Madrid: Siruela.
— (2004 [1999]): *Esferas II. Globos. Macroesferología*. Madrid: Siruela.
Stead, W. T. (ed.) (1902): *The Last Will and Testament of Cecil John Rhodes with Elucidatory Notes to which are added some Chapters describing the Political and religious Ideas of the Testator*. Londres: "Review of reviews" Office.

Romina Wainberg
Writing about Writing Amidst the End of Worlds
An Invitation

> Pourquoi ne cesse-t-il pas d'écrire?
> Maurice Blanchot[1]

Amid a global pandemic, unprecedented environmental catastrophes, egregious military occupations, an increasing number of forced displacements, femicides and genocides, rampant socioeconomic inequalities, and an ongoing wave of massive layoffs (including the closure of entire humanities departments), Blanchot's question returns with the wit of a provocation, if not with the weight of an accusation: Why don't we just stop writing? Why, exactly, among the rubble of a planet in ruins?

This question is urgent and deceivingly plain. We are now self-evidently no longer in a position where our responses can delight in their own overstatements about the "disruptive agency" of literature and the "political power" of literary studies. The very fact that our impotence has become self-evident – in the twofold sense of "flagrant to everyone" and "clear to us" – should give us pause. How many red flags have we mistaken for red herrings along the way? How long have we been taking for granted the significance of our jobs quite solitarily? A tentative answer: at least twenty-seven years.

In 1994, within the framework of the so-called Science Wars (1994–2000) that would climax with the Sokal Affair[2], biologist Paul R. Gross and mathematician

---

[1] See Blanchot (1955: 20).
[2] In 1996, physicist Alan Sokal "intentionally wrote [an] article so that any competent physicist or mathematician (or undergraduate physics or math major) would realize that it is a spoof [. . .] the editors of *Social Text* felt comfortable publishing [this] article on quantum physics without bothering to consult anyone knowledgeable in the subject" (Sokal 1996: n.p.). According to Sokal, while his method was satirical, his motivation was "utterly serious". To his mind, *Social Text*'s acceptance of his article "exemplifie[d] the intellectual arrogance of Theory – postmodernist literary theory, that is – carried to its logical extreme. No wonder they didn't bother to consult a physicist. If all is discourse and 'text,' then knowledge of the real world is superfluous" (Sokal 1996: n.p.). Curiously, this concern towards an overbroad notion of "text" was voiced *within* the humanities at least a decade prior to The Sokal Hoax. Take, for instance, analytic philosopher Richard Shusterman's words from 1986: "Radical philosophical

---

Romina Wainberg, Stanford University

∂ Open Access. © 2023 the author(s), published by De Gruyter. This work is licensed under the Creative Commons Attribution-NonCommercial-NoDerivatives 4.0 International License.
https://doi.org/10.1515/9783110762143-005

Norman Levitt published their best-selling *Higher Superstition: The Academic Left and Its Quarrels with Science*. Although Gross and Levitt's main thesis is rehearsed, stated, and rehashed many times throughout the volume, the following passage discloses the book's agenda with particular candor:

> The humanities, as traditionally understood, are indispensable to our civilization. [. . .] The indispensability of professional academic humanists, on the other hand, is a less certain proposition. Scientists are deeply cultured people, in the best and most honorable sense. [. . .] The range of knowledge of music, art, history, philosophy, and literature to be found in a random sample of scientists is, we know from long experience, extensive. As humanists, scientists are autodidacts. One obvious consequence of this fact is to undercut the argument that traditional humanities departments [. . .] are indispensable. (Gross/Levitt 1994: 243)

Irrespective of the heated discussions held in the context of the Science Wars, at the heart of whose "hard" side were precisely Gross, Levitt, and Sokal, few scholars on the "soft" side took this assault on their disciplines seriously enough to think that it could pose a real threat to the humanities' existence[3]. At most, the problem that the Sokal Hoax in particular was presenting seemed to be about a specific way of doing humanistic scholarship, not about the pertinence of the field as such. Yet, Sokal's provocation – overtly inspired by the reading of Gross and Levitt – hit the core rather than the "mantle" of humanistic research. To the still-incalculable benefit of contemporary neoliberal academia, in the mid-1990s there were influential spokespeople sufficiently confident to state (to put in writing): "We can have humanism without the humanities. Are humanities scholars even capable of giving a well-construed reason why universities still need them?"

This was almost three decades ago. Already then, the question of whether the humanities had the right to exist was posable, and in fact openly posed in the public sphere, with much resonance. The deadlock that our departments are presently experiencing may be new in its implications, but its roots (at least its epistemological ones) predate both the COVID-19 crisis and the 2008 socio-economic collapse. If we are just now beginning to witness the resurfacing and the consequences of questionings such as Sokal, Levitt, and Gross's, it is not because their stances have been dismantled along the road, but because they were simply put in reserve: *pre*-served for a better (or a worse) time.

---

deconstructors [. . .] are abolitionist Unionists who work to break down the distinctions between literature, criticism, and philosophy [by] treating all three as forms of what we would call 'writing', a general, undifferentiated, and thus unprivileging textuality [. . .] Rejecting these distinctions, however, seems only to lead us to a much wider and pernicious essentialism, an engulfing and unstructured monism of expression or textuality" (Shusterman 1986: 22–31).

3 Exemplary minimizations of The Hoax's consequences are Derrida (1997) and Latour (1997).

Now is that time. Now is the time when decades-long suspicions towards the humanities are being harnessed to shrink and shut entire university departments with unsettling ease. Coupled with the open cynicism and the entrepreneurial drive of both alt-right politics and institutional corporatism, epistemological slander becomes combustible. It is hence feasible that at present – as much as in the 1980s and 1990s – giving good reasons for the pertinence of our work will not suffice. But it is also the case that today, more patently than ever, it is impossible for us to keep doing business as usual.

Latin Americanists foresaw the possibility of our current deadlock. Mariano Siskind in particular cautioned us against doing-business-as-usual in "Towards a Cosmopolitanism of Loss". In what remains one of the most compelling and heartbreaking essays of the decade, Siskind prompted us to stop working under the often-shared assumption that humanistic research and aesthetic sensibility have an immediately relevant and politically disruptive role in public debates. "The notion that we are effectively politicizing our *shtick* because of our materialist analytical frame", writes the critic, "depends on an excessive and ostensibly voluntaristic self-representation of the role that humanistic research and aesthetic sensibility have in public debates today [. . .] I truly believe there is *very little* we can do with art and literature" (Siskind 2019: 228; my emphasis).

There is, I think, an indispensable double gesture contained in this passage: a compound generosity that allows us to think both retro and prospectively. On the one hand, Siskind's words are soberingly oracular – the accuracy of their vision urges us to retroactively revise the style, the consistency, and the impact of our previous work. On the other hand, the critic's argument does not point to the irreversibility of our discipline's impotence, but to the potency afforded by the very little we can still do from our epistemological and institutional standpoints. When considering the full gamut of this "very little", Siskind proposes "offering the discursive spaces we inhabit (our pedagogical, critical and aesthetic practices) as sites of [not-so-melancholic] mourning" (Siskind 2019: 227)[4]. My intervention –

---

[4] It is key to note how Siskind's proposal differs from superficially similar positions on the state of the art and the role of literary criticism. Indeed, a decade before the publication of "Towards a Cosmopolitanism of Loss" (2019), Stephen Best and Sharon Marcus were already warning literary scholars against the tendency "to equate their work with political activism" and were correspondingly asking the question of "why literary criticism matters if it is not political activism by another name" (Best/Marcus 2009: 2). Furthermore, Best and Marcus were advocating for a criticism whose role would be "a relatively modest one" (Best/Marcus 2009: 11). Still, these scholars' counterproposal to the state of the art of the discipline was to displace its epistemological focus from "symptomatic reading" to "surface reading" (Best/Marcus 2009: 1–13). What was being questioned then was not whether literary scholars should keep doing business-as-usual, but how business-as-usual should be conducted. Siskind's proposal thus

meant as an addition rather than a criticism towards Siskind's proposal – posits that opportunities may lie not only in the opening of spaces, but also in the carving out of times.

***

Let me elaborate by recapping and expanding Blanchot's initial question: "Pourquoi ne cesse-t-il pas d'écrire?", asks the essayist. "Pourquoi ne cesse-t-elles pas d'écrire?", could be asked about us. Why don't we stop writing precisely *now*? Why do *we* insist? Why do we, literary scholars or literary-scholars-to-be, insist not only upon writing, but upon *writing about writing*[5]?

Conveniently enough, I see a possible response hidden in my last extended formulation – a formulation that, also conveniently, refers to what literary scholars do. Through the phrasing "why do we keep writing about writing", I seem to be exploiting the homophony inherent in the term "writing" to refer to two different signifieds: first, an act of ongoing, continuous, or recurrent inscription ("why do we keep writing . . ."); secondly, a corpus of already written pieces (". . . about writing"). A common-sense interpretation of my phrase, which would also entail a general understanding and a questioning of our job, would thus be: "Why do we keep writing about the written, about written pieces of literature"? This inquiry sounds quite pertinent and descriptive. Indeed, most of the effort of twentieth and twenty-first century literary criticism has been directed to the study of writing as *corpus*: we read, theorize, examine, and build our analyses upon writing as always-already-the-(a)-crafted-(piece). In other words, we begin already in the *space* of writing, we focus on the extension of the already written.

---

differs from Marcus and Best's position not solely for its content, but also for the level at which he considers the discussion should be held. Not only is the critic's stance more modest in that it implies its own self-criticism, but it also operates at a more fundamental level. To be clear: Siskind's effort is not oriented towards favoring an epistemological agenda within an already functioning field but aimed at advancing structural questions about the field's very dynamics and *raison d'être*. Finally, one additional – hopefully self-explanatory – remark: the fact that Siskind's proposal engages with the role of the critic as professor (as *docente*) makes all the difference.

5 Needless to say that some of us, especially literary-scholars-to-be, keep writing about writing because we cannot economically afford to stop. Writing is, after or above all, part of our job description. My inquiries do not ignore that not all literary scholars are in the same position when it comes to writing, writing about writing, or writing about writing about writing. From my precarious vantage point, I wish to find more consistent ways of elucidating and explaining the relevance of our work (both to ourselves and to others). We may find an explanation behind the work we already do; we may need to change the ontological and epistemological understanding of our job before we find a sufficiently robust answer for our times.

But what about the *time* of writing? What about the *meantime* when writing is still in the process of its own spacing, of its making room for itself and of making itself a room for us to explore, to dwell, and to inhabit? What if, in the formulation "why keep writing about writing", the first and the second occurrence of the term were to mean the same? What if both occurrences of "writing" were to refer to the process of inscription as it progressively unravels? Could there be an underexplored possibility in the examination of writing in its undetermined, gradual deployment? My tentative answer is: "yes"! To justify my confidence and to show the modest though real potential of considering (the) penning (as) process, I propose to examine two twenty-first century Latin American novels that, within their already written spaces, stage writing as spacing. Put it simply, these novels feature scenes of writing as it gradually, continuously unfolds in time.

The first piece that I wish to explore is Rodrigo Hasbún's *El lugar del cuerpo* (2018 [2007]). The book is centered on Elena, an elderly Latin American writer based in the United States who, upon the imminence of her death, decides to recount her life story. At first, this project seems to be about healing the wounds caused by a single event: Elena's rape by her brother at the age of seven. From that moment on, and regardless of the character's prolific career and affective (after)life in the United States, it seems that her whole sense of worldliness[6] has irreversibly crumbled: Elena's is, indeed, the experience of the errant orphan "for whom no longer is a world underfoot and who can only afford to dwell in the time and place of [her] own dislocation" (Siskind 2019: 227). There is no personal, local, national, or universal signifying frame that could possibly substantiate the character's actions: the horizon of homeliness seems as alien to her as the horizon of her (or a) self.

And yet, amidst her corroded sense of world, within this permanent state of unworldling, *something* is still worth pursuing. Elena's words: "*Desarrollo, continuidad. No me importan. Con tal de lograr una textura, aire, color [. . .] Pero es*

---

[6] I use the concept of "world" as Heidegger characterizes it in "The Origin of the Work of Art", as that which "structures and simultaneously gathers around itself the unity of paths and relations in which birth and death, disaster and blessing, victory and disgrace, endurance and decline acquire for the human being the shape of its destiny. The all-governing expanse of these open relations is the world of this historical people" (Heidegger 2002 [1950]: 21). This concept of world is not incompatible with Mariano Siskind's historicized understanding of the term as "the symbolic structure that used to sustain humanistic imaginaries of universal emancipation, equality and justice" (Siskind 2019: 206). In the context of this essay, to "lose own's own sense of worldliness" entails both partaking in the corrosion of humanistic horizons of universal emancipation *and* experiencing the untying of knots that used to gather and hold a particular community together.

escribir o colgarse. Es escribir o cruzar la calle justo cuando pasa el bus. Es escribir o que el filo de un cuchillo se abra paso" (Hasbún 2018 [2007]: 83; emphasis in the original). As we can infer from this excerpt, writing is, for the character, quite literally vital. It is *that* which inscribes a dividing line between living and dying. Furthermore, writerly exercises seem here to serve as redeeming forms of suturing or, at least, as therapeutic modes of confronting the trauma of rape in such manner that unrepairable pain does not lead to suicide.

The identification of writing with a therapeutic tool may be a comforting – that is, a conclusive – interpretation. However, this thesis does not hold once we read the above-cited passage in concert with other scenes of writing featured in the novel. I take the following episode to be particularly revealing, but there are many:

> Yo en esta sala, sintiendo este frío, recordando estas cosas, intentando escribir este libro. Movimientos secretos del alma atribulada. Alma es una palabra que usa por primera vez. Sonríe después de teclearla. Realmente me estoy haciendo vieja, escribe, sus dedos delicados pero firmes sosteniendo un ritmo constante, como de disparo de ametralladora [. . .] Una tiene que disfrutar lo que va saliendo mientras va saliendo, escribe Elena, los dedos delicados pero firmes sosteniendo un ruido constante, como de disparos de ametralladora, y yo a estas alturas del párrafo he dejado de hacerlo. Luego mira hacia la ventana y se queda quieta durante varios minutos. (Hasbún 2018 [2007]: 68–69)

In this scene, writing emerges as a rather ambivalent, unpredictable practice: the exercise starts off with a dry enumeration of facts, only to move on to the rather grandiloquent expression "movimientos secretos del alma atribulada", a phrase whose unexpected inclusion of the word "alma" surprises Elena herself and makes her burst into laughter. This laughter is soon followed by a bitter reflection ("realmente me estoy hacienda vieja"), which is in turn succeeded by the playful orchestration of the character's fingers as she tries to keep the same constant rhythm, a rhythm that is itself disturbing, as it resembles the cadence of a machine gun. Finally, and without any solution of continuity, Elena devotes herself to staring at the window, her thoughts remaining inaccessible to the reader.

The fluctuating plasticity, the pliancy of this writerly process – its making room for the dry, the bitter, the risible, the unexpected, and the pleasurable – does not contradict but surely complicates the hypothesis suggested by the first passage. What the second excerpt and similar ones disclose is that, if the writerly praxis seems to Elena to be a lifesaver, it is not necessarily because it is always therapeutic or cathartic, but chiefly because writing opens a rather safe space of unpredictability. The very engagement with the texture of language, with the materiality of the computer, with the temperature in the room, with the salience of the bright window, this alternating interaction with the ecology of beings and events co-present in the moment of drafting (and afforded by that moment) – the entire dynamic guarantees that, at the very least, while writing is in place, life will not be subjected to traumatic predictability.

The writing process thus introduces the possibility of novelty into the homogeneity of a time that is otherwise lived as bare and unbearable pain. In other words, writing, in its own processual seriality, exteriority, and open-endedness, in the differences sprouting from its very form of reiteration, unparalyzes an experience of time caught in the repetition of the same. Hence, what we find in this scene are two temporal experiences of reiteration: that of the time of writing (which affords difference throughout its unbounded openness, porousness, and exteriorization) and that of the replay of the scene of rape (which amounts to a self-identical and thus increasingly asphyxiating form of repetition).

The twofold account of temporality displayed in Elena's scene has, I argue, philosophico-practical implications. These implications go against and simultaneously complement late-twentieth and twenty-first-century characterizations of the act of inscription. What Hasbún's novel affords in its depiction of the writerly process is a viewpoint complementary to the now too-well-established association between writing and dying. Indeed, it may be the case that, as twentieth-century thinkers have taught us well, "absence", "destruction", and "loss" are inherent in any writerly practice[7], *but insofar as it remains a process (and for as long as such process involves a human) writing is of the living.* It

---

[7] Reflections on the relationship between writing, loss, and death constitute the bulk of *The Space of Literature* (1955), even if Blanchot sides with the non-side of "the neutral". The very first page of Barthes's iconoclast "The Death of the Author" already involves the affirmation: "The author enters his own death, writing begins" (1977: 142). Giorgio Agamben's *Language and Death* (1982) surveys the relationship between language, being(s), negativity, and death in Western philosophy and poetry. Although the "paradigma deconstructivo" has been closely associated with an "énfasis excesivo en la muerte" (Esposito paraphrased by Moreiras 2019: 136), Derrida himself does not subscribe to characterizations of writing as either pure life or its complete exhaustion (1998 [1967]: 17). Still, the critique of "the metaphysics of presence" implies a corrective emphasis on non-presence understood as a necessary condition of possibility for all modes and activities of *archi-écriture*, including writing and speaking. I propose a reemphasis on vitality that takes Derrida's lessons as a premise. In this vein, my focus on (alphabetic) writing-as-spacing could be read as an instance of Derrida's twofold conceptualization of "*différer*". According to the theorist, "*Différer* in [one] sense is to temporize, to take recourse, consciously or unconsciously, in the temporal and temporizing mediation of a detour that suspends the accomplishment or fulfillment of 'desire' or 'will' [. . .] this temporization is also temporalization and spacing, the becoming-time of space and the becoming-space of time [. . .] The other sense of *différer* is the more common and identifiable one: to be not identical, to be other, discernible" (Derrida 1982: 8). If I depart from Derrida's viewpoint in my analyses, it is not only to place particular emphasis on the vital dimension of arche-writing, but also to

necessitates life even if it is traversed by the trails of death. And this lively, not necessarily vitalist but vital condition of the operation of writing, this process that in its exteriorized materiality is open to and opens the possibility of the unpredictable, of an unpredictable that does not come from sudden "unmediated inspiration" but from embodied compenetration, this more-than-human experience of extimacy makes all the difference to a character trapped in a growingly introspective, baleful form of monotony.

***

The above would be too grand to be my last words. They would stand too close to an overstatement to fulfill the promise of Siskind's "very little . . .". As I am determined to keep that promise, I wish to briefly examine an additional scenario– a scene where the stakes accorded to the decision of writing or not writing are lower than in Hasbún's novel. Ultimately, what I must prove is that writerly exercises also afford intriguing possibilities to those whose lives are not in immediate danger.

This is the case of the characters featured in Conceição Evaristo's novella "Sabela" (2016). In this piece, a community based in an unspecified area of Brazil retells the story of a flood that, years before, almost obliterated their village. The book is thus composed of diverse accounts of the same event, all collected orally, and then put in writing by the novella's eponymous protagonist. In the beginning, what the character aims to craft is a narrative as close to the actual event of the flood as possible. Since the only version Sabela has heard over the years is the one she has co-crafted in dialogue with her Mamãe, the daughter decides to ask other members of the community for their versions. "[P]ara un melhor entendimento do que foi a chuva", she explains, "não carece da escuta de outras falas. Quem sabe se ajuntando pedaços de falas [. . .] não poderia eu chegar a uma narração mais próxima do realmente acontecido. Digo mais próxima, porque penso que diante de certos acontecimentos, a palavra é muda" (Evaristo 2016: 86).

As this passage already suggests, Sabela's initial presupposition is that – although the event is itself unspeakable, constitutively unsurmountable – the weaving of different narratives will allow the community to get a more cohesive sense of what happened. Yet, as the character engages in an enterprise that demands "transcribing" the cadence and the specificity of the experience of others in their own terms, she finds herself writing sentences such as: "falo do prazer que o dilúvio me causou" (Evaristo 2016: 97), "[d]ebaixo das chuvas, eu

---

examine the distinct historical role that voice and the written letter have played (and still play) in more-than-Western or non-Western societies.

me sentia limpa e igual a todos" (Evaristo 2016: 96), "das chuvas me encanta o mistério" (Evaristo 2016: 102), and "eu não temi nada, estávamos numa prazeroza brincadeira, cada qual se molhava e molhava o outro" (Evaristo 2016: 91). Immediately after recording accounts on this joyful note, Sabela would find herself inscribing: "O que mais vi foi uma correnteza de naúfragos [. . .] Não esqueço também que as águas me levaram mamãe [. . .] Quando me equilibrei e olhei para traz, ainda vi parte da sua mão, no esforço do nado o do nada, como se estivesse dizendo adeus" (Evaristo 2016: 91–92).

A surprising, rather uncomfortable contrast thus emerges from the tension between Sabela's initial conceptualization of the flood as a solemnly unsurmountable event, and the complex, intermittently playful, often self-contradictory experiences that are revealed to her through aurality and inscription. In the end, the protagonist cannot but conclude that "muitos se perderam, mas muitos se encontraram nas e pelas águas" (Evaristo 2016: 76) – many died, but many found each other amidst turbulent waters. A structure of worlding crumbled while emerging senses of worldliness surged out of this communal experience.

To be sure, Evaristo's story does not aestheticize the deadly aftermath of the flood nor environmental catastrophe; on the contrary, there are many instances where coloniality, territorial occupation, modern extractivism, and long-term capitalistic resource mining are contested by the story's narrating voices (Evaristo 2016: 67, 70, 77). However, the novella is simultaneously invested in showcasing the irreducibility of experience to any hygienic, aprioristic, and uniform moral standard. As soon as it gives itself to the processes of remembrance, of externalization, of dialogic exchange, of unraveling, experience (both personal and collective) proves to be thornier, muddier, far less cohesive, and thus harder to convey than expected. From the perspective of Sabela, different *vivências* appear in all their convolutedness and unpredictability first in the process of listening and, more nuancedly, in the process of writing– a process that goes from the drafting of her first notes to the "curatorial" practices of reviewing, contrasting, and interlacing all recorded narratives in a single text.

The fact that the convolutedness of experiences seems to appear more intricately during the writing process prompts questions that, despite falling outside the scope of this essay, are worth noting. First, what is the historical standing of writing vis-à-vis speech in this community? When the protagonist concludes that "palavra alguma, seja ela falada, escrita, consagrada, repudiada, inventada, nada diz todo" (Evaristo 2016: 104), what is at stake? Is there a supplementariness, a tension, or a confrontation between writerly and oral (and between official and extra-official) accounts of communal experience? What is Sabela's status such that she may self-appoint to write on behalf of the collective? What is the relationship between words, bodies, and water in the context of this flood? Given that the story recounts the event in detail, including the deaths of those *que se perderam nas e pelas águas*, what can be inferred from the ones who got to live? Is there a criterion that can be retroactively retrieved and that separates deceased from survivors? To borrow Samir Sellami's delicate phrasing: what can we derive from the "I can breath [again][8]" that happens only for few after the flood and that functions as a condition of possibility for Sabela's plural-though-partial story?

That these questions make us uncomfortable is salutary. As it happens with Hasbún's work, Evaristo's piece does not allow for the reduction of her protagonist to a one-dimensional archetype (be it that of the heroine or the antiheroine). Concomitantly, the story prevents us from identifying writing with a cathartic, comforting or conclusive activity. Once again, writerly unfolding is deployed as an interval where open-ended, unsettling, and porous encounters emerge. By displaying these encounters as inherent in any writerly praxis, Evaristo's work also replaces the public image of literature as a self-enclosed, unmediated activity with a kinetic, thickly mediated characterization of composition: insofar as writing happens in life, it cannot but engage in porous rapports involving human and non-human agents. Finally, Sabela's penning process implies, as much as Elena's, an exercise in attentiveness to one's own body and to others' presences: in Hasbún's story, these others are non-human; in Evaristo's flood narrative, manifold human and non-human embroilments come about.

***

This anthropodecentric and dynamic characterization of the writerly practice, already present in Hasbún's work and richly expanded by Evaristo's piece, bears new theoretico-practical fruits. First and foremost, we gain an increasing awareness of the transformations that the representation of writing has undergone in the Latin American tradition. As I elaborate elsewhere[9], processual depictions of writing can already be found in mid nineteenth-century novels, and their presence becomes increasingly prominent in mid twentieth-century metaliterary works. However, the emphasis on the enmeshment between human and

---

8 In Samir Sellami's "The Poetics of Respiration", an unpublished manuscript, the critic reflects on whether "we are hearing a potential shift in our political discourses from Logos to *pneuma tou stomatos* and from the demand 'listen to me' to the statement 'I can't breathe'". Further studies may disclose unexpected links between *Dézafi*'s "frightening world where suffocation is the rule and breathing almost a miracle" (Sellami) and *Sabela*'s intermittent characterization of the flood as a "sufocamento da chuva" (Evaristo 2016: 80).

9 My dissertation-in-progress examines representations of the act of writing in the Latin American novel from the nineteenth to the early-twentieth centuries, with a particular emphasis on temporality.

non-human bodies, the complication of the status of writing vis-à-vis speech, and the focus on attentiveness and patience as values– all these seem to be peculiar to the twenty-first century.

I am currently working on ratifying (or regretting having proposed) this hypothesis on representations of writing in the Latin American novel. In the meantime, let us focus on the one fruit that is within reach, and allow me to recapitulate for the final harvest: This is a devastating historical moment for and beyond our field.

In this peculiar context where, in Mark Fisher's auspiciously borrowed words, "it is easier to imagine the end of the world[10] than it is to imagine the end of capitalism" (Fisher 2009: 2)[11], practices that lend themselves to modest surprises, to patient attentiveness, to reflection and exchange, to unexpected results, to no results at all! Practices *just like writing* are most welcome. Crucially, though, in order for these praxes to remain safe modes of unpredictability, their processual, mercurial, and porous unfolding needs to occur not in continuity, but in responsible (and sometimes inevitable) discontinuity with politics.

These writerly events, as displayed in Hasbún and Evaristo's works, would be an occasion of what Alberto Moreiras dubs "infrapolitics": a spacetime[12] where thought and perception can exist on the sidelines of a dialectical circularity between "politics" and "life" whereby everything, absolutely everything, is either

---

10 I am here referring to the threefold Heideggerian-Siskindian-planetary sense of term "world".

11 According to Fisher, the phrase was first attributed to Slavoj Žižek and Fredric Jameson (Fisher 2009: 2). To my knowledge, the idea first appeared in print in Jameson's *The Seeds of Time* (1994). The "Introduction" reads: "It seems to be easier for us today to imagine the thoroughgoing deterioration of the earth and of nature than the breakdown of late capitalism" (Jameson 1994: xii). That these words have begun to widely resonate with humanists fifteen years after their coinage may be another testament to our belatedness.

12 Although Moreiras uses the spatial metaphors of "la dimensión infrapolítica" (Moreiras 2019: 37) and "la región infrapolítica" (Moreiras 2019: 32), the infrapolitical enterprise (Moreiras 2019: 41) – as an always-ongoing adventure in thought/being at the margins of the circularity between life and politics – presupposes at least two kinds of temporality: a) a factic temporality (i.e., the time of existence where infrapolitics amounts to an ontological imperative, to the fact that life and politics are de facto non-coextensive) and a reflective temporality (i.e., all instances of explicit recognition and harnessing of infrapolitical facticity as an existential imperative, as that which does not let existence be reduced to the either-or of life and politics). The active carving out of writerly moments would be a case of reflective infrapolitics carried out within the inevitable constraints of factic time; writerly moments as such, though constrained by the imperatives of factic time, may combine different sorts of reflective experiences of temporality (some of which might be infrapolitical).

political or apolitical. As Moreiras's himself puts it, if we accept that there is nothing but life and politics, bare existence or political subjectivation, then "no hay salida, solo la aceptación mansa de una dialéctica [vida-política] que se mueve hacia la asimilación total, que es también la total transparencia [. . .] equivalencia plena y total disponibilidad, continuo ilimitado: vida y política [. . .] Y lo que se ha excluido es la posibilidad de dar un paso atrás para buscar un lugar de acogida" (Moreiras 2019: 29).

I cannot in good faith promise that all non-instrumental writerly practices will be homely places ("lugares de acogida"), but I am confident enough to suggest that many of them will stand as relatively *safe* spacetimes to rehearse avenues of thought that may only make themselves available through an open, attentive, patient, and hopefully collaborative process of inscription. Maybe, for us who are passionate about doing, studying, and teaching literature, for us who, for better or worse, have placed a bet on language and are still stubbornly betting on it, a question to add to our critical repertoire could be *what kinds of under-explored writing and after-writing experiences we can assemble, bring to bear, put to work, and socialize?* In other words: what kinds of writerly intervals can we carve out during those pockets of weekly time that we share with our peers and students– those pockets which are the only mode of "very little" that we definitely have (for now)? Which specific, untried, unorthodox strategies can we still put at others' disposal, perhaps because we wish to help them mourn, perhaps because writing allows precisely for that which we cannot predict?

As I hope to have shown with my analyses of Hasbún and Evaristo's scenes, our search for writerly praxes need not start from scratch: we may begin by (re)turning to Latin American literature for ideas.

Works Cited

Agamben, Giorgio (1991) [1982]: *Language and Death: The Place of Negativity*. Minneapolis: University of Minnesota Press.

Barthes, Roland (1977) [1967]: "The Death of the Author". In: *Image-Music-Text*. Transl. Stephen Heath. New York: Hill & Wang, pp. 142–148.

Best, Stephen/Marcus, Sharon (2009): "Surface Reading: An Introduction". In: *Representations* 108, 1, pp. 1–21.

Blanchot, Maurice (1955): *L'espace littéraire*. Paris: Gallimard.

Derrida, Jacques (1998) [1967]: *Of Grammatology*. Transl. Gayatri Chakravorty Spivak. Baltimore, London: Johns Hopkins University Press.

— (1997): "Sokal et Bricmont ne sont pas sérieux". In: *Le Monde*, p. 17.

—— (1982): *Margins of Philosophy*. Transl. Alan Bass. Baltimore, London: Johns Hopkins University Press.
Evaristo, Conceição (2016): "Sabela". In: *Histórias de leves enganos e parecenças*. Rio de Janeiro: Malê Editora, pp. 59–105.
Fisher, Mark (2009): *Capitalist Realism: Is There No Alternative?*. Hampshire: John Hunt Publishing.
Gross, Paul R./Levitt, Norman (1998) [1994]: *Higher Superstition: The Academic Left and Its Quarrels with Science*. Baltimore, London: Johns Hopkins University Press.
Hasbún, Rodrigo (2018) [2007]: *El lugar del cuerpo*. La Paz: El Cuervo.
Heidegger, Martin (2002) [1950]: "The Origin of the Work of Art". In: *Off the Beaten Track*. Transl. Julian Young and Kenneth Haynes. Cambridge: Cambridge University Press, pp. 1–56.
Jameson, Fredric (1994): *The Seeds of Time*. New York: Columbia University Press.
Latour, Bruno (1997): "Y a-t-il une science après la guerre froide?". In: *Le Monde*, https://lemonde.fr/archives/article/1997/01/18/y-a-t-il-une-science-apres-la-guerre-froide_3740724_1819218.html (Last Visit: 12/07/2021).
Moreiras, Alberto (2019): *Infrapolítica*. Santiago de Chile: Palinodia.
Shusterman, Richard (1986): "Analytic Aesthetics, Literary Theory, and Deconstruction". In: *The Monist* 69, 1, pp. 22–38.
Siskind, Mariano (2019): "Towards a Cosmopolitanism of Loss". In: Müller, Gesine/Siskind, Mariano (eds.): *World literature, Cosmopolitanism, Globality. Beyond, Against, Post, Otherwise*. Berlin/Boston: De Gruyter, pp. 205–235.
Sokal, Alan (1996): "A Physicist Experiments with Cultural Studies". In: *Lingua Franca*, https://linguafranca.mirror.theinfo.org/9605/sokal.html (Last Visit: 12/07/2021).

2 Anthropocene Narratives I: Geo-Poetics

Ursula K. Heise
The Vanishing Metropolis
Environmental Justice and Urban Narrative in Latin America

1 Environmentalism and Environmental Justice between Place and Planet

Since its emergence in the 1960s and 70s, the modern environmental movement has been fertile ground for the imagination, re-imagination, and counter-imagination of globalisms and globalization. Environmental movements, in the plural; struggles for the conservation of nature – have never been cut of one cloth across different regions, languages, and cultures. Some strands of environmentalism have emphasized the urgency and necessity of global perspectives: from René Dubos' slogan "Think globally, act locally" and the adoption of the 'Blue Marble' image produced by the Apollo 17 mission in 1972 to Stewart Brand's *Whole Earth Catalog* and contemporary activism around climate change, planet Earth in its entirety and the more abstract concept of "planetarity" have been central figures of thought for environmentalism. Planetarity, understood as a counter-term to globalization, approaches Earth as "an undivided 'natural' space rather than a differentiated political space" (Spivak 2003: 72). To the extent that environmentalism seeks to understand the interconnectedness of planetary ecological systems, processes, and crises, it continues to be fundamentally invested in certain types of globalism. The highly influential notion of the Anthropocene, proposed as a new geological era of pervasive human influence on global ecosystems by the scientists Paul Crutzen and Eugene Stoermer (Crutzen and Stoermer 2000), continues this kind of thinking about planet Earth in its entirety.

This understanding, however, has often entered into complex and sometimes contradictory combinations with commitments to localities, bioregions, or nations[1]. From the association of indigenous identities with particular territories in the Americas and Australia to the call for a "sense of place" as an indispensable prerequisite for environmental ethics in the North American environmentalist movement, localisms have played a central role in conflicts over the uses and

---

[1] For a detailed discussion of the dialectics between local, regional, and global orientations in environmentalist thought, see Heise 2008: 17–67.

Ursula K. Heise, University of California, Los Angeles

misuses of nature in many parts of the world. At times, such localisms have been based on a spiritual, political, and ethical commitment to local communities or ecosystems, at other times on the pragmatic reasoning that political participation and legal change are defined and shaped by citizenship. Given the relative strength of local and national institutions compared to the limited political power of supranational organizations, environmentalist activism at these levels has arguably been more successful than for the planet as a whole. But it is also true that local knowledge and engagement do not invariably guarantee environmentally desirable outcomes (for example, when local residents benefit materially from the exploitation of fossil fuel resources), and that they can sometimes lead to NIMBYism and the outsourcing of hazardous industries and waste sites from privileged to less powerful and environmentally protected communities (for instance, the export of European and North American plastic trash and other waste to China before the 2018 ban).

For these reasons, and in view of continuing world-wide ecological crises such as biodiversity loss, ocean pollution, and climate change, I proposed the concept of "eco-cosmopolitanism" in *Sense of Place and Sense of Planet* (Heise 2008). Building on a quarter-century of theories of cosmopolitanism in anthropology, literary studies, political science, and philosophy that sought to rethink cosmopolitan citizenship outside its historical framework of European privilege, eco-cosmopolitanism seeks to "envision individuals and groups as parts of planetary 'imagined communities' of both human and nonhuman kinds", to "explore the cultural means by which ties to the natural world are produced and perpetuated, and how the perception of such ties fosters or impedes regional, national, and transnational forms of identification" (Heise 2008: 61). At a historical moment when collective action in response to such crises as climate change and global pandemics is ever more urgent, the need for this kind of critical cosmopolitan thinking has only increased.

Unlike the humanisms and universalisms that underwrote European, North American, and East Asian imperialisms of the past, eco-cosmopolitanism seeks not to generalize one human community's way of living in and with nature as a universal parameter, but instead to understand and negotiate the true diversity of ecological inhabitation across different ecosystems, cultures, and languages. Eco-cosmopolitanism therefore entails a focus on the unequal distribution of geopolitical power and the inequities generated by differences of class, gender, race, ethnicity, religion, and language. Whether an animal species is endangered because poor communities turn its forest habitat into subsistence farmland or because affluent communities consume it for food or medication, for example, makes a difference not only in how we assess the crisis in ethical terms, but also what practical conservation measures are likely to be successful.

Whether a coastal city is able to protect itself from sea level rise, more frequent king tides, and hurricanes depends crucially on its material wealth and its political influence. Whether climate change is even perceived as an important problem or not depends on historical memories and the relative urgency of other problems such as housing, employment, health care, and access to clean water. In these instances and many others, the ecological embedding of a human community cannot be understood, negotiated, and transformed without a simultaneous grasp of its historical experiences and memories, its current socio-economic structures, and its cultural frameworks for approaching nature.

Eco-cosmopolitanism converges in some of its emphases with the environmental justice movement, which has gained increasing importance for environmental theory and activism worldwide since the turn of the millennium. In the US, the environmental justice movement emerged in the late 1980s, putting an emphasis on the unequal exposure of different communities to environmental risks and their unequal access to environmental benefits. Work by the African American sociologist Robert Bullard, and later the Latinx studies scholar Laura Pulido, highlighted the siting of hazardous industries and waste disposal sites near poor communities and communities of color, a process that they came to refer to as "environmental racism". This term was adopted by the US federal government under Bill Clinton in 1994, and the first National People of Color Environmental Leadership Summit, which was held in Washington in 1991, proposed 17 principles of environmental justice.

Internationally, issues of human rights and particularly indigenous rights came to be discussed increasingly in connection with environmentalism, and an international environmental justice movement took shape that was not always as focused on racism as the one in the United States, but engaged with a broad range of environmental inequalities. By "taking shape", I do not mean that such movements were newly instituted – though some, of course, were, such as the movement for climate justice. In many cases, social movements that had already existed came to be recognized as "environmentalisms" for their important ecological dimensions. The sociologist Ramachandra Guha and the political scientist Juan Martínez-Alier contributed crucially to this recognition with analyses of environmental movements in India and Latin America, respectively, in their jointly authored book *Varieties of Environmentalism: Essays North and South* (1997). They argued that struggles in these regions that were mainly anti-colonial fights for social justice often contained important environmental elements: the fight against the construction of megadams or the Chipko movement's struggle against deforestation in India, for example; or Chico Mendes' advocacy for the rights of peasants, rubber tappers, and indigenous people in the Brazilian rainforest, which also included advocacy for forest preservation. Such movements might not have labeled themselves "environmentalist" as European and North American organizations in the late twentieth century did, Guha and Martínez-Alier argued, but they were nevertheless working in practice for natural conservation. Often, this work was not done with the goal of preserving nature for its own sake or for aesthetic and leisure enjoyment as it often was in the global North, but in order to preserve the foundations of local peoples' subsistence. Hence, Guha and Martínez-Alier argued, they should be counted among the "varieties of environmentalism" and be acknowledged as the "environmentalism of the poor".

This phrase has come to be widely used in environmentalist thought from the turn of the millennium onward, and it shifted common narratives in the global North about the emergence and spread of modern environmentalism. While North American environmentalists in particular had tended to portray the modern environmental movement as emerging from the United States – with Rachel Carson's *Silent Spring* (1962) as a global catalyst – the prevailing narrative from the 1990s onward offered a far more varied picture, seeing movements for the conservation of nature as having emerged in many different places at different moments during the twentieth century, with varying motivations, goals, and organizational structures. In this expanded sense, environmental justice came to be recognized as a far more global phenomenon than it had been considered before.

Environmental justice theories and activisms differ by region and have gone through their own transformations. In the United States, environmental justice started out with a focus on distributive justice, that is, the question of who benefits from environmental resources and who does not, who is exposed to environmental risks and who is not or has the means of shielding themselves from the consequences (Bullard 2018). In parts of Africa, Asia, and Latin America, the question of who might be disadvantaged by environmental activism itself – for example, local communities whose uses of local resources are curtailed or who are displaced when a national park or wildlife sanctuary is established – became a focus of political confrontation (see Agrawal and Redford 2009; Dowie 2009). Subsequently, especially with the work of David Schlosberg (Schlosberg 2007) and David Pellow (Pellow 2007), environmental justice was expanded to include other dimensions. Participatory justice addresses the questions of who is involved in environmental decision-making, who implements these decisions, and who has the right to veto them. Capabilities justice asks who has the practical ability to attain well-being, not just a theoretical right to it. Recognition justice, finally, revolves around the acknowledgment that Western science does not always have the last say on environmental matters, but that other knowledge systems and epistemologies (for example, indigenous cosmologies in the Americas and Australia) deserve to be respected and included as a foundation of ecological knowledge and management.

Regional differences add to the complexity of the body of theory as well as the legal and political practices that surround environmental justice today. The emergence of environmental justice as a movement that was separate from – if connected to – "mainstream" environmentalism is to some extent specific to North America. As Bullard has frequently pointed out, the first wave of North American environmentalism attracted mostly white and middle or upper-class followers but did not successfully integrate working class and non-white nature advocates. In addition, the valuation of wilderness untouched by humans as the ideal form of nature to be conserved (Cronon 1995) – as distinct from the idealization of rural and other human-altered landscapes in Asian and European environmental movements – made connections with other forms of social struggle more difficult to conceive.

In other regions, however, the substance and demographics of what came to be called environmental justice emerged in quite different ways. "Environmental justice, in fact, is an important part of popular environmentalism in much of the world", David V. Carruthers has argued (Carruthers 2008: 2). He elaborates:

> While environmental justice in Latin America is not anchored in the hazardous siting inequities that fueled its rise in the United States, environmental concerns are deeply woven into the fabric of Latin American popular mobilization for social justice and equity. Environmentalism in Latin America generally begins with a stronger social justice component than its counterpart in the United States. [. . .] Environmental resistance weaves into existing struggles for social justice because people face environmental threats in every corner of their daily lives (Carruthers 2008: 7).

Across Latin America and the Caribbean, Carruthers emphasizes, environmental justice issues have emerged in the context of urban movements and shantytown dwellers' organizations, women's movements, labor movements, struggles for the autonomy and recognition of indigenous communities, fights between landowning elites and land-poor peasants, movements for the rights of farmworkers and for *campesino* identity, and battles against the imposition of the Washington Consensus and economic liberalization, among others (Carruthers 2008: 9–14). In other words, while it makes sense to identify such concerns as "environmental justice" in Latin America, it is important to recognize that they did not arise in the context of a movement specifically intended to address them, as they did in the United States, but in broader struggles for social, political, and economic justice. For these reasons, some Latin American researchers such as the Mexican economist and sociologist Enrique Leff have preferred to draw on the vocabulary of political ecology rather than that of environmental justice (Porto-Gonçalves and Leff 2015)².

With these differences as a background, Latin American institutions have given crucial impulses to environmental justice thinking over the past two decades. Amazonian indigenous cosmologies as investigated by Philippe Descola and Eduardo Viveiros de Castro rely on what Viveiros de Castro has called a "multinatural perspectivism" that does not rely on the same categorical distinction between humans and nonhuman species as that envisioned by European-based science and philosophy (Viveiros de Castro 1998; cf. Descola 1986 and Latour 2009), and thereby enables fundamentally different relationships and ideas of justice between species. The question of how human rights and indigenous rights intersect with environmental justice has been given been given powerful new impulses by the new constitutions of Ecuador (2008) and Bolivia (2009), both of which rely on indigenous ideas that translate into Spanish as "vivir bien" and into English as "good life" or "living well" (cf. Acosta 2013; Cadena 2015). They attribute legal rights to a nature understood as the "Madre Tierra" or "Pachamama" of indigenous cosmologies, defined in the Bolivian "Ley de derechos de la Madre Tierra" of 2010 as "el sistema viviente dinámico conformado por la comunidad indivisible de todos los sistemas de vida y los seres vivos, interrelacionados, interdependientes y complementarios, que comparten un destino común" (*Ley 71* 2010: Art. 3). "Para efectos de la protección y tutela de sus derechos, la Madre Tierra adopta el carácter de sujeto colectivo de interés público", the same law continues (*Ley 71* 2010: Art. 5)³. How such rights might be legally implemented and enforced is still an open question. But it is true that these legal texts are as close as any currently living environmentalist will come to eco-utopian visions with actual legal force (cf. Heise 2016: 122), and they also present an interesting model for eco-cosmopolitanism in their combination of secularism and the discourse of rights with regionally specific and spiritual conceptualizations of the natural environment. These relatively recent Latin American developments have yet to be fully integrated into theories of environmental justice that have, to date, principally relied on the work of scholars from Australia, Canada, and the United States. They promise to take

---

[2] Political ecology and environmental justice address many of the same issues. As Eric Sheppard at the Department of Geography at the University of California, Los Angeles, has highlighted, political ecology tends to focus more on the structural causes of environmental inequity, whereas environmental justice tends to focus on its consequences (personal communication). In practice, the two overlap, and Leff has also used the term "justicia ambiental" (Leff 2001).

[3] For a more detailed discussion, see Heise (2016: 111–122) and Hindery (2013).

environmental justice theory and practice to a new level, including the idea of "multispecies justice" (Heise 2016: 166–167, 202–204) as well as other types of justice that environmental movements have recently focused on: climate justice, energy justice, just transition, food justice, spatial justice, shade equity, and housing justice, to name a few.

2 Urban Narrative and Environmental Justice

Reasoning about justice is often intertwined with storytelling: as Michael Sandel's magisterial volume *Justice* shows, narrative scenarios are often useful for exploring what principles and assumptions are at stake in our ethical and legal decision-making. Environmental justice, nourished as it is by activism on specific issues and in particular contexts, is no exception, and the narrative templates that stories about environmental justice and injustice follow are of course of particular interest to narratologists and cultural studies scholars. Such story templates matter in particular for comparative analysis, since they offer a set of tools for analyzing why and how different communities approach what scientists would define as identical ecological problems – for example, pollution, biodiversity loss, or deforestation – as very different issues depending on their historical memories, cultural frameworks, and social practices.

This essay will focus on stories about environmental justice that are set in cities. Given the association of many environmental justice conflicts in Latin America with struggles for indigenous rights, land ownership, and resource extraction, this focus may at first appear counterintuitive. Yet cities are of central importance – on the one hand, because urbanization is one of the most salient characteristics of the Anthropocene. Today at least 50% of the global human population lives in cities, and this proportion is expected to rise to 70% by midcentury (UNDESA 2008). On the other hand, since the late nineteenth century, cities have often functioned as the imaginative and narrative territories where conflicts, convergences, and negotiations between local, national, regional, and global interests occur, from the novels of Honoré de Balzac, Charles Dickens, and Fyodor Mikhailovich Dostoevsky to those of James Joyce, Virginia Woolf, Alfred Döblin, and John Dos Passos. They are therefore narrative sites of particular interest for the analysis of global, anti-global, and post-global impulses – as later texts in the Latin American tradition such as Carlos Fuentes' *La región más transparente* (1958) about Mexico City and Julio Cortázar's *Rayuela* (1963), which unfolds in Paris and Buenos Aires, clearly demonstrate.

Socio-economic injustice as well as gender and racial discrimination form part of many if not all of these classic urban narratives. What we now call environmental injustice is a reality in many cities in the global North as well as the South, in that residents of megacities often have unequal access to infrastructures of water, electricity, and sanitation, unequal exposure to pollution, and unequal access to housing, green spaces, and biodiversity. Especially but not only in the global South, such inequalities are compounded by what urban studies researchers call "informal urbanism": uncertain or undocumented property rights, building codes that are either non-existent or not enforced, and a lack of electricity, water, and sanitation infrastructures. The geographer Mike Davis has therefore warned that rapid urban growth in many parts of the world may ultimately lead to a "planet of slums" (Davis 2006).

The North American literature on urban environmental injustice from Robert D. Bullard's *Dumping in Dixie: Race, Class, and Environmental Quality* (1990) onward has analyzed in detail how the distribution of environmental risks maps onto that of poverty and race. Recent work on the future of cities in the age of climate change has highlighted similar associations across various regions of the world between the risks of rising sea levels, increased flooding and drought, and more hurricanes and wildfires, on one hand, and socio-economic, racial, and ethnic inequalities, on the other, as nonfiction books such as Jeff Goodell's *The Water Will Come: Rising Seas, Sinking Cities, and the Remaking of Civilization* (2017), Ashley Dawson's *Extreme Cities: The Peril and Promise of Urban Life in the Age of Climate Change* (2017), and David Wallace-Wells' *The Uninhabitable Earth* (2019) show.

North American works of fiction have foregrounded similar patterns, from the Latina workers exposed to unemployment, poverty, and toxicity in Ana Castillo's *So Far from God* (1993) to the so-called "pleeblands" in Margaret Atwood's *Oryx and Crake* (2003) and the African American working-class characters who experience a Katrina-like hurricane in Jesmyn Ward's *Salvage the Bones* (2011). Some Latin American authors explore similar scenarios. The Nicaraguan writer Gioconda Belli, for example, features a toxic incident based on a real scenario in her novel *Waslala* (1996), where it functions as a paradigm of the reality that the protagonist must return to after searching for, and finding, the eponymous utopian community. Melisandra, the main character, sets out on a quest for Waslala to find utopia and also her parents, who disappeared decades earlier during their own search for it. Her journey takes her through varied landscapes in the fictional country of Faguas that the novel is set in.

On the way to Waslala, Melisandra and her companions pass through the city of Cineria, "'la gran ciudad señorial, la más antigua de Faguas, quemada y reconstruida varias veces'" (Belli 1996: 149). Their main contact in Cineria is a woman named Engracia, who runs an enterprise of trash that is brought to the city from around the nation and the globe, including materials so toxic that not even the Policía Ambiental wants to investigate them. Landfills in the global South where the commodities discarded by the global North end up have, of course, functioned as one of the main icons of global environmental injustice for several decades now, and the enormous inner courtyard of the complex where Engracia does the recycling "parecía la playa donde la civilización moderna depositara los despojos de su naufragio" (Belli 1996: 157). Cineria, in other words, functions as a global garbage dump underneath its majestic historical appearance. Engracia listens to but dismisses warnings about the dangers of the materials she processes.

But in spite of her physically and intellectually towering presence, she and her crew of orphaned boys fall victim to the global garbage they process. A container with a bluish powder that glows in the dark becomes the main entertainment at a party they celebrate, with Engracia and her crew covering themselves with the powder. Too late, her lover Morris, a scientist, discovers that the powder is the radioactive chemical Cesium 137, which is used in nuclear power recycling and disposing generation. Covering their bodies with Cesium condemns Engracia and five members of her crew to death from radioactive poisoning within a week. As she waits for her death, Engracia decides to use her coming end as a way of striking a blow to the wealthy, drug-trafficking Espada family that has oppressed the city and the region for decades. She and her contaminated crew members cover themselves once again with Cesium 137 and cross the city with their ghostly appearance in the night to blow up the barracks from where the Espadas exercised their dictatorial control of the region and of Faguas more generally. She thereby turns a moment of grave environmental injustice into an act of revolution that, through the presence of an American journalist in Melisandra's company, is sure to reach the world outside Faguas. This is the real world that Melisandra, after finding her mother in the remote community of Waslala, whose utopian aspirations have foundered because of a mysterious decline in fertility, has to return to and live her life in[4].

Belli indicates in an afterword to the novel that even though the events in Cineria may appear to be among the most fantastic in the novel, they are based on a real incident in the Brazilian city of Goiania in 1987 (Belli 1996: 381–382). Here, too, Cesium 137 was improperly deposited and went through the hands of several poor trash handlers to end up at the birthday party of a girl who subsequently died from the contamination, along with six others who had been

---

[4] For a more detailed analysis of utopian thought in Waslala, see DeVries (2013: 282–286).

exposed to the substance. Both Belli and Eduardo Galeano, who wrote about the incident, highlight the contrast with the nuclear accident in Chernobyl the year before: whereas Chernobyl was covered extensively in the international press, Goiania was barely noticed, a translation of environmental injustice into the realm of media that Belli's novel seeks to redress by fictionalizing the incident. Arguably, the explosion in Cineria is what makes it possible for Melisandra to reach Waslala – Engracia leaves her a pet parrot who ends up being her guide through the mountain forests around the utopian community – but also what makes her decide to return to the everyday world of environmental inequality after finding the community. Through this plot structure, the city as the site of national history as well as international environmental injustice comes to function as a crucial pole in the dialectic between lived reality and utopian imagining that the novel outlines, as well as in the dialectic between local and global contamination crises.

3 Environmental Injustice and the Vanishing Latin American Metropolis

But if Belli's *Waslala* highlights the exposure of the poor in Latin America to the toxic wastes of the entire globe in ways that resonate with North American thinking about urban environmental justice, other Latin American writers have constructed quite different narratives about the city and its ecological injustices. In part, this divergence may have to do with different urban realities. As Carruthers has emphasized,

> clear correlations between race or poverty and environmental risk do not typically appear in Latin American cities. Instead, studies suggest that industrial hazards are distributed widely throughout metropolitan zones and outskirts. While factories and waste-storage facilities might be concentrated in industrial parks, in most cases they are dispersed across many neighborhoods of all social classes. The risks that lower-class and working-class urban Latin Americans face are not consistently greater than those of middle-class and upper-middle-class residents. (Carruthers 2008: 5–6).

But the difference is one of literary strategy as much as of divergent urban realities. While questions of humans' relation to urban and non-urban environments and experiences of ecological crisis loom large in Latin American literature, such environments and crises are often as much allegories of social and political upheavals as they are engagements with nature itself. Jorge Marcone has shown how the journeys of the protagonist from the city to the forest and back to the city in the *novela de la selva* of the late nineteenth and early twentieth centuries function as allegories for Latin America's engagement with modernity (Marcone 1998; cf. DeVries Ch. 4). George Handley has found a similar pattern on a more transcontinental scale in Alejo Carpentier's *Los pasos perdidos*, which takes the protagonist on a voyage from a North American metropolis into the Latin American rainforest and back to the city (Handley 2011). When ecological crises surface as a topic in Latin American novels of the late twentieth and early twenty-first centuries, they often function in a similarly double fashion as allegories for political or economic turning points. But by the same token, an ecocritical approach can unearth the ecological underpinnings of such allegories to highlight their implications for current crises of ecosystems and environmental injustices. Two novels will serve as examples of such a reading: the Brazilian novelist Ignácio de Loyola Brandão's *Não Verás País Nenhum (Memorial Descritivo)*, published in 1981 during the military dictatorship, and Pedro Mairal's *El año del desierto* (2005), which engages with the Argentinian economic crisis of 2001 and the country's history at the same time that it explores environmental and multispecies justice.

Não Verás País Nenhum presents a dystopian allegory of Brazil's military dictatorship that was, at the time the novel was published, in its last few years. In Loyola Brandão's futuristic São Paulo, so-called "mili-techs" rule and have divided the city into different districts that residents can only cross into with special passes, often getting caught in violent conflicts between the mili-techs and criminal gangs. The city suffers from intense heat, drought, and crowding, from which the privileged shelter in "Superquadras Climatizadas" (Loyola Brandão 1981: 297). Slums proliferate, basic services have been rationed or have disappeared, and the media are censored. Civil liberties have been abrogated: Souza, the novel's protagonist and first-person narrator, is a former history professor who has been blacklisted. When he finds himself one morning with a mysterious hole in one hand, he begins to search not just for medical help but also the ontological explanation for something that should not be logically possible, and his life begins to degrade. His wife's nephew, who is part of the regime, moves strangers into his apartment; his wife moves out and disappears; and as his physical space shrinks, his options for action equally diminish. National space also shrinks: the military regime has sold some northeastern parts of Brazil to other countries as "Multinational Reserves", and displaced persons from these areas end up in Souza's apartment. Souza himself is gradually pushed out of his apartment by these new arrivals and his nephew. He meanders around various sites in and beyond São Paulo, witnessing many of the city's darkest sides. As Souza's wanderings progress, Loyola Brandão articulates a scathing critique of Brazil's so-called "Economic Miracle" and the market-driven economy the military dictatorship fostered with the help of enormous loans from the IMF and the

World Bank, as well as of the growth of socio-economic inequality under this regime.

Nature forms a surprisingly central part of this satirical and speculative portrait of urban and national life under a dictatorship. *Não Verás País Nenhum* has recently come to be seen as an environmentalist novel and has been included in the canon of "cli-fi", climate fiction, because of the outsized role that intense heat, drought, and water shortages play in its portrayal of São Paulo[5]. Extreme heat functions as an allegory for the way in which daily urban life becomes unlivable under conditions of extreme political oppression, but it is described in its very literal consequences in ways that resonate with climate change: water shortages that in recent years have become a bitter part of urban reality in São Paulo and heat pockets so intense that they instantly kill unprotected pedestrians. The entire Amazon basin and large parts of the rest of Brazil have turned into the largest desert in the world. Animals have completely died out, and plants have become a luxury commodity available only to rich collectors who buy them in art galleries and water them illegally. The livable and aesthetically pleasing parts of nature, in this scenario typical of environmental injustice, have become the privilege of the wealthy elite.

As his nephew takes him farther and farther away from his apartment, Souza witnesses the city itself disintegrating under the impact of heat and political oppression:

> À medida que andávamos, os bairros iam se modificando, os conjuntos residenciais eram mais simples, cada vez mais feios, maltratados. Cruzamos uma grande avenida e mergulhamos numa zona em completa decadência. Mais um pouco, atravessamos blocos de ruínas sombrias (Loyola Brandão 1981: 238).

"Ainda estamos em São Paulo?" Souza asks (Loyola Brandão 1981: 229), in a first indication that he is losing his ability to cognitively map the city in which he has lived all his life. He undergoes a momentary reprieve when he runs into a fellow history professor, Tadeu Pereira, a friend who has also been blacklisted. Pereira, it turns out, runs a secret compound on the outskirts of São Paulo where he raises a few animals and grows real vegetables, in a glimpse of a resistance movement. But when a hungry mob discovers the secret farm and consumes or destroys all it has to offer, Pereira lapses into depression and commits suicide, and Souza's own experience of urban space becomes ever more disjointed. Suffering from hunger and being arrested by security forces, he

---

[5] The novel's ecological dimensions have been explored by Gouveia (2017a and 2017b) and Pereira dos Santos and Libanori (2018); it has been analyzed as climate fiction by Anderson (2019).

becomes more and more disoriented as he is transported in prison trucks to parts of the city he does not know, and as he is chased away from neighborhoods he does not recognize.

At the end of the novel, the loudspeakers of "O Esquema" announce that a giant concrete marquee has been constructed as a shelter from the sun – obviously an absurd and cynical project of urban climate resilience, and Souza is transported to this shelter. "Digo que nem saímos de São Paulo. Tenho a impressão que conheço aquelas ruínas de freeway que se vê aqui", a woman with whom Souza strikes up an acquaintance remarks. But he dismisses even this rudiment of spatial recognition: "Podem ser de qualquer estrada. Eram todas iguais" (Loyola Brandão 1981: 353). The city has vanished as a recognizable entity, let alone as a livable space: none of the refugees under the marquee know whether they are still inside São Paulo, or if not, how far from the city they might be. Even as the physical city crumbles, its psychological representations evaporate for the refugees who are no longer able to recognize or map it: the ultimate consequence of environmental injustice is the narrative disappearance of the metropolis.

While Souza waits under the marquee, he discovers a lonely plant and the remote possibility of some rain on the horizon: a weak hope for at least temporary relief from the environmental crisis that may or may not materialize. Loyola Brandão's novel, then, remains relentlessly dystopian in its joint portrait of injustice in the environmental as well as civic domains. But it has become an increasingly important text in the decades since its publication even as political conditions in Brazil have changed, as its vision of warming climate and intensifying injustice has turned out to be increasingly prophetic of the challenges many other cities face under conditions of global climate change.

The vanishing metropolis is also the structuring motif of the Argentinian novelist Pedro Mairal's *El año del desierto* (2005). The novel describes the one-year journey of the protagonist, María Valdéz Neylan, through Argentinian landscapes that allegorize stages of the nation's history all the way back to the moment of European arrival. Starting in Buenos Aires at about the time of the 2001 financial crash, María works as a receptionist at the financial company Suárez & Baitos. She loses her job when the streets become insecure and she can no longer commute to work, and the city and her own life gradually decline. She works as a nurse's assistant in a hospital, as a maid, and finally as a prostitute before moving out to the countryside. After some time in a poor farming community, she falls in among bandits, and finally ends up living with an indigenous tribe. When the Indians undertake an exploratory survey of Buenos Aires, she is captured by her former bosses, now turned savages and cannibals, and deported onto a ship that takes her back to the country of her ancestors, Ireland, from where she writes her account.

The novel's chronological structure – its move backward through historical periods as María moves forward in space and ages by a year – has been commented on in detail and with great lucidity, as has its critique of finance capital and of military and other dictatorships (Campisi 2019; Zimmer 2013). What befalls Buenos Aires and gradually erases it over the course of the novel is called the "intemperie" – a term that fluctuates between several different meanings. It means economic crisis. It refers to the collapse of effective government and military conflict between different political factions. It also evokes a both political and ecological process whereby Argentina's provinces rebel against the capital and gradually invade it, reconverting it to countryside. Further, it is mentioned in connection with an environmental crisis that brings heat and floods – climate change, in other words. And it seems to refer to an ontological crisis whereby areas that are affected by the "intemperie" turn into wastelands, with buildings not just falling into ruin, but simply disappearing. As the concept of the "intemperie" oscillates between these different meanings, it evokes layers of injustice that range from the present to the colonial past and from local urban space to the global networks of imperialism and capital markets.

El año del desierto is detailed and graphic in its portrayal of the structures of injustice that propel María from a middle-class life into various forms of prostitution, slavery, and exploitation. Her bodily and psychological condition, the food and clothing she has access to, and the kinds of labor she learns to perform clearly signal her gradual deterioration. Already in the different districts of Buenos Aires she moves through, and afterwards in the landscapes she traverses, María is incessantly silenced, constrained, exploited, abused, beaten, abducted, robbed, raped, and held captive, mostly by men, more rarely by other women. Through the declines and humiliations María has to endure, *El año del desierto* foregrounds a long history of gender injustice. It also, almost invariably, juxtaposes the treatment of women with the treatment of nonhumans. This parallel is most obvious in the animal character that accompanies María through almost her entire story: a dog that originally belongs to the neighbors to whom María's father rents their suburban house after he and María move downtown. This dog, sometimes called Anit and more often Negra, barks insistently at María when she goes to collect the rent in the first phase of the crisis, to María's surprise:

No paraba de ladrar, como si estuviera advirtiéndome todo lo que me iba a pasar en los meses siguientes, todas las penurias que íbamos a terminar pasando juntas. Era raro porque siempre le ladraba a papá y no a mí; esa mañana parecía realmente decirme algo. (Mairal 2005: 34)

When María goes back at a later and more destitute stage when the house itself has collapsed, Negra starts to follow her. And she keeps reappearing at every stage of María's journey through Argentina, though it is not always clear how she manages to follow her. The dog ages far more than María: "ya estaba vieja y huesuda", María comments during her stay with the indigenous "ú" tribe toward the end of the novel (Mairal 2005: 260). Negra is left behind on the shore when María is put on a rowboat that takes her toward the ship to Europe: "Avanzamos hacia atrás mirando la orilla. Oí el ladrido y la vi a la *Negra* ladrándome, mi sombra, mi perra vieja. Se perdió en la costa. Se habrá sumado a las jaurías que corrían por el campo o se la habrán comido los hombres que se quedaron" (Mairal 2005: 272, emphasis in the original). Negra functions, then, as María's animal alter ego, and perhaps also as the quintessentially Argentinian part of herself that she has to leave behind as she departs for the land of her European ancestors. The dog stands for the domestication of nature that gradually unravels as the novel moves backward in time, from urban commodity consumption to rural small-scale farming, to hunting and gathering, and finally to the indigenous stewardship of nature. Negra is the residue of the urban connection with the nonhuman world that remains with María almost until the end. But she also signals the violence and brutality that is inflicted on nature in this process of domestication, and the invisibility that so often afflicts domestic animals, women, and more rarely nonwhite characters in the novel. Through the parallels between these mistreatments, *El año* foregrounds what I have called multispecies justice: it portrays humans as inextricably entangled with animals and sometimes even with trees, and all caught in the same networks of inequality and injustice (cf. Heise 2016: Ch. 5).

The city of Buenos Aires also deteriorates as María and Negra do. María first lives in an apartment complex that is gradually turned into a sort of fortress by its residents as a defense against rural invaders – similar to the fortified apartment complex Souza inhabits at the beginning of *Não Verás País Nenhum*. Like Souza, María is forced to leave the complex and has increasing difficulty recognizing even familiar boulevards and plazas as the "intemperie" erases the city: "La calle estaba alfombrada de volantes. Agarré uno. Decía: 'La intemperie que el Gobierno no quiere ver'. Tenían fotos de una cuadra antes y después de la intemperie. En el *antes*, había casas una al lado de la otra y, en el *después*, se veían sólo los baldíos" (Mairal 2005: 15, emphasis in the original). As the building residents look at a map of city districts affected by the advancing "intemperie", "era como una lista demuertos" (Mairal 2005: 48). Later, María moves through neighborhoods she barely knows – as does Souza – before migrating to the countryside.

The city itself shrinks as the countryside overruns it: "La Provincia ha decidido que el municipio de la Capital ya no tenga 18 mil hectáreas sino 4 mil" (Mairal 2005: 141), and "[e]l campo se estaba comiendo la ciudad" (Mairal 2005: 149). Environmental changes contribute to its deterioration, with warming temperatures, a monstrously flooded river, and an unprecedented snowfall (Mairal 2005: 31, 117, 121). Buenos Aires gradually loses its material reality: "El avance de la intemperie me había hecho sentir que toda la ciudad, a medida que se borraba de la realidad, debía quedar grabada en mi cabeza. Yo tenía la obligación [. . .] de memorizar cada rincón, cada calle, cada fachada, y no dejar que los nuevos terrenos baldíos se superpusieran sobre la nitidez de mi recuerdo" (Mairal 2005: 176). The "intemperie" that the novel revolves around, then, unfolds from its historical urban center in Buenos Aires in 2001 through concentric circles of environmental and especially multispecies injustice that spread out to the Americas and Europe and far back into the history of humans' domestication of nature. Modern economic globality, through the backward temporal movement, gradually vanishes along with the city of Buenos Aires, which shrinks and becomes increasingly diffuse. It is replaced by a different globality that encompasses both humans and nonhumans – characterized by relationships of violence and oppression between humans and their nonhuman Others, but also allowing for relationships of solidarity and even identification, as particularly María's stay with the indigenous ú tribe makes clear.

In North American novels and films that focus on social and environmental injustice, cities sometimes persist while their natural components are degraded and inhabitants lose their health or lives; but in many cases, they are destroyed in a spectacular manner, with flood waves or hurricanes smashing them to pieces. Cities in Latin American novels vanish under the onslaught of environmental change and political injustice in more subtle ways, even as the main characters survive – though barely. While effective resistance is not within the power of the protagonists I have discussed here, their survival and their narratives function as stinging reminders and scathing critiques of economic modernity and global capitalism. Climate change – whether it is oppressive urban heat in São Paulo or unprecedented snowfall in Buenos Aires – allegorizes the impact of global networks of power and finance that ultimately erase even cities with deep histories. In the context of the Anthropocene, such political allegories acquire literal meanings by staging the ways in which global ecological change reinforces existing structures of social and environmental injustice. As built urban structures become unrecognizable, diffuse, or disappear, the structures of environmental injustice that have shaped them emerge all the more clearly.

Works Cited

Acosta, Alberto (2013): *El buen vivir: Sumak kawsay, una oportunidad para imaginar otros mundos*. Barcelona: Icaria Editorial.
Agrawal, Arun/Redford, Kent (2009): "Conservation and Displacement: An Overview". In: *Conservation and Society*, 7, pp. 1–10.
Anderson, Mark (2019): Ignacio Brandão's *And Still the Earth* (1981): Political Cli-fi". In: Goodbody, Axel/Johns-Putra, Adeline (eds.) *Cli-fi: A Companion*. Oxford: Peter Lang, pp. 35–40.
Atwood, Margaret (2003): *Oryx and Crake*. New York: Anchor Books.
Belli, Gioconda (1996): *Waslala: Memorial del futuro*. Managua: anamá Ediciones Centroamericanas.
Bullard, Robert D. (2018 [1990]): *Dumping in Dixie: Race, Class, and Environmental Quality*. New York: Routledge.
Cadena, Marisol de la (2015): *Earth Beings: Ecologies of Practice Across Andean Worlds*. Durham: Duke University Press.
Campisi, Nicolás (2019): "El retorno de lo contemporáneo: Crisis e historicidad en *El año del desierto* de Pedro Mairal". In: *Cuadernos LIRICO* 20, https://journals.openedition.org/lirico/8361 (last visit 02/01/2022).
Carruthers, David V. (2008): "Introduction: Popular Environmentalism and Social Justice in Latin America". In: Carruthers, David V. (ed.). *Environmental Justice in Latin America: Problems, Promise, and Practice*. Cambridge, MA: MIT Press, pp. 1–22.
Castillo, Ana (1993): *So Far from God*. New York: Norton.
Cronon, William (1995): "The Trouble with Wilderness; or, Getting Back to the Wrong Nature". In: Cronon, William (ed.): *Uncommon Ground: Rethinking the Human Place in Nature*. New York: Norton, pp. 69–90.
Crutzen, Paul J., and Eugene F. Stoermer (2000): The "'Anthropocene'". In: *Global Change Newsletter*, 41, pp. 17–18.
Davis, Mike (2006): *Planet of Slums*. London: Verso.
Descola, Philippe (1986): *La nature domestique: Symbolisme et praxis dans l'écologie des Achuar*. Paris: Maison des Sciences de l'Homme.
DeVries, Scott M. (2013): *A History of Ecology and Environmentalism in Spanish American Literature*. Lewisburg: Bucknell University Press.
Dowie, Mark (2009): *Conservation Refugees: The Hundred-Year Conflict between Global Conservation and Native Peoples*. Cambridge, MA: MIT Press.
Gouveia, Saulo (2017a): "A Collision of Disparate Historical Timescales in Ignácio de Loyola Brandão's *And Still the Earth*". In: *Latin American Literary Review* 44, 87, pp. 24–33.
— (2017b): "O catastrofismo ecodistópico: Perspectivas do Brasil e da América do Norte". In: *Revista Moara* 48, pp. 35–53.
Guha, Ramachandra/Juan Martínez-Alier (1997): *Varieties of Environmentalism: Essays North and South*. London: Earthscan.
Handley, George B. (2011): "Postcolonial Ecology of the New World Baroque: Alejo Carpentier's *The Lost Steps*". In: DeLoughrey, Elizabeth, and George B. Handley (eds). *Postcolonial Ecologies: Literatures of the Environment*. New York: Oxford University Press, pp. 117–135.

Heise, Ursula K. (2016): *Imagining Extinction: The Cultural Meanings of Endangered Species*. Chicago: University of Chicago Press.
— (2008): *Sense of Place and Sense of Planet: The Environmental Imagination of the Global*. New York: Oxford University Press.
Hindery, Derrick (2013): *From Enron to Evo: Pipeline Politics, Global Environmentalism, and Indigenous Rights in Bolivia*. Tucson: University of Arizona Press.
Leff, Enrique (ed.) (2001): *Justicia ambiental: Construcción y defensa de los nuevos derechos ambientales culturales y colectivos en América Latina*. Mexico City: Programa de las Naciones Unidas para el Medio Ambiente/Oficina Regional para América Latina y el Caribe and Universidad Nacional Autónoma de México/Centro de Investigaciones Interdisciplinares en Ciencias y Humanidades.
Ley 71: Derechos de la Madre Tierra (2010): In *LexiVox: Portal jurídico libre*. http://www.lexivox.org/norms/BO-L-N71.html (last visit 02/01/2022).
Latour, Bruno (2009): "Perspectivism: 'Type' or 'Bomb'?" In: *Anthropology Today* 25, 2, pp. 1–2.
Loyola Brandão, Ignacio de (1981): *Não Verás País Nenhum: Memorial Descritivo*. Rio de Janeiro: Codecri.
Mairal, Pedro (2005): *El año del desierto*. Buenos Aires: Interzona.
Marcone, Jorge (1998): "De retorno a lo natural: La serpiente de oro, la 'novela de la selva' y la crítica ecológica". In: *Hispania* 81, 2, pp. 299–308.
Pellow, David Naguib (2007): *Resisting Global Toxics: Transnational Movements for Environmental Justice*. Cambridge, MA: MIT Press.
Pereira dos Santos, Estela/Evely Vânia Libanori (2018): "Questões ecológicas em *Não Verás País Nenhum*, do escritor Ignácio de Loyola Brandão". In: *Travessias* 12, 2, pp. 89–104.
Porto-Gonçalves, Carlos Walter/Leff Enrique (2015): "Political Ecology in Latin America: The Social Re-Appropriation of Nature, the Reinvention of Territories and the Construction of an Environmental Rationality". In: *Desenvolvimento e Meio Ambiente*, 35, pp. 65–88.
Schlosberg, David (2007): *Defining Environmental Justice: Theories, Movements, and Nature*. Oxford: Oxford University Press.
Spivak, Gayatri Chakravorty (2003): *Death of a Discipline*. New York: Columbia University Press.
UNDESA (United Nations Department of Economic and Social Affairs), Population Division (2008): *World Urbanization Prospects: The 2007 Revision*. New York: United Nations, www.ipcc.ch/apps/njlite/srex/njlite_download.php?id=5849 (last visit 02/01/2022).
Viveiros de Castro, Eduardo (1998): "Cosmological Deixis and Amerindian Perspectivism". In: *Journal of the Royal Anthropological Institute*, 4, 3, pp. 469–488.
Ward, Jesmyn (2011): *Salvage the Bones*. New York: Bloomsbury.
Zimmer, Zac (2013): "A Year in Rewind, and Five Centuries of Continuity: *El año del desierto*'s Dialectical Image". In: *Modern Language Notes*, 128, 2, pp. 373–383.

Jobst Welge
Post-Natural Histories
Mimicry and Deep Time in Pola Oloixarac's *Las Constelaciones Oscuras* and Carlos Fonseca's *Museo Animal*

A Post-Global Aesthetics and (Post)-Natural History

Let me begin with the question of how the urgency of climate change and the notion of the Anthropocene have impacted the practice and discourse of the humanities in recent years. The recent critical studies in the field of post-colonial history, Dipesh Chakrabarty's *The Climate of History in a Planetary Age* (2021) and Ian Baucom's *History 4° Celsius* (2020) bear mentioning here. They see mankind at a "planetary conjuncture", pointing out how "anthropocenic explanations of climate change spell the collapse of the age-old humanist distinction between natural history and human history" (Chakrabarty 2021: 201). Chakrabarty argues that the axiom of man-made history, going back to philosophers such as Giambattista Vico and only slowly challenged by historian Fernand Braudel and newer developments of environmental history, has now led to a situation where the recorded history of globalization needs to be complemented by the "deep history of human beings", namely "species history" (Chakrabarty 2021: 219, 220) as a collective geological and planetary force. Baucom, building partly on Chakrabarty, sees climate change as "one of the outer frontiers of a new theory of historical time" (Baucom 2020: 5), involving "dizzying jumps between temporal scales" (Baucom 2020: 6). He calls for a foregrounding of the natural history of the modern world, namely "the planet's anthropogenetically altered 'natural' or *postnatural* history" (Baucom 2020: 7).

In the present essay on contemporary fiction, I am obviously not concerned with historiography as such, nor even with the question of method in literary studies. Rather, the postcolonial historians' programmatic statements prompt me to ask how two contemporary novels respond to these challenges on their own terms. In fact, it has been stated that the unsettling of the boundary between human and natural history has posed new challenges for reading and for literary representation (Heise 2008: 54). I hope to show that the novels to be

Jobst Welge, Leipzig University

discussed here, Pola Oloixarac's *Las Constelaciones Oscuras* (2016) and Carlos Fonseca's *Museo Animal* (2017), share in some sense the historians' agenda of "elongate[ing] our scales of time and [. . .] dispers[ing] conceptions of agency across a mingled human and natural spectrum" (Baucom 2020: 12), so that the categories of the "human" and the "natural" elements tend to coincide (Chakrabarty 2009: 201–207).

Furthermore, I want to show how the two novels are self-consciously conceived as going beyond the paradigm of the global. They may be tentatively grouped as planetary novels. The term has been used, for instance, by Susan Stanford Friedman: "I use the terms *planetary* and *planetarity* in an epistemological sense to imply a consciousness of the earth as planet, not restricted to geopolitical formations and potentially encompassing the non-human as well as human" (Friedman 2015: 347, n.9). The planetary novel, therefore, denationalized and deterritorialized, is associated with "a relationality of being toward others", including the "historical other of prehistory", geological or "deep" time, as well as habits of imagining the other (Keith 2018: 272–275). The two novels considered here may be part of "a much larger trend of recent novels that have fashioned narrative and formal efforts to animate or represent the occluded relationships linking 'close living substance' to the planet" (Keith 2018: 280). If for the contemporary Latin American novel the subject of nature has for a long time appeared as something like an exhausted resource itself, my examples suggest a return of nature – not as a picturesque backdrop or national reservoir, as in the heydays of Romanticism and Regionalism – but in the shape of a *natural history* that affects the very form of the novel. The contemporary novelistic reworking of natural history appears to be a distinct phenomenon, yet its broader engagement with 'Nature' certainly also resonates with the role of natural materialism and extractivist themes explored recently by Héctor Hoyos (Hoyos 2019).

Yet how is natural history connected to temporality? For a long time, conceptually, man-made and natural history have been kept apart. The traditional *historia naturalis*, going back to the Roman encyclopedist Pliny the Elder (ca. 22–78), was essentially ahistorical and incremental, even as it underwent a process of temporalization during the latter half of the eighteenth century, not least in response to new discoveries in the "New World" (Findlen 2006: 437). While the atemporal character of natural history was often adduced to emancipate the domain of History as such, Immanuel Kant began to see the first signs of an "archeology" *of* nature, for which he cites the geological theories of Linnaeus (Lepenies 1976: 57–58) – which is remarkable since Linnaeus is commonly associated with a static, merely classificatory conception of nature. In fact, as Wolf Lepenies has shown, the temporalization of natural history occurs within the writings of Linnaeus and Buffon themselves, as their static systems are increasingly pressured to accommodate biological forms as 'points of transition' between different species (often rationalized as 'monstrosities'), and thus raising the question of their transformation (Lepenies 1976: 61, 64). As we will see, the literary adoption of natural history is inscribed into temporality, yet not necessarily a progressive, evolutionary one. Furthermore, the term "post-natural" in the title of my essay indicates that, while the two authors variously explore the semantics and rhetoric of natural history, the very concept of nature has changed and is no longer conceived as the opposite of human history.

Las Constelaciones Oscuras: Interconnected Times and Species

The Argentine writer Pola Oloixarac's novel *Las Constelaciones Oscuras* (2016) exemplifies the multiplication of temporal scaling by grafting different narrative levels unto each other, suggesting a mobile, reiterative relation between different historical periods, rather than a strictly developmental logic of history, thereby echoing certain (post)-modern approaches to the historical imagination in the novel (Kaakinen 2017). Thus, Oloixarac's novel features one shorter, late nineteenth-century thread around the fictional European botanist Niklas Bruun; a further thread located during the 1980s–1990s, at the time of the emergence of the internet as well as subculture hacker communities, centers on the hacker Cassio Brandão; and finally, one around the year 2024 with a dystopian regime of state-directed DNA-tracking, featuring the biologist Piera, who develops a genetic virus to be implanted into Cassio's own body. Cassio moves from Brazil to Bariloche in Argentina, and through its various references to Brazilian and Argentine participations in international projects and political alliances, the novel fleshes out a continent-inflected version of the "global" Latin American novel (Hoyos 2015), while it explicitly (and somewhat idiosyncratically) dates the Anthropocene to the use of nuclear energy in the year 1945 (Oloixarac 2016: 42).

The thread around Niklas Bruun's expedition into the Brazilian jungle, significantly set in the year of Charles Darwin's death, 1882, introduces a fantasy running counter to Darwin's developmental theory of natural selection, namely a mode of natural science that investigates the hybrid transformations between humans, animals, and plants, and that is repeatedly associated with an explicitly subterranean imaginary (Oloixarac 2016: 15, 18, 101, 137): "Sus notas trazan sistemas de cuevas que se hunden cientos de kilómetros en el Atlántico negro: reinos enteros donde los seres se apartan de la representación de la naturaleza" (Oloixarac 2016: 24). According to this historically situated, visionary form of natural science the different natural species would no longer reproduce but rather enter and invade each other at the level of present existence: "Los cambios eran mucho más rápidos: ocurrían durante la vida misma del individuo, se daban por contactos inesperados y por mímesis que no esperaban el trabajo silente de ciclos reproductivos que se seleccionan los mejores rasgos" (Oloixarac 2016: 140). The phenomenon of mimesis – in the sense of natural beings taking on the appearance of others, and here understood in a decisively non-evolutionary fashion – has come to be associated especially with the tropical region of the Amazon rainforest, as I will further discuss below. Oloixarac's interest in the cultural history of the region is attested by her earlier libretto for a chamber opera on Hercule Florence (*Hércules en el Mato Grosso*, 2014), a nineteenth-century traveler and early photographic experimentalist[1], as well as a planned non-fiction work on the Amazon, *Atlas literario del Amazonas* (Brizuela 2014; Blasco 2021).

First, I want to highlight that the motive of the travelling natural scientist in the tropical forest recalls a central constellation of the modern Latin American novel, namely its association with an archive of knowledge about nature (Echevarría 1998). More specifically, as Bieke Willem has persuasively argued in a recent article, Oloixarac's novel self-consciously inscribes itself within the lineage of the distinctively Latin American genre of the *novela de la selva*, echoing some of its formal and thematic elements (Willem 2020). For her part, Elisabeth Heyne has shown in great detail how the novel dialogues with new trends in (Amazonian) ethnographies and their interest in alternative epistemologies of perception (Heyne 2020). For instance, Oloixarac herself has acknowledged being influenced by the work of Brazilian ethnologist Eduardo Viveiros de Castro, who has described the animist world-view of indigenous people in terms of what he calls a "multinaturalist" alternative to the Western mode of objectivism: "To know is to personify, to take on the viewpoint of that which is to be known; [. . .] for the shamanist knowledge shows a given 'something' as a 'someone', another subject or agent. The form of the Other is a person" (Viveiros de Castro 2017: 311; my translation).

While the nineteenth-century plot line of a botanical expedition into the Amazon occupies only a part of the narrative, the apparently neat tripartite temporal structure of the novel (1882 – 1983 – 2024) is complicated by the fact

---

[1] The fictional naturalist expedition of Niklas Bruun appears to be partially modelled on a historical one by Georg Heinrich von Langsdorff (1824–1828), in which Hercule Florence participated. For instance, the novel alludes to the Brazilian emperor Pedro II's interest in photography (Oloixarac 2016: 207). For her knowledge on Florence Oloixarac draws on Brizuela (2012).

that the 'early' plot line also reappears in the later sections. The novel is thus constructed around the resonances that the literal and literary jungle entertains with the metaphorical jungle of data, genetic, and digital codes since the twentieth century. For instance, human and sexual relations, such as the one between Cassio and a girl named Mora, are described as if occurring in a natural habitat: "un animal en la selva oscura"; "su medio natural" (Oloixarac 2016: 73). The nerd Cassio is characterized as an "organismo fotofóbico" (Oloixarac 2016: 85), which corresponds in turn with Niklas' eschewing of human relations and his obsession with non-human beings, the "más allá del humano" (Oloixarac 2016: 136, 138). As Willem notes: "Oloixarac recycles the trope of a cosmic unity by repeatedly (in fact, almost *ad nauseam*) using metaphors based on comparisons between the human and the nonhuman and between the animal and the non-animal" (Willem 2020: 138). Moreover, the novel explicitly suggests an analogy between the Amazon region and the discovery of the "new world" of data, including their common challenge to "traditional" modes of perception: "El enorme, nuevo continente de datos representaba el nuevo mundo por descubrir: había que diseñar los sentidos, el tacto, la vista, que pudieran percibir ese laberinto" (Oloixarac 2016: 166). Accordingly, coding languages and algorithms are compared to species of plants: "[. . .] los primeros lenguajes informáticos, específicos y porosos, variegándose como especies de plantas" (Oloixarac 2016: 68).

Moreover, *Las Constelaciones oscuras* is distinguished by a peculiar style, through which the characters are presented less as novelistic subjects and more as products or transmitters of genetic codes. In fact, towards the end of the novel Bruun joins a "speculative botanist", traveling with him towards the interior of the Amazon, where they end up in the laboratory of a rat-like being, named Hoichi, who cultivates a species of hallucinogenic flowers ("*Crissis pallida*") said to look like spiders, for their implantation into the bodies of women (Oloixarac 2016: 216). This cyber-punk like aesthetic in the novel may be understood as a parodic development of central tropes in literary discourses about the Amazon, such as the often-noted perceptive problem of identifying distinct forms in the tropical surfeit (Anderson 2014; Willem 2020: 133; Lindquist 2008). The visual impenetrability of the jungle is echoed by the comment of the mutant rat Hoichi in his laboratory: "Hay tantas cosas que nos miran y no vemos" (Oloixarac 2016: 104) which is in turn an echo of the theme of technological surveillance. The decentering of the human in Oloixarac's text gestures not only at an ecologically intertwined world, it also carries dystopian tones, since the novel tells of the construction of an entity called "Stromatoliton", a gigantic archive of biometric data-gathering and optical surveillance. Such temporal parallels and echoes, between nineteenth-century naturalism and modern information technology, between real and metaphorical jungles, are complemented by geographical and genealogical connections, namely by the fact that Cassio's mother is an Argentine ethnologist who had conducted research in Brazil.

The contradictory alliances between natural and human actors, the mutual entanglement between nature and technology, as well as the confrontation between different temporalities show how Oloixarac self-consciously inserts her novel into discourses both about the Anthropocene and the Amazon (Andermann 2018: 192). Literary and novelistic representations of the Amazon forest are notable not only for their mapping impulse, but also for their explorations of different regimes of temporality – from Euclides da Cunha's writings on Amazonia to Alejo Carpentier's *Los Pasos Perdidos* (1953). Oloixarac's novel takes up precisely this notion of time travel as associated with the Latin American tropics:

> Remontaron el río. Era como volver a los inicios de la creación, cuando la vegetación estallaba sobre la tierra. [. . .] Los pastizales se deshacen a medida en que se internan en riachos tornasolados, que los árboles cortan como castillos, bajando en ramas desde lo alto para volver a alzarse, líneas de materia vegetal líquida y dura uniendo la tierra con el cielo. Seguían avanzando, y los vapores nubosos envolvían el follaje, y sólo algunos árboles se perdían en lo alto como fantasmas, en pináculos de rocas que empezaban a descender, en dirección al cráter oculto por la ley del barro que reina en todas direcciones. Por donde miren, el manglar se despliega en un laberinto de manos hundidas en el barro, las manos olvidadas de seres enormes crispándose bajo el río. Niklas cierra los ojos para guardar las imágenes, mientras su mano se mueve sobre el cuaderno. (Oloixarac 2016: 208–209)

There is an obvious allusion here to *Los Pasos Perdidos*, notably in the first line of the passage (Willem 2020: 136). Yet temporality is not only linked to the idea of travel, it is materially sedimented and genetically transmitted through links of deep time. For instance, Bruun is associated with the deep time of genetic history: "Entonces los visitantes empiezan a mezclarse con las nativas, ingresando en un torrente de sangre y semen en la historia genética de la isla" (Oloixarac 2016: 17).

Likewise, temporality is inscribed in the genetic bank of Stromatoliton. The term is explained as being derived from stromatolite, a stone resulting from the petrification of once-living bacteria. The different layers are to be understood as different sedimentations of time. Of course, during the early nineteenth century the scientific method of geology, as represented by Georges Cuvier, was precisely the field that played a crucial role for the temporalization of natural history, by suggesting the notion of a "deep time" in both vertical and horizontal terms (Dünne 2016: 41)[2]. In this sense, Oloixarac's novel asks to be read as a

---

[2] Dünne (2019) explicitly refers to Oloixarac's novel as a "cosmogrammatic fiction", situating it in a longer genealogy of the concern with geology in Argentine fiction (46).

planetary text, insofar as it engages far-ranging chronologies and foregrounds spatial and other forms of comparison and interconnectedness: "The planetary operates through different temporalities, including geologic and prehistoric time, which prefigure and thus destabilize the nation (as well as the West and the human ultimately) as an organizing rubric, opening the novel instead to much wider-ranging temporal and spatial sets of relations and influences" (Keith 2018: 275).

Such a notion of deep time is echoed by the narrator's tendency to sometimes reach back millions of years, to millenarian trees (Oloixarac 2016: 18), to past colonies of cockroaches, to the parallel emergence of civilizations among both humans and insects, to the memory of the human species made possible by the genetic data library of Latam, partly instigated by the Argentine trauma of "personas desaparecidas" (Oloixarac 2016: 83). This universal genetic bank makes it possible to track down a person, a process which is again described in metaphorical terms, putting the "person" in the position of the object searched for in the impenetrable surface of the jungle: "Como un animal, la persona se esconde en los bosques; no pasa mucho tiempo hasta que es encontrada" (Oloixarac 2016: 83).

Oloixarac's novel, then, destabilizes the distinction between humans and nature, thereby invoking the "temporal and spatial expansions invisible to man" (Oloixarac 2016: 24). In the context of jungle imagery, the notion of natural mimesis is also associated with alternative indigenous mythologies, as those theorized by Viveiros de Castro: "En la mitología tupinambá, los encuentros entre especies diferentes son sucesos del orden maravilloso. Una especie comienza por imitar a otra, empieza por poseer sus gestos para después comérsela; es una historia de amor cuya temporalidad excede al arco humano" (Oloixarac 2016: 36–37).

Through its invocations of genetic, volcanic-geological (Oloixarac 2016: 19) and cosmological temporalities, the novel programmatically gestures toward a planetary frame. Its title, *Dark Constellations*, refers to the notion that in the southern hemisphere darkness overpowers the light of the stars (Oloixarac 2016: 144); to the Inca's 'negative' astronomical constellations made up of dark clouds, and hence, by extension, to an alternative to epistemologies of the Western Enlightenment, in short, to a "parallel natural history" (Heyne 2020: 3.1), said to coincide with the "constelaciones oscuras de la historia de la ciencia del continente del Antropoceno" (Oloixarac 2016: 144). Although the novel is planetary in its orientation, it mobilizes a specifically Latin American modernity, combining indigenous epistemologies and alternative histories of scientific and technological knowledge.

Museo Animal: Natural History and Mimicry

The nameless narrator of Carlos Fonseca's novel *Museo Animal* works in a museum for natural history in New Jersey. The English translation of the novel (Fonseca 2020) modifies the title to *Natural History*, an interesting choice in light of Fonseca's pronounced affinities with the work of W. G. Sebald, whose essay *Luftkrieg und Literatur* (1999; 'Aerial war and literature') has in turn been translated as *The Natural History of Destruction*. The initial and programmatic association of the narrator with a museum of natural history points to Carpentier's *Los Pasos Perdidos*, where the male protagonist also works in a museum, as a curator of indigenous musical instruments. Thus, similar to Oloixarac, Fonseca inscribes his novel self-consciously into the tradition of naturalist voyages and the specifically Latin American tradition of fictions of the archive (Welge 2021; Echevarría 1998). Thus, he acknowledges the influence of Alexander von Humboldt, among others: "On *The Natural History* [*Museo animal*] I wanted to play with this tradition of natural voyages, to reflect upon their meaning and artificiality, to reimagine the jungle as something more than a lost paradise" (Azurdia 2020). Classical 'archival' Latin American novels incorporated the early discourses on natural science by European travelers, since they promised the valuation of autochthonous nature and were generally associated with progress (Echevarria 1998: 102). While Fonseca revisits this idea of the archival novel, it is now no longer conceived in a national or even continental mode; rather, it gestures at a "planetary" form, that is, it aims not at the representation of the planet, but it encourages connections between different times and places (Keith 2018: 275).

At the beginning of the novel, the first-person narrator learns of the passing of his friend Giovanna Luxembourg, a fashion designer from New York. The day after Giovanna's death, the narrator receives a shipment of documents and records, the nightly reading of which introduces him more and more to the story of her family origins. Through this reading, the narrator becomes immersed in the life of an Israeli photographer with Hispanic roots, Yoav Toledano (who will eventually turn out to be Giovanna's father), who is trying to escape his country's 1960s climate of war and who has developed a fascination with Latin America since his youth. From Haifa he travels first to Spain, "[. . .] como si todo viaje transatlántico pidiese una repetición del viaje de Colón" (Fonseca 2017: 115).

The novel thus emphasizes that Toledano's travel plans are a sort of individual rehearsal of colonial tropes, the paradigms of colonial travel and discovery. Of course, these tropes had already been reworked in *novelas de la selva*, where they appeared under the signs of irony and mimicry. While also taking distance from these regional novels, it is apparent that Fonseca's novel takes its cue from the meta-textual trajectory in this tradition. As Jens Andermann has described it: "Ese discurso narrativo caracterizado por la inautenticidad y el mimicry, [. . .] ya no puede enfocar la selva como un silencioso afuera del texto sino que la abarca como intertexto, como aquello que media entre un corpus y su reescritura" (Andermann 2018: 227; cf. Wylie 2009: 1–3).

The last and longest part of the novel describes, in relative temporal slowness, a voyage young Giovanna and her parents take into a South American, yet geographically undefined jungle. Instead of untouched purity, there they encounter a "gringo", who invokes an entire "genealogy" of previous travelers to the Latin American tropics: "[. . .] pasan por sus tormentosas frases Cristóbal Colón y el barón Alexander von Humboldt, Hernán Cortés y Moctezuma, los indios de Cipango y el temible Aguirre" (Fonseca 2017: 342). If the travel and quest motif in the classical Latin American novel was often linked to the experience of disillusionment (Welge 2018), Fonseca's novel stresses the "negativity" of the travel experience with respect to previous, paradigmatic journeys. Connected to Toledano's being a photographer, the novel uses the metaphorical semantics of the negative image in the sense of a "sombra histórica de lo que fue" (Fonseca 2017: 125):

> Le sigue una travesía latinoamericana que es una suerte de reverso negativo de aquellas grandes travesías clásicas de los grandes viajeros. Allí donde Humboldt encontró la imagen de una América silvestre y sublime, ellos encontraban la imagen de una naturaleza ruinosa, repleta de basura. [. . .] Allí donde Franz Boas encontró la naturaleza de lo desconocido, ellos parecen encontrar un siniestro espejo de sí mismos. (Fonseca 2017: 156)

The narrator and Giovanna had become friends because of their common fascination for animal mimicry. In fact, Giovanna understands fashion as "un arte del camuflaje y del escondite" (Fonseca 2017: 39). This isotopic field of associations also includes allusions to Subcomandante Marcos, the Mexican leader of the Zapatista movement, whose masked *guerilleros* are said to return the jungle to its anonymity: "En esas máscaras la selva volvía a perderse en su anonimato" (Fonseca 2017: 63). The art exhibition, projected originally by Giovanna together with the narrator figure, would have been dedicated to different aspects of masking and hiding. Remembering these plans, the narrator muses on the implications of mimicry, namely the erasure of the boundary between man and nature: "[. . .] traer a un animal vivo al museo, elaborar una anatomía de la mirada, llenar la sala con retratos de ojos hasta que se confundiesen las miradas y ya nadie supiese cuáles eran los animales y cuáles los humanos" (Fonseca 2017: 90).

Such a scenario is reminiscent of a page in W. G. Sebald's novel *Austerlitz* (2001), where photographs of the eyes of humans and animals are juxtaposed, suggesting the levelling of different modes of seeing (Sebald 2001: 11) (Figure 1). Similar to Oloixarac, then, Fonseca mobilizes the "tropical" aesthetics of mimicry via a re-contemporization of late nineteenth-century discourses. For instance, Alexander von Humboldt is an important point of reference both in *Museo animal* and in

er, durch dieses, weit über jede vernünftige Gründlichkeit hinausgehende Waschen entkommen zu können aus der falschen Welt, in die er gewissermaßen ohne sein eigenes Zutun geraten war. Von den in dem Nocturama behausten Tieren ist mir sonst nur in Erinnerung geblieben, daß etliche von ihnen auffallend große Augen hatten und jenen unverwandt

forschenden Blick, wie man ihn findet bei bestimmten Malern und Philosophen, die vermittels der rei-

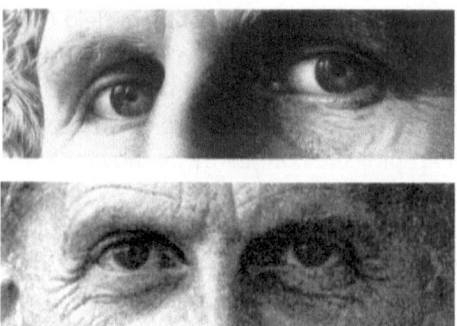

nen Anschauung und des reinen Denkens versuchen, das Dunkel zu durchdringen, das uns umgibt. Im üb-

− 7 −

Fig. 1: W. G. Sebald (1997), *Die Ringe des Saturn*. Frankfurt: S. Fischer.

Fonseca's critical study *The Literature of Catastrophe* (2020), where the Prussian explorer, via his scientific interest in earthquakes and volcanology, is associated with the temporalization of natural history and the introduction of eventfulness into its previously tableau-like order: "Catastrophe presents itself as the event that disrupts the continuity of the catalogue, the harmony of its taxonomy, leaving in its place a pure multiplicity" (Fonseca 2017: 29)[3].

Humboldt, for his part, had commented that tropical nature is distinguished by an overload that produces visual confusion, which challenges the scientific ideal of panoptic vision, leading to a constant relation between fragment and totality (Humboldt 2004: 7; Lindquist 2008: 231). Such visual confusion, arising in the tension between immediate perception and objectifying distance, is a recurring theme within the work of the Victorian evolutionary biologist Henry Walter Bates (1852–1892), in his naturalist travel book *The Naturalist on the River Amazon* (1863). Bates' narrative comments on animal mimicry in the Amazon forest distance themselves from the Linnean tradition of the static isolation of natural objects and instead foreground the processual nature of vision as it unfolds in the Amazon's "many wonders in its recesses" (Bates 2010: 11). This means that the naturalist is taking on the position of the animal being deceived. As Will Abberley has put it, Bates and other naturalists "sought to simulate a crypsis as a sensory-cognitive experience for readers" through ekphrasis and other verbal means (Abberley 2020: 29), and where the "vivid immediacy for personal impressions came at the cost of scientific detachment" (Abberley 2020: 32). The analogy between human and animal vision implies the levelling of the distinction between the naturalist and animal. This phenomenon may also be observed in the volume's illustrations and the animal. This may be seen in the frontispiece, which shows Bates himself, having shot a toucan, now surrounded by a flock of the birds, which had been hidden by the tropical vegetation (Fig. 2). The illustrators, Wolf and Zwecker, mimic Bates' moment of visual confusion as the birds emerge from hiding, suddenly taking on forms[4]. A similar scene occurs in Fonseca's novel. Here the narrator remembers a foundational childhood experience, namely a visit to the zoo, where the boy is transfixed by the visual enigma of animal mimicry, in the form of an insect, the so-called walking stick:

> Allí, detrás del cristal, se hallaba la vida como enigma a descifrar. La vida a modo de rompecabezas o de estereograma. [. . .] Era frente a esas cajas aparentemente vacías donde yo me postraba, a la expectativa de que súbitamente surgiese la figura hasta entonces oculta: la singular mariposa que se confundía con el ramaje [. . .] Me encantaban esos pequeños trópicos en cautiverio en donde la nada se hacía finalmente visible. (Fonseca 2017: 92)

---

[3] On the dynamization of natural history, in relation to the catastrophic theory of Georges Cuvier, see also Dünne (2016: 39–48).
[4] For a detailed discussion of this image, see Abberley (2020: 46–47).

Fig. 2: Henry Walter Bates (1863): *The naturalist on the River Amazons: a record of adventures, habits of animals, sketches of Brazilian and Indian life and aspects of nature under the Equator during eleven years of travel*. London: J. Murray, 1863. Image: https://www.loc.gov/item/49032931/.

This emblematic scene repeats the discourse about the visual perception of the tropics (Humboldt, Bates), yet in does so in the mode of zoological domestication. Therefore, it multiplies and heightens the sense of re-presentation. When the narrator tells us that his early fascination for the phenomenon of camouflage was later complemented by the reading of a book by a French philosopher, concerned with the "devouring" of an original object by its copy (likely an allusion to Jean Baudrillard's *Simulacres et Simulations*, 1981), then it becomes clear that the narrator conceives of the biological phenomenon of camouflage also in an aesthetic, poetological sense. *Museo animal* repeatedly invokes acts of vanishing, which, through the character of Virginia MacCallister, Giovanna's mother, are also associated with the artistic practices of the avant-garde (Shell 2012: 17–18)[5].

The Novel and/as Natural History

In an interview for the *Los Angeles Review of Books* Carlos Fonseca commented on his early interest in the paradigm of natural history:

> I still remember a book that left a strong impression on me when I was 16 or 17 and starting to get into literature. It was not a novel but rather Strabo's *Geography*, where the narrator tells us about about the many lands and the forms of nature he has seen. I remember reading that book and first feeling tempted to write a novel: a novel without characters, where the true character would be nature itself. I think that, to some extent, that bizarre idea has remained with me up until today. I think that explains, as well, my interest in natural histories, be it Alexander von Humboldt's travel notebooks or the works of Sebald (Sequeira 2020).

The novel repeatedly invokes the utopia of such a poetics. Thus, the lawyer character Gerardo Esquilín, intent on defending a collective art project designed by Giovanna's mother, which was based on "plagiarism", finally muses on the possibility of a post-anthropocentric form of history. This utopian concept of history is specified as a critique of modernity that reconnects with older practices of the historical avant-garde as well as with the paradigm of natural history:

> [. . .] la imagen de una historia mucho más amplia dentro de la cual el juicio que lo ocupaba era apenas la punta del iceberg, una historia amplia y extensa como las cartografías que de niño dibujaba sobre el techo de su casa. Una historia impersonal e inhumana como los viejos catálogos de historia natural. (Fonseca 2017: 205)

---

[5] The study by Shell is explicitly cited by Fonseca as an inspiration for his novel (Fonseca 2017: 429).

This sentiment is echoed by further passages that convey a meta-poetic perspective. For instance, there is the character of a writer, named Juan Dinis, who cherishes the idea of a post-anthropocentric type of novel, where not human subjects are the protagonists, but where fire is the subject of history:

> Según pasó a explicar, la novela estaba a punto de entrar en una nueva etapa: una etapa inhumana, como le gustaba llamarla, en la que poco importaba la experiencia urbana. [. . .] Una novela vacía, repleta di polvo y aire, una novela geológica, que retrate en un instante absoluto el monumental paso del tiempo. Una novela archivo, eso es [. . .]. (Fonseca 2017: 242–243)

This is further echoed by the comment of a priest travelling through the jungle, who also speculates about a new historiography, concerned not with humans, but with geology: "Una historia universal que procede a paso geológico y no humano. [. . .] Una historia escrita a otra escala: a escala natural en vez de a escala humana, escrita con el ritmo de las corrientes subterráneas, escrita sobre la corteza de los árboles" (Fonseca 2017: 347). In fact, it might be said that Fonseca's novel is indeed less interested in the psychological development of its characters, but rather aims to construct a network of symbolic relations in space and time. Because of its global as well as encyclopedic ambition, the novel may be classified as a "maximalist novel", as defined by Stefano Ercolino. According to Ercolino, this form of novelistic totality comprises centrifugal as well as centripetal tendencies. Furthermore, the narrative digressiveness of this type of novel is structured and harmonized through metaphors and metonymies (Ercolino 2014: 113), in this case mostly visual ones (photography, camouflage).

For its digressive style (and the inclusion of photographs), the novel is especially indebted to the poetics of Sebald. The most direct allusion to Sebald is via a shared reference to the English baroque author Thomas Browne (1605–1682). As mentioned above, on the first pages of the novel the narrator receives a parcel from Giovanna; it is marked by five black dots, which seem to resemble a domino (Fonseca 2017: 17). Yet soon the narrator realizes that this is indeed the sign of the so-called Quincunx, and which is described as the programmatic encounter between nature and culture (Fonseca 2017: 20). This sign is traced to Thomas Browne's *The Garden of Cyprus*, where it is said to be defined in the following way: "[. . .] la prevalencia del patrón quincunque en la naturaleza como demostración de un diseño divino" (Fonseca 2017: 20). Years later, he even had authored article on this topic in an academic journal: "Variaciones del patrón quincunce y sus usos para la lepidopterología tropical" (Fonseca 2017: 20).

Here, readers familiar with the work of Sebald recognize – mediated by the explicit citation of Browne – an implicit allusion to the beginning of the novel *The Rings of Saturn* (*Die Ringe des Saturn*, 1995). Here the narrator speaks about

Browne's attempt to recognize in nature – which resists a totalizing, comprehensive representation – a recurring geometrical pattern: "[. . .] it befits our philosophy to be writ small, using the shorthand and contracted forms of transient Nature, which alone are a reflection of eternity. True to his own precept, Browne records the patterns which recur in the seemingly infinite diversity of forms, in *The Garden of Cyprus*, for instance, he draws the quincunx, which is composed by using the corners of a regular quadrilateral and the point at which its diagonals intersect (Sebald 1998: 16–17).

For all three authors the quincunx works as a meta-poetic sign. For Sebald and Fonseca, the figure of Browne embodies the anachronistic science of natural history, revisited as a model for postmodern literature, marked by an unstable speaking position, a fragmented, discontinuous sense of totality, and the logic of association and correspondence rather than one of cause and effect (Morgan 2013: 224). Fonseca thus also perhaps shares other motives of Sebald's passage on Browne, namely the "science of the disappearance in obscurity" as well as the typically baroque (and Benjaminian) notion of history as catastrophe (Sebald 1998: 36). As seen above, Toledano is even said to write a "natural history of fire", bearing the (Sebaldian) title *A Brief History of Destruction* (Fonseca 2017: 355). As Kaisa Kaakinen has recently argued, Sebald has been an enabling figure for a variety of contemporary authors. In this context, she also remarks that Browne's concept of the quincunx may be related to a deeper principle of narrative organization, whereby digressive, paratactically organized narratives are brought into an overarching coherence and a network of relations (Kaakinen 2017: 194-195), similar to the logic observed by Ercolino.

Fonseca's novel contains a postscript by the external narrator who finally receives notice of the posthumous exhibition designed by Giovanna, in a gallery of contemporary art in Puerto Rico. Since the nameless narrator (like the author) grew up in Puerto Rico, this final chapter is shadowed not only by posthumous memories, but by a sense of *nostos*, both epic and ironic, a return to origins, to the "green of the tropics" (Fonseca 2017: 409). The description of the exhibition includes various quotations and images of the technique of camouflage, straddling the border between science and art, including a photograph of a boy, which again resonates with the page from Sebald's *Austerlitz* (Fig. 3). The boy depicted is Abbott Handerson Thayer (1849–1921), a New England painter, naturalist, and pioneer of evolutionary biology, who has become a crucial figure for "multidisciplinary speculations" (Shell 2012: 28). Thayer was especially interested in a universal theory of protective coloration, that is, the idea that animals evolve according to the momentary possibility to blend in with the natural environment, namely through a technique of so-called "counter-shading" which diminishes their outlines against the natural background (Abberley 2020: 54).

Fig. 3: Buckingham's Inc. Abbott Handerson Thayer as a boy, ca. 1861. Abbott Handerson Thayer and Thayer Family papers, 1851–1999. Archives of American Art, Smithsonian Institution. Digital ID: 8659.

The phenomenological experience of crypsis was employed to erase the boundaries between science and art, while Thayer himself insisted on the difference between camouflage and mimicry: "Mimicry makes an animal appear to be some other thing, whereas this newly discovered law makes him cease to exist at all" (Shell 2012: 29).

The novel subscribes to a concept of subterranean history as well as the practice of natural history, distinguished by temporal and spatial interconnections. The topos of visual indeterminacy, associated with the Latin American tropics, is translated into the poetics of the text (camouflage, mimicry), aiming at a conceptual dissolution of the boundaries between humanity and nature, art and nature, past and present.

Conclusion: Other Worlds and Histories

Both novels discussed here, through their respective depictions of voyages into the forest, or through their metaphorical rewriting of jungle imagery, play on the metaphor of the "new world" and of new world discovery; they employ the idea of travelling towards "los inicios de la creación" (Oloixarac 2016: 208), but there is also the sense that their travelers "llega[n] tarde" (Fonseca 2017: 396). In fact, in contrast to the Latin American jungle novel, as mostly associated with the vogue of regionalism, the novels by Oloixarac and Fonseca relinquish the very idea of the realist representation of nature. In contrast to the earlier literary image of the tropics as embodying arrested time and a realm distinct from the history of modernity, the contemporary novels associate the tropical space with deep time and emphasize the continuity of humans with non-humans[6]. According to this very scheme, in *Las Constelaciones Oscuras*, Bruun disappears toward the end of the novel, or is possibly himself transformed into a hybrid being (Oloixarac 2016: 148), thus echoing the figure of Cassio, who, in his capacity as a techy nerd, is associated with the "arte de desaparecer" (Oloixarac 2016: 224). Both characters are also compared with a camouflaging serpent (Oloixarac 2016: 84, 136). Fonseca's novel ends with the frame narrator's comment that he has succeeded in becoming an "incomprehensible animal" (Fonseca 2017: 425).

Furthermore, both novels feature a scene of "una biblioteca encerrada en el medio de la selva" (Oloixarac 2016: 210; Fonseca 2017: 387), thus self-consciously alluding to the "traditional" function of the Latin American novel as archive, collection, or museum, as overwriting of previous discourses. Disappearance into the natural background, camouflage, or species transformation – both novels suggest

---

[6] This latter aspect, however, is already visible in Carpentier's *Los Pasos Perdidos* (Saramago 2021: 63, 90).

the human subject's continuity with nature, yet, in contrast to the nineteenth century backdrop of natural science, arguably a nature that is itself conceived as post-natural. Optical games of hide-and-seek, negative photographic images, dark constellations: both novels invoke such visual metaphors in order to emphasize a perspectival shift with regard to the perception of the world. If Alexander Beecroft has argued that the technique of narrative *entrelacement* is the novelistic equivalent of the paranoid connectedness in the age of globalization (Beecroft 2014: 283), temporal strata and the mimesis or mingling of species are self-conscious novelistic devices that seek to convey the deep time of the Anthropocene.

Works Cited

Abberley, Will (2020): *Mimicry and Display in Victorian Literary Culture. Nature, Science and the Nineteenth-Century Imagination*. Cambridge: Cambridge University Press.
Andermann, Jens (2018): *Tierras en trance: Arte y naturaleza después del paisaje*. Santiago de Chile: Metales pesados.
Anderson, Mark (2014): "The Natural Baroque: Opacity, Impenetrability, and Folding in Writing on Amazonia". In: *Hispanic Issues On Line* 16, pp. 57–83.
Azurdia, Diego (2020): "A Conversation with Carlos Fonseca". In: *Music and Literature*, https://www.musicandliterature.org/features/2020/8/2/a-conversation-with-carlos-fonseca (last access: 06/2020).
Bates, Henry Walter (2010): *A Naturalist on the River Amazon*. Cambridge: Cambridge University Press.
Baucom, Ian (2020): *History 4° Celsius. Search for a Method in the Age of the Anthropocene*. Durham: Duke University Press.
Baumgärtner, Patrick (2017): "Naturgeschichte". In: Öhlschläger, Claudia/Niehaus, Michael (eds.): *W. G. Sebald-Handbuch. Leben-Werk-Wirkung*. Stuttgart: Metzler, pp. 213–219.
Beecroft, Alexander (2014): *An Ecology of World Literature. From Antiquity to the Present Day*. London: Verso.
Blasco, Lucía (2021): "'El Amazonas es un paraíso de culturas que no conocemos': entrevista con la escritora Pola Oloixarac". In: *BBC Mundo*, https://www.bbc.com/mundo/noticias-55676337 (last access: 26/ 01/2021).
Brizuela, Natalia (2014): "Light Writing in the Tropics". In: *Aperture* 215, pp. 32–37.
—— (2012): *Fotografia e império. Paisagens de um Brasil moderno*. São Paulo: Companhia das Letras.
Chakrabarty, Dipesh (2021): *The Climate of History in a Planetary Age*. Chicago: Chicago University Press.
—— (2009): "The Climate of History: Four Theses." In: *Critical Inquiry* 35 (2), pp. 197–222.
Dünne, Jörg (2019): *Kosmogramme. Geohistorische Skalierungen romanischer Literaturen*. Berlin: August Verlag.

—— (2016): *Die katastrophische Feerie. Geschichte, Geologie und Spektakel in der modernen französischen Literatur*. Konstanz: Konstanz University Press.
Echevarría, Roberto González (1998): *Myth and Archive. A Theory of Latin American Narrative*. Durham: Duke University Press.
Ercolino, Stefano (2014): *The Maximalist Novel. From Thomas Pynchon's 'Gravity's Rainbow' to Roberto Bolaño's '2666'*. Transl. Albert Sbragia. London: Bloomsbury.
Findlen, Paula (2006): "Natural History". In: Park, Katharine/Daston, Lorraine (eds.): *The Cambridge History of Science*. Cambridge: Cambridge University Press, pp. 435–468.
Fonseca, Carlos (2020a): *The Literature of Catastrophe. Nature, Disaster and Revolution in Latin America*. New York: Bloomsbury.
—— (2020b): *Natural History*. Transl. Megan McDowell. New York: Farrar Strauss.
—— (2017): *Museo animal*. Barcelona: Anagrama.
Friedman, Susan Stanford (2015): *Planetary Modernisms: Provocations on Modernity Across Time*. New York: Columbia University Press.
Heise, Ursula (2008): *Sense of Place and Sense of Planet: The Environmental Imagination of the Global*. Oxford: Oxford University Press.
Heyne, Elisabeth (2020): "Wahrnehmungshygiene und Baumpuderrausch. Kleine amazonische Sinneslehre (Lévi-Strauss, Restany, Viveiros de Castro, Kohn, Oloixarac)". In: *Kulturwissenschaftliche Zeitschrift* 5, 1, pp. 91–110.
Hoyos, Héctor (2019): *Things with a History: Transcultural Materialism and the Literatures of Extraction in Contemporary Latin America*. New York: Columbia University Press.
—— (2015): *Beyond Bolaño. The Global Latin American Novel*. New York: Columbia University Press.
Humboldt, Alexander von (2004 [1807]): *Ansichten der Natur*. Frankfurt am Main: Eichborn.
Kaakinen, Kaisa (2017): *Comparative Literature and the Historical Imaginary. Reading Conrad, Weiss, Sebald*. London: Palgrave.
Keith, Joseph (2018): "The Novel as Planetary Form". In: Bulson, Eric (ed.): *The Cambridge Companion to the Novel*. Cambridge: Cambridge University Press, pp. 268–283.
Lepenies, Wolf (1976): *Das Ende der Naturgeschichte. Wandel kultureller Selbstverständlichkeiten in den Wissenschaften des 18. und 19. Jahrhunderts*. Munich: Hanser.
Leys Stepan, Nancy (1976): *Picturing Tropical Nature*. London: Reaktion Books.
Lindquist, Jason Howard (2008): *A "pure excess of complexity": Tropical surfeit, the observing subject, and the text, 1773-1871*. Dissertation. Indiana University.
Morgan, Dawn (2013): "The World after Progress: The Thomas Browne of W. G. Sebald". In: *ESC* 39, 2–3, pp. 217–242.
Oloixarac, Pola (2019): *Dark Constellations*. Transl. Roy Kesey. New York: Soho Press.
Oloixarac, Pola (2016): *Las Constelaciones Oscuras*. Barcelona: Random House Mondadori.
Saramago, Victoria (2021): *Fictional Environments. Mimesis, Deforestation, and Development in Latin America*. Evanston, Ill.: Northwestern University Press.
Sebald, W. G. (2004): *On the Natural History of Destruction*. London: Penguin.
Sebald, W. G. (2001): *Austerlitz*. Munich: Hanser.
Sebald, W. G. (1998): *The Rings of Saturn*. Transl. Michael Hulse. New York: New Directions.
Shell, Hannah Rose (2012): *Camouflage, Photography, and the Media of Reconaissance*. New York: Zone Books.

Sequeira, Jessica (2020): "'One thinks through Fictions': A Conversation with Carlos Fonseca". In: *Los Angeles Review of Books*, https://lareviewofbooks.org/article/one-thinks-throughfictions-a-conversation-with-carlos-fonseca/ (last access: 31/7/2020).

Viveiros de Castro, Eduardo (2017): *A inconstância da alma selvagem*. São Paulo: Ubu.

Welge, Jobst (2021): "Natur, Geschichte und die Poetik des globalen Romans: Alexander von Humboldt und Carlos Fonseca". In: *Abhandlungen der Humboldt-Gesellschaft* 44, pp. 193–211.

—— (2018): "The Jungle Novel. International Permutations of a Genre". In: Lay Brander, Miriam (ed.): *Genre and Globalization. Transformación de géneros en contextos (post-) coloniales/Transformation des genres dans des contextes (post-) coloniaux*. Hildesheim: Olms, pp. 207–229.

Willem, Bieke (2020): "A 'New Continent of Data': Pola Oloixarac's *Dark Constellations* and the Latin American Jungle Novel". In: *Lit: Literature Interpretation Theory*, 31, 2, pp. 129–145.

Wylie, Lesley (2009): *Colonial Tropes and Postcolonial Tricks: Rewriting the Tropics in the Novela de la Selva*. Liverpool: Liverpool University Press.

Jenny Haase
"Para contarte de la isla"
entrelazamientos corporales,
ecológicos y económicos
en la poesía de Rosabetty Muñoz

Permanecer aquí, en este momento del desarrollo
personal y comunitario, es resistir activa y
productivamente frente a un sistema que absorbe
toda manifestación local.
(Muñoz 1997: s.p.)

Crisis mundial, perspectivas post-globales y propuestas latinoamericanas

En los últimos años, la crisis ecológica llegó a cambiar substancialmente nuestra percepción de la relación entre el ser humano y su 'medio ambiente'. Transformaciones ecológicas fundamentales como el calentamiento global o la extinción de las especies se desarrollan y nos afectan a escala planetaria y ya no se pueden reducir a problemas y constelaciones locales. Sin embargo, los efectos de estas transformaciones cada vez más aceleradas se perciben de manera específica y distinta en cada lugar y están estrechamente relacionadas a las condiciones geopolíticas, económicas y sociales locales. En este sentido, quisiera referirme a la noción de lo 'post-global' como marco de reflexión crítica tal como ha sido propuesto por los editores de este volumen. Según Alfred López, que retoma la noción del economista italiano Mario Deaglio, lo post-global se hace visible precisamente en estos momentos en que el discurso hegemónico de la globalización llega a tropezar y la crisis de la economía neoliberal mundial se hace palpable: "The global South diverges from the postcolonial, and emerges as a postglobal discourse, in that it is best glimpsed at those moments where globalization as a hegemonic discourse stumbles, where the latter experiences a crisis or setback" (López 2007: 1). Lo post-global, entonces, describe la relación dinámica entre la experiencia de los efectos locales de la globalización por un lado y el

Jenny Haase, Universidad de Halle-Wittenberg

posicionamiento crítico frente a los discursos y las prácticas que la legitiman, por el otro. El concepto también hace referencia a las relaciones conflictivas entre políticas globales y activismos locales, así como a las asimetrías de poder que las fomentan.

En las literaturas y culturas latinoamericanas contemporáneas (y también históricas) los entrelazamientos entre las asimetrías económicas y geopolíticas, las estructuras de poder y la explotación ecológica se pueden apreciar de manera especialmente expresiva. Al mismo tiempo, las narraciones y filosofías autóctonas y las prácticas sociales locales llegan a constituir el trasfondo para un pensamiento socio-ecológico *otro*. En el marco del debate post-global, cabe preguntarse entonces por el aporte específico de los discursos latinoamericanos a la hora de generar economías, políticas, ecologías y epistemologías alternativas frente al sistema de la globalización implementado en los últimos decenios a escala global. ¿De qué manera el saber local situado y las estéticas locales entran en diálogo con los discursos literarios y teóricos mundiales? ¿Cómo describir estas epistemologías resistentes que nos plantean autoras y autores, artistas y activistas del Sur americano sin caer en nuevos esencialismos y dicotomías?

Nuestra lectura de la poesía de Rosabetty Muñoz parte de estas preguntas. Tras una breve presentación de la autora, nos interesa explorar la sensibilidad con la que la poeta indaga en las condiciones físicas compartidas entre seres humanos, animales, plantas y elementos en el archipiélago de Chiloé, es decir, en un lugar concreto y específico, y las relaciona con aspectos socioeconómicos y de género. En este contexto, preguntaremos también por el papel de la religión en el debate sobre nuevas subjetividades post-globales y post-antropocéntricas. Finalmente, exploraremos las consecuencias poetológicas de estas epistemologías alternativas que se hacen visibles en la poesía de Rosabetty Muñoz.

Hablar desde el Sur de Chile: Rosabetty Muñoz

Rosabetty Muñoz es una de las voces líricas chilenas más perfiladas de la actualidad. Nació en 1960 en el archipiélago de Chiloé en el Sur de Chile donde reside hasta ahora. Las islas de Chiloé desempeñan un papel central en su poesía: como tema y motivo, pero también como lugar de enunciación destacado. Desde 1981 hasta ahora, la poeta publicó más de diez poemarios y ganó múltiples premios, además es miembro de la Academia Chilena de la Lengua.

Su obra multifacética se inscribe tanto en la cultura regional de Chiloé como en los discursos de la literatura mundial. Su poesía se despliega a partir de un sujeto lírico múltiple que rompe con estereotipos y convenciones desde una posición marginalizada a nivel geográfico, cultural, económico y político en diálogo crítico con la realidad social local.

Entre los temas de su lírica destacan la última dictadura militar y el exilio, la violencia, el dolor y la soledad, así como como la destrucción ecológica y cultural; pero también la empatía, la solidaridad, el deseo y la esperanza. Los críticos han leído la obra de Muñoz desde perspectivas feministas y postcoloniales; sin embargo, la autora misma rechaza estas categorías limitativas tanto como las de 'poeta chilota' o 'sureña' (Labarthe/Rau 2019: 202–203; Travis 2018: 221)[1]. En los últimos años, críticos como Mauricio Ostrias González (2010) o Christopher M. Travis (2018) han destacado el impulso ecocrítico de sus textos y con ello la han situado dentro de una larga tradición chilena de poetas como Nicanor Parra, Raúl Zurita, Cecilia Vicuña o Juan Pablo Riveros.

"Navajuelas, cangrejos, cochayuyos": el cuerpo del archipiélago

La presencia del archipiélago de Chiloé y el entrecruce de cuerpos y paisajes, anatomía y geografía, caracterizan la obra de Muñoz (Prado Traverso 2011: 118). De manera parecida, la relación dinámica entre tierra y agua atraviesa sus textos. En este contexto, la geografía física del paisaje también lleva una capa cultural. Cada pieza del archipiélago remite a un recuerdo que se debe conservar – como en el siguiente poema del poemario *Hijos* (1991) que se desarrolla en la playa de la isla Metalqui:

> Metalqui
>
> Navajuelas machos y hembras,
> cangrejos, cochayuyos, hasta piedras
> guardaré.
> Para contarte de la isla,
> como era antes
>   de los depredadores.
> (Muñoz 2020a: 237)

El texto —como muchos otros del poemario— comunica la melancolía de una pérdida. En las capas materiales de las numerosas islas del archipiélago se des-

---

[1] "A eso aspiro: a ser leída con toda mi particularidad en el ámbito total de la poesía sin apellidos" (Labarthe/Rau 2019: 205).

cifran historias de represión solapadas y relacionadas a la colonización, al régimen militar, a la violencia de género y a la explotación económica. No obstante, el mundo animal y vegetal remite también a la posibilidad de un futuro *otro* y, con ello, a una forma de esperanza (Travis 2018: 222). Llama también la atención cómo la voz poética marca el lugar de enunciación decididamente local al usar un vocabulario específico de las costas chilenas del Sur. El poema da lugar a una reflexión metapoética: para narrar la isla, poetizarla y preservar su memoria cultural, nos dice la voz poética, es preciso entrar en contacto con el entorno físico y hacerles caso a los animales, las plantas y los elementos. Así, la dimensión material llega a ser el fundamento y la condición de posibilidad de una poética de los sentidos y de lo local que Rosabetty Muñoz desarrolla en sus poesías. Solo a través de la materialidad física de los caracoles y de las piedras concretas y singulares es posible acercarse a la historia cultural de Chiloé.

La condición física del ser humano muchas veces representa la base del dolor y de la vulnerabilidad en los textos de la poeta chilote. Esta vulnerabilidad se hace especialmente visible en los poemas que tematizan motivos como el aborto, el infanticidio, el incesto o la prostitución, como en el poemario *En nombre de ninguna* (2008). En estos textos, los cuerpos de los niños muertos son transportados en bolsas de basura. Y las mujeres jóvenes son desnucadas igual que los cisnes:

> Fue un año de exterminio.
> Cisnes de cuello negro
> caían en bandada;
> [. . .]
> Y las sardinas
> por ciento varaban en las playas.
> [. . .]
> Como las aves
> ciertas muchachitas respiraron
> un aire cargado de toxinas
> y curvaron el gracioso cuello
> sobre el altar del placer.
> (Muñoz 2008: s.p.)

Varias veces, Muñoz paraleliza la violencia contra los niños y las mujeres jóvenes con el sufrimiento de los animales. Esta perspectiva entrecruzada tiene un efecto doble: por un lado, se destaca la empatía por y el aprecio de los animales; por otro lado, la animalidad del ser humano mismo, su corporalidad y vulnerabilidad, se hacen visibles. En este sentido, Muñoz se inscribe en una "poética de la criatura" (Pick 2011) que parte de la vulnerabilidad física de todos los seres vivos y deja al mismo tiempo traslucir una huella religiosa y espiritual, como veremos más abajo[2].

Los textos del volumen *Este ocio de amar* de 2002 también sugieren una relación estrecha entre la existencia de animales y humanos. En el fondo, la voz lírica pone en duda la separación entre la naturaleza-objeto y el sujeto humano en términos más generales ya que el yo lírico cada vez se vuelve más animal o planta, especialmente en el contexto amoroso y erótico, como en el poema siguiente que sugiere ya desde su título un sujeto animal:

Medusa

Ondean mis tentáculos.
Se humedece el perímetro de mí.

Buceo
en el ansia sumergida.
Ciega y colmada
la marea empuja esta redondez
hacia la playa.
(Muñoz 2012: 107)

En cambio, en el poema "Gruta" se puede apreciar una estética vegetal, como en la siguiente imagen simbiótica en la que fusiona la voz enunciativa con el mundo de las plantas: "Plácida/ me crecen flores/ en el nido de la axila" (Muñoz 2012: 108). Hay cierta afinidad aquí con la poesía de Juana de Ibarbourou, en el ámbito americano, o incluso con Rosalía de Castro, en el contexto español, en esta estética sensual, muy conectada al mundo vegetal. En otro poema, el "tú" al que se dirige la voz poética oscila entre un amante humano y una especie de árbol salvaje. Además, la imagen del amante está estrechamente relacionada con los elementos de la tierra y del viento: "Fangoso el territorio de tu aliento" (Muñoz 2012: 109), le dice el sujeto a su amado.

Bien se podría objetar que las metáforas vegetales y las comparaciones entre los seres humanos y animales son tan viejas como el acto de narrar y la poesía misma. En este sentido, las referencias al mundo natural siempre han sido consideradas como figuras retóricas y formas de expresión figurativa. Sin embargo, en el uso poético de las palabras siempre trasluce la capa de significado literal, con la consecuencia de que el sentido literal y el sentido metafórico se superponen. Si leemos los poemas de un modo 'materialista', entendido

---

[2] "The creaturely is not only a synonym for the material and corporeal. It carries within it (as inflection, as horizon) an opening unto a religious vocabulary of creation and created, and so attempts a rapprochement between the material and the sacred." (Pick 2011: 17).

como una manera de rescatar el sentido literal del significante, entonces dejamos al descubierto la semántica de lo vegetal y de lo animal como método constitutivo de estos textos. Desde esta perspectiva los poemas de Rosabetty Muñoz enfatizan la materialidad y la cercanía a la tierra, el devenir dinámico del sujeto – cualidades que comparte con los animales y las plantas. En los textos se construye entonces una subjetividad frágil y dinámica que no solo podríamos calificar como post-global sino también como post-antropocéntrica, en el sentido de que parte desde las experiencias físicas y afectivas compartidas con otros seres vivos y se caracteriza por una vulnerabilidad existencial.

"Dios nos puso en el jardín": una espiritualidad terrenal

En este contexto de la construcción material de la subjetividad poética, quisiéramos brevemente mencionar el papel complejo de la religión en Rosabetty Muñoz ya que las imágenes cristianas, referencias bíblicas y alusiones a la liturgia católica abundan en su poesía, impregnada de una espiritualidad sensible. Cabe destacar que el cristianismo, por un lado, puede ser considerado como una religión antropocéntrica por antonomasia si solo se piensa en el dogma de la encarnación o en la posición privilegiada programática del hombre en relación a los animales y plantas en la narración bíblica del Génesis. Por otro lado, no obstante, el concepto de un Dios-Creador trascendente también remite a una espiritualidad teocéntrica en la que el ser humano se ve completamente *sujeto* a la potencia divina.

Los motivos religiosos abarcan en Muñoz desde el distanciamiento irónico y la crítica a veces severa de la Iglesia católica hasta las relecturas de las narraciones bíblicas, y en especial, del libro de los profetas. A primera vista puede resultar sorprendente que esta semántica religiosa no constituya una oposición a la predominancia de lo físico y lo material en los textos de Muñoz. Recordemos, sin embargo, que en el pensamiento católico, el sufrimiento físico, la vulnerabilidad carnal y la transitoriedad de la vida en la Tierra son figuras de pensamiento esenciales. Rosabetty Muñoz llama a esta condición física del ser humano "la presencia mortal que somos" (Muñoz 2012: 144). Así, en la siguiente cita del volumen inédito *De sitios fugaces* (2003), se hace visible cómo el sujeto poético siempre es formado por la sombra de su futura disolución:

> soy yo, con mi carga de muerte
> el olor a tumba

> las larvas de la descomposición
> bullendo en el músculo.
> (Muñoz 2012: 144)

En otros textos, la voz lírica se inscribe en el círculo material de la vida, al hacer alusión a la liturgia católica:

> y es que uno respira
> el polvo de los huesos suspendidos en el aire.
> Polvo que será moho en los puentes
> pátina en las manillas de las puertas
> musgo descolgándose del techo.
> (Muñoz 2012: 145)

El mismo acto de respirar se puede leer aquí de manera metonímica, indicando una concepción holística e integral de la vida en la que todo ser, todo elemento está estrechamente relacionado con todas las otras entidades vitales y la respiración figura como elemento mediador. "La experiencia de la fe está ligada a la comunión en tanto fusión cárnea con otros" (Labarthe/Rau 2019: 210), comenta a este respecto la poeta. Así, en el poema citado, el aliento a su vez encarna una manera igualitaria de relacionarse con el otro, un símbolo de una trascendencia inmanente u horizontal y una referencia autorreflexiva a la labor del poeta, como lo formulara Amy Hollywood:

> Breath [. . .] is the concealed but still material source of a human transcendence that is horizontal and nonhierarchical, a movement out toward the other [. . .]. The silent, moving source of existence, the air requires that we take the risk of opening ourselves to the other if we are to experience presence within language. (Hollywood 1999: 64)

En un poema más reciente del libro *Santo oficio* (2020) —libro que por lo general se centra mucho en la condición física y corporal— leemos, además de un guiño intertextual a Quevedo, una idea muy parecida pero más distanciada todavía del pensamiento católico convencional ya que se insinúa otra vez la continuidad material inmanente en distanciamiento explícito a la fórmula funeral:

> Pero el acontecimiento definitivo
> el drama
> es esta materia
>   que se desmorona.
> Será polvo en el polvo.
> Así sea
>   pero no cenizas.
> (Muñoz 2020b: 13)

En otro lugar, la voz lírica expresa una espiritualidad muy conectada a la tierra que corresponde con muchas cosmologías indígenas, como, entre otras, la mapuche, cuando dice: "La tierra entera es un santuario"[3]. Finalmente, en la siguiente cita, la referencia bíblica al Jardín de Edén se puede leer como una crítica manifiesta a la explotación de los océanos y del abuso de la Tierra en términos generales, y a las prácticas pesqueras abusivas ejercidas en las costas chilenas sureñas por las empresas multinacionales en concreto:

Dios nos puso en un jardín decían
Y lo perdimos

Fueron cerrando los ojos
porque no querían ver.

Vendrán otros peces
de ojos comestibles y pieles calcáreas

Tendrán escamas con mensajes cifrados
que tampoco entenderemos.
(Muñoz 2019:12)

La crítica a la ignorancia y al menosprecio de los humanos frente a los animales y las plantas parece evidente. Al mismo tiempo se comunica la experiencia de una alteridad existencial, puesta en evidencia por medio de la metáfora de los "mensajes cifrados", transmitidos por los peces, y que nosotros, los seres humanos no somos capaces de descifrar. Quizás esta imagen la podemos leer también como una alegoría más amplia de la alienación humana y de una poética que en vez de apropiarse de la alteridad externa privilegie la escucha atenta del Otro, humano y no-humano.

"Mi voz contra la tierra ahogada": posicionamientos éticos y estéticos

Finalmente, quisiéramos proponer una lectura de la poesía de Rosabetty Muñoz desde una perspectiva ecocrítica basada en algunas vertientes del pensamiento materialista actual, y más específicamente, en la ética post-antropocéntrica que ha desarrollado la filósofa norteamericana Jane Bennett y la propuesta feminista planteada por la socióloga Verónica Gago.

---

[3] Los conceptos de la tierra (*mapu*) y de la Tierra Madre (*Ñuke Mapu*) empeñan un papel esencial en la filosofía mapuche. Ver, p.ej., Ñanculef Huaiquinao (2016: 23/38).

En su ya clásico estudio *Vibrant Matter*, Bennett propone un posicionamiento ético cuya base sería la materialidad compartida y experimentada de todos los seres vivos y, también, de las entidades no vivas, como las piedras y otros elementos inorgánicos. Dice Bennett:

> For the vital materialist [. . . . .] the starting point of ethics is [. . .] the recognition of human participation in a shared, vital materiality. [. . .] Vital materiality captures an "alien" quality of our own flesh, and in so doing reminds humans of the very radical character of the (fractious) kinship between the human and the nonhuman. (Bennett 2010: 112)

Partiendo del pensamiento monista de Espinoza, el vitalismo de Bergson y las ideas del *assemblage* de Deleuze, entre otros, Bennett busca crear una conciencia de los complejos entrelazamientos del ser humano con su entorno. La consecuencia de tal pensamiento sería una sensibilidad ecológica que no tiene como objetivo borrar por completo las diferencias entre hombres, animales, plantas y materia inorgánica, sino más bien reconocer el ensamblaje constitutivo de toda vida y, por tanto, la existencial interdependencia y condición de expuesto del ser humano. Tal como declara Bennett: "In a knotted world of vibrant matter, to harm one section of the web may very well be to harm oneself." (Bennett 2010: 13).

Por su parte, en su estudio reciente, *La potencia feminista o el deseo de cambiarlo todo*, la socióloga argentina Verónica Gago destaca los estrechos enlaces entre el sistema económico neoliberal, las estructuras patriarcales de poder y el abuso de los recursos naturales desde una perspectiva decididamente feminista y latinoamericana. En su análisis de los movimientos y huelgas feministas actuales en Argentina y toda América Latina, Gago propone nuevas maneras de resistencia colectiva que reúne grupos muy diferentes y de contextos sociales diversos. Al hacerlo, destaca también la existencial interdependencia del sujeto con las estructuras sociales y las condiciones materiales que lo rodean: "¿Qué es tener un cuerpo? ¿Qué es tener un territorio? En primer lugar, se 'tiene' en el sentido de que se es parte. No se tiene como propiedad, no se posee. Ser parte implica entonces reconocer la 'interdependencia' que nos compone, que hace posible la vida." (Gago 2019: 98). Así, a su vez hace hincapié en la imposibilidad de "recortar y aislar el cuerpo individual del cuerpo colectivo, el cuerpo humano del territorio y del paisaje." (Gago 2019: 97). La investigadora argentina, además, enfatiza los orígenes coloniales de las asimetrías económicas y sociales latinoamericanas actuales y paraleliza así la violencia de género, la violencia antropocéntrica y la violencia colonial: "La subordinación de las mujeres, de la naturaleza y de las colonias como lema de la 'civilización' inaugura la acumulación capitalista y pone así las bases de la división sexual y colonial del trabajo." (Gago 2019: 95–96).

En la poesía de Muñoz, desde sus primeras publicaciones o bien *avant la lettre* podemos reconocer una perspectiva similar en las numerosas reflexiones poéticas sobre las estrechas conexiones entre las exploraciones ecológicas, culturales y económicas del archipiélago. O, como formula la poeta: "Aquí, donde los canales angostos no son estrictamente mar sino sinuosas aguas que lamen costas y las lomas parecen los recovecos femeninos, cuerpo y territorio son una sola materia viva." (Labarthe/Rau 2019: 206). Ya en el texto "El Arribo" (*Baile de señoritas*) de 1994 la poeta remite a la tala masiva de los bosques regionales conectándola con los procesos coloniales y neo-coloniales y con la situación histórica y actual de las mujeres en Chiloé:

> El arribo
>
> Traían los dedos agarrotados
> y el mar metidos en las coyunturas.
> Los ojos blandos y desbordados.
>
> Desaparecieron árboles, cercos, todas
> las minucias.
> Sólo nosotras permanecimos,
> mudas y palpitantes
> mirando sus faenas de atraque.
> (Muñoz 2020a: 141)

En estos versos, aspectos coloniales, ecológicos, económicos y de género se entrelazan y se condicionan entre sí. Además, llama la atención como el yo lírico adapta la voz de un colectivo femenino al cambiar de la primera persona singular a la plural; estrategia textual que se puede interpretar como una manera de resistencia y solidaridad femeninas.

En los últimos años, Rosabetty Muñoz no solo publicó textos poéticos comprometidos con la protección del medioambiente sino que también intervino de manera periodística y política en el discurso público en Chile – denunciando, entre otros, el desastre ecológico de la llamada "marea roja" en las costas chilenas del Sur. Se trataba de una plaga de algas tóxica en el año 2016, provocada aparentemente por el calentamiento de los mares y, sobre todo, por miles de toneladas de salmones muertos echadas al Océano Pacífico por la salmoneras nacionales e internacionales. En la sección con el mismo título –"Marea roja"– de uno de sus poemarios más recientes, *Técnicas para cegar a los peces* (2019), la poeta vincula la marginalización geopoética con las condiciones laborales precarias, el sexismo, la sociedad de consumo y el desastre ecológico, abriendo así un campo asociativo de múltiples relaciones:

> Ahora la ciudad tiene otro orden.
> Bajo un cielo sucio
> las micros desechadas por la capital, circulan
> tragando turnos de obreros que van a las pesqueras.
> Se abren choperías, cafés con piernas
> en los nuevos nait clubs las vecinas bailan,
> sin ningún tipo de miramientos
> (Muñoz 2019: 21)

Las estructuras de poder que se hacen visibles en estos versos conciernen tanto la relación asimétrica entre metrópolis y periferia como las asimetrías económicas entre los hombres poseedores del capital y los trabajadores, al igual que la violencia que la violencia estructural de una sociedad patriarcal y sexista dirigida hacia el consumo y el placer rápido. El cuerpo sensible, vital y frágil, capaz de sentir placer y dolor, humano o no-humano, es el centro de todas estas reflexiones poéticas de Muñoz. Con Gago (2019: 100), se podría argumentar que "el cuerpo como cuerpo-territorio es el lugar concreto desde donde hoy se confronta el extractivismo ampliado: todas las formas de desposesión, despojo y explotación (del extractivismo literal de materias primas al extractivismo digital y financiero) que articulan la máquina de valorización capitalista."

A modo coral y repetidas de manera variada, descripciones de las medusas muertas entrecortan los fragmentos poéticos de la sección "Marea roja" una y otra vez:

> (El mar, en oleadas, vomita
> medusas muertas y envases plásticos)
> (Muñoz 2019: 21--22)

> (Ahí están todas esas medusas agonizando.
> Enlazados sus tentáculos ambarinos
> cubren playas y campos.)
> (Muñoz 2019: 27)

> (en marejadas, el mar sigue vomitando medusas muertas)
> (Muñoz 2019: 35)

Los comentarios lacónicos tienen un efecto eufemístico. Puestos entre paréntesis, en realidad constituyen el subtexto central y dominante del poemario entero. Así, el tema ambiental no representa de ningún modo un decoro pintoresco ni tampoco únicamente un paisaje social y cultural, sino que llega a ser la materia existencial que une y conecta todas las entidades materiales, sujetos humanos y no-humanos. Al mismo tiempo, la poeta destaca la constante ignorancia de las sociedades frente a la crisis ecológica desplazada hasta los márgenes del discurso público.

De este modo, la responsabilidad ecológica y la justicia social de ninguna manera se contradicen en Rosabetty Muñoz sino que convergen y se posibilitan una a la otra mutuamente, en el sentido más amplio del concepto de "justicia ambiental", concepto que ha desarrollado una especial relevancia en el continente latinoamericano (Heffes 2014). Es decir, que la mirada post-antropocéntrica de la poeta de ningún modo equivale a una perspectiva anti-humanista en el sentido del descuido de las injusticias sociales en favor de la protección ambiental. Sino que se trata de un enfoque más-que-humano que incluye la preocupación social y que reconoce la indisoluble interdependencia entre el ser humano y su entorno en un lugar geopolítico específico. Desde este posicionamiento ético nace al final de "Marea roja" un posicionamiento poetológico decidido:

> Abriré la boca y pegaré los labios al confín de las raíces.
>
> Mi voz contra la tierra ahogada.
> Que el silencio actúe como concha de ostra
> mientras dentro de sí se concentra la materia de una perla.
>   Desde ahora.
>
> (Muñoz 2019: 47)

A modo de conclusión

En su poesía, Rosabetty Muñoz nos habla desde un lugar geopolítico y cultural muy específico: del archipiélago de Chiloé en el Sur del continente americano. Al mismo tiempo, destaca los efectos, conexiones y consecuencias de una globalización económica y cultural cada vez más acelerada. La voz poética reflexiona sobre las relaciones estrechas y complejas entre el sistema económico neoliberal, las asimetrías sociales, la violencia de género y el abuso de los animales y de la naturaleza. Con ello, propone una poética sensible a las condiciones físicas y materiales del lugar geográfico, del medioambiente y del cuerpo humano y no-humano. Lo que llama la atención es que la poesía de Muñoz evita las abstracciones, dirigiendo su atención hacia las experiencias diarias, los objetos cotidianos, a veces a lo cruel y lo feo, pero también a la belleza de lo cercano. Este enfoque en la materialidad cotidiana, combinado con una alta sensibilidad por las injusticias económicas, sociales, culturales y de género, comparte algunos rasgos con la perspectiva feminista de Gago (2019: 124), quien sostiene que "el materialismo que nos importa, el que problematizan los cuerpos diversos del trabajo y de los bienes comunes entendidos desde la perspectiva feminista y su expresión en distintos territorios y conflictos, es uno que combate la abstracción." De modo parecido, los textos poéticos de Muñoz nos hablan desde el cuerpo, denunciando el sufrimiento y el dolor, pero también reivindicando el deseo y la esperanza "desde el placer y la resistencia al avance neocolonial" (Gago 2019: 103):

> Cultivar un cuerpo
>   que no está en el mercado
> una apariencia que no se expone.
> (Muñoz 2020b: 51)

Al mismo tiempo los textos poéticos de Muñoz despliegan un alcance mucho más amplio y nos afectan más allá de los intereses locales, regionales o incluso nacionales al expresar una conciencia profundamente sensible, humana. Humana no en el sentido del humanismo antropocéntrico tradicional sino en el sentido de una mirada holística que da cuenta de los entrelazamientos indisolubles entre los humanos y su entorno vital, "the complicated web of dissonant connections between bodies" (Bennett 2010: 5), y de nuestro 'ser naturaleza'. De cierto modo, entonces, figuras de pensamiento del materialismo dialéctico con su enfoque en las condiciones socioeconómicas y del materialismo ecocrítico con su atención en la materialidad compartida de todos los seres vivos se cruzan y convergen en la poesía de Muñoz. El punto de encuentro es siempre "[el] cuerpo en tanto territorio, composición de afectos, recursos y posibilidades que no son 'individuales', sino que se singularizan porque pasan por el cuerpo de cada quien en la medida que cada cuerpo nunca es sólo 'uno', sino siempre con otr*s, y con otras fuerzas también no-humanas." (Gago 2019: 98).

La poesía deviene la forma ideal para reflejar todas estas vinculaciones e interconexiones vitales existentenciales. No solo porque, como dijera Jonathan Culler, el discurso poético siempre ha privilegiado otras subjetividades, humanas y no humanas, al invocar los árboles, el viento o conceptos abstractos como el amor o la poesía misma. "A specific effect of [lyrical] address is to posit a world in which a wider range of entities can be imagined to exercise agency, resisting our usual assumptions about what can act and what cannot, experimenting with the overcoming of ideological barriers that separate human actors from everything else" (Culler 2015: 242). Sino también porque desde siempre la poesía ha transmitido una lógica *otra* que se basa, precisamente, en lo asociativo, en las conexiones entre diferentes elementos semánticos, fonéticos o estructurales.

En sus textos, Muñoz incluye una cantidad de voces diversas, desde las capas sociales más marginalizadas, los obreros, los niños o las mujeres maltratadas, hasta los bosques, los caracoles, los mariscos y las plantas, atravesando tiempos y espacios, haciendo hincapié en las conexiones entre cuerpos, sistema económico y ecología. Leemos una crítica severa a las estructuras neocoloniales, la injusticia ambiental y la violencia económica y de género, pero también una celebración del archipiélago chilote, su naturaleza y su rica historia cultural. Así, la propuesta poetológica de Rosabetty Muñoz siempre también incluye un posicionamiento ético.

Bibliografía

Bennett, Jane (2010): *Vibrant Matter. A Policial Ecology of Things*. Durham/Londres: Duke University Press.
Culler, Jonathan (2015): *Theory of the Lyric*. Cambridge, MA: Harvard University Press.
Gago, Verónica (2019): *La potencia feminista o el deseo de cambiarlo todo*. Madrid: Traficantes de Sueños.
Heffes, Gisela (2014): "Introducción. Para una ecocrítica latinoamericana: entre la postulación de un ecocentrismo crítico y la crítica a un antropocentrismo hegemónico". En: *Revista de crítica literaria latinoamericana*, 40, 79, pp. 11–34.
Hollywood, Amy (1999): *Sensible Ecstasy. Mysticism, Sexual Difference, and the Demands of History*. Chicago/Londres: The University of Chicago Press.
Labarthe, José Tomás/Rau, Cristián (eds.) (2019): *La viga maestra. Conversaciones con poetas chilenos 1973–1989*. Santiago de Chile: Ediciones Universidad Diego Portales.
López, Alfred J. (2007): "Introduction: The (Post) Global South". En: *The Global South*, 1, 1, pp. 1–11.
Muñoz, Rosabetty (2020a): *Misión circular. Antología*. Santiago de Chile: Lumen.
—— (2020b): *Santo oficio*. Santiago de Chile: Ediciones Universidad Diego Portales.
—— (2019): *Técnicas para cegar a los peces*. Valparaíso: Universidad de Valparaíso.
—— (2012): *Polvo de huesos. Antología*. Santiago de Chile: Edición Tácitas.
—— (2008): *En nombre de ninguna*. Valdivia: Ediciones Kultrún.
—— (1997): "Acallo la loba que contengo". En: *Uchile*, https://web.uchile.cl/publicaciones/cyber/15/vida1e.html (última visita: 20/8/2021).
Ñanculef Huaiquinao, Juan (2016): *Tayiñ mapuche kimün. Epistemología mapuche – Sabiduría y conocimientos*. Santiago de Chile: Universidad de Chile.
Ostrias González, Mauricio (2010): "Notas sobre ecocrítica y poesía chilena". En: *Atenea*, 502, pp. 181–191.
Pick, Anat (2011): *Creaturely Poetics. Animality and Vulnerability in Literature and Film*. Nueva York: Columbia University Press.
Prado Traverso, Marcela (2011): "Poesía, espacio/paisaje e identidades en las literaturas latinoamericanas". En: *Cuadernos del Pensamiento Latinoamericano*, 17, pp. 108–123.
Travis, Christopher M. (2018): "'Mi voz contra la tierra ahogada'. La consciencia ecopoética de Rosabetty Muñoz". En: *Anales de literatura chilena*, 19, 30, pp. 217–230.

3 Anthropocene Narratives II: Exhausted Resources

Nicolás Campisi
Documentary Mines
Archives of Ecohorror in the Anthropocene

In Valeria Luiselli's "Agua negra (Fragmento del ensayo sonoro *Echoes from the Borderlands*)", a chorus of women's voices traces parallels between the history of copper mining and the violence against the female body through the invention of the intrauterine contraceptive device, or IUD. The family of women is led by a mother who tells the story of her visit to a copper mine in Bisbee, Arizona, and her subsequent realization that the IUD that she harbors inside of her body has turned her into "una mina excavada, empinada, erosionada en espirales" (Luiselli 2020: 135). The mother is frequently interrupted by "Hermana 1", who puts together a genealogy of the IUD that reveals its entanglement with the enslavement of women, anti-Semitism, and the dispossession of communal territories, and "Sobrina 1" who declares that "La minería es una forma de acumulación, para algunos, y de despojo, para todos los demás" (Luiselli 2020: 131). Other voices include that of "Sobrina 2" who recalls US interventionism in the coup against Salvador Allende following the nationalization of Chile's copper mines, the voice of Northern Cheyenne activist Tia Oros Peters, and the collective voice of a "Coro" that denounces the actions of the "señores" who enlarge their bank accounts on the back of women's labor. The choral voices of Luiselli's "Agua negra" set up a space for reclaiming a body and a territory in which to exist, as well as the interdependence of one with the other at a time when nature and culture are being conjured as separate entities by large-scale extractive enterprises.

Moreover, the chorus of female voices in Luiselli's sound-essay establishes clear links between contemporary capitalism's conception of natural territories as bodies to be pillaged and human bodies as disposable commodities, reflecting the ecofeminist ways of organizing that are taking place in Latin America today. This positing of a collective female voice in the face of the erasure of bodies and ecosystems is representative of the way in which contemporary literature is responding to the disasters left behind by mining and hydroelectric enterprises across the Americas. We could call it a strategy of "undermining" as Lucy Lippard has theorized it – a "political act" of subversion that lays bare the scars on the earth and the body that are tied to extractive activities such as drilling or drainage of acidic water in coal, copper, and uranium mines (Lippard 2014: 2). It is a strategy of unlearning the institutional and imperial structures

---

Nicolás Campisi, Georgetown University

∂ Open Access. © 2023 the author(s), published by De Gruyter. [CC BY-NC-ND] This work is licensed under the Creative Commons Attribution-NonCommercial-NoDerivatives 4.0 International License.
https://doi.org/10.1515/9783110762143-009

that have led us to conceive of the land as a vault to be plundered and the body as a commodified property, and a call to protect the commons and forge new alliances with human and nonhuman beings alike. This subversion takes the form of artworks that do not easily fit the boundaries of traditional aesthetic categories such as the novel, the essay, or the book of photographs, leaving room for the reader or the spectator to ethically engage with scenes of a decaying planet. Moreover, critical engagement with archival documents such as maps, municipal reports, or newspaper clippings displays the violent formation of the imperial archive and serves as a basis for a new conception of history that does not rely on modern myths of progress, development, and the embrace of the new.

While connecting the long-lasting scars on the bodies of workers with the degradation of the environment and the appropriation of ancestral territories, some contemporary writers are making use of the archive to go back in time to specific moments of the original accumulation of capital to recover the voice of the voiceless and create entanglements between the human and the nonhuman, as well as between the living and the dead. Even though the literature of ecohorror traverses environmental issues such as pesticide poisoning, global pandemics, and animal rights in the slaughterhouse industry, I will focus on two contemporary works that depict the dismaying working conditions of miners and the toxic waste left behind by the mining industry's booms and busts. I am especially interested in contemporary works that incorporate archival materials to raise awareness about the relationship between extractive capitalism and the violent construction of institutional archives that excluded the knowledges and temporalities of those considered to be noncitizens by the nation-state. More specifically, I will examine two literary works that recover little-known mining disasters in 20th century Mexico. Yuri Herrera's nonfictional book *El incendio de la mina El Bordo*, or *Silent Fury* (2018) in Lisa Dillman's translation, reconstructs a forgotten mining tragedy that occurred in the Mexican state of Hidalgo in 1920 by piecing together the scarce sources that remain of the accident: newspaper articles, expert reports, and public monuments. Verónica Gerber Bicecci's *La Compañía* (2019) is a photo-novella that tells the story of the exploitation of the mercury mines of Nuevo Mercurio, Zacatecas, a place that has become a repository of nuclear and industrial waste. Both Gerber Bicecci and Herrera develop a new aesthetic category that I call ecohorror, which seeks to turn the negative affects and dystopian realities of the climate crisis into tools that lay bare the utopian fabric of collective human action.

The Buried Archive

Almost a hundred years after a mining tragedy in his native Pachuca killed at least eighty-seven workers, Yuri Herrera's *Silent Fury* brings this forgotten event back to public attention by examining the few traces that remain of it in municipal archives, public libraries, and urban memorials. By writing the book from the perspective of a citizen concerned with the violence that lies dormant in the archives, Herrera situates this mining tragedy within a genealogy of Mexico's necropolitical violence and shows that this event offers a window onto the practices that hegemonic institutions such as mining companies use to justify dispossession of land, enslavement, and murder. Herrera's account of the fire could be inscribed within the tradition of Latin American investigative journalism inaugurated by Rodolfo Walsh's 1957 *Operación masacre*, as it largely focuses on the seven survivors of the massacre who were still inside the mine when the company decided to seal its shafts. Unlike Walsh's foundational *crónica*, however, Herrera tackles the tragedy from the mediation of the archive, which contributed to the "persistent silence" (Herrera 2018: 12) or the "silent fury" that has rendered the event a virtual vacuum in Mexican history. The task of Herrera, then, is to disentangle the lives of these unknown workers and their families from the violence that has made them appear as property of the mining company and mere tools for the pursuit of profit. Hence the payment reports that Herrera copies verbatim in the body of the text, in which their last names, frequently misspelled, appear next to the amount that they were paid for their services.

In *Silent Fury*, Herrera does not speak for the archive but lets the archive speak for itself, reading between the lines to point its contradictions and undo its manipulations. The tone of the book subverts the supposed objectiveness of journalistic writing by questioning each of the sources: the coverage of the event by reporters from *El Universal* and *Excélsior*, statements by the company's bosses that portrayed miners as being "in a perfect state of health but starving to death" (Herrera 2018: 44), and court documents that speak for the families of the deceased because these could not read nor write. In line with contemporary historiographical efforts to narrate counter-histories of the present such as in the work of Saidiya Hartman, Herrera reckons with the stories of the missing and the forgotten by shifting attention to the ways archives are formed. Especially telling is the chapter that narrates how the expert report of the tragedy was assembled through a series of translations or mediations that transformed reality "into a neutral universal voice that fits the legal codes used in proceedings" (Herrera 2018: 61). Herrera sheds light on the creation of an innocuous archive that staged the theater of imperial violence and proposed the linear temporality of progress, represented by the American mining company, as the only possible option. Herrera is careful not to introduce photographs in the text, instead choosing to describe them with his own words. He is keenly aware of the way in which photographs have been manipulated by the authorities to convey a deceitful portrait of history, as in the picture of the funeral procession carrying the workers' bodies through the streets of Pachuca, at a period when there were hardly any cars in the city. In this way, Herrera reproduces the silence of the archive and makes the reader go on a search for the original sources. It is his way of pointing out the imbrication of photography with institutional and corporate structures of power, the way that the camera's shutter, as Ariella Azoulay reminds us, perpetuates the transformation of peoples and worlds into "raw material" and "imperial resources" (Azoulay 2019: 8).

In a chapter entitled "The Women's Fire", Herrera reveals the links between extractive capitalism and patriarchal social structures that have represented women in the archives "as incomplete, silent beings" whose testimony in the El Bordo case was transcribed and manipulated by male clerks (Herrera 2018: 50). Herrera inserts in this chapter the documents that the all-male representatives of the mining company crafted to exonerate themselves by taking advantage of the illiteracy of the miners' relatives, who were mostly women of indigenous descent. The book lays bare the predatory legal practices that forced women to provide all kinds of personal information about themselves, including proof of their status as "untainted women", in order to include them in the historical record. It is telling that the clerks, while asking women about their untainted status, were putting together the legal justification for the boundless pillage of nature, casting both women and nonhuman environments as beings without agency. In addition to being denied access to the historical archive, women were not allowed to enter the mines before or after the tragedy "out of a superstition: a woman in the mine was a terrible omen" (Herrera 2018: 49). In *Silent Fury*, Herrera weaves a parallel between the mine and the archive, two entities that have been controlled by male forces throughout history, in order to show that male reason has made nation building run parallel with the destruction of nature. By illuminating how men were associated with reason and indigenous women with illiteracy and tamed nature, Herrera reveals that the guardians of the archive have been the same male agents who excluded women from the formation of the modern nation-state.

Silent Fury assembles an archive of ecohorror by depicting the historical record as a common grave in which miners have been deprived of their humanity. Herrera dedicates an entire chapter to the description of the grave that the mining company dug to bury the bodies of the miners before they were even pulled out of the mines. The horror of this tragedy derives not only from the environmental devastation caused by the mine fire, but from the treatment of the miners' bodies before and after their deaths: "ex-humans" whose postmortem biographies could not be reconstructed because of the bodies' state of decimation (Herrera 2018: 84). By recognizing the impossibility of fully piecing together the lives of these miners, Herrera writes against the linear time of the nation-state, as an archeologist of the temporalities that interfere with the forward-motion of extractive capitalism. He performs this task by reading not what the case files say, but what they conceal, placing them within a juridical effort to control public life and discourse[1]. For instance, Herrera introduces the guidelines that the district judge handed over to the inspector to conduct the investigation, followed by the blank spots that, according to him, the inquiry left aside, such as inspecting the mine before cleaning it or closing the shafts after making sure that no miners were trapped inside. When Herrera ends the book by stating that "down below people were still, are still, alive" (Herrera 2018: 100), "down below" refers both to a spatial movement and a temporal one, both to the underworld of the mines and the injustices of the historical archive.

The hundred years that separate Herrera from the events of the El Bordo mine fire have seen the degradation of the environment, the intensification of underground and open-pit mining, the privatization of Indigenous lands, and the transformation of ancestral territories into abandoned and toxic remnants of modernity's fables of progress. A hundred years that Herrera refers to as "the many days that followed", in which a succession of mining tragedies, the demands for better working conditions, and the unionization of miners across the continent have not necessarily prevented the reduction of people into tools for extractive capitalism's empty promises. The fury in the book's title may be interpreted in a number of ways that confirm the tangled relationship between nature and culture and between nature and the archive. It may refer to the silent fury of a natural landscape that comes back to haunt the humans who intervened it, to the "slow violence" (as Rob Nixon has famously termed it) that has been brewing for centuries and is now impacting the most vulnerable communities of the developing world. But the title might also be pointing to the colonial formation of the archive as a regime of exclusion and exploitation of living beings, because as Silvia Rivera Cusicanqui reminds us via Walter Benjamin, "if the preservers of the archive succeed, the past cannot escape the fury of the enemy" (Rivera Cusicanqui 2020: 49). For Rivera Cusicanqui, "Words

---

[1] Mirta Alejandra Antonelli coins the expression "mineral modernity" to refer to the lobby of mega-mining enterprises that are exempted from the juridical framework of human rights through the silences and omissions of institutional and media discourses (Antonelli 2012: 67).

have a peculiar function in colonialism: they conceal rather than designate" (Rivera Cusicanqui 2020: 12). By responding to this colonial taxonomy through a documentary poetics, Herrera oftentimes resorts to speculation to underscore the void of the archive and the official strategies to bury evidence under countless expert reports, lists, and testimonials. Moreover, by inserting this tragedy in a timeline of dispossession of peoples and territories, Herrera delineates a cyclical version of history: capitalism erased this tragedy from the face of the earth – literally buried it alive, just as it buried the El Bordo miners before their actual deaths – by materializing in paper the colonial practices of expropriation, looting, and enslavement.

The classification of miners into hierarchical categories that are profitable for the colonial project illustrates the forms of violence characteristic of the imperial archive. Assigning differential roles to sectors of the population is an archival practice that dates back at least to the Spanish empire's exploitation of people and natural resources in the Potosí silver mines beginning in the sixteenth century. The Imperial Villa of Potosí serves as a dark precedent of mineworker abuse in the Americas through Viceroy Francisco de Toledo's *mita* draft. The *mita* was a system of labor that forced Andean villages to contribute 16 percent of their men, known as *mitayos*, to perform nonstop work in the Potosí mines, where they were grossly underpaid and were subjected to high mortality rates (Lane 2019: 72). According to Azoulay, the representation of people as "archival records" serves the purpose of subjecting them to the power of governing authorities, who act as the patrons of these "files" (Azoulay 2019 172). In *Silent Fury* Herrera includes the classification of workers by job and wage, from the deputy foreman down to the day laborers, that was commissioned by the inspector. The figure of the inspector, which evokes the administrative control performed by the *visitadores* during the Spanish conquest, lays bare the continuities between the governing body of the colonial and republican eras in their cataloguing and subjection of people through differential roles.

In contrast to this imperial system of classification, Herrera recounts the oral history of the tragedy through the people whose testimony was discredited for not fitting into the administrative channels of the modern nation. This is a historiographical method that counters the notion that the archive is a factual representation of the past. Herrera's account makes clear that there is also a people's history of the fire that stands against the institutional version. He lists the existence of a pamphlet written by a member of the community, Deputy Alberto Vargas, whose aim was to reproduce the peoples' conviction that the company was guilty. When he was called as a witness to the case, the deputy was unable to provide evidence as the administrators had already cleaned the scene of the crime. Herrera also mentions that there are still people in Pachuca who keep alive the memory of the tragedy despite the success of the state in burying the case in a "dead file" (Herrera 2018: 100). Among these people is his brother Tonatiuh, who first passed the story on to him. Herrera's challenge to the institutional version of the tragedy enacts his archival right to recover these voices out of the refuse of history and make them active participants in the construction of the commons.

In reading official discourse against the grain, Herrera's account of the El Bordo mine fire does not only encompass the files that distorted the events of the tragedy, but also the public monuments that were erected to exculpate its perpetrators. The book ends with the analysis of a plaque that is found in Pachuca's Parque Hidalgo, "A Gift from the American Community to the State Government", unveiled a few months after the fire. As a writer-historian who remains attentive to the omissions of the archive and the lives reduced to waste, Herrera interprets the subtext of the plaque to be the mutual exoneration of guilt by the American corporation and the state government. This is furthered by the material of the plaque – metal – that hides the stories of the miners as it does not mention the fact that it was extracted by the very victims of the fire. By writing this account of the fire at a time of social and environmental violence, Herrera proposes a new form of citizenship in which the human and the nonhuman become entangled, an entanglement that allows readers and spectators to reconsider the *res publica*, the modern project of the nation-state that has come under fire in the face of unprecedented damages to the geosphere.

The Ecological Houseguest

In addition to writing nonfictional accounts of the archive's destruction of shared worlds, Latin American writers are narrating alternative histories of the region's modernization through procedures of recycling, collage, and postproduction that have been characteristic of the visual arts during recent decades. According to Nicolas Bourriaud, the aesthetic procedure of postproduction has been used by contemporary artists to "descongestionar el mundo, usar lo que ya existe, rehabilitar el desecho o reciclar las sobras" (Bourriaud 2020: 77). By repurposing existing materials instead of producing new ones, contemporary artists are searching for new interlocutors in the realm of the nonhuman and thus opposing the cycle of infinite consumption promoted by neoliberal capitalism. This procedure of postproduction is at the heart of what Cristina Rivera Garza has termed *necrowriting* to refer to "writing practices that both bear witness to and resist the violence and death resulting from the neoliberal state that has embraced maximum profit as a guiding principle" (Rivera Garza 2020: 5). Rivera Garza introduces the concept of *disappropriation* to name these strategies that challenge traditional notions of authorship and property by cooperating with other people, both dead and alive, in the creative process. Moreover, she posits that these documentary practices that recover the voices of others as "material existences" play an important role in the redefinition of the communal and the questioning of the language of neoliberalism (Rivera Garza 2020: 6). In dialogue with Achille Mbembe's notion of necropolitics and Josefina Ludmer's concept of postautonomous literatures, Rivera Garza's theorization of documentary necrowriting is useful to redefine the place of literature at a time of unprecedented changes to the planet, especially in contexts of expropriation of territories, dispossession of Indigenous and Afro-Latino bodies, loss of biodiversity, and displacement of entire communities.

The works of Mexican writer Verónica Gerber Bicecci are an example of these communal and counter-hegemonic writing practices insofar as they ask us to unlearn the mechanisms of progressive history. Her book-objects rewrite literary tradition and national history through a communal practice that combines the voices of the living and the dead, of illustrious writers and minor historical figures, in order to derive forms of resistance at a time when literature and the arts have fallen prey to the interests of capital. The two books that Gerber Bicecci published in 2019 at the same publishing house – Mexican publisher Almadía – use this procedure to reflect on the scope of human agency in the Anthropocene and to show that the audience's active engagement might contribute to ecological awareness and political action. One of them, *otro día. . . (poemas sintéticos)*, is a rewriting of Juan José Tablada's book of haiku poetry, *Un día. . . poemas sintéticos*, a hundred years after its original publication, in which the representation of an idyllic natural landscape gives way to toxic settings that have been interposed by the technoscientific creed. The volume also reproduces contemporary anxieties over the end of nature. Gerber Bicecci's other book, *La Compañía*, mixes textual and visual techniques to undo dualist ontologies between nature and culture. The book's title plays with the double meaning of "company" as both the multinational firm that exploited Nuevo Mercurio's natural resources and left behind a post-natural landscape of devastation, and the collective forms of resistance that emerge out of the interdependence between human and nonhuman beings.

La Compañía is divided into two sections: part a. is a retelling of Amparo Dávila's short story "El huésped", or "The Houseguest", whereas part b. uses a collage of oral testimonies, science books, short stories, and visual diagrams to tell the story of the discovery, exploitation, and abandonment of a mining site in the state of Zacatecas. The first part of *La Compañía* uses procedures of sampling and postproduction to re-contextualize Dávila's short story in a subtext of ecological danger. In short, "El huésped" tells the story of an entity that we are unable to describe as either human or animal. It enters the home of a rural family after the husband brings it from a work trip, convinced that the "houseguest", as he calls it, is harmless. However, the wife-narrator and the domestic worker Guadalupe view it as a sinister presence that has come to interrupt the family's peaceful routine, especially after it attacks Guadalupe's son. Both the narrator and Guadalupe decide to seal the room until the houseguest dies, in a move that echoes the sealing of the El Bordo mine's shafts in Herrera's book.

Gerber Bicecci intervenes in Dávila's "El huésped" in at least three ways. First, she moves the original location of the story, which takes place in an unnamed "town that was almost dead, or about to disappear" (Dávila 2018: 14), to the mining town of Nuevo Mercurio, Zacatecas, which was insatiably exploited by American and Mexican mining companies beginning in the nineteen-thirties. Ever since the mining corporations halted their activities in the late nineteen-seventies, the town became a repository of industrial and nuclear waste and the companies walked away without enduring any legal sanctions. Further, Gerber Bicecci changes the verb tense of Dávila's short story from the past to the future, introducing a vertiginous temporality that recreates the feeling of imminent danger that is caused by the contemporary ecological crisis. In Gerber Bicecci's intervention, the character of "el huésped" becomes "la Compañía", with a capital C, whereas Guadalupe becomes "la máquina". The book reveals anxieties associated with the biotechnological intervention in our everyday lives by multinational corporations, as well as with the simultaneous commodification of nature and the human body. As the Company takes control of the family space, the photographs reveal a no man's land in which the only index of human presence are ruins and toxic waste – an example of what has come to be known as "waste capitalism", the practice of dumping toxic materials among the populations that are most vulnerable to epidemics and climate change. In fact, the room on the corner where the houseguest lives in Dávila's short story becomes the storage space for the barrels of polychlorinated biphenyl (PCB), a carcinogenic chemical produced by Monsanto. Finally, Gerber Bicecci transforms the third person narration of Dávila's short story into a second person voice that reconfigures the role of the readers-spectators in the search of the origins of the crisis.

The photographs that appear in the first part of the book come from archival sources or were taken by Gerber Bicecci herself. There are photographs of the dirt roads leading up to Nuevo Mercurio, the abandoned mining site, the warning signs that point to its health hazards, the collapsed buildings, and the barrels containing toxic chemicals. Some of the photographs are infiltrated by pictograms extracted from Manuel Felguérez's *La máquina estética*, a project that the Mexican artist undertook in the nineteen-seventies – the same decade of the abandonment of the Nuevo Mercurio mines – alongside systems engineer Mayer

Sasson. According to Felguérez, the goal of this project was to equip computers with an artificial sensibility that would result in the autonomous creation of works of art, an artistic technique that anticipated the contemporary field of machine learning (Felguérez/García 2019: 24). By constellating different temporal orders, the pictograms embedded in the photographs disrupt the linear conception of history, as they point towards Aztec codices as well as towards a posthuman future (or present) in which machines have a sensibility of their own. Moreover, the juxtaposition of pictograms in photographs that document the ruins of extractive projects reveals the links between the digital world and climate change, as can be perceived in the massive production of techno fossils: a new geological layer composed of plastics and other materials that are distributed on a global scale.

The fact that the photographs that Gerber Bicecci inserts are high-contrast proves that her intention is to conceal as much as it is to reveal. The photographs of the company's ruinous and toxic extraction site oscillate between what Déborah Danowski and Eduardo Viveiros de Castro call "'a world without us,' that is, the world after the existence of the human species; and an 'us without the world,' a worldless or environmentless humankind, the subsistence of some form of humanity or subjectivity after the end of the world" (Danowski/Viveiros de Castro 2016: 21). The book's photographs become representations, not so much of what we have in front of us, as of the ghostly presence of things and beings that are no longer here. The ruins of the company's buildings are populated by the ghosts of the former miners, who persist in the objects with which they interacted, such as a Coca Cola vending machine that has been left behind as another proof of capitalism's techno fossils. The photographs are sites of mourning for the irretrievable world of the missing. In presenting the landscape and the miners as representations of the living dead, as hieroglyphs whose lexicon we need to learn how to decipher, Gerber Bicecci is giving us a portrait of the present in its transition from the human to the post-human, from the natural to the post-natural[2].

The selection of Dávila's short story as the intertext may be explained by the contributions of the Gothic, and more specifically by the figure of the parasite, to the representation of human agency during the Anthropocene. Gerber Bicecci is not the first Mexican writer who returns to Dávila's story to trace the parallels between bodily and environmental degradation through the invasion

---

[2] Martín Arboleda charts the "Fourth Machine Age" in the mining industry through the implementation of new technologies such as AI, GIS, and robotics. These methods have expanded the extractive activities of corporations to include mineral deposits that were difficult to mine with older technologies (Arboleda 2020: 49).

of a parasite. The narrator of Guadalupe Nettel's *El huésped* (2006) is seized by an entity, The Thing, which removes her vision and takes control of her actions, and whose existence she links to Mexico City's polluted atmospheric conditions: "el *smog* o la lluvia ácida del verano en la ciudad de México" (Nettel 2006: 30). In these rewritings of Dávila's short story, the figure of the host designates the parasitic condition of human beings in the Anthropocene, given that, as Michel Serres points out, "a parasite – which is what we are now – condemns to death the one he pillages and inhabits, not realizing that in the long run he's condemning himself to death too" (Serres 1995: 38). By representing the company as a parasite, Gerber Bicecci traces a clear distinction between the responsible actors for the ecological crisis and the main victims of capitalist dispossession, which is also a criticism of the way a term such as Anthropocene groups together all sectors of the human population as if they were equally responsible for the crisis. Gerber Bicecci's rewriting sides with the struggles of Indigenous and ecofeminist activists across Latin America who denounce the various forms of appropriation of nature by governments that, instead of protecting it in the wake of extractive encroachment, reduce it to a mere economic resource.

Gerber Bicecci's adoption of this type of communal writing is useful to think about contemporary forms of resistance to the commodification of nature, a being-with-others that is based on the borrowing of the words of fellow citizens, the same way that Indigenous notions such as *buen vivir* prioritize the welfare of the community and the ecological wellbeing over the exaltation of the self that is characteristic of the neoliberal frame of mind. Moreover, her documentary fiction puts forward a symbiotic relationship between bodies and territories, or what Verónica Gago has called "cuerpos-territorios", the way that ravishing communal territories means to plunder the body of each member of the community (Gago 2019: 90). In tune with the work of feminist theorists such as Verónica Gago and Rita Segato, Gerber Bicecci develops a writing practice that traces the continuities between the individual and the collective body, and that thinks about nature and culture not as private property, but as a communal corpus that can be reused and reappropriated (Gago 2019: 91–92). This writing strategy echoes the idea that the commons is a body-territory that is exploited by the extractive machine and that can be countered by recognizing the interconnection between all human and nonhuman beings.

In rescuing the voices of people who have been swallowed by the capitalist work of destruction and who have not participated in the formation of the sovereign archive, *La Compañía* assembles new forms of citizenship that do not entail belonging to the same nation-state. Gerber Bicecci's *La Compañía* proposes a counter-hegemonic archive of the present in which to be with others, both living and dead, human and nonhuman, becomes a way to resist the separation of past from present and the current state of dispossession of lands and necropolitical violence. At a time when the narratives of modern citizenship are based upon the destruction of shared worlds and the exclusion of entire populations, Rivera Garza points out that literature may derive its role of resistance out of a poetics of "mutual care and the protection of the common good" (Rivera Garza 2020: 5). Instead of appropriating the experience of others just as extractive capitalism expropriates communal lands, these strategies of necrowriting gather a chorus of voices that disrupt the supposed neutrality of the archive that both nation-states and private industries endorse. Rivera Garza derives her notion of communal property and authorship out of the writings of *mixe* theorist Floriberto Díaz, who defines communality through a series of principles that oppose the "aislamiento egocéntrico" (Díaz 2018: 38) of the citizens of the West. These tenets include consensus decision-making, the rights of mother nature, collective work, and Indigenous ceremonies as expressions of the "don comunal" (Díaz 2018: 40).

Gerber Bicecci appropriates this concept of collective social organization, which Díaz refers to as *tequio*, by conjuring the voices of scientists who have documented the disposal of nuclear waste in the company's mining site and journalists who researched the toxic effects of mercury among Nuevo Mercurio's residents. It also includes excerpts of official documents such as the letter of a state representative who asked the Mexican government to export the barrels of toxic chemicals to countries that have the proper infrastructure to dispose of them. Nowadays, these voices embody the ecofeminist assemblies that are denouncing the patriarchal conception of nature and culture across the continent. Gerber Bicecci does not represent the exploitation of the Nuevo Mercurio mines as an isolated event but as one among the many abuses of bodies-territories in the Americas, as when she cites a critical history of neo-extractivism that dates it back to the conquest and colonization of the continent. Just as feminist theorists like Gago conceive of the human body as an entity that is always already crisscrossed by a series of affects and possibilities that transcend the individual, Gerber Bicecci thinks of the literary text as a corpus of subjectivities in dispute that embody the mechanism of the assembly, insofar as it is through the collective intelligence of the assembly that voices and bodies become one and the same and are therefore able to invent new horizons of time.

As a representative of the documentary writing tradition, *La Compañía* belongs alongside works that posit an alternative history of modern development by registering the devastating effects of extractive enterprises and the anonymous existence of its labor force. Two of the works that Rivera Garza mentions in *The Restless Dead* as examples of documentary necrowriting are Muriel Rukeyser's *The Book of the Dead* (1938) and Mark Nowak's *Coal Mountain Elementary* (2009), which record the sacrifice of miners who worked in extremely precarious circumstances in the name of capitalism's modernizing promises. Rukeyser writes about the Hawks Nest industrial disaster in 1930s West Virginia, where more than 500 miners died of silicosis, a type of lung disease, while building a tunnel. On the other hand, Nowak puts together a kaleidoscope of testimonials, photographs, newspaper clippings, and school syllabi by the American Coal Foundation in order to connect a series of mining disasters that took place across the world. Through aesthetic procedures that precede and foreshadow the ones employed by Gerber Bicecci, these authors show that our understanding of history is mediated by a cluster of discourses that hegemonic institutions impose to hide the pile of debris that they produced while invoking humanity's progress. By standing against a linear conception of history, *La Compañía* creates a communal archive that records the voices of those who seek to preserve a shared world when private and state-sponsored enterprises oppose the positing of alternative models.

While the notion of communality promotes new ways of conceiving the nature-culture divide, *La Compañía* seeks to decenter our field of vision by focusing on the material traces that humans are leaving behind. The nature without humans that Gerber Bicecci depicts in *La Compañía* shows that in the Anthropocene, what we formerly perceived as inanimate matter has come to rule our world. In times of generalized crises and possible civilizational collapses, Gerber Bicecci shows that literature can generate relational practices that echo these communal ways of organizing. Maristella Svampa argues that the defense of the commons is at the heart of "la búsqueda de un nuevo paradigma emancipatorio" that protects people from the neoliberal policies of austerity and privatization, among the many other forms that neoliberalism takes up across Latin America (Svampa 2019: 29). Communality favors those visions that stand against Western dichotomies between nature and culture and rescues Indigenous cosmologies that think about the continuities between human and nonhuman beings. The multiple voices that make up the communal tissue of *La Compañía* show that a remote place such as Nuevo Mercurio, Zacatecas deserves a prominent spot in the history of modern extractivism, alongside several other far-flung places where institutions and multinational companies set up their operations to exonerate themselves from the crimes that they commit.

The book illuminates the close relationship between capitalism's machine of war and environmental destruction through Nuevo Mercurio's role during the Second World War, when it provided the United States with mercury for ammunition and explosives. Given that some of this mercury ended up polluting terrestrial and marine environments, *La Compañía* tells a history of the "Great Acceleration" that took place after the war by putting a chemical element (mercury) at center stage. Gerber Bicecci thus reframes the temporal and spatial scales of the novel, a genre that evolved alongside capitalist modernity and reduced its scope to the dramas of the human. In *La Compañía*, by contrast, the human body is depicted only in relation to the substances and affects that cross through it, just as contemporary works of art in which the human figure appears, according to Bourriaud, "disuelta en una *solución* (en el sentido químico)" (Bourriaud 2020: 222). When the inhabitants and former miners of Nuevo Mercurio appear in *La Compañía*, it is only to relate the psychosomatic effects that they suffer nowadays, such as silicosis, anthracosis ("[la] inflamación crónica de los bronquios y pulmones"), cancer, miscarriages, and hallucinations, given that some of the intoxicated workers started to see elves coming out of the mines (Gerber Bicecci 2019: 121). The establishment of a new Nuevo Mercurio four kilometers away from the original site serves only to mitigate but not to entirely erase the series of toxic poisonings, as some inhabitants still live among the ruins of the old town.

La Compañía unfolds in the discontinuous temporality of the allegorist who, in the wake of the expropriation of communal lands and the dispossession of bodies, conceives of new ways to unwind linear history and compile an archive of voices that are not assimilable to the narrative of modern progress. Through a fragmented textual corpus, Gerber Bicecci assembles a collective "allegory of the Anthropocene", as Elizabeth DeLoughrey designates the use of montage to engage the reading public as co-participants in the creative process, "calling out attention to our responsibility as witnesses to states of waste in the age of the Great Acceleration" (DeLoughrey 2019: 101). The metaphor of writing as a form of recycling is useful to think about the recovery of those lives that leave scattered traces among landscapes of ecological devastation, the "wasted lives" – as Zygmunt Bauman has referred to them – of refugees, stateless people, or the miners who suffer in their own skin the environmental impact of extractive activities. In addition to using the procedures of interviewing and transcription that an author such as Svetlana Alexievich employed to register the consequences of the Chernobyl nuclear disaster, Gerber Bicecci rescues the voices of unknown regional writers who have been omitted from the construction of the literary cannon, as well as scientific studies that provide empirical evidence to corroborate the word of the victims. In this way, Gerber Bicecci compiles a counter-hegemonic archive in which the act of being together with these forgotten figures, who suddenly disrupt the complacent picture of the present put forward by extractive corporations and provides strategies to resist the dispossession of bodies-territories in the Americas.

The relational poetics of *La Compañía* seeks to decenter the role of human beings in the conception of history, showing that the end of humanity is not equivalent to the end of the world as we know it. Gerber Bicecci's book tells the story of a remote population that, after a century of insatiable extractive activities, has been left without a world to inhabit, outside of the networks of institutional protection and lacking true consciousness about its involvement in processes of environmental destruction. The collaboration of multiple voices in the construction of the book reveals that the idea of companionship – the ethics of caring for others and defending the common good – is at the center of the search for sustainable alternatives to the current models of industrial development. The book ends with the image of a population that resists extractive encroachment through the establishment of an industry of ecotourism based on the guano produced by the bats that live inside of the abandoned mines. This project of eco-touristic development that the inhabitants of Nuevo Mercurio set up by taking advantage of the role of the bats in the "control biológico de plagas" (Gerber Bicecci 2019: 182) is key for the elaboration of means of life and use value amidst sites of devastation, embodying the kind of local knowledge that plays a fundamental role in ideas such as post-development and post-extractivism. By revealing the existence of other worlds within this one, *La Compañía* calls for the creation of strategies of co-citizenship and alternative ways of inhabiting the planet that are within our reach.

Conclusions

By rescuing unknown mining tragedies in modern Mexican history, Herrera and Gerber Bicecci reflect on the constitution of the archive as a technology that normalizes its methods of selection and erasure. They remind us that extractive corporations may reduce environmental tragedies to oblivion through the construction of the archive as a neutral entity and the imposition of colonial timelines. Whereas the colonial project depended on the subjugation of human and nonhuman others, these writers show us that in the Anthropocene archives are not centralized institutions but include the temporality of nonhuman actors such as metals and chemical substances. The Anthropocene has come to prove that the "New World" that colonial enterprises treated as *terra nullius*, and therefore as a resource to be pillaged, has led to a new world in which nature has turned against us and is outside of our control. In linking the guardians of the archive with the people who ordered the closing of the mine shafts, Herrera demonstrates that archival writing in the Anthropocene consists in undermining the mechanisms through which institutions construct hygienic versions of history to continually justify the extractive paradigm. Gerber Bicecci, on the other hand, undermines the genre of the novel by creating a hybrid image-text format that incorporates the agency of nonhuman beings whose temporality exceeds the history of capital and the modern nation-state. Both writers undo the linear timeline of progress through the recovery of voices that were rendered obsolete by the nation-state's consignment of subaltern roles. Where extractive capitalism creates graveyards of communal territories, contemporary writers such as Herrera and Gerber Bicecci conjure archives of natural destruction to display records of survival and collective resilience.

Works Cited

Antonelli, Mirta Alejandra (2012): "Mega-minería transnacional y espectros de lo justo. Tiempos de impunidad y territorios de inmunidad". In: Massuh, Gabriela (ed.): *Renunciar al bien común: Extractivismo y (pos)desarrollo en América Latina*. Buenos Aires: Mardulce, pp. 59–84.
Arboleda, Martín (2020): *Planetary Mine: Territories of Extraction under Late Capitalism*. London: Verso.
Azoulay, Ariella (2019): *Potential History: Unlearning Imperialism*. London: Verso.
Bourriaud, Nicolas (2020): *Inclusiones: estética del capitaloceno*. Transl. Eduardo Berti. Buenos Aires: Adriana Hidalgo.
Danowski, Déborah/Viveiros de Castro, Eduardo (2016): *The Ends of the World*. Transl. Rodrigo Nunes. Cambridge: Polity Press.
Dávila, Amparo (2018): "The Houseguest". In: *The Houseguest and Other Stories*. Transl. Audrey Harris and Matthew Gleeson. New York: New Directions, pp. 14–19.
DeLoughrey, Elizabeth (2019): *Allegories of the Anthropocene*. Durham: Duke University Press.
Díaz, Floriberto (2018): *Escrito: Comunalidad, energía viva del pensamiento mixe*. Mexico City: Universidad Nacional Autónoma de México.
Felguérez, Manuel/García, Pilar (2019): "La pulsión de crear: una conversación". In: *Manuel Felguérez: Trayectorias/Trajectories*. Mexico City: MUAC (Museo Universitario Arte Contemporáneo), pp. 10–35.
Gago, Verónica (2019): *La potencia feminista: o el deseo de cambiarlo todo*. Buenos Aires: Tinta Limón.
Gerber Bicecci, Verónica (2019): *La Compañía*. Mexico City: Almadía.
Herrera, Yuri (2018): *A Silent Fury*. Transl. Lisa Dillman. Cáceres: Periférica.
Lane, Kris (2019): *Potosí: The Silver City That Changed the World*. Oakland: University of California Press.
Lippard, Lucy R. (2014): *Undermining: A Wild Ride Through Land Use, Politics, and Art in the Changing West*. New York: The New Press.
Luiselli, Valeria (2020): "Agua negra (Fragmento del ensayo sonoro *Echoes from the Borderlands*)". Transl. Marta López. In: Jáuregui, Gabriela (ed.): *Tsunami 2*. Mexico City: Sexto Piso, pp. 125–144.
Nettel, Guadalupe (2006): *El huésped*. Barcelona: Anagrama.
Rivera Cusicanqui, Silvia (2020): *Ch'ixinakak utxiwa. On Practices and Discourses of Decolonization*. Transl. Molly Geidel. Cambridge: Polity Press.

Rivera Garza, Cristina (2020): *The Restless Dead: Necrowriting and Disappropriation*. Transl. Robin Myers. Nashville: Vanderbilt University Press.

Serres, Michel (1995): *The Natural Contract*. Transl. Elizabeth MacArthur and William Paulson. Ann Arbor: University of Michigan Press.

Svampa, Maristella (2019): "Antropoceno, perspectivas críticas y alternativas desde el Sur global". In: Speranza, Graciela (ed.): *Futuro presente: perspectivas desde el arte y la política sobre la crisis ecológica y el mundo digital*. Buenos Aires: Siglo Veintiuno, pp. 19–36.

Azucena Castro and Luis I. Prádanos
Retos estéticos del postdesarrollo
imaginarios no extractivos y futuros postfósiles en medios culturales andinos

La teoría del postdesarrollo en Latinoamérica está cada vez más presente en la crítica cultural decolonial que entiende las dinámicas desarrollistas como articulaciones discursivas neocoloniales con consecuencias socioecológicas nefastas, como neoextractivismo, descampesinización, acumulación por desposesión, agro-toxicidad, desigualdad. Este ensayo explora manifestaciones culturales recientes en la región andina que no solo aportan una resistencia reactiva a dichos discursos y prácticas tóxicas, sino que tejen lo que podríamos llamar *subjetividades postdesarrollistas* en tanto que sugieren imaginarios alternativos al de la globalización económica. En "la disputa por el desarrollo" en América Latina, la zona andina —altamente afectada por las actividades extractivas— ha articulado desde comienzos de este siglo un frente de resistencia indígena y campesina por los derechos culturales, ecológicos y territoriales de las comunidades locales (Svampa 2008: 11–12). Este frente se manifiesta en movimientos y organizaciones sociales, pero también en medios culturales y estéticos, de los que nos ocuparemos en este trabajo. Los retos de estas manifestaciones culturales radican en generar estéticas postdesarrollistas, lo que Prádanos (2018) denomina "imaginarios postcrecimiento" (*postgrowth imaginaries*), en tanto que constituyen epistemes pluriversales que estimulan o articulan deseos, identidades y procesos de subjetivación, politización y sensibilización decoloniales radicalmente diferentes a los imaginarios desarrollistas provenientes de la petrocultura consumista.

En este capítulo reflexionamos sobre las siguientes preguntas: ¿Cuáles son las circunstancias que motivan la proliferación de manifestaciones culturales andinas alineadas con la lógica del postdesarrollo? ¿Cuáles son los retos estéticos, no ya solo políticos, a los que se enfrentan estas manifestaciones culturales para hacer atractiva, deseable, expresable e imaginable la transición del imaginario dominante a otros imaginarios postextractivistas, pluriversales, decoloniales, emancipadores y regeneradores? ¿Existen diferencias temáticas y formales significativas entre las estéticas postdesarrollistas y las estéticas fósiles en el contexto andino? Para discutir estas preguntas, nos enfocamos en expresiones culturales

Azucena Castro, Stockholm University, University of Buenos Aires
Luis I. Prádanos, Miami University

Open Access. © 2023 the author(s), published by De Gruyter. This work is licensed under the Creative Commons Attribution-NonCommercial-NoDerivatives 4.0 International License.
https://doi.org/10.1515/9783110762143-010

multimodales —performance, ecopoesía, instalaciones, cine, literatura— que no solo elaboran una crítica al desarrollo y extractivismo, sino que imaginan formas alternativas de organización ecosocial que difieren radicalmente de los modelos impuestos por la Modernidad occidental hegemónica y el capitalismo verde contemporáneo.

Desarrollo como extractivismo

Maristella Svampa (2019) identifica tres momentos fundamentales en el pensamiento latinoamericano crítico con la monológica del desarrollismo económico: "the critique of consumer society (1970s–1980s); the post-development critique (1990s–2000s); and critical perspectives on extractivism (early 2000s–present)" (18). El discurso del desarrollo —que en teoría asume que toda la humanidad debe seguir una temporalidad lineal y jerárquica hasta que todas las regiones del planeta se desarrollen imitando a los países 'desarrollados' del norte global— supone una imposibilidad biofísica: si todas las regiones del planeta se 'desarrollaran' en base a la industrialización de la naturaleza harían falta los recursos de más de cuatro planetas Tierra. La realidad es que la globalización económica no solo no puede cumplir sus promesas de universalizar el modo de vida de las sociedades opulentas, sino que lo que realmente consigue con su expansión es colapsar los sistemas vivos planetarios e intensificar procesos extractivos de acumulación por desposesión. La globalización económica ha intensificado un extractivismo (neo)colonial que compromete la viabilidad y supervivencia de cada vez más cuerpos y comunidades. Si bien los discursos sobre los límites biofísicos del crecimiento económico global irrumpen de manera significativa en los años 70, es a partir de los 90 cuando las teorías latinoamericanas del postdesarrollo dejan claro que el modelo de crecimiento económico constante que se está imponiendo como modelo global no solo es ecológicamente inviable (es una ideología de muerte que destruye el tejido de la vida), sino que tampoco es deseable socialmente, pues se trata de un modelo etnocéntrico, antropocéntrico, neocolonial, violento, racista y patriarcal que manufactura escasez, exacerba la desigualdad y fomenta una geopolítica imperialista. En este contexto, Arturo Escobar, Gustavo Esteva o Alberto Acosta son algunas de las voces más representativas del postdesarrollo latinoamericano. Estas voces ponen de manifiesto que el modelo hegemónico de desarrollo equiparado con crecimiento económico no solo no puede cumplir sus promesas de prosperidad generalizada, sino que, cuanto más se expande, más rápido provoca extinción, escasez y desigualdad. Los problemas sociales y ecológicos actuales no solo no se pueden resolver desde la lógica hegemónica del crecimiento económico, sino que cuanto más se expande más intratable se vuelve la crisis ecosocial. Por ello, es crucial desplazar el imaginario hegemónico responsable de la aniquilación de la vida y generar imaginarios afines al postdesarrollo que no solo resistan la seducción de la cultura económica dominante, sino que hagan deseables otros caminos posibles que sean socioecológicamente regenerativos (Kothari et al. 2019). Las expresiones culturales críticas hacia la lógica del desarrollo juegan un papel fundamental en esta transición de imaginarios sociales, pero no son pocos los retos estéticos y políticos que tienen que sortear para poder articular imaginarios decididamente contrahegemónicos que nos impulsen a buscar caminos transformadores.

Las humanidades energéticas (*energy humanities*) han dejado claro que existe una relación intrínseca entre modernidad tecno-industrial, insostenibilidad y consumo energético creciente (Szeman/Boyer 2017). A su vez, la ecología política y la ecología social reconocen que la crisis ecológica hunde sus raíces en relaciones de poder injustas, asimétricas y explotadoras. Se trata de dinámicas neocoloniales interconectadas que se apoyan necesariamente en estructuras de desigualdad y extractivismo. De hecho, no es de extrañar que estemos presenciando una intensificación dramática del extractivismo justo en el momento en el que la urgente situación ecosocial a escala global —pico del petróleo y de muchos minerales, cambio climático desbocado, aniquilación biológica, pérdida de soberanía alimentaria por descampesinización y agro-corporativismo— requeriría una transformación y un decrecimiento progresivo y controlado del metabolismo material y energético de la economía a escala planetaria. Lejos de fomentar esa transición decrecentista necesaria, lo que la globalización económica incentiva es una intensificación y aceleración del extractivismo global sin precedentes, incluso cuando se hace con la excusa de luchar contra el cambio climático. Latinoamérica es un punto neurálgico de este extractivismo extremo global y la zona andina en particular constituye uno de sus nodos centrales. Atendiendo a la historia medioambiental latinoamericana, se observa una continuidad del extractivismo (neo)colonial andino que une la primera extracción de plata a gran escala en el cerro de Potosí en el 1600 con la creciente extracción contemporánea de litio en los salares andinos. Por ello, las manifestaciones culturales postdesarrollistas más relevantes hoy surgen de la resistencia a dicha intensificación del metabolismo extractivo desde una crítica ecofeminista y decolonial que muchas veces surge en el seno de las luchas de comunidades campesinas e indígenas. En cierto sentido, estas resistencias al extractivismo desde el feminismo decolonial suponen un correctivo al feminismo liberal eurocéntrico que no reconoce límites al crecimiento capitalista y, por ende, se apoya en el extractivismo, la exclusión y la explotación neocolonial de cuerpos-territorios menos privilegiados (cadena de cuidados globales). La mayoría de las políticas desarrollistas en Latinoamérica se materializan en dinámicas de extractivismo extremo y descampesinización forzada con consecuencias ecológicas y sociales nefastas. Desde la perspectiva del ecofeminismo decolonial antiextractivista resulta obvio que regenerar, descolonizar y despatriarcalizar van de la mano y son condiciones necesarias para superar la lógica extractivista, desarrollista y economicista responsable de la crisis ecológica y la desigualdad social.

Para entender las respuestas culturales postdesarrollistas a la intensificación extractivista es importante comprender los cambios organizacionales, logísticos y tecnológicos que ha experimentado la industria extractiva en los últimos años, así como recordar algunas aportaciones teóricas claves que ayudan a exponer la lógica tóxica (patriarcal, racista, colonial) que ha hecho posible la aceleración e institucionalización de procesos socialmente corrosivos y ecológicamente devastadores. La lógica dominante fomenta el desarrollo y el crecimiento a cualquier precio, ya que equipara progreso con un desarrollo económico basado en la extracción que va inextricablemente asociado a un ataque directo sobre las bases materiales y culturales sobre las que se apoya la vida de las comunidades humanas y no humanas.

John Locke justificaba la desposesión de los nativos americanos de sus tierras ancestrales porque suponía que los colonizadores europeos 'mejoraban' la tierra mediante la agricultura intensiva (Dawson 2020: 129). Basándose en las investigaciones de Kathryn Milun, Ashley Dawson explica cómo muchas categorías legales occidentales (ahora internacionalizadas) continúan perpetuando estos discursos legales coloniales para facilitar la acumulación por desposesión en relación con los espacios comunes: "the international law of the global commons works as a kind of technology of accumulation by dispossession" (156). Hoy día se continúa justificando la desposesión de comunidades indígenas y campesinas en nombre del desarrollo en forma de extractivismo. Lo cierto es que ni la agricultura intensiva colonial (mucho menos la tóxica agroindustria corporativa actual que es una de las mayores responsables de la pérdida de biodiversidad), ni la actividad extractiva mejoran la tierra, sino que, al contrario, destruyen el suelo y el tejido de la vida a un ritmo sin precedentes. Esta lógica de desposesión y destrucción (neo)colonial se articula hoy de manera perversa ya que el 'capitalismo verde' utiliza la crisis climática y la transición energética como excusa para continuar —e incluso intensificar— procesos de desposesión y extracción. La ecología política ha demostrado los efectos devastadores del *green grabbing*, una nueva forma de extractivismo que continúa desplazando comunidades indígenas de sus tierras en varios lugares de Latinoamérica. En esas tierras, se desarrollan megaproyectos corporativos relacionados con energías 'renovables' y con conservación de la biodiversidad con la excusa de la mitigación climática, como los enormes parques de energía eólica en México (Dawson 2020: 159–160). Estos macroproyectos no solo no suelen beneficiar a las comunidades locales —de hecho, muchas veces las desplaza— sino que además generan una demanda creciente de minerales para la infraestructura 'verde' impulsada por las transiciones energéticas de otras regiones hacia energías renovables. Las consecuencias son intensificar todavía más las dinámicas extractivas a costa de la salud de ecosistemas y comunidades, como es el caso de la extracción masiva de litio, 'el oro del siglo XXI', en Bolivia y otras áreas de la zona andina.

En *Planetary Mine*, Martín Arboleda (2020) deja claro que en los últimos años ha habido un cambio cualitativo en la modernización tecnológica y organizacional de la industria extractiva. Los avances en robótica e inteligencia artificial han permitido una escala de intensificación en los procesos extractivos sin precedentes y con unas huellas ecológicas monstruosas (11–13). En dicha reorganización e intensificación extractiva planetaria, el Pacífico se ha posicionado como el epicentro del comercio global de materias primas y Latinoamérica ha adquirido un papel central como exportador (31): "The balance of trade between China and Latin America has expanded dramatically in recent years, going from $15 billion in 2009 to a staggering $200 billion in 2011" (Arboleda 2020: 14). Este neodesarrollismo extractivo intensificado, además de tener consecuencias ecológicas devastadoras y dejar legados tóxicos intratables, provoca una descampesinización sin precedentes en la historia humana que desplaza y transforma a las poblaciones campesinas en mano de obra migrante y precaria (Arboleda 2020: 21; 37; 207).

Si la narrativa del Antropoceno, la era que evidencia el impacto sin precedentes de la actividad humana sobre los sistemas geológicos y climáticos, supone un intento desesperado de mantener un diseño globalizador ante el desbaratamiento de los discursos optimistas sobre globalización económica, una estética postdesarrollista debe, por definición, escapar de estas tentaciones globalizantes, neocoloniales y ecomodernistas para vislumbrar imaginarios pluriversales. Según Kathryn Yusoff (2019), si el Antropoceno apunta al fin del mundo, "imperialism and ongoing (settler) colonialisms have been ending worlds for as long as they have been in existence" (xiii). Mientras que la abstracción globalizante del discurso del Antropoceno soslaya cuestiones de raza y colonialidad (Yusoff 2019: 18), la estética del postdesarrollo insiste en visibilizarlas. En este estudio nos inspiramos en la propuesta de Yusoff de alterar las maneras de pensar e imaginar las relaciones geológicas en modos no extractivos que permitan la expresión de percepciones situadas —postglobales— de la experiencia. Como propone Yusoff (2019: 66), la organización y comprensión de la materia es crucial para visibilizar los imaginarios de desposesión y racialización que fomenta el sistema capitalista. En lo que sigue, por tanto, nos enfocamos en cómo la organización y la comprensión del mundo material en una serie de medios culturales andinos configuran modos no extractivos y epistemes postfósiles que articulan imaginarios postdesarrollo, necesarios frente a la emergencia planetaria contemporánea.

Estéticas del postdesarrollo y resistencia al extractivismo

En las siguientes páginas identificamos cuatro rasgos frecuentes —sin pretensión de exhaustividad— que se encuentran en muchas manifestaciones culturales andinas con sensibilidades postdesarrollistas. Este tipo de expresiones culturales confrontan el imaginario extractivista y desarrollista dominante mediante la incorporación simbólica, performativa y temática de varios aspectos que acercan las expresiones culturales a estratos del suelo y capas de la atmósfera y, con ello, proponen maneras alternativas de relacionarnos y reconectarnos con la biósfera. A continuación, discutimos una serie de obras de la región andina que ejemplifican los cuatro aspectos que consideramos característicos de la estética postdesarrollista que venimos delineando: estética vegetal, cuerpo-territorio, temporalidades pluriversales, diversificación agencial.

Biomímesis y estética vegetal. Bajo este aspecto, consideramos un conjunto de obras que se inspiran en la manera en que se relacionan las plantas con la comunidad biótica. De esta manera, la obra de arte puede entenderse como un diseño vegetal donde se incluyen material y simbólicamente elementos relacionados con raíces, rizomas, tejidos orgánicos, semillas, entre otros. También se concibe la obra —igual que la vida— como el resultado de una colaboración entre especies. Por último, se apela a la necesidad de una soberanía alimentaria y una relación comunitaria y regenerativa con la producción de comida. Esta estética se comunica, por tanto, con la agroecología como estrategia de dignidad y autonomía comunal revalorizando la vía campesina. Si el extractivismo supone una descampesinización forzada, la estética postdesarrollo celebra la recampesinización (regenerativa, decolonial y no patriarcal) como estrategia para sanar el suelo y la comunidad.

Al conectar biósfera y palabra, la poesía y el arte visual andino proponen reconexiones entre humano y nohumano, ciencia y arte. En este eje, la obra de Cecilia Vicuña —artista chilena que involucra saberes indígenas de las Américas y, entre ellos, de la zona andina— desarrolla un activismo por la semilla en contra del monocultivo, la apropiación y el patentamiento de semillas. Queremos destacar, en particular, la obra poético-visual *Semi Ya* (2000) de Vicuña, una instalación montada en la galería Gabriela Mistral de Santiago que expone objetos 'precarios' formados por semillas, fibras, maderas, huesos y hojas junto con poesía. Estos ensamblajes entre poesía y objetos articulan un "semillar" del lenguaje mezclando palabras, botánica, ecología y literatura, como manera de alterar el pensamiento y descolonizar las maneras utilitaristas de percibir el medioambiente[1]:

Fig. 1: Catálogo de la muestra *Semi Ya* de Cecilia Vicuña en la Galería Gabriela Mistral.

Como vemos en los versos e imágenes, la instalación conecta el potencial generativo del lenguaje con la potencia regeneradora de vida de las semillas y produce un entrelazamiento de las categorías, las especies y las culturas, apelando a un 'gesto comunitario' contra la destrucción del medioambiente. Esta obra configura así una botánica disidente que relacionamos al postdesarrollo, pues genera un bioarchivo poético para el presente y futuro donde predominan entendimientos del medioambiente ancestrales y locales que enfatizan la germinación, a diferencia del discurso científico occidental que enfatiza la catalogación y clasificación. Asimismo, esta estética propone una "justicia multiespecie" (Heise 2016: 167), pues considera el bienestar y la conservación tanto humana como no humana, no solo desde un punto de vista biológico sino también cultural, ya que la semilla es tanto fuente de vida de la planta como de las culturas ancestrales que las custodian. Proyectos como el de Vicuña no pretenden representar las semillas, sino incluir su diversidad y capacidad regeneradora de vida en nuestros imaginarios

---

[1] Las imágenes que contiene este capítulo (Figs. 1–5) están reproducidas en blanco y negro debido a normas editoriales, pero las imágenes originales son a color. Ver la bibliografía para acceder a las fuentes en color original.

culturales, para pensar *con* las semillas e imaginar otras maneras de relacionarnos con la comunidad biótica. En este sentido, la obra de Vicuña pone de manifiesto lo que Marder (2013: 12–13) propone como la herencia vegetal del pensamiento humano que lo retrotrae hacia raíces, tubérculos y semillas acercándonos a un sentir vegetal y botánico. La transformación en verbo de la semilla, "semillar", en el ecoarte visual de Vicuña propone un activismo postdesarrollista contra la siembra transgénica caracterizada por el crecimiento acelerado, la exclusividad de un tipo de semilla y la estética de muerte puesto que necesita de pesticidas que eliminen todo lo que crece alrededor para que la planta transgénica subsista: "La semilla genéticamente alterada rompe el ritmo de una música terrenal / Violencia que la tierra devuelve en tempestad" (Vicuña 2000: 19). Esta práctica poético-visual elabora así una poética de regeneración y reconexión local con la tierra que es radicalmente opuesta al panorama del avance acelerado de monocultivos transgénicos y privatización de las semillas que se viene intensificando desde 2005 en Latinoamérica.

En la relación entre poesía y medioambiente en el contexto andino, la ecopoesía del poeta peruano Samuel Cárdich en *Heredar la tierra* (2018) nos confronta con la idea de *legado* de la tierra obligándonos a mirar más allá del individuo, la propiedad privada y el presente. El poemario entreteje animales y vegetales locales con animales lejanos en peligro de extinción como el panda, o animales extintos como el pájaro dodo y, con ello, propone un pensamiento local y planetario. Esta ecopoesía subvierte el tono elegíaco que mira hacia atrás añorando una naturaleza pasada, para ejercer un urgente llamado lírico-político a la preservación de lo que queda de la naturaleza y, con ello, nos insta a un cambio en los modos de pensamiento y acción. En las diversas secciones del poemario, que incluyen un canto natural, migraciones, extinciones de especies y poluciones, el poema articula una estética del cuidado y la solidaridad al unir acontecimientos locales con las peripecias medioambientales sufridas por otras comunidades del Sur Global, como en la sección "Homenaje al Continente Africano". De esta manera, este poemario elabora un vínculo biomimético entre el sufrimiento humano y nohumano y nos obliga a repensar lo que dejaremos a futuras generaciones. Así, esta ecopoesía involucra temporalidades más allá de la línea de vida del individuo moderno y su capacidad de progreso, y es en este sentido que pensamos esta estética como postdesarrollista. La sección de oración que cierra el poemario insta a la acción por la conservación de cara al futuro, reflexionando sobre qué legamos a las generaciones venideras: "Que de aquí a mil o cien mil años, no florezca /el desierto sino matas de jazmines" (Cárdich 2018: 107). Nos interesa destacar en esta expresión cultural, el pensamiento sobre el legado futuro en temporalidades y vidas por venir como una estética que desafía la idea de crecimiento infinito en los imaginarios del desarrollo. En los dos casos que discutimos de Vicuña y Cárdich, el arte involucra cuerpos y temporalidades en los márgenes de la actividad capitalista: animales extintos o en peligro de desaparecer, semillas y objetos precarios. En este sentido, estos trabajos producen nuevas percepciones de la relación entre ser humano y medioambiente que promueven subjetividades postdesarrollistas, en tanto que sugieren otros posibles entramados socioecológicos más regenerativos.

Ensamblaje cuerpo-territorio. La estética postdesarrollo ejemplifica lo que el ecofeminismo decolonial latinoamericano conceptualiza como "cuerpo-territorio" (Sempértegui 2021: 199), es decir, el reconocimiento de la continuidad e interdependencia entre el cuerpo y el territorio. Desde dicha perspectiva, cualquier agresión hacia el territorio se considera violencia sobre los cuerpos que lo habitan y, por ende, todo proceso extractivo supone un ataque y una violación inaceptable al cuerpo-territorio.

Si bien en este estudio nos ceñimos a la zona andina, es preciso mencionar que el arte visual y performático femenino latinoamericano cuenta con una fecunda tradición que pone de relieve la relación cuerpo-territorio como dupla de resistencia. Podemos pensar el legado artístico del uso del cuerpo en contacto con la materialidad del suelo en el *land art* de la artista cubano-norteamericana Ana Mendieta desde los años 60, y las performances corpóreas de la artista guatemalteca Regina José Galindo, quien usa su cuerpo como extensión del territorio en contra de la violencia tanto de la máquina extractiva como del conflicto armado que produjo el genocidio de campesinos, indígenas y mujeres en los años 60 y 70. Más específicamente, en el contexto contemporáneo de la puna jujeña argentino-boliviana, la artista y *drag queen* indígena Maximiliano Mamani en su nombre artístico de Bartolina Xixa, cholita *drag*, utiliza su cuerpo y su identidad trans en una resignificación del territorio andino a la luz de los desastres socioambientales en la región. Empleando el folklore tradicional en danzas como la vidalita coreografiada a través de su cuerpo indígeno-*queer*, la música y performance de Bartolina Xixa documenta la pobreza, la discriminación y el racismo en el norte andino, así como los efectos del extractivismo y la contaminación. En su hit del 2019, *Ramita Seca, La colonialidad permanente*, Xixa[2] no solo aborda desde la música y la danza la repetición de la colonialidad sobre los cuerpos y territorios andinos, sino que hace comunidad con el paisaje tóxico y contaminado de basura (el video fue filmado en el basural a cielo abierto de Hornillos en la Quebrada de Humahuaca), y con ello cuestiona el imaginario neoliberal dominante:

---

2 Esta estética musical tiene relación con el rap decolonial de la cantautora chilena Ana Tijoux y aún con el trap quechua de la artista peruana Renata Flores.

Fig. 2: Captura de imagen del video *Ramita Seca, La colonialidad permanente*.

Como vemos en la imagen del video musical, la performance de Xixa expone su cuerpo indígeno-*queer* en vestimentas tradicionales de la cholita, forjando una estética del despojo y la toxicidad que vemos en la toma del cuerpo yaciendo en un vertedero con el trasfondo del paisaje andino y con el rostro cubierto con una máscara de gas. Esta estética inquieta al espectador mientras documenta un cuerpo resiliente que involucra la comunidad LGBTQ, la comunidad indígena, la pobreza y marginalidad social de las comunidades quechua y aimara a partir de la evocación de Bartolina Sisa, la heroína indígena en el periodo de la conquista que luchó contra la colonización de su comunidad. En este sentido, esta estética pone de manifiesto "geographies of erasure" (Yusoff 2018: 35) puesto que presenta paisajes borrados de las narrativas de progreso y subjetividades desposeídas que documentan los efectos de las violentas políticas desarrollistas en esta zona. Afín al arte ecofeminista y ecológico *queer*, esta estética produce intersecciones entre género, raza, sexualidad y medioambiente mostrando las interrelaciones entre las diversas categorías y la imposibilidad de encontrar soluciones viables a la crisis medioambiental que no involucren justicia social y epistémica. El entretejido entre lo indígena y ecofeminista en este arte no diferencia entre cultura y naturaleza. Así, se estimula un imaginario transformador que tiene el potencial de señalar "what causes this collective inabiliy to imagine a sustainable future without economic growth in the Anthropocene" (Prádanos 2018: 13–14) y, con ello, de producir rasgaduras en el imaginario neoliberal y desarrollista que propone crecimiento infinito.

Entre las expresiones culturales andinas que producen quiebres en el imaginario desarrollista encontramos la novela *Montacerdos* (1981) de Cronwell Jara, que podría considerarse un ejemplo precursor de una sensibilidad postdesarrollista en el contexto andino peruano. En un mundo hostil donde una familia marginalizada y enferma vive y come de la basura en un gran vertedero, se desarrolla una amistad inusual entre humano y cerdo. La novela de Jara se enfoca en el desarraigo forzado y la marginalidad social de Griselda, la madre del adolescente protagonista llamado Yococo, quien, junto con un cerdo, el Celedunio, se desplazan de un lado a otro cargando cartones que son su hogar, "pequeño laberinto de colgajos" (9). Usando quechua o castellano quechuizado, la novela relata los lazos que forma una familia pobre y desposeída buscando refugios junto con sus llagas corporales que crecen, como describe el protagonista "Muertos vivos. Pudriéndonos [. . .] Hermanos con cucarachas, ratones y alacranes" (11). En esta situación de despojo social e insalubridad medioambiental (ya que esta familia habita vertederos tóxicos y ríos contaminados), Yococo entabla una relación de camaradería con un cerdo, también enfermo y pestilente, que fue arrojado por su dueña. Juntos, ambos enfrentan los intentos de la sociedad moderna por hacerlos desaparecer, ya que ponen de manifiesto nuestra cercanía a la tierra, el mundo no humano y lo insalubre y sucio. Esta inusual alianza entre pepenador-cerdo señala los límites de la ideología del crecimiento que no solo devasta las comunidades no humanas y el planeta, sino que también recorta el futuro de las comunidades humanas más vulnerables que reciben los impactos socioambientales del capitalismo, pues el joven protagonista humano fallece sin atención médica y el cerdo huye esquivando que lo maten. De este modo, es crucial combinar la crítica del Antropoceno con teoría decolonial para dar cuenta de cómo los procesos de acumulación y saqueo son racializados hacia las comunidades vulnerables y cómo estos procesos se comunican con la historia colonial de la Modernidad Occidental desde donde se desprende el ideal de progreso y civilización.

Temporalidades pluriversales y regenerativas. Las manifestaciones culturales postdesarrollo invitan a experimentar con varias temporalidades humanas, vegetales o incluso minerales. Estas temporalidades resultan más compatibles con ritmos corporales sanos y ciclos ecológicos regenerativos que con los tiempos acelerados y estresantes del capital y los ritmos infernales del extractivismo tecno-industrial y sus procesos de urbanización planetaria que violentan los cuerpos-territorios y hacen inviable la vida digna de cada vez más comunidades humanas y no humanas.

En esta dimensión, obras especulativas como los cuentos de la escritora boliviana Liliana Colanzi incluidos en la colección *Nuestro mundo muerto* (2017) abordan temporalidades no unidireccionales ni jerárquicas que irrumpen en la linealidad progresiva del imaginario moderno orientado al crecimiento. En particular, en el cuento "Chaco", el espíritu de un indio asesinado se adueña de la conciencia del personaje del abuelo en Santa Cruz, desde donde la cosmovisión indígena comienza a fundirse con la línea histórica de la vida del abuelo:

> Poco después la voz del mataco se metió en mi cabeza. Cantaba, sobre todo (. . .) Ayayay cantaba. Yo soñaba sus sueños: manadas de taitetuses que huían en el monte, la herida caliente de la urina alcanzada por la flecha, el vapor de la tierra yéndose a juntar con el cielo. Ayayay [. . .] Ya no hay más vos ni yo, de aquí en adelante somos una sola voluntad. (Colanzi 2017: 82)

Como vemos en la cita, esta estética pone de relieve una matriz ancestral que disuelve las dualidades forjadas por el imaginario de la Modernidad occidental (cielo-tierra, sujeto moderno-indígena, tiempo histórico-tiempos geológicos y cósmicos). Este cruce en las conciencias de los dos personajes, el abuelo y el indio, produce un entrelazamiento entre temporalidades, con lo que el tiempo adquiere densidad y trascurre ensamblando espacios y personajes. Por tanto, el tiempo se diferencia de la narrativa lineal, progresiva y ascendente que caracteriza el imaginario occidental moderno. La temporalidad es protagonista en esta expresión cultural andina y permite entrecruzar el trauma de la historia colonial latinoamericana con el trauma terrestre del Capitaloceno. La tematización y corporización temporal comunica el tiempo psíquico interior de la conciencia de los personajes con el tiempo cósmico y el futuro posible del planeta, a través del canto ancestral andino del indio, quien, al cantar sobre la muerte del mundo, también revaloriza la cosmovisión indígena ayorea para repensar nuestra relación con el planeta.

Inspirada en la mitología ayorea de Bolivia, pero con una estética diferente, la propuesta del cortometraje boliviano-danés *Abuela grillo* (2009) dirigido por Denis Chapon cuenta el viaje del personaje cosmológico, Abuela Grillo, por paisajes andinos rurales y urbanos. A través de la cosmovisión indígena de las Tierras Bajas bolivianas, donde la abuela es un grillo cuyo canto produce la lluvia, pero también controla el clima y puede ocasionar desastres naturales, este cortometraje nos zambulle en las políticas medioambientales relacionadas con el agua en esta región andina. El cortometraje cuenta la historia de la Abuela Grillo, raptada y obligada a producir agua para una corporación y finalmente rescatada por una movilización popular para liberar el agua, lo que resuena con las Guerras del Agua en Cochabamba en el 2000. El formato de cortometraje animado con voces en off propone una estética que apela tanto a adultos como a jóvenes, y la música andina interpretada por Luzmila Carpio, con sus tonos altos que imitan el canto de los pájaros, configura una reconexión con las epistemes ancestrales y el agua en tanto que materia y espíritu, más allá de la temporalidad lineal del imaginario del crecimiento económico (ver Fig. 3).

El cortometraje contrasta el aprisionamiento de la Abuela Grillo, que simboliza la privatización del agua, con la regeneración de la vida que produce el agua y la lluvia, como vemos en la imagen citada que ocurre al final de la narración. Esta estética, que podríamos llamar de interdependencia, quiebra así

Fig. 3: Captura de pantalla de *Abuela Grillo*.

la temporalidad y ritmo del progreso en varias temporalidades ensambladas que unen la vida de las comunidades humanas y no humanas en torno al agua. De tal manera, este cortometraje articula un imaginario postdesarrollo en tanto que no solo critica los planes gubernamentales y corporativos de explotación medioambiental y de apropiación de los recursos, sino que propone sensibilidades culturales de reconexión con la biósfera en torno a los saberes ancestrales que fueron soslayados por el imaginario neocolonial y neoliberal.

Finalmente, queremos destacar la instalación multimedia *Selva jurídica* (2014), un proyecto de Ursula Biemann y Paulo Tavares en las selvas vivientes entre la Amazonía ecuatoriana y la cordillera de los Andes, que también opera con temporalidades regenerativas desde un imaginario postdesarrollo. Este proyecto artístico produce un diálogo con el biotopo selvático y con las comunidades locales que lo habitan en el cruce con los conflictos medioambientales que atraviesan estas zonas y las movilizaciones populares para influir en la legislación medioambiental siguiendo las cosmopolíticas indígenas. La instalación multimedial involucra textos, videos y cartografías alternativas que descentran la idea unitaria de objeto artístico y abren la experiencia sensorial a expresiones de la selva amazónica basadas en la comunidad y lo común (ver Fig. 4).

En la imagen, el activista shuar narra las luchas contra la explotación petrolera en esa región y las 'guerras subterráneas' de las corporaciones contra la tierra y el suelo buscando los minerales y yacimientos. Recogida en el libro de nombre homónimo, esta instalación dialoga con *El contrato natural* (1990) de Michel Serres y utiliza su apertura ensayística para dar forma a una cosmopolítica de la zona subtropical. Tras una serie de batallas jurídicas ya emblemáticas que están surgiendo en Ecuador y Bolivia, donde se ha establecido constitucionalmente que la naturaleza es un sujeto con derechos, la instalación pone de relieve la agencialidad de la selva y la necesidad de renegociar nuestra supervivencia y

Fig. 4: Domingo Ankwash, activista shuar. Imagen reproducida de *Selva Jurídica* (Biemann/Tavares 2017: 127).

la subsistencia de la población local de campesinos, contra la intervención capitalista. Las disputas en torno a los bosques del Amazonas entrelazan la geografía inmediata de la región con la escala planetaria en tanto que los ecosistemas amazónicos están directamente relacionados con la desestabilización climática global, la pérdida de biodiversidad y la contaminación tóxica que afectan a la población mundial. Este arte multi-genérico (ensayo, video, imagen, texto, instalación) involucra intervenciones de comunidades locales reconociendo a la selva como interlocutor y voz protagonista. Con ello, se generan nuevos lenguajes artísticos que no solo critican a las petroleras multinacionales y al estado por el manejo mercantil de los territorios ancestrales, sino que estimulan a imaginar mundos postfósiles a través de la cosmopolítica indígena donde el bienestar de la comunidad nohumana implica también la supervivencia humana.

Diversificación del poder y sanación de relaciones. La estética del postdesarrollo representa empoderamientos diversos que cuestionan los modelos de liderazgo petromasculinos que han transformado la biosfera en una mina planetaria y sugieren formas de organización social más benignas. Para Cara Daggett (2018), la petromasculinidad emerge de la relación "between fossil fuels and white patriarchal orders [. . .] environmentalism itself has become masculinised, as a result of the dominance of science and security frames for understanding climate change" (28–29). Estos marcos, según Daggett, conllevan optar por soluciones dentro de los imaginarios patriarcales, produciendo a "'downgrading of ethical concerns' like justice, health, or economic equity" (Daggett 2018: 29, citando a Sherilyn MacGregor). Así, ha surgido el imaginario ecomodernista, prominente entre hombres de elite occidentales para proponer soluciones tecnológicas y comerciales a problemas ecológicos preservando la matriz del crecimiento económico (33). Por tanto, la petromasculinidad, que se reproduce en el ecomodernismo no considera la ética del cuidado, la compasión y el duelo como parte de las aproximaciones afectivas a las cuestiones medioambientales.

Por su parte, Jennie Stephens en *Diversifying Power* (2020) reconoce que la crisis ecológica es una crisis de liderazgo. El paradigma de liderazgo patriarcal y poco diverso que ha dominado durante la petromodernidad se ha basado en la dominación, la exclusión y la competición, ha facilitado la acumulación de poder y riqueza, ha exacerbado todo tipo de desigualdades y ha negado el carácter urgente y sistémico de la crisis climática al enfocarse en soluciones técnicas. En cambio, Stephens aboga por un tipo de liderazgo feminista, antirracista y diverso basado en la colaboración, la inclusión y la participación, que priorice la distribución de poder y riqueza y reduzca todo tipo de desigualdades, que invierta en las comunidades locales y conecte los diversos problemas socioecológicos. Este tipo de liderazgo privilegiaría la innovación social y no solo la tecnológica para enfrentar los desafíos climáticos.

Como propuesta postfósil más allá de la hegemonía petromasculina en el contexto andino queremos destacar la producción cinematográfica independiente de los hermanos peruanos Diego y Álvaro Sarmiento. En particular, el documental poético *Sembradoras de vida* (2019) propone un viaje hablado en quechua por paisajes del cambio climático que afectan la tierra y la subsistencia de comunidades locales. Este documental poético retrata la vida de cinco lideresas conectadas con el suelo de los andes peruanos que realizan una agricultura ancestral con semillas tradicionales atenta a la renovación de los suelos. Las cinco protagonistas muestran el significado de sus prácticas campesinas de agricultura lenta, no solo para la comunidad sino como alternativa sustentable frente al cambio climático, el avance de los transgénicos y el monocultivo en América Latina y la agroindustria:

Fig. 5: Captura de imagen de la película de *Sembradoras de vida* (2019).

En la imagen vemos a una de las mujeres realizando la siembra tradicional. Se pone de relieve el empleo orgánico del suelo en una práctica circular (más que unidireccional como la extracción), que relacionamos a la idea de "compostaje" (Haraway 2016: 5), pues no genera basura, más bien, disemina ideas de lo integrable, orgánico y biodegradable. La estética poética de este tipo de documental con largas tomas resalta la vitalidad de los colores del suelo y la vestimenta permitiendo apreciar prácticas ecosociales regenerativas. Asimismo, mientras el ecocidio incluye el etnocidio y la desaparición de las lenguas y culturas nativas en la carrera por el progreso moderno, expresiones culturales como la de los hermanos Sarmiento estimulan un imaginario postdesarrollista que revaloriza lenguas y culturas indígenas, así como propuestas regenerativas de recampesinización y producción de alimento más compatibles con el planeta. Las relaciones entre seres humanos y biósfera que propone el documental infiltran los nuevos medios como el cine y la fotografía para producir otros lenguajes culturales, nuevos vocabularios socioambientales y maneras de hacer comunidad respetando la agencia de la naturaleza y alejándose, como propone Stephens, de los imaginarios extractivos típicos de las hegemonías patriarcales (2020: 104).

Conclusión

En el recorrido analítico aquí propuesto emerge una cadena con eslabones claros: semillas, mujer empoderada, cuerpo-tierra, relaciones socioecológicas no limitadas por la lógica heteropatriarcal, cuerpos vulnerables, creativos, diversos y resilientes, ontologías relacionales (convergencia de dimensiones materiales, espirituales y cosmológicas) y temporalidades no lineales. En medios culturales andinos de Bolivia, Perú, Ecuador, Chile y la Puna argentina discutimos cuatro aspectos interrelacionados de la estética postdesarrollo. Esta estética no solo manifiesta una visión crítica con el capitalismo, sino que también articula lenguajes alternativos que estimulan acercamientos inspirados en formas biosemióticas, ciclos ecológicos, formas de comunicación más-que-humanas, cosmopolíticas pluriversales y liderazgos diversos. Frente al imaginario extractivo y petromasculino, el semillar poético-visual de Vicuña, la preocupación por el legado futuro en la ecopoesía de Cárdich, la performance musical de la cholita *drag* Bartolina Xixa, el cortometraje animado *Abuela Grillo*, la instalación multimedia *Selva jurídica*, el cuento "Chaco" de Liliana Colanzi y la cinematografía de los hermanos Sarmiento proponen una estética y ética basada en el cuidado, la solidaridad y la ralentización y transformación del metabolismo económico global. Mientras creemos en el potencial transformador y activista de estas obras para promover un imaginario postdesarrollo, también notamos la necesidad de intensificar la crítica al imaginario economicista dominante que distingue entre desarrollo y subdesarrollo. Los imaginarios culturales postdesarrollo emergentes deben trascender dicha división, pues se trata de dos caras de la insostenible moneda desarrollista que genera simultáneamente desarrollo consumista (urbanización del capital y agro-corporativismo) y subdesarrollo extractivo (descampesinización y marginalización). Ambos son procesos mutuamente constitutivos.

Uno de los retos estéticos del postdesarrollo es no caer ni en la celebración ecomodernista del urbanismo *smart* y verde, ni estetizar la otra cara de su moneda y limitarse a espectacularizar la pobreza manufacturada y la desigualdad socioespacial que genera el desarrollo extractivista. El reto es vislumbrar otros mundos posibles postglobales y postfósiles que puedan emerger de las semillas e imaginarios alternativos existentes. Ramón Grosfoguel (2018) explica las diferencias entre cómo se percibe la modernidad desde el pensamiento decolonial y desde el postcolonial, dependiendo de dónde identifica cada uno el origen de la historia colonial (en el siglo XVI o en el XVIII). Para el pensamiento postcolonial, al pensar la historia colonial a partir del siglo XVIII, "la modernidad y la colonialidad aparecen como procesos simultáneos, pero no mutuamente constitutivos uno del otro" (68-69). Para el pensamiento decolonial, en cambio, la historia colonial comienza en 1492 y, por tanto, "la modernidad y la colonialidad son dos caras de la misma moneda. Son proyectos que están mutuamente constituidos el uno del otro" (71). El postdesarrollo latinoamericano bebe del pensamiento decolonial y reconoce que la modernidad no existe sin la colonialidad, así como el desarrollo económico y la acumulación de capital no existen sin extracción, descampesinización y desposesión. El imaginario postdesarrollo que hemos trazado a través de medios culturales andinos apunta a diseños regenerativos que desde lo cultural, político y medioambiental generan maneras de *sentipensar* que reconocen, como dice la vidalita de Xixa, que "sin agua muere la vida". En este sentido, las obras culturales discutidas articulan *subjetividades postdesarrollistas* en tanto que están ancladas en procesos locales y geológicos que entretejen un pensamiento planetario más allá de la globalización económica.

Las estéticas del postdesarrollo que hemos discutido *vis-à-vis* medios culturales andinos se alinean, por tanto, con el ecofeminismo decolonial y contrarrestan la petromasculinidad tóxica, la violencia extractiva y la colonialidad epistémica. Al visibilizar la interdependencia socioecológica y la vulnerabilidad del cuerpo-territorio, estas expresiones también ponen de relieve y disuelven las fantasías (neo)liberales de cuerpos independientes y desconectados social y ecológicamente, cuyas consecuencias catastróficas para el planeta repercutirán en futuros profundos. Ante las nuevas formas de apropiación y desposesión capitalista, las estéticas del postdesarrollo incitan a redescubrir o reinventar, y hacer deseables, prácticas comunales para la reproducción de vidas dignas y sostenibles.

Bibliografía

Abuela Grillo (2009): Película dirigida por Denis Chapon. Bolivia-Dinamarca.
Arboleda, Martín (2020): *Planetary Mine. Territories of Extraction Under Late Capitalism*. Brooklyn: Verso.
Biemann, Ursula/Tavares, Pablo (2014): *Forest Law – Selva Jurídica*. East Lansing, Michigan: Eli and Edythe Broad Art Museum, https://cpb-us-e1.wpmucdn.com/sites.ucsc.edu/dist/0/196/files/2015/10/Biemann-Tavares-Forest-Law.compressed.pdf (última visita: 06/08/2021).
Cárdich, Samuel (2018): *Heredar la tierra*. Lima: Amotape.
Colanzi, Liliana (2017): "Chaco." En: *Nuestro mundo muerto*. Buenos Aires: Eterna Cadencia.
Daggett, Cara (2018): "Petro-masculinity: Fossil Fuels and Authoritarian Desire." En: *Millenium: Journal of International Studies* 47,1, pp. 25–44.
Dawson, Ashley (2020): *People's Power. Reclaiming the Energy Commons*. Nueva York/Londres: OR Books.
Grosfoguel, Ramón (2019): "De la crítica poscolonial a la crítica decolonial: similaridades y diferencias entre las dos perspectivas." En: Tobar, Javier (ed.): *Diversidad epistemológica y pensamiento crítico*. Popayán: Editorial Universidad del Cauca, pp. 65–78.
Haraway, Donna Jeanne (2016): *Staying with the Trouble: Making Kin in the Chthulucene*. Durham: Duke University Press.
Heise, Ursula K. (2016): *Imagining Extinction: The Cultural Meanings of Endangered Species*. Chicago: The University of Chicago Press.
Jara, Cronwell (1981): *Montacerdos*. Lima: Lluvia Editores.
Kothari, Ashish/Salleh, Ariel/Escobar, Arturo/Demaria, Federico/Acosta, Alberto (eds.) (2019): *Pluriverse. A Post-Development Dictionary*. Nueva Delhi: Tulika Books.
Marder, Michael (2013): *Plant-Thinking: A Philosophy of Vegetal Life*. Nueva York: Columbia University Press.
Prádanos, Luis I (2018): *Postgrowth Imaginaries: New Ecologies and Counterhegemonic Culture in Post-2008 Spain*. Liverpool: Liverpool University Press.
Ramita Seca, La colonialidad permanente (2019): Video musical de Maximiliano Mamani/Bertolina Xixa. Argentina. En: Youtube, https://www.youtube.com/watch?v=-2-wFmNnFDc (última visita: 06/08/2021).
Sembradoras de vida (2019): Película dirigida por Diego y Álvaro Sarmiento. HDPERU y Conteo Regresivo Films.
Sempértegui, Andrea (2021): "Indigenous Women's Activism, Ecofeminism, and Extractivism: Partial Connections in the Ecuadorian Amazon". En: *Politics & Gender*, 17, pp. 197–224.

Stephens, Jennie C (2020): *Diversifying Power. Why We Need Antiracist, Feminist Leadership on Climate and Energy*. Washington D.C.: Island Press.
Svampa, Maristella (2008): "La disputa por el desarrollo: territorio, movimientos de carácter socio-ambiental y discursos dominantes". En: Maristella Svampa: *Cambio de época. Movimientos sociales y poder político*. Buenos Aires: Siglo XXI, pp. 1–31.
Svampa, Maristella (2019): "The Latin American Critique of Development." En:Szeman, Imre/ Boyer, Dominic (eds.) (2017): *Energy Humanities: An Anthology*. Baltimore: Johns Hopkins University Press.
Vicuña, Cecilia (2000): "*SEMI YA.*" En: *Galería Gabriela Mistral*, https://static1.squarespace.com/static/53343bb6e4b0b47198d89031/t/559925d5e4b069786e90eb26/1436100053889/semiya_catalogue.pdf (última visita: 27/08/2021).
Yusoff, Kathryn (2018): *A Billion Black Anthropocenes or None*. Minneapolis, MN: University of Minnesota Press.

Jan Knobloch
Globalization Reversed
Reading Scales of Collapse in Pedro Mairal's
El año del desierto

Globalization and Collapse

If we want to consider the dark underside or double of the globalization project[1], one of the possible starting points would be to study its notion of time. Whether we are talking about cultural or economic globalization; the enthusiastic rhetoric of the global vision has been underpinned, from the beginning, by a narrative of progress and the specific temporality connected to it. At least since the second half of the 20th century, globalization's proponents have argued that the free exchange of commercial and cultural goods will lead to an equalization of living standards between societies, universal well-being, democracy, and a dissolution of the old nation states. In this decentered network of free societies, cultures and economies will deal productively with one another, while cosmopolitan subjects engage in liberal-minded, non-dogmatic interaction. We could call this conception of time not *linear*, but *utopian*: with time, things will get better. The current realization that the necessary ground for things to "get better" in this particular way does not exist on this Earth produces materialist anguish, as Bruno Latour writes: "The soil of globalization's dreams is beginning to slip away" (Latour 2018 [2017]: 4). Utopia, seen from this perspective, is not a non-place in space or time, but the possibility of continuous development itself.

It comes as no surprise, then, that the global transformation of the ways we imagine the future has had a disastrous effect on discourses of globalization. The increasing impossibility of thinking about the future in terms of progress severs our connection to globalization's utopian foundation. In her seminal study *The Future as Catastrophe,* Eva Horn has described this general turn in expectations as a pessimistic reinterpretation of how we think of what is to come: she diagnoses the "disintegration of a temporal order in the modern age

---

[1] For a short discussion of discourses and cultural theories of globalization since the 1990s, see Heise (2008: 4–9) or Reati (2006: 20–31), as well as the extensive work of Gesine Müller on global processes of cultural circulation (e.g. Müller/Siskind 2019).

Jan Knobloch, University of Cologne

in which the future was still an 'auratic key concept,' a space of hope and planning, a locus of utopia" (Horn 2018 [2014]: 5). Pessimist outlooks, one might object, have existed throughout cultural history (they might even constitute the normal case). What is new in the era of climate catastrophe is the robustness of the scientific data – the measurements, models, and instrumentation on which fears about the future are based – as well as the fact that many of the actions that bring about this future have *already been* done (Latour 2017 [2015]: 9–10, 24–33, 41–74). Underlying the current sense of impending catastrophe, then, is a new, data-driven *grand récit* shaping the present: the narrative of an imminent collapse, linked to the Anthropocene, the destruction of the environment, the extinction of species and the dismantling of the conditions that make life on Earth possible. The intimate connection between the time order of globalization, the destruction of ecosystems, and what Laura Barbas-Rhoden has termed "ecoapocalypse" has been reflected in Latin American fiction at least since the 1990s (Barbas-Rhoden 2011: 139–168). Contrary to the utopian time of globalization, the conception of time inherent in the narrative of collapse is apocalyptic or, in more secular terms, cataclysmic: collapse describes a radical break in time at which linearity is broken off, with no or almost no transition[2].

While global warming and the climate catastrophe are increasingly seen as planet-wide dangers (Chakrabarty 2015: 153–156), their perception differs locally and seems to be rooted in a strong "sense of place" (Heise 2008). These varying degrees of how catastrophic we imagine the future to be are not always coherent with the distribution of local vulnerabilities. A look at Europe, for example, shows that – according to a study published in 2019 – 71% of Italians and 65% of French citizens agree with the belief that civilization as we know it will collapse in the coming years, while only 39% of Germans agreed when asked the same question (Ifop 2019). In Latin America, young people, when asked in 2013, were rather optimistic about the future, while questions of climate and ecology did not play a major role (Observatorio de la Juventud en Iberoamérica 2013). However, if we take fiction as an indicator, a different picture of the cultural sensibilities

---

[2] Collapse, understood as the sudden breakdown of societies, civilizations, species populations, and ecosystems, has been studied from a variety of disciplinary angles. While early archaeological approaches link it to complexity (Tainter 1990), more recent investigations from the realm of philosophy (Dupuy 2002), cultural history (Diamond 2005) or cultural studies (Citton/Rasmi 2020) stress the connection to environmental destruction and climate change. More activist approaches (Servigne/Stevens 2015) use the term to create a sense of urgency in their readers. In the context of this essay, it refers to a secular form of apocalypse, one without empire or revelation.

related to temporalities of the future emerges[3]. In the last decades, commentators have noted a post-apocalyptist turn in certain strands of Latin American fiction (Logie 2008, Fabry 2012: 20, Salvioni 2013). In view of the multiple crises and downfalls that characterize the region, these theorists argue, fear of the future has often been replaced by the feeling that collapse has already happened, that one is living after the event. From the point of view of these imagined futures, the present appears as a landscape of trauma, riddled with signs and symptoms to be decoded (Berger 1998). In *Los rituales del caos*, a collection of *crónicas* and parables describing daily life in Ciudad de Mexico published in 1995, Carlos Monsiváis notes:

> Y éste es el resultado: *México, ciudad post-apocalíptica*. Lo peor ya ocurrió (y lo peor es la población monstruosa cuyo crecimiento nada detiene), y sin embargo la ciudad funciona de modo que a la mayoría le parece inexplicable, y cada quien extrae del caos las recompensas que en algo equilibran las sensaciones de vida invivible. (Monsiváis 1995: 21)

For Monsiváis, the postapocalyptic condition of Mexico City is not so much linked to a catastrophic event or an imagery of destroyed landscapes but is entrenched in the socio-economic realities of everyday life. The end is "immanent rather than imminent" (Kermode 1967: 101), the temporal mode is not so much apocalyptic as it is post-apocalyptic. The worst has already happened, and the mystery is continuity itself (i.e. why Mexicans keep on living in and moving into "la ciudad más contaminada del planeta", and why this apocalyptic mode of dwelling can be the source of a festive, paradoxical joy). Another post-cataclysmic case could be made for Venezuela (see Gustavo Guerrero's article in this volume) or for Argentina, a country that went from being one of the richest nations in the world in the 1920s to completely disintegrating economically by the end of the century. It may seem almost too banal to note, but it was precisely during the period of intensified globalization that the country saw some of its biggest economic and political crises (notably that of 2001). As Fernando Reati has shown, there is a clear link between the neoliberal policies of the years from 1985 to 1999 and the surge in the publication of dystopian novels, a genre that had until then been unusual in Argentina's narrative tradition. Already during the 80s and 90s, expectations of the future tended to shift toward

---

[3] The question how actors and collectives from Latin America imagine the future has recently received increasing scholarly attention, see for example the program of the International Research Training Group "Temporalities of Future" at the Free University of Berlin, the Heidelberg Käte Hamburger Centre for Apocalyptic and Postapocalyptic Studies (CAPAS), or the museum of imagined futures at *Futuros imaginados*, https://2084futurosimaginados.org (last visit: 12/11/2021).

the negative (Reati 2006: 32–34), the predominant feeling being the possibility of an abrupt ending at any moment. This became true for example for the so-called "nuevos pobres", former members of the middle class who suddenly lost everything during the years of hyperinflation. The peak of this development was reached during the crisis of 2001, with damage to the social fabric at un unprecedented scale, unemployment rates above 20%, and more than half of the population living in poverty (Novaro 2010: 279–287).

For Argentina during the mid 2000s, the worst, in the words of Monsiváis, had thus already happened. Defining the relationship between globalization and collapse from this point of view is insightful: what at first glance seems a simple opposition – that is, that the breakdown of natural and social systems radically questions the progressivist narrative on which globalization depends – becomes a dialectical relationship upon closer inspection. If we follow through with globalization, it *always already* carries within itself the event of collapse. Collapse, then, has to be read as the *Aufhebung* of globalization in a truly Hegelian sense, meaning its negation, but also its conservation and its elevation to another level of being. What form this new being takes is one of the most pressing questions of today's debate around the Anthropocene.

Scaling Time: History and Narration in the Work of Pedro Mairal

A novel that puts into action or plots this dialectical[4] relationship between progress and collapse in the Argentinian context is Pedro Mairal's *El año del desierto* (2012 [2005]). In the novel, the reverse side of the globalizing dynamic is incarnated by the so called "intemperie", a devastating disaster that hurtles Argentina back into pre-modern conditions. While it remains unclear whether the disaster is ecological, socio-economic, or fantastic in nature, what is certain is that here, the global paradigm of development and growth is confronted with its negative, inverted double. Within just one year, the so-called *desierto* of the pampas reclaims Argentina as a whole, dissolving all urban structures and retaking the land. The systems formerly guaranteeing stability – commerce, food supply, transport, electricity, policing, agriculture, money, financial and healthcare

---

[4] Zac Zimmer's (2013) eloquent interpretation of Mairal's "dialectical image" mainly refers to the ending of the novel, revealing the arrival of the colonizers as the originary American apocalypse.

systems, democratic institutions – collapse into chaos and brutality. Global integration is reversed as the country breaks up into small communities and groups at war with each other. The exchange of goods and information between different regions, as well as with the outside world, comes to a halt.

Published one year before *The Road* (2006), Cormac McCarthy's international bestseller, *El año*'s depiction of collapse departs from a less global, more specifically Argentinian context: the 2001 economic crisis, and, more broadly, the perceived decline of the country from 1930 to 2003. Yet the novel continues still further back in time. The narrator-protagonist María, who survived the collapse, lives through a regression or "involución" (Hallstead/Dabove 2012: xxiv), going backwards on "a return journey through Argentina's history, told in reverse chronological order" (Zimmer 2013: 374). From the neoliberal years of the 90s, Argentina develops into a situation that closely resembles the social struggles of the first half of the 20th century, including the years of mass immigration from Europe. Supra-communal forms of organization crumble, as María moves on to work on an *estancia* in a 19th-century setting, where she is captured by the *braucos*, a tribe of modern city-dwellers turned nomadic. After finally "going native" with the premodern "Ú" tribe, in an inverted depiction of colonization, María leaves the country on a ship to return to Europe (probably Ireland, where her European ancestors had come from). Time progressing in the novel, then, is also the time of historic regression (Zimmer 2013: 376). The reverse image of progress and globalization is an inversion of the opposition between so-called *civilización* and *barbarie*, a dichotomy that shaped the Argentinian national project of *desarrollo* since Domingo Faustino Sarmiento's *Facundo*.[5] The cannibalistic practices that María finds her boss Suárez engaged in when, at the end of the novel, she returns to her old workplace at the Torre Garay, an office tower in the center of Buenos Aires, demonstrate that the *barbarie* is not actually emerging from the pampas to haunt the civilized world of the city or resulting from its reclamation, but that it was inherently present, located right at modernity's center (Zimmer 2013, Bonacic 2015).

While the narrative device of accelerated time in reverse (or "rewind", as Zimmer calls it) has often been read as a powerful tool for producing national allegory (Drucaroff 2010, Hallstead/Dabove 2012: xii–xviii, Bonacic 2015, Campisi 2019), it also constitutes a solution for a crucial problem of representation.

---

[5] There is a whole tradition of texts that link writing about the *desierto* to the reversal, contestation or playful parody of Sarmiento's famous categories, probably starting from Sarmiento's own complications of the opposition in *Facundo* to José Hernandez' *Martín Fierro* to certain *cuentos* of Borges (e.g. "Historias de jinetes" or "Historia del guerrero y de la cautiva") to César Aira's aestheticist inversion in *Ema, la cautiva*.

As Timothy Clark (2012), Jörg Dünne (2019), Eva Horn (2019), and other theorists have argued, some of the most pressing questions of literary representation in the Anthropocene concern incompatibilities of scale: spatial scales are disturbed by the fact that climate change ties local actions to global responsibilities. Temporal scales are superimposed in ways that create deranging effects, for example when human time suddenly collides with the geological frames of deep time, or when human history becomes a factor in natural history (Chakrabarty 2009). Processes of collapse, even if they are not "hyperobjects" (Morton 2013), entail their own set of scalar distortions. Representing them means connecting the scale of national history – in the Argentinian case more or less 500 years, with an ecosystem that has a history of tens of thousands of years – to the scale of individual history and plot time (the time of representable action in the narrated world). To this end, Mairal uses two devices. First, he inscribes the temporality of decay into the space of the narrated world, a topography in constant, supernaturally rapid decomposition (buildings disintegrate quickly, city districts disappear, plants grow and rot faster). At one point in the novel, this acceleration is symbolized by the change of an orange: "Si la miraba constantemente, no notaba ningún cambio, pero si la miraba cada diez minutos, notaba que se iba achicharrando" (Mairal 2012: 24). Second, the arrangement of historical references indicates the backward progression of time. As María advances through the space of the diegesis, references to national history, but also brand names, places, cultural elements, and historical trivia point towards an epoch further away from the present. While not strictly chronological, Chapter II ("Suárez & Baitos") starts in the present, Chapter III ("Como un fuerte") reaches back into the 1940s, 50s and 60s, and Chapter IV ("Un mismo cuerpo") assembles references to the beginning of the 20th as well as to the end of the 19th century. The historical time of the nation is plotted onto the time-space of narration. Narrating time and narrated time are brought into great tension. It is this acceleration that allows the novel to condense the long process of dissolution and collapse into one year. By downscaling collapse in this way, the novel makes tangible what would otherwise remain outside the scope of human perception. What we see before our eyes is a process of radical degrowth that would otherwise take at least decades to happen. The invisible "slow violence" of collapse, to use Rob Nixon's term (Nixon 2011), becomes visible in fast-forward.

As Buenos Aires is eaten up street by street by the *intemperie*, the city reprovincializes. Where building blocks have been swept away, informal settlements arise. Advancing in concentric circles, the *intemperie* operates as a force of horizontalization: all vertical, human built structures break down, leaving only dust, weeds, and ombú trees behind. Urban verticality becomes horizontal *desierto* (Mairal 2012: 170). Only when this process reaches the central areas of Buenos Aires do the inhabitants of the capital envision the possibility that they too might be concerned. Mairal's novel thereby illustrates how social inequality influences the perception of the temporality of collapse: the urban elites do not (want to) believe in the reality of the coming catastrophe until their own lifeworld is directly affected by it. In the face of power outages, Suárez, the head of an international investment firm, buys electricity generators to keep the elevators and the air conditioning running. These partial measures to keep up the façade of business as usual appear as social forms of denial. "—Quedate tranquilo, de acá no nos movemos. ¿Qué puede pasar? ¿Cortan todas las rutas? Compramos diez helicópteros. ¿Aumenta la temperatura de la tierra? Compramos el aire acondicionado más grosso que exista" (Mairal 2012: 28). Something similar is true for the public demonstrations: the "marcha contra la intemperie" (Mairal 2012: 5) is nostalgic because it holds on to the logic of political struggle in a world that has decoupled itself from human engagement. Illusions of stability (Hallstead/Dabove 2012: xx), fantasies of agency; both are symptoms of what Jean-Pierre Dupuy has termed the "time of catastrophes"– an inversed temporality in which catastrophe is an intrusion of the possible into the impossible, retrospectively creating its own possibility (Dupuy 2002: 9–13) [my translation]. Catastrophe seems impossible before it happens, while after the event, it appears necessary, as if it could not have happened otherwise.

Mairal's narrative acceleration moreover permits us to observe the processuality of collapse. An example of this is María's work in the hospital in chapter IV. María, until then a classic office worker, has to learn practical skills suitable for a decomplexifying economy in order to obtain food and a place to sleep. The disintegration of the hospital mirrors the disastrous effects of neoliberal cost-cutting policies: in just a couple of weeks, the building structure of the hospital falls apart. Power cuts endanger the lives of patients, certain medications begin to run out, and complex medical practices can no longer be performed. In the novel, this causes stress and disbelief in certain doctors who have trouble adjusting to the new realities. Old routines, forged during decades of relative material wealth, continue to exercise power over people's actions, even though the conditions that made them possible have been eliminated. While medical standards fall, anachronistic methods of treatment return. Many patients die. In a powerful image, Mairal connects this process of erosion to the Argentinian politics of the 20th century:

> Los múltiples arreglos del piso habían dejado un mapa de la desidia y la falta de continuidad en los programas de salud pública. Según donde se tropezara, la jefa insultaba al gobierno responsable de la reparación. Así fui entendiendo que las baldosas ajedrezadas eran originales de los tiempos del presidente Roca; las celestes, de los tiempos de Perón; las de cerámica, de la Revolución Libertadora; unas medio beige, del final de la dictadura; las de vinilo símil madera curvadas por la humedad, del tiempo del segundo

> fracaso radical; y los arreglos con parches de cemento pelado, de los peronistas de los últimos años. (Mairal 2012: 84–85)

One could interpret the passage as a rewriting of the Apocalypse as described in the book of Daniel (Dan. 2) where, in Nebuchadnezzar's dream, the progressive decay of kingdoms is symbolized by the body parts of a statue: its head made of gold, its torso made of silver, the feet made of clay. However, the passage also illustrates the intimate doubling of utopian and catastrophic time. The declining quality of the floor tiles progresses in parallel with the advance of the national project; globalization and progress, in the accelerated time of the novel, can indeed be seen as indistinguishable from cataclysmic temporality.

At this point, it seems legitimate to ask about the reasons for collapse in the novel. *El año*'s relationship to the climate crisis is hard to pin down, as it is not clear if the *intemperie* is a human-made natural disaster (even if it does seem to have effects on climate and the environment, from increased heat and light (20) to floods (153) and the melting of glaciers (126), to epidemics (Mairal 2012: 161)). What *is* clear, though, is that the *intemperie* incarnates the massive agency of the Earth system, while at the same time successively shrinking the agency of the human characters in the novel. As Bruno Latour (2017) has argued, what we used to consider the backdrop or *décor* of human actions enters the stage in the Anthropocene to become a powerful actor in and of itself, limiting the possibilities of human action. The novel stages this animation of the setting: *intemperie* is nothing but the name for the increasing agency of the *desierto* itself. Consequently, it is the expansion of the *desierto* that drives the backward evolution of the country, successively depriving humans of the possibility to act and limiting them to modes of reaction, dependency, and acceptance. When towards the end of the novel, María's freedom depends on a match of an archaic, brutal version of football ("ful") between the *braucos* and a group of visitors, this loss of agency is symbolized by an image of absence:

> Me quedé así largo rato, entregada a esa voluntad que me era ajena y que me seguía arrastrando de acá para allá, esa fuerza que era algo parecido a Dios, pero también era la desintegración, y lo invisible, y también la intemperie y el viento, la soledad de ese lugar vacío, el dios del mundo sin gente. No sé cómo explicarlo. Un yuyo seco doblándose en el viento, algo que nadie ve, un lugar igual a cualquier otro en ese desierto donde hasta los bichos ciegos escarbaban sus cuevas para huir del desamparo del cielo. (Mairal 2012: 262)

The force before which humans disappear as a *quantité négligeable* is unsayable. It is a figure of the sacred as much as it is the eternal force of becoming that is nature, but also emptiness, the strangeness of the planet itself. It is important to note the almost total absence of animate, organic matter in this description of the *desierto*, except for the weed and the blind animal. In an image of the mathematically sublime (the subject disappears before the vastness of the object), Mairal, following authors like Echeverría, Sarmiento or Ezequiel Martínez Estrada, transforms the emptiness of the pampas into a figure of human insignificance and dependence on planetary forces. Only, where in classic theories of the sublime from Burke to Kant to Schopenhauer the moment of intimidation of the subject is cancelled out by an opposing movement of empowerment by way of reason, the body, or contemplation, here, María's shrinking into passivity in the face of a disintegrated "mundo sin gente" seems complete[6].

Zooming In: Organizing Collapse

Recent studies have suggested that fictions of the future do not exclusively consist of projections derived from past and present tendencies, but that they can also operate as a form of fictional anticipation, imagining possible futures that, despite being fictive, format the field of the possible (Bayard 2016, Horn 2018 [2014], Citton/Rasmi 2020: 129–152). Reading novels as *scenarios* in this way means focusing on the "*margins* and *backgrounds* of the fictional world[]", its "conditions of possibility" (Horn 2018 [2014]: 18). Scenario-based readings treat the diegesis not as a symbolic or allegorical space, but as though it exists in the material sense, allowing us to heuristically explore "the strange universes of fiction as *possibilities* for our real environment" (Horn 2018 [2014]: 19). In the present context, this implies scaling down our reading by means of a negation or suspension of the allegorical interpretation of the novel, instead "zooming in" (Heise 2008: 66) on its concrete, present elements.

El año seems particularly suitable for such a reading. This is because the processuality of the unfolding scenario permits it to critically portray different stages of political, social, and economic organization during and after the collapse. Allegorical readings pass over these thick textures all too quickly. European discourses on societal collapse – so-called French "collapsology", for example – often argue that survival in a catastrophic future will depend on the cultivation of "local resilience", meaning the strengthening of the local social ties in order to limit the physical and psychological damages associated with the breakdown (Servigne/Chapelle 2017). According to this vision, informal and non-democratic networks of mutual aid will pop up, as solidarity between neighbors replaces the nation state. It is surprising to see how some of these thinkers, skeptical and darkly pessimistic when it comes to national politics,

---

6 On the transformation of the sublime in the Anthropocene see Latour (2017: 40).

adopt a light, enthusiastic, almost utopian tone when they sketch out possibilities for local initiatives. Within the local realm, they argue, ethics and cooperation between survivors come about naturally. After the collapse, politics end. This naïve, harmonic vision of the local has been criticized by commentators as apolitical, unethical, and naturalist. As Pierre Charbonnier puts it:

> Playing to quite genuine and legitimate fears, [the collapsologists] have unwittingly promulgated a survivalist discourse that is fundamentally apolitical in nature. This discourse maintains that tomorrow's survivors will be those most able to adapt to a post-technological world. It espouses a form of purifying disintegration, addressing a community of the enlightened. (Charbonnier 2019: 2)

To return to the Argentinian context, in Pedro Mairal's novel, if the *intemperie* does break up the country into small communities and groups at war with each other, this does *not* bring about the end of politics. Two chapters are especially illuminating on this subject: Chapters III and VII, with the former modelling post-cataclysmic forms of local organization in the urban space, and the latter doing the same in a rural context. In both chapters, local forms of survival intensify power relations instead of abolishing them, further increasing inequality instead of softening it.

In Chapter III, entitled "Como un fuerte", urban survivors entrench themselves in their houses. Every block of buildings, shielded against the outside world but connected by an inner *patio*, becomes a fortress, harboring a local community with its own micro-society, economy, and politics. While these fortresses constitute protected inner spaces, the streets become their exteriors, filled with provincial revolutionaries and people who did not make it into houses. Significantly, then, after some deliberation, the middle-class occupants of the houses choose to close and defend the buildings rather than seeing those who wander the streets as potential allies or refugees: "Al final, en toda nuestra manzana, el miedo y la desconfianza tuvieron más poder. La idea de abrir la puerta de calle se descartó" (Mairal 2012: 51). It is important to note that there is no determinism here, but the representation of a political decision process: under external pressure, the small communities *choose* a Schmittian logic of enmity, opting for closure over solidarity. (This closure, as María Semilla Durán notes, is illusionary because the inhabitants of the buildings are forced to adopt the practices of the *villas miserias* themselves, Semilla Durán 2010: 331). The identity of those in the streets is unknown, but the mere fact of finding oneself inside or outside determines group affiliation.

Later in the chapter, the fortresses of the *manzanas* are connected by an intricate system of tunnels and bridges, making it possible to circulate between blocks without setting foot on the street. The city space is transformed to mirror the new two-class society. Yet political, economic, and sexual power inequalities also become prominent inside the buildings. Leaders are elected for each "censo" (1200 people), where food, jobs, and water are distributed centrally, a provisional system of healthcare is set up, and defense is organized. One of the main problems identified by the novel is that the old logic of individualism, central to the market economy, is still present, as inhabitants keep the best food for themselves, hide things, or refuse to accept the tasks assigned to them. María, who has almost no practical skills, is forced to do laundry – physically painful and repetitive labor. No new collective subjectivity can emerge here, precisely because there is no recognizable class structure left that could act as the motor force of history, as Marx would have called it: "Era todo muy confuso y arbitrario" (Mairal 2012: 76). The utopian horizon of development which had been an integral part of leftist emancipatory politics has collapsed along with the old order. Instead, cooperation and participation are now demanded under threat of punishment by the new leaders. Mairal demonstrates the difficulty of switching to collectivist, local thinking after being socialized in a globalized market economy. Neither does the replacement of money with barter lead to more fairness or altruism, as when María must pay "cuatro turnos de lavar ropa" (Mairal 2012: 74) for a pair of old shoes. While at first, a new form of solidarity between the inhabitants seems to replace the anonymity of previous urban life (Mairal 2012: 53), with increasingly scarce supplies of food and water, the logic of egotism, corruption, and violence takes hold. As apartments are requisitioned for collective purposes, displacement sets in, and private space becomes public. Without privacy, María feels more and more confined and sexually vulnerable. The two parties in the building, the "puentistas" and the "tuneleros", struggle for control, weapons, power, and privilege. Democratic mechanisms of deliberation fail, as there are no institutions to guarantee them. Mairal's Argentinian scenario, it seems, deconstructs the idea that the problems of the old world might not transfer into life after collapse. And it is precisely the rhetoric of harmony and mutual aid that obscures the underlying politics, as the case of the murdered Presidente de Consorcios shows:

> A pesar de todo, algunos en la manzana insistían con que había sido gente de afuera. No podían aceptar que hubiera pasado puertas adentro, donde se suponía que habían quedado los "vecinos respetables", los que nos ayudábamos entre nosotros y compartíamos todo. Ahora se susurraba en los pasillos, se confabulaba en los balcones. Teníamos miedo cuando andábamos solas por las escaleras. (Mairal 2012: 63)

In the urban space, then, Mairal does not present a functioning new model of political organization in conditions of scarcity. Instead, the novel represents the lack of a guiding utopian horizon by demonstrating the absence of the new. In this fictional future, trauma is not resolved, but repeated (Berger 1998). What returns are the well-known problems of corruption, impunity, inequality, authoritarianism, and general distrust that plagued Argentinian 20th century politics.

In Chapter VII ("La Peregrina"), rural space comes into view. Still in Buenos Aires, a customer at Ocean Bar describes the joys of rural life in fantastic terms:

> —Ustedes, chicas, tienen que irse a Luján. Arriendan tierra por unos pesos. Se puede vivir bien. Tiran dos semillas y a la mañana siguiente ya asoma el tallo. Se ve la caña del maíz subir y crecer. En unos días, tienen tomates, lechuga, papas... No hay que obedecer a un patrón y con remover la tierra un poco cada día y regar, ya está. (Mairal 2012: 165)

It is striking to see how Mairal's novel deconstructs this rural promise. The first part of the statement, which sounds the most fantastical, proves to be true, as the *intemperie* not only accelerates processes of decay, but also makes plants grow faster. Instead, what turns out to be the stuff of fantasy is the last sentence, in which the abolition of power and the end of hard work are promised: "No hay que obedecer a un patron".

Upon arriving in Luján, María and her three companions try to rent some land. By now, the *intemperie* has dissolved large chunks of Buenos Aires. The dissolution of the city into *desierto*, as well as a circulating epidemic, have triggered a massive migration out into the countryside[7]. Fertile soil has become the most valuable good, while money, an institution based on interpersonal trust, has lost most of its value (Mairal 2012: 198). Nevertheless, there seems to be plenty of land on offer: "Al parecer, todos eran dueños de tierras" (Mairal 2012: 205). After persuading an owner to rent out an inundated pasture, María and her companions find out that their business partner did not really own what he claimed was in his possession. After the collapse, land division and ownership rights have become unclear. With the breakdown of authority, land markers have ceased to exist. Again, reversed globalization does not engender local utopia or functioning counter-communities (be they Marxist, socialist, localist or naturalist), but an intensification of the tensions already in place. The results are bad for everyone, as land lies fallow instead of being used for food production. As María puts it: "La tierra ya no era ni del que la pudiera comprar ni del que la pudiera sembrar, la tierra era del que la pudiera defender" (Mairal 2012: 208). The Hobbesian undertones of Mairal's vision of the rural are further accentuated when María's group returns the favor by stealing from the man who stole from them. The collapse of the globalized economy does not

---

7 More precisely, the novel outlines two phases of migration: first, people flee towards the center of Buenos Aires as the *orillas* of the city are destroyed; then, when the center comes under attack, mass migration turns towards the countryside.

lead to reterritorialization, understood as the "attempt to realign culture with place" (Heise 2008: 53), but to the local distribution of goods by force.

This local dynamic of inclusion and exclusion continues at the second chronotope of the chapter: the *estancia* "La Peregrina", a large, centrally organized farm that offers a place to stay and food in exchange for hard, manual labor. Having almost no knowledge in practical matters, the arrivals from the city are violently exploited on the *estancia*, where slavery and absolute dependency on their bosses are the rules of the day. References to slavery and its post-slavery substitute, *peonaje por deudas* (Mairal 2012: 216), merge with modern forms of neoliberal exploitation and cheap labor. While the chapter is clearly a reverse rewriting of national history, concerned with the first half of the 19th century (citing a range of *topoi* from the *caudillo* to the *frontera*, the *cautiva,* and the *malónes*, evoking the fight between indigenous people and settlers under Juan Manuel de Rosas), it can also be read as a gloomily realist imagination of the consequences of degrowth. In rural zones where food is produced, survival is possible, but the rapidly shrinking economy brings about a hardening of living conditions, heavy physical work, economic and sexual dependence, and submission to the mercy of land-owners. Degrowth also puts into place a re-hierarchization of knowledge: city residents like María, who has a literary education, lack practical knowledge, for example in handling horses (193, 198, 200), sowing grain (205) or milking cows (Mairal 2012: 211). Even if María *does* progress (later in the novel, she benefits from having learned how to gut animals and uses the basic medical skills she picked up at the hospital), she and her companions regularly find themselves in the lower ranks of the group because their areas of expertise have lost their relevance.

In the rural space, then, after collapse, local communities gather around monopolies of land ownership, connecting resilience and survival not to harmony, but to antisocial and undemocratic models of resource exploitation. In the novel, it is the centralization of power on the farm that permits the production of food, while in Luján, fields lay bare. Mairal draws on the historical experience of Argentina to demonstrate this pessimist point. What the novel seems to suggest is that the process of degrowth must be completed if the traces of old power distribution are to be eliminated. Even the *braucos*, a hybrid tribe of modern people turned nomad, are an unequal, patriarchal society that excludes weaker members, perpetuating the history of violence and domination. Only the "Ŭ", pre-modern *indígenas* untouched by Western thought, transcend the ego. Their members do not bear proper names but are named according to their *oficios*, which change every few days – a practice that results not only in non-alienated forms of work, but also in a temporal, collective, non-essentialist conception of the subject (Mairal 2012: 280–290). Time in this context is not a linear succession of events pointing towards a *telos*, but an oscillation between repetition and change that can be inhabited: "Nadie me molestaba. Nadie me quería mal. Si un trabajo me resultaba difícil, bastaba con esperar dos o tres días para que me tocara rotar. El tiempo se dejaba habitar. *El pasado no dolía*. Podía vivir en esa especie de eternidad" (Mairal 2012: 290, my emphasis).

Even if the novel seems to fall prey to a certain Neo-Rousseauist idealization here, the idea that the past must be destroyed to quit the cycle of trauma and repetition appears as the consequent, albeit radical, conclusion of the rural experience. It is no coincidence that María's self-imposed obligation to remember the streets, places and facades of the destroyed city ceases precisely when she enters the *desierto*: "Entrar en el campo me libraba de ese mandato, lo borraba todo de una vez, al menos, en mi cabeza" (Mairal 2012: 192). As we know from the first chapter, speaking, remembering, and writing the past will only become possible once María has returned to Europe, in the timeless space of the library where maps help imagine what has been lost: "Acá las cosas no cambian" (Mairal 2012: 2).

Zooming Out: Towards a Planetary Reading of the Argentinian Scenario

After *zooming in* on the concrete aspects of the novel in the last section (analyzing the scenario on the scale of individuals and local communities), the following section will take the opposite approach of *zooming out*. Departing from Ursula Heise's claim that environmental consciousness in a globalized world entails grounding local knowledge in "an environmentally oriented cosmopolitanism" (Heise 2008: 59), the question arises as to what can be said about the relationship between the local and the global, or the local and the planetary scale, for that matter. I would like to propose three possible readings.

First, the novel can be seen as a scenario very much grounded in the local – local national history, local literary and intertextual tradition, the local imaginary of the urban and the rural *desierto*. This reading starts out from the perspective of what Dipesh Chakrabarty has called the "homo", meaning "humanity as a divided political subject" (Chakrabarty 2015: 173). *El año del desierto*, then, appears as a story about the damages and inequalities created by globalization, the Capitalocene (Jason Moore), and postcolonial politics. From this perspective, Mairal articulates a very national sense of perpetual crisis and dissolution of social cohesion. While the Argentinian *novela de anticipación* of the 90s projects the fears and obsessions of the *década menemista* into a dystopic future to produce an ironic commentary about the present (Reati 2006: 15), Mairal, writing after the crisis of 2001, paints a future that consists in the collision of the present with the past (Campisi 2019). We can see how this allegorical mode of reading privileges an archeological rather than a futurological interpretation: it frames María's trajectory as an exploration of the historical roots of the Argentinian crisis.

A second possible reading of the novel would be set on a radically different scale. It is grounded in the perspective of humanity as *anthropos*, or what Chakrabarty has called the "zoecentric view" (Chakrabarty 2015: 154). As Chakrabarty has argued, if we want to make sense of the current epoch of anthropogenic global warming, we must accompany the history of capital with a history of life on the planet. In this non-homocentric view, humans appear as "collective and unintended forms of existence of the human, as a geological force, as a species" (Chakrabarty 2015: 173–174). The history of political, economic, and social systems is embedded into the history of the Earth system. Zooming out in this way also means distancing ourselves from the assumption that we are the central actors in this story: "The idea of anthropos decenters the human by subordinating human history to the geological and evolutionary histories of the planet" (Chakrabarty 2015: 173). Reading the novel from this perspective provides us with a much broader and, in a sense, universal insight about the increasingly conflictual interaction between human and non-human agents. What is important to note here is that this reading does not cancel out the first one, but remains problematic, in permanent suspense, precisely *because* of the possibility of the first reading. In the context of this second reading, zooming out from the national scale converts Argentina into a symbol of planetary anticipation, a place with seismographic relevance in terms of the experience of progressive loss that humanity faces. It is by its local specificity that the national becomes indicative of the planetary. The act of reading operates as a double allegorical upscaling: individual experience (María) stands as an allegory for national history, but the national in turn becomes an allegory for the planetary. If we read the novel through this lens, *the central protagonist is not María, but the intemperie itself*, the effects of which are indicated or mirrored by María's behavior and emotions. The fact that the consequences of the *intemperie* are represented while its processes remain largely invisible or inexplicit in the novel is itself a scale effect. From the perspective of the human as *Being-in-the-world* (Heidegger), the spatiotemporal order of the *intemperie* as a geological force is not immediately perceptible. Instead of being the driver of the plot, María's central function consists in the visualization of the invisible.

Rather than highlighting the actions of the protagonist, then, we should focus on the *re*actions, the forced inactivity, the passive modes of dependency, acceptance and nostalgic refusal that define the human characters in the novel.

Often, this can be seen at the fringes of the diegesis – for example through María's father, who retreats into the world of television. Another instance is when the destruction of the outer city space forces the inhabitants to migrate to the center of Buenos Aires where, in turn, other inhabitants react by locking themselves up in their houses. This process mirrors the reactive politics of wealthy states like the USA or members of the European Union towards displaced people who, more and more frequently, flee due to weather-related disasters or food shortages triggered by climate change (UNHCR 2020: 9). Here, too, the human-altered, non-human world is the driving agent, compelling humans to a chain of reactions (which is not to say that the possibility that governments could change their policies does not exist – what I want to highlight is the redistribution of agency).

Another important aspect of this process in the novel is the unequally rapidly shrinking agency of women. Towards the end of her trajectory, María reflects on the connection between collapse, agency, and gender: "No era tanto el miedo que tenía sino el hartazgo de estar a merced de los hombres, así fueran *cafishos*, patrones, braucos, revolucionarios o caníbales. Quería poder decidir qué hacer y qué no hacer. Todos estos hombres me estaban llevando y arreando hacía meses" (Mairal 2012: 274). A final example of how to read the *intemperie* as the novel's main character would be to analyze how Mairal represents the increased workload that is necessary to guarantee subsistence. On the farm, work is the only activity left: "No había siesta, ni domingo, ni feriado" (Mairal 2012: 211). The link between the intensification of work and the agency of the *intemperie* is further accentuated by the acceleration of the process of desertification: "Había que desmalezar todos los días [. . .]; había que arrancarlas [las malezas, J.K.] de raíz, rebrotaban constantemente" (Mairal 2012: 211). Plants become so animated that they create fear among humans who try to control them: "Daba un poco de miedo la huerta. Parecía que respiraba. Las guías de los tomates se me enredaban en el pelo, como agarrándome, cuando las acomodaba" (Mairal 2012: 211–212). The geological force causing collapse is the negative protagonist of the novel, an active absence that negates human civilization and is only visible in its consequences and further limitations on human capacities to act.

However, this planetary reading is not an obvious one. Mairal, like many Latin American authors of *literatura de anticipación* (Reati), places national allegory in the foreground. This is why the planetary reading must be a reading against the grain, as the novel does not easily lend itself to it (making such a reading an all the more possible one). The operation of scaling is thus mostly one of reading, not of the text itself (Clark 2012). This is not only the case on the thematic and plot levels, but also on the level of syntax: regarding María's actions, the reader has to imagine an inversion of active sentences into passive ones and vice-versa. This operation is the grammatical counterpart to what new-materialist environmental historians propose when they claim that plants, animals, and minerals must be recognized as historical "actors whose agency rivals that of the human players" (Miller 2007: 2). Moreover, the *resistance* that the novel puts up against this move, actively felt by the reader, is a symptom that holds its own potential for recognition. It is precisely the resistance that our human-centered, politically-shaped perception of the world mounts against the decentering perspective of the *anthropos*. Resistance is an indicator of how the world of the New Climate Regime (Latour) negates our humanocentric attempts to make sense of it. Finally, this reading also restores the novel's futuristic aspect: we are not exclusively revisiting episodes of the past but also witnessing a projected future in which human history will be tightly limited by the growing agency of the non-human.

Naturally, the objections that postcolonial thinkers have brought forward against such a reading (namely that it conceals the politics of inequality by means of a false universalism) cannot simply be rejected outright. A third reading of *El año* comes into focus precisely when we meditate on the relationship between the first and second ones. The reciprocal negation or bracketing of interpretations uncovers their respective blind spots and repressions. From the horizon of each reading, we can see what the other one refuses to think or omits. The local is negated by the planetary dimension of the climate crisis, while the planetary is negated by the social critique of false universalism. This third reading brings forward, reflects on, and "inhabit[s] the tension" (Chakrabarty 2015: 181) between the homocentric and the zoecentric, the visible and the invisible protagonist, histories of capital and the history of life – without ever resolving any of them. Making this tension inhabitable, Chakrabarty suggests, has something to do with the conversion of the colorless, placeless narrative of climate change into a "mood"; an affective experience, tied to the concreteness of place, in this case an experience of Heideggerian thrownness – "the recognition of the otherness of the planet itself" (Chakrabarty 2015: 183). If making available to us what escapes perception necessitates constant shifting between interdependent scales by routing the experience of the "more-than-human planet [. . .] through our all-too-human communities" (Nugent 2020: 456), then Mairal's novel permits us to playfully operate this shifting by reading the text against the grain.

Works Cited

Barbas-Rhoden, Laura (2011): *Ecological Imaginations in Latin American Fiction*. Gainesville: University Press of Florida.
Bayard, Pierre (2016): *Le Titanic fera naufrage*. Paris: Minuit.

Berger, James (1998): *After The End: Representations of Post-Apocalypse*. Minneapolis/London: University of Minnesota Press.
Bonacic, Dánisa (2015): "La barbarie y el retrato mítico de la catástrofe en *El año del desierto* de Pedro Mairal". In: *Confluencia*, 31, 1, pp. 110–119.
Campisi, Nicolás (2019): "El retorno de lo contemporáneo: Crisis e historicidad en *El año del desierto* de Pedro Mairal". In: *Cuadernos LIRICO*, 20, https://journals.openedition.org/lirico/8361 (last visit: 11/12/2021).
Chakrabarty, Dipesh (2015): *The Human Condition in the Anthropocene*. The Tanner Lectures in Human Values at Yale University, <https://tannerlectures.utah.edu/_resources/documents/a-to-z/c/Chakrabarty%20manuscript.pdf> (last visit: 11/12/2021).
—— (2009): "The Climate of History: Four Theses". In: *Critical Inquiry*, 35, 2, pp. 197–222.
Charbonnier, Pierre (2019): "The splendor and squalor of collapsology. What the survivalists of the left fail to consider". In: *Revue du Crieur*, 2, pp. 88–95.
Citton, Yvey/Rasmi, Jacopo (2020): *Générations collapsonautes. Naviguer par temps d'effondrements*. Paris: Seuil.
Clark, Timothy (2012): "Scale". In: Cohen, Tom (ed.): *Telemorphosis. Theory in the Era of Climate Change*, Vol. 1. Ann Arbor: Open Humanities Press, pp. 148–166.
Diamond, Jared (2005): *Collapse: How Societies Choose to Fail or Survive*. New York/London: Viking Penguin/Allen Lane.
Drucaroff, Elsa (2010): "Narraciones de la intemperie. Sobre *El año del desierto*, de Pedro Mairal y otras obras argentinas recientes". In: *Lunes por la madrugada*, http://lunesporlamadrugada.blogspot.com/2010/06/narraciones-de-la-intemperie.html (last visit: 11/12/2021).
Dünne, Jörg (2019): *Kosmogramme. Geohistorische Skalierungen romanischer Literaturen*. Berlin: August.
Dupuy, Jean-Pierre (2002): *Pour un catastrophisme éclairé. Quand l'impossible est certain*. Paris: Seuil.
Fabry, Geneviève (2012): "El imaginario apocalíptico en la literatura hispanoamericana: Esbozo de una tipología". In: *Cuadernos LIRICO*, 7, https://journals.openedition.org/lirico/689 (last visit: 11/12/2021).
Hallstead, Susan/Dabove, Juan Pablo (2012): "Introducción". In: Pedro Mairal: *El año del desierto*. Edición a cargo de Susan Hallstead y Juan Pablo Dabove. Doral, FL: Stockcero, pp. vii–xxxiv.
Heise, Ursula K. (2008): *Sense of Place and Sense of Planet. The Environmental Imagination of the Global*. New York: Oxford University Press.
Horn, Eva (2019): "The Aesthetics of the Anthropocene". Talk given at ICI Berlin, 4. 12.2019, https://www.ici-berlin.org/events/eva-horn/ (last visit: 11/12/2021).
—— (2018 [2014]): *The Future as Catastrophe. Imagining Disaster in the Modern Age*. New York: Columbia University Press.
IFOP (2019): *Enquête internationale sur la 'collapsologie'*, https://www.jean-jaures.org/wp-content/uploads/drupal_fjj/redac/commun/productions/2020/1002/enquete_collapso.pdf (last visit: 11/12/2021).
Kermode, Frank (1967): *The Sense of An Ending. Studies in the Theory of Fiction*. New York: Oxford University Press.
Latour, Bruno (2018 [2017]): *Down to Earth. Politics in the New Climatic Regime*. Transl. Catherine Porter. Cambridge/Malden: Polity.

—— (2017 [2015]): *Facing Gaia. Eight Lectures on the New Climatic Regime*. Transl. Catherine Porter. Cambridge/Malden: Polity.
Logie, Ilse (2008): "Avatares de un mito: Manifestaciones del Apocalipsis en la literarura rioplatense contemporánea: El caso de *Insomnio* de Marcelo Cohen". In: *Biblioteca Virtual Miguel de Cervantes*, http://www.cervantesvirtual.com/nd/ark:/59851/bmc05801 (last visit: 11/12/2021).
Mairal, Pedro (2012 [2005]): *El año del desierto*. Edición a cargo de Susan Hallstead y Juan Pablo Dabobe. Doral, FL: Stockcero.
Miller, Shawn William (2007): *An Environmental History of Latin America*. Cambridge/New York: Cambridge University Press.
Monsiváis, Carlos (1995): *Los rituales del caos*. Mexico City: Era.
Moore, Jason W. (ed.) (2016): *Anthropocene or Capitalocene? Nature, History and the Crisis of Capitalism*. Oakland, CA: PM Press.
Morton, Timothy (2013): *Hyperobjects. Philosophy and Ecology after the End of the World*. Minneapolis: University of Minnesota Press.
Müller, Gesine/Siskind, Mariano (eds.) (2019): *World Literature, Cosmopolitanism, Globality. Beyond, Against, Post, Otherwise*. Berlin/Boston: De Gruyter.
Nixon, Rob (2011): *Slow Violence and the Environmentalism of the Poor*. Cambridge, MA/London: Harvard University Press.
Novaro, Marcos (2010): *Historia De La Argentina: 1955–2010*. Buenos Aires: Siglo Veintiuno.
Nugent, Carlos Alonso (2020): "Latinx Literature in the Anthropocene". In: *ISLE*, 27, 3, pp. 453–471.
Observatorio de la Juventud en Iberoamérica (2013): "El futuro ya llegó. 1ª Encuesta Iberoamericana de Juventudes", https://oji.fundacion-sm.org/el-futuro-ya-llego-primera-encuesta-iberoamericana-de-juventudes/ (last visit: 11/12/2021).
Reati, Fernando (2006): *Postales del porvenir. La literatura de anticipación en la Argentina neoliberal (1985–1999)*. Buenos Aires: Biblos.
Salvioni, Amanda (2013): "Lo Peor ya ocurrió. Categorías del Postapocalipsis hispanoamericano: Alejandro Morales y Marcelo Cohen". In: *Altre Modernità, Numero Speciale: Apocalipsis 2012*, pp. 304–316.
Semilla Durán, María A. (2010): "El Apocalipsis como deconstrucción del imaginario histórico en *El año del desierto* de Pedro Mairal". In: Fabry, Geneviève/Logie, Ilse/Decock, Pablo (eds.): *Los imaginarios apocalípticos en la literatura hispanoamericana contemporánea*. Oxford: Peter Lang, pp. 327–343.
Servigne, Pablo/Chapelle, Gauthier (2017): *L'entraide. L'autre loi de la jungle*. Paris: Les liens qui libèrent.
Servigne, Pablo/Stevens, Raphaël (2015): *Comment tout peut s'effondrer: Petit manuel de collapsologie à l'usage des générations présentes*. Paris: Seuil.
Tainter, Joseph (1990): *The Collapse of Complex Societies*. Cambridge: Cambridge University Press.
UNHCR (2020): *Global Trends. Forced Displacement in 2020*, https://www.unhcr.org/60b638e37/unhcr-global-trends-2020 (last visit: 11/12/2021).
Zimmer, Zac (2013): "A Year in Rewind, and Five Centuries of Continuity: *El año del desierto*'s Dialectical Image". In: *MLN*, 128, 2, pp. 373–383.

4 Digital Worlds: Trends and Traps

Carolina Gainza C.
Pensar la condición digital desde la literatura digital latinoamericana
apropiaciones, decolonización y tecnodiversidad

Pareciera que hoy las tecnologías y algoritmos digitales no solo eluden a los estados, manejados por las grandes empresas transnacionales de la tecnología y postergando aún más a los territorios del sur, sino que también estas mismas tecnologías buscan ir más allá de lo humano, a través del desarrollo de tecnologías de Inteligencia Artificial. Siguiendo al filósofo Yuk Hui (2000), las narrativas dominantes sobre las tecnologías contemporáneas no son más que una reelaboración del discurso del progreso occidental y moderno, lo cual implica la persistencia de ciertas formas de comprender la relación humano-tecnología, estableciendo una forma hegemónica de abordarlas y de comprender su lugar en el mundo; o, como diría el mismo filósofo, siguiendo a otros como Gilbert Simondon (2007), sus condiciones de existencia.

En los países latinoamericanos se discute la necesidad de generar tecnologías, fomentar la innovación y capacitar personas para alcanzar la sociedad de la información, convertido en el nuevo hito civilizatorio. La sociedad de la información se ha constituido como la nueva meta del progreso, un modelo, como fue antes la sociedad moderna industrial, ahora encarnado por un tipo de sociedad informacional, red, o postindustrial. En este modelo, se imponen nuevas formas de colonialismo, representados por la datificación, la algoritmización de la vida y formas de colonización de los conocimientos. Ante este panorama, poco nos hemos detenido a pensar sobre la sociedad que estamos construyendo y que queremos construir, desde Latinoamérica, lo cual implica pensar las nuevas formas de colonialidad, la relación humano-máquina desde un punto de vista situado – la tecnodiversidad como la denomina Yuk Hui (2000)–, y las formas de subjetividad que están emergiendo en este contexto.

La literatura no es ajena a estos procesos. En particular, en la literatura digital, un campo creativo que utiliza intensamente las tecnologías digitales en la creación de nuevas formas, géneros, escrituras y temáticas, es posible observar, a través de una particular experiencia estética, la relación con estas tecnologías, cómo son significadas y apropiadas. Mi interés es delinear un análisis situado de la literatura digital en América Latina desde una mirada decolonial.

Carolina Gainza C., Universidad Diego Portales, Santiago de Chile

Open Access. © 2023 the author(s), published by De Gruyter. This work is licensed under the Creative Commons Attribution-NonCommercial-NoDerivatives 4.0 International License.
https://doi.org/10.1515/9783110762143-012

Mi objetivo es explorar la siguiente pregunta: ¿De qué forma la literatura digital latinoamericana nos puede servir para pensar la relación con algoritmos y existencias digitales desde una perspectiva histórica (situada) y posthumana, que no reproduzca la visión moderna occidental, sino que fomente la tecnodiversidad e imaginarios divergentes?

En este artículo abordaré, entonces, la relación con las tecnologías digitales y los algoritmos, analizando las formas de apropiación y el campo de experiencia estética que podemos observar en la literatura digital latinoamericana. No busco respuestas definitivas, sino que más bien identificar algunos nodos problemáticos y presentar reflexiones que nos permitan abordar la cultura digital desde una perspectiva latinoamericana.

Máquinas sensibles

Uno de los fenómenos más sorprendentes del último tiempo es el de AlphaGo, aquella Inteligencia Artificial creada por el equipo de DeepMind, que ganó tres a uno a Lee Sedol en 2016, el campeón mundial de Go. Como cuenta Marcus du Sautoy (2019), 19 años antes, frente a la victoria de DeepBlue en el juego de ajedrez frente a Kaspárov, el astrofísico Piet Hut declaró al New York Times: "Seguramente habrá que esperar cien años para ver cómo un ordenador consigue ganar al Go a un ser humano, quizá más" (du Satoy 2019: 41). A pesar de los escepticismos respecto a los avances tecnológicos, en las últimas décadas el desarrollo de algoritmos inteligentes ha superado toda expectativa.

Como con toda tecnología, este desarrollo creciente ha generado toda clase de miedos y visiones apocalípticas. El ámbito de la creación artística es quizás uno en que la tecnología genera mayor recelo. Escuchamos todo el tiempo frases como: "una máquina nunca podrá reemplazar la creatividad humana" o "un algoritmo no tiene la sensibilidad que se requiere para crear". En este sentido, la creatividad artística es entendida como una característica intrínseca del ser humano, algo que, como la razón, nos separaría de otras especies y objetos, naturales y tecnológicos. La creación artística pareciera ser uno de los terrenos en los cuales nos negamos a aceptar la posibilidad de entrada de otras especies, menos de las tecnologías. Nos negamos a que una entidad no humana pueda crear algo bello. E incluso, poniendo en cuestión el concepto de belleza, que los algoritmos sean capaces de crear algo que pueda tener otra sensibilidad o estética no capturable por nosotros, humanos. De alguna manera, AlphaGo demostró que los algoritmos sí pueden crear, lo cual se ha extendido a otros ámbitos, como la pintura, la música y la literatura.

Moviéndonos hacia la literatura, podemos preguntarnos: ¿Puede escribir una máquina? Frente a esta pregunta podríamos responder, considerando diversos experimentos escriturales realizados con algoritmos e Inteligencias Artificiales, "claro que puede". Ahí surge otra pregunta, que se deriva de la anterior, ¿puede tener una máquina la sensibilidad para realizar una obra de arte que nos enmudezca, nos haga pensar, nos emocione o nos interpele? También podríamos decir que sí. Sin embargo, así como los algoritmos inteligentes o la Inteligencia Artificial nos llevan a revisar el concepto de inteligencia humana, y explorar otros tipos de inteligencia, lo mismo ocurre con la creatividad, la sensibilidad y la experiencia, en relación con los algoritmos que generan obras de arte o escrituras literarias. Entonces, en contra de las perspectivas apocalípticas respecto al fin del autor, de la literatura o del arte, me interesa pensar en las posibilidades que abren estas experimentaciones digitales y cómo podemos pensar, a partir de éstas, la relación entre tecnología, cultura y política en América Latina. En relación con esto considero que lo peor que podemos hacer es aferrarnos o volvernos hacia formas de humanismo conservadoras, sino que más bien es importante abrirnos a pensar los diversos modos de existencia, tanto de los humanos como de las máquinas.

Una perspectiva latinoamericana respecto a la relación humano-tecnología que podemos observar en las literaturas digitales, y que puede constituir una vía para identificar formas situadas de la relación humano-tecnología, debería considerar los estudios culturales y decoloniales realizados desde hace varias décadas en nuestra región y que no han sido suficientemente relacionados con el fenómeno tecnológico contemporáneo. En este sentido, en este artículo se busca establecer puentes entre la literatura digital latinoamericana, el pensamiento cultural latinoamericano y una concepción posthumana de la existencia. Pienso que las formas que adquieren los usos de las tecnologías digitales y sus lenguajes algorítmicos en la literatura digital latinoamericana pueden entregarnos algunas luces para comprender la particular configuración que adquiere la cultura digital en Latinoamérica.

Literatura digital latinoamericana

La literatura digital Latinoamericana ha crecido como campo creativo y teórico en los últimos veinte años. Dada la cantidad creciente de experimentaciones escriturales con las tecnologías digitales, así como las reflexiones teóricas en torno a esta, es posible afirmar que se trata de un campo que se ha consolidado en la región. Claudia Kozak, Anahí Ré, Verónica Gómez, Nohelia Meza, Rejane Rocha,

Alckmar Luiz Dos Santos, Jaime Alejandro Rodríguez, Leonardo Flores, Milton Läufer, Elika Ortega, Osvaldo Cleger, Perla Sasson, Luis Correa Díaz, Scott Weintraub, Roberto Cruz Arzabal, Thea Pitman, Claire Taylor, Mónica Nepote, Maria Andrea Giovine, Belén Gache, son algunos de los muchos autores que han contribuido en estas décadas a esta consolidación, siendo algunos de ellos escritores de literatura digital también. Si bien se utiliza casi indistintamente el concepto de literatura electrónica y digital (Kozak 2012) en este campo, considero que el de literatura digital es más apropiado para el tipo de escrituras a las cuales me referiré en este artículo, las cuales están basadas en la utilización de códigos digitales. Esto convierte a la literatura digital en un subconjunto de la literatura electrónica, en cuanto esta última considera expresiones analógicas, como por ejemplo la videopoesía y obras multimedia realizadas con tecnologías no digitales.

Desde mi trayectoria de investigación en literatura digital latinoamericana, considero que es posible distinguir ciertas fases de su desarrollo. Durante los noventa y principios de la primera década del siglo XX predominaron los hipertextos, hipermedias y literaturas interactivas. En una segunda fase, desde mediados de la primera década del 2000, comienzan a proliferar narrativas y poéticas generativas. Si bien este último género es anterior, en esta época se desarrolla con más fuerza utilizando el lenguaje de código digital y da origen a una reflexión sobre las posibilidades poéticas del código. Finalmente, en una tercera fase, desde el 2010 en adelante, la aparición y masificación de las redes sociales, como Facebook, Twitter e Instagram, entre otras, impulsan el desarrollo de literaturas en redes sociales. En este periodo aparecen nuevos géneros, como la *instapoesía* y la *twiteratura*. Mi interés es vincular estas etapas con una particular relación entre tecnologías digitales y creatividad en la cultura digital latinoamericana. Sin caer en esencialismos nacionalistas o regionalistas, mi hipótesis de investigación, en la que pretendo avanzar en este artículo, es que la forma que adquieren las literaturas digitales regionales está profundamente asentada en la manera de concebir la relación con la técnica y la cultura, la cual, a su vez, está marcada por procesos coloniales y perspectivas situadas. Esto permitiría comprender por qué en nuestros países se siguen ciertas trayectorias, predominan ciertas prácticas creativas, géneros y usos de software, sin caer en explicaciones simplistas respecto al atraso tecnológico latinoamericano o la copia de modelos foráneos como formas de justificar las diferencias con aquellos países y regiones que demuestran un desarrollo tecnológico más avanzado. Por supuesto esto no significa que las prácticas literarias latinoamericanas se encuentran aisladas de los fenómenos mundiales, sino que más bien me interesa abordar la pregunta por la convivencia conflictiva con estas tendencias.

Leonardo Flores cuestiona esta vinculación con tradiciones literarias nacionales o regionales, afirmando que "[l]as narrativas de continuidad son más reconfortantes que las de ruptura" (Flores 2017:11), y propone que las tecnologías digitales producen tal ruptura que vuelve inviable vincularlas con tradiciones situadas, sino que más bien surgen al alero de tendencias internacionales. Flores se pregunta: "Pero ¿qué tal si las tecnologías digitales traen un cambio de paradigma tan radical y tan ajeno a los movimientos literarios tradicionales que se puede considerar como un movimiento internacional y hasta posnacional? ¿Qué tal si la literatura electrónica sucede *a pesar* de las literaturas nacionales?" (Flores 2017: 11). De esta manera, identifica tres momentos en la literatura electrónica, los cuales serían universales en cuanto incluyen a la literatura desarrollada en las distintas regiones del mundo. Flores denomina a estos momentos "generaciones". Las dos primeras provienen de la categorización realizada por Katherine Hayles (2004), donde la primera incluye toda obra creada antes de la web, "incluyendo géneros como hipertexto, obra generativa, ficción interactiva, videopoesía y obras multimedia creadas con programación y distribuidas en medios físicos: papel impreso, disco, videocassette, CD-ROM y los comienzos de obras en redes digitales" (Flores 2017: 11). La segunda generación es situada por Flores en la mitad de los años noventa, posterior al nacimiento y popularización de la web, "se caracteriza por obras multimedia e interactivas diseñadas para distribución y recepción a través de medios digitales. Esto incluye obras creadas en HTML, JavaScript, CSS, Director, Flash y otros lenguajes de programación y programas de autoría multimedia" (Flores 2017:11). Esto es lo que corresponde en mi tipología y definición al surgimiento de la literatura propiamente digital. La tercera generación corresponde, según Flores, a "plataformas comerciales como tabletas y teléfonos inteligentes, recursos digitales que ofrecen conexiones via API (Application Programming Interface) y medios sociales como Facebook y Twitter" (Flores 2017:11). En esta tercera generación se habría producido la masificación de la literatura electrónica, dado que se trata de plataformas más accesibles y que no necesariamente requieren de conocimientos de programación.

Sin embargo, a pesar de la utilidad de las tres generaciones definidas por Flores para identificar un desarrollo general de la literatura electrónica, considero que no dan cuenta del desarrollo de la literatura digital en América Latina, porque en esta región es posible encontrar estas generaciones en otros momentos y con otras características, como definí en párrafos anteriores, y analizaré en lo que continúa de este artículo. En este sentido, me parece un ejercicio de adaptar el desarrollo de la literatura digital en América Latina a otras temporalidades, especialmente a la forma como se dio el desarrollo de la literatura electrónica en Estados Unidos, donde la relación y acceso a las tecnologías se desenvuelve de otra forma. El peligro de esta adaptación es invisibilizar las características de la cultura digital latinoamericana y sus políticas, así como la imposición de una idea de progreso, en este caso de la literatura digital, donde nuestra región siempre pareciera quedar atrás, junto con homogeneizar una idea de desarrollo que responde a las generaciones de la literatura digital observables en Estados Unidos principalmente.

Claudia Kozak, identifica la existencia de tres momentos de desarrollo de la literatura digital en América Latina que difieren de los señalados por Flores. Lo destacable en esta periodización es que Kozak da cuenta de una relación entre tendencias globales de las tecnologías y cómo las prácticas identificadas se insertan en tradiciones literarias y culturales Latinoamericanas, siendo al mismo tiempo apropiadas y subvertidas. Lo anterior permite dar cuenta de unos ritmos diferentes, prácticas colaborativas en algunos casos, y una relación con la tecnología que Kozak denomina "tecnologías sociales disruptivas" (2018: 3), siguiendo la conceptualización de tecnologías sociales realizada por Flavia Costa (2012).

La separación entre lo local y lo global que realiza Flores no me parece productiva para pensar la forma que adquiere la cultura y la literatura digital en un espacio particular, sino que más bien es importante analizar cómo interactúan. Por supuesto que existen influencias globales, pero eso no necesariamente provoca que las literaturas digitales se desanclen totalmente de las tradiciones regionales, sino que más bien continúan dialogando con las cosmovisiones locales. Esto es lo que autoras como Claudia Kozak (2012) y Mariela Yeregui (2020) han llamado "tecnopoéticas". Este concepto, a diferencia de la propuesta de Leonardo Flores, permite pensar unas literaturas digitales postcoloniales.

En efecto, como señala Yuk Hui, "[e]l modo en que vemos la tecnología como mera fuerza productiva y mecanismo capitalista para incrementar la plusvalía nos impide vislumbrar en ella el potencial descolonizador y la necesidad de desarrollar y preservar una tecnodiversidad" (2020: 13). Considero que la literatura digital es un espacio que nos permite pensar esa tecnodiversidad, es decir la relación con la tecnología desde el pensamiento latinoamericano. La literatura, entonces, como espacio desde donde es posible recuperar e imaginar diversas relaciones entre humanos y tecnologías desde una resignificación de los lenguajes a través de nuevas formas poéticas.

El objetivo de construir un archivo y preservar la literatura digital Latinoamericana, entonces, se vincula con la importancia de resguardar esa "tecnodiversidad" literaria. Es decir, visibilizar, estudiar y generar perspectivas críticas que tomen en cuenta las particularidades de este tipo de literaturas, los imaginarios que las informan y la especificidad de sus poéticas y las relaciones humano-tecnología que podemos observar en ellas.

Políticas de los archivos y repositorios digitales latinoamericanos

En la investigación desarrollada en el proyecto "cartografía crítica de la literatura digital Latinoamericana", partimos desde preguntas vinculadas a las escrituras y lenguajes digitales, sus estéticas y las formas de apropiación tecnológica. En este contexto, construimos una *Cartografía de la literatura digital latinoamericana*[1], proyecto de investigación que dirijo desde el año 2018 junto a Carolina Zúñiga, también de la Universidad Diego Portales. El proyecto tiene como objetivo generar una visualización de datos y un archivo de las obras recopiladas, que hasta ahora son 193 en español. En el proceso trabajamos en estrecha colaboración con el proyecto ATLAS[2], dirigido por la investigadora brasilera Rejane Rocha (Universidad Federal de Sao Carlos, Brasil). La visualización de datos presenta un mapa de Latinoamérica que tiene la potencialidad de expandirse y transformarse a medida que incorporamos obras. De esta manera, queríamos dar cuenta sobre cómo la literatura digital cuestiona los límites, tanto geográficos, por la movilidad de los escritores y artistas, así como la definición misma de literatura, sus géneros y lenguajes. Al entrar en alguna de las obras se accede a una ficha con información y a un enlace que dirige al archivo, el cual cuenta con imágenes de las obras y videos de navegación.

El criterio para reunir las obras obedece a la siguiente definición de literatura digital: "obras creadas para ser reproducidas en un dispositivo electrónico y que presentan estructuras hipertextuales, hipermedias e interactivas imposibles de trasladar al formato libro, o en cuyos procesos de creación se utilizan intensivamente lenguajes de programación o tecnologías de Inteligencia Artificial (bots, proyectos generativos, entre otros)". El código digital es fundamental en esta definición, ya que se trata del lenguaje que posibilita la existencia de este tipo de literatura. En este sentido, no podemos hablar de literatura digital sin hacer referencia a estos lenguajes, como señala Katherine Hayles en su ya canónico libro "Electronic Literature": "Electronic text remains distinct from print in that it literally cannot be accessed until it is performed by properly excuted code" (2008: 5).

El acto de archivar y generar repositorios de literaturas digitales se ha convertido en un eje importante de trabajo y reflexión en este campo de estudios en Latinoamérica. Podemos identificar, además de la cartografía y el proyecto

---

[1] https://www.cartografiadigital.cl/.
[2] https://atlasldigital.wordpress.com/.

ATLAS de Brasil, el repositorio Broken English[3], E-literatura[4] del Centro de Cultura Digital de México, Antología de la literatura electrónica Latinoamericana y Caribeña[5], el archivo de netart[6] que contiene algunas obras de literatura digital latinoamericana, y el proyecto "Cultura Digital" de Chile[7]. Consideramos que mapear las obras constituye una acción importante en cuanto no solo buscamos preservar e intentar garantizar el acceso a estas piezas en el futuro, sino que además nuestro objetivo es político: visibilizar la literatura digital latinoamericana en el contexto de la literatura mundial. Existe una fuerte presencia de literaturas digitales estadounidenses y europeas, con sus asociaciones, organismos y archivos que les dan una visibilidad mayor en el campo de la literatura electrónica, donde las literaturas digitales del sur parecieran no existir o tener que depender de estos espacios para ser vistas. Los repositorios y archivos de literatura digital desarrollados en América Latina permiten situar la producción literaria regional y contrarrestar no solo la perpetuación de formas de colonialismo literario, sino que también la lógica de "visibilidad algorítmica".

En efecto, los repositorios y archivos mencionados dan cuenta de un movimiento descolonizador. No solo agrupan y visibilizan obras y autores, sino que instalan preguntas respecto a formas de apropiación, regímenes estéticos y sus políticas, la existencia de relaciones diversas con la tecnología, y cómo esta es resignificada y permea la construcción de subjetividades latinoamericanas en el contexto global actual. De alguna manera, estas literaturas dan cuenta de lo que Yuk Hui llama cosmotécnicas. Hui opone a la concepción hegemónica, moderna-occidental, de la tecnología como universal antropológico, la siguiente antítesis, que constituye el eje central de su argumento: "La tecnología no es un universal antropológico; es posibilitada y constreñida por cosmologías particulares que van más allá de la funcionalidad o utilidad. Por consiguiente, no existe una única tecnología, sino múltiples cosmotécnicas" (2020: 11). Llevando la propuesta de Hui a la literatura digital latinoamericana, estas nos interrogan respecto a las formas particulares en que los lenguajes algorítmicos son utilizados, tematizados y apropiados, configurando estéticas que sitúan las tecnologías en contextos culturales determinados. Esto provoca una ruptura respecto a la idea que desde el sur global somos "consumidores" de tecnologías y literaturas, porque considera otras epistemologías y regímenes estéticos que dan un nuevo marco a la tecnología. De esta manera, en las obras de literatura digital podemos

---

3 http://brokenenglish.lol/.
4 https://editorial.centroculturadigital.mx/eliteratura.
5 http://antologia.litelat.net/.
6 https://netart.org.uy/.
7 http://culturadigitalchile.cl/.

observar ejercicios de descolonización y producción de pensamiento respecto a cómo incorporamos y transformamos las tecnologías, así como también podemos identificar el surgimiento de narrativas y poéticas que elaboran sobre los lenguajes algorítmicos, generan imaginarios, potencialidades y problematizan el lugar de estos lenguajes en la diversidad de culturas latinoamericanas.

En las literaturas incluidas en la cartografía encontramos hipertextos, hipermedias, poesía y novelas generativas —en las cuales parte o la totalidad de ellas ha sido generada por un algoritmo—, bots poéticos, y literatura creada por Inteligencia Artificial. En todas éstas existe una interacción, menor o mayor, con el lenguaje de código. En algunas, como en hipertextos e hipermedias, la programación fomenta la interacción entre lenguajes y con los operadores/lectores, donde estos son llamados a activar los códigos de estas obras a través de diversos recursos, desde presionar enlaces, activar imágenes en movimiento, realizar ejercicios de escritura, proveer de información a la obra, entre otros. En los bots y la literatura generativa encontramos escrituras automatizadas, donde los algoritmos realizan acciones que van desde ejercicios combinatorios utilizando una base de datos de escrituras hasta "aprender" de la información entregada por el programador, donde una Inteligencia Artificial genera un texto propio.

¿Puede escribir un algoritmo?

Dentro de la literatura generativa, entendida como aquella que es generada parcialmente o en su totalidad por algoritmos, en la cartografía predomina la primera, es decir, aquella en que podríamos decir que existe una "coautoría" con el algoritmo. Solo tenemos una obra incluida en la cartografía que es propiamente generada por Inteligencia Artificial, a la cual me quiero referir en este artículo. Me interesa abordarla por las preguntas que plantea respecto a las posibilidades de escritura de los algoritmos inteligentes. Se trata de la colección de cuentos *Mexica* del programador mexicano Rafael Pérez y Pérez. Si bien las primeras versiones de *Mexica* datan de fines de los noventa, la colección de veinte cuentos en formato impreso, en español e inglés, fue publicada por la editorial Counterpath en el año 2017.

La obra fue creada por un sistema de Inteligencia Artificial también llamado Mexica, el cual genera tramas de historias acerca de este pueblo mesoamericano, popularmente conocido como Azteca. El objetivo de utilizar Inteligencia Artificial, declara su autor, era investigar los procesos involucrados en la escritura creativa, a través de su simulación en este sistema. Veamos un extracto de la historia 2 contenida en el libro:

> Molesta, la princesa humilló al enemigo.
> El caballero ocelote observó al enemigo y lo atacó
> Decidido, el enemigo tomó una piedra grande y descalabró al caballero ocelote.
> La princesa le administró al caballero ocelote la poción que había preparado. Él mejoró rápidamente.
> Repentinamente, el caballero ocelote y el enemigo se enzarzaron en una dura riña.
> Sin dudarlo, el caballero ocelote le quitó hasta el último aliento de vida al enemigo.
> El caballero ocelote cortó las ataduras de la princesa. ¡Libre al fin!
> Fin. (Pérez y Pérez 2017: 5)

En esta historia podemos apreciar cómo el sistema Mexica genera una secuencia narrativa en que se narra un conflicto y cómo es resuelto. Para generar estas historias, el programa emplea una base de datos que se forma a través de "historias ejemplo", es decir es provisto de historias a partir de las cuales genera otras nuevas, de acuerdo con procesos de aprendizaje del algoritmo sobre "secuencias lógicas" de las historias. Pérez y Pérez lo describe de la siguiente manera:

> Por ejemplo, el sistema registra que cuando el caballero ocelote está enamorado de la princesa (contexto con una liga emocional), es lógico llevarle un ramo de flores, invitarla a una cena romántica, o conocer a su familia (tres posibles acciones lógicas a ejecutar); de la misma manera, si el caballero está herido (contexto con un conflicto), un acontecimiento razonable para continuar el relato es que la princesa lo cure o que el caballero muera (dos posibles acciones lógicas a ejecutar). (Pérez y Pérez 2017: 69)

Luego de evaluar estas opciones, el programa decide cuál es el camino más lógico para continuar la narrativa, siguiendo una estructura tradicional que consiste en una introducción, desarrollo, clímax y resolución, y finalmente lleva a cabo un ejercicio de autoevaluación, donde califica su propia historia y entrega un reporte de resultados. Esto último es realizado por el algoritmo, comparando la historia creada con las que se encuentran en la base de datos. Como señala su autor, "MEXICA tiene un estilo propio" (2017: 67) y agrega, "quizás algún día se reconozca este tipo de relatos como pertenecientes al estilo MEXICA" (2017: 68).

A diferencia de lo que ocurre en muchas poéticas generadas por algoritmos, en Mexica el lenguaje de códigos digitales no se limita a repetir o recrear un relato, sino que es capaz de aprender a partir de la información obtenida y generar una estética particular. Podemos ser críticos respecto a la "calidad" de estos cuentos, especialmente por la reproducción de roles de género, pero no olvidemos que el principal objetivo de Mexica no es estético- literario, sino que la creación de una poética es secundaria en relación con el objetivo de estudiar el proceso de escritura a través de la acción de una Inteligencia Artificial. Esto no significa que la misma Inteligencia Artificial no desarrolle una poética particular, y eso es justamente lo que está en discusión. La pregunta acá es: ¿puede escribir un algoritmo? Y en este sentido, la pregunta es positiva. Pero, más allá de eso, cabe preguntarse sobre la posibilidad de pensar una "estética del algoritmo" cuyas características aún no se han problematizado en profundidad y que quizás escapen a los criterios de calidad establecidos hasta el momento.

En efecto, Hayles (2017) se refiere a la necesidad de abordar una cognición no consciente de los objetos digitales y naturales, donde operan procesos que generan ensamblajes entre actores humanos y agentes no humanos. Al respecto señala:

> For example, a computer algorithm, written as instructions on paper, is not itself cognitive, for it becomes a process only when instantiated in a platform capable of understanding the instruction set and carrying it out. *That interprets information*: interpretation implies a choice. There must be more than one option for interpretation to operate. In computational media, the choice may be as simple as the answer to a binary question: one or zero, yes or no [. . .] Moreover, these commands may be nested inside each other to create quite complex decision trees. Choice here, of course, does not imply "free will" but rather programmatic decisions among alternative courses of action. (2017: 25)

Mexica toma decisiones y a partir de esto, escribe historias. Pero, más allá de separar acciones humanas y no humanas, lo relevante es comprender las complejas relaciones que ocurren tanto dentro del medio que permite la existencia de un objeto digital (Hui 2016), como con las interacciones con las acciones humanas. Una crítica de las estéticas y políticas de los objetos digitales necesariamente debe tomar en cuenta los ensamblajes y relaciones que ocurren entre los lenguajes algorítmicos y humanos. En este sentido, una cisión antropocéntrica de las máquinas no constituye un aspecto productivo para la discusión de las potencialidades creativas de los algoritmos inteligentes, así como tampoco un enfoque que sólo esté centrado en el poder de acción de los algoritmos. Como señala Hui (2016), es necesario pensar los objetos digitales y sus interacciones con los humanos desde una perspectiva relacional.

Abordar una estética de los algoritmos pasa por dejar de pensar que estos actúan para nosotros, sino que, como es posible apreciar en *Mexica*, las posibilidades de actuar y pensar con ellos. En la actitud de desinterés que se aprecia en las humanidades latinoamericanas por pensar la tecnología es posible identificar un discurso apocalíptico subyacente en el que prima la idea de que las tecnologías van a reemplazarnos—a los autores, a los libros, al ejercicio del arte. Otros investigadores de diversas áreas, tanto de las humanidades como de las ciencias de la computación, afirman que las máquinas no pueden pensar y que hacen lo que se les dice que hagan. Probablemente, los algoritmos programados llegan a los resultados esperados, pero ¿cómo lo hacen? En el campo de la Inteligencia Artificial muchas veces los mismos programadores desconocen el proceso de aprendizaje y cómo la máquina obtiene los resultados esperados. Podríamos decir que en *Mexica* el algoritmo no entiende lo que procesa, y en ese sentido es un autómata que procesa información entregada por un humano. Pero, siguiendo a Hayles (2017), esta afirmación supone una comparación con la cognición humana, y quizás ese es justamente el problema: no reconocer el "modo de existencia", como señala Simondon refiriéndose a los objetos técnicos (2007), pero, en este caso, de los objetos digitales. Las Inteligencias Artificiales y los algoritmos simulan la escritura humana en estas literaturas, pero, al mismo tiempo, van más allá de las capacidades humanas; por ejemplo, en la posibilidad de procesar grandes cantidades de información y crear algo en tiempos que los humanos no seríamos capaces de hacerlo. Pero más allá de procesar información, también imprimen una estética, una poética y generan significados. El foco, entonces, debería ser analizar la relación de co-creación entre humano y algoritmos, desde una perspectiva que reconoce el modo de existencia de este sistema y su potencialidad de creación, lo cual configura lo que llamo "la condición digital", es decir, una en que la subjetividad se construye en diálogo con las máquinas y sus formas de acción. A partir del análisis de *Mexica* es posible pensar la relación humano-tecnologías digitales, donde, como ocurre frecuentemente en la literatura digital, el trabajo con las tecnologías difumina el límite entre las disciplinas, e incluso nos lleva a preguntarnos qué es la literatura. La experimentación con los lenguajes nos lleva a hacernos preguntas disciplinares. Pero, dado que la literatura no es ajena al contexto en que surge, también es útil analizar las interrogantes que surgen de ellas para nuestra convivencia con los objetos digitales presentes en tantos aspectos de la vida contemporánea.

Esta y otras obras latinoamericanas generadas por algoritmos nos permiten reflexionar no solo sobre los lenguajes de programación como lenguajes poéticos y la función literaria que cumplen, sino que también sobre una especial configuración en la relación humano- algoritmos digitales que estas literaturas propician. En una era en que es fundamental pensar la técnica y nuestra relación con ésta, las literaturas digitales latinoamericanas establecen relaciones situadas con las tecnologías, enlazando estas experimentaciones con la tradición literaria experimental latinoamericana, así como con una particular incorporación de las tecnologías en la cultura. Nos invitan, también, a analizar las condiciones coloniales que abre la datificación y la digitalización, y, desde la literatura, cómo estas tecnologías se vinculan con la construcción de subjetividades y abren espacios para imaginar otros regímenes estéticos.

La cartografía, y otros archivos y repositorios de literatura digital generados en Latinoamérica, permiten establecer las trayectorias de uso de las tecnologías digitales en la literatura. Desde la creación de tecnologías propias, apropiaciones, uso de lenguas indígenas —una deuda de la literatura digital latinoamericana es poner atención a estas prácticas—, encontramos en la literatura digital una especial relación con los lenguajes algorítmicos digitales, los cuales son descentrados de su función hegemónica vinculada a la eficiencia, para ser ensamblados con tradiciones literarias locales. Hay una estética-política aquí, un reparto de lo sensible, como diría Rancière (2014 [2000]), donde las literaturas digitales dislocan las formas de percepción, de sensibilidad y experiencia estética establecidas, y al mismo tiempo, interrogan los usos de las tecnologías, los llevan a un terreno común, subvirtiendo sus usos.

La literatura digital como espacio para pensar la tecnodiversidad

Así como la literatura no es ajena a las tecnologías, tampoco, como bien sabemos, es ajena a diversas formas de colonialismos. En la historia del colonialismo presente en Latinoamérica, hemos vivido muchas colonialidades, la del ser, poder y del saber (Quijano 2020 [2005]), a lo que podríamos agregar la colonización tecnológica, que de alguna manera cruza las otras tres en la actualidad. Como señala Yuk Hui, la manera de relacionarnos con la técnica fue impuesta desde una visión moderna occidental, donde la tecnología moderna "sincroniza las historias no occidentales" (Hui 2020: 74), y respecto a esto señala: "Uno de los grandes fracasos del siglo XX ha sido la incapacidad de articular la relación entre lo local y la tecnología, y la dependencia de un pensamiento ecológico prácticamente estandarizado dotado de un fuerte humanismo europeo" (Hui 2020: 127). Desde esta hegemonía occidental-moderna, que continúa imponiéndose de diversas maneras, siempre surge la figura de la imitación desde nuestros países, es decir, todo lo que hacemos pareciera ser una copia de lo que se hace en occidente. La narrativa del atraso Latinoamericano en la carrera del progreso continúa presente y se reinventa en relación con lo digital: un horizonte deseado que nunca podemos alcanzar.

La escritura, entendida como tecnología, así como el libro, también constituyeron herramientas de colonización. Y así ocurre con cada tecnología hasta hoy. Sin embargo, en esos procesos, estas mismas tecnologías son subvertidas, transformadas, se crean otras, se copian, se liberan, y son apropiadas en nuestros territorios. Así, el desarrollo de las tecnologías forma parte de la cultura, y en este sentido, quizás debamos pensarlas más allá de las configuraciones hegemónicas del saber-poder. Me llama la atención que los estudios postcoloniales y decoloniales latinoamericanos actuales le pongan tan poca atención al desarrollo y usos de las tecnologías digitales, y es quizás justamente porque la tecnología no se ha pensado realmente desde las epistemologías del sur, sino que siempre ha sido vista como un dispositivo de dominación occidental-moderno. Como señala Hui, los conceptos de naturaleza y técnica "han sido heredados como universales sin ser interrogados" (Hui 2020: 80). Así, surgen las siguientes preguntas: ¿es posible establecer nuevas direcciones para nuestra relación con la técnica, desde un pensamiento situado, que abra nuevas posibilidades? ¿Cómo han sido las trayectorias de las tecnologías en Latinoamérica? ¿Cómo han sido creadas, utilizadas y apropiadas? ¿Qué tipo de relaciones humano-máquina podemos identificar en las diversas expresiones culturales locales?

Comenzando por las trayectorias, podríamos partir con la escritura occidental, como una técnica que se impone desde la conquista de América. Podríamos decir, siguiendo a Ángel Rama en *La Ciudad Letrada* (2004 [1984]), que la escritura, como proyecto represivo de las elites y representativo del proyecto moderno-colonial, es también una técnica, que junto a la tecnología libro, encarnaron ese proyecto. Sin embargo, como el mismo Rama señala, esta escritura fue constantemente intervenida por los lenguajes populares, a partir de lo cual fue apropiada, transformada y resignificada. Como señala Monsiváis en su prólogo a *La Ciudad letrada*: "Si la ciudad letrada organiza las técnicas para obtener la sumisión, de ella también provienen los proveedores de alternativas" (Monsiváis 2004: 22). Por otro lado, esta visión de mundo dominante —moderna y colonial— que viene con la escritura, convivió con las visiones de mundo de las poblaciones locales, donde, por ejemplo, en las poblaciones amerindias la relación entre naturaleza y cultura, así como entre lo humano y no humano, era diferente. Si bien se ha estudiado bastante la cosmovisión de poblaciones amerindias respecto a la relación naturaleza y cultura (Danowski/Viveiros de Castro 2019), poco se ha considerado el lugar de la tecnología en esa relación. En Latinoamérica, antes de la llegada de los españoles, es posible distinguir distintas culturas que habían alcanzado altos grados de desarrollo social, cultural, político y también tecnológico. Según Lechtman "[l]as sociedades andinas sirven como un excelente punto de partida para el estudio de la tecnología en la cultura" (1981: 17).

El proyecto colonial construyó un imaginario donde el progreso y la modernización se oponían a estas formas de ver el mundo, siendo consideradas atrasadas, prehistóricas y "mágicas". En el caso de las cosmologías andinas, la relación entre la naturaleza y lo humano implicaba que la tecnología tenía un límite: la naturaleza misma. Pero para el proyecto moderno, esto no existe: la naturaleza es un objeto para ser explotado por el ser humano, no tiene agencia. La imposición del proyecto colonial, como señala Quijano (2020 [2005]), no sólo se plantea como una superioridad étnica del europeo (colonialidad del poder), sino que también esta superioridad se establece en el plano epistémico (colonialidad del saber). Occidente no sólo monopolizó las relaciones de producción que serían la base del capitalismo, sino que además concentró bajo su hegemonía la producción de conocimiento. Actualmente persiste la colonialidad bajo otras técnicas, conceptos y formas de hegemonía: una colonialidad digital que obedece a un nuevo discurso del progreso apoyado en las tecnologías de la inteligencia artificial, la datificación y la algoritmización de la vida. Problematizar esta forma hegemónica de concebir la tecnología, especialmente desde los estudios culturales y postcoloniales latinoamericanos, constituye tanto un imperativo como una oportunidad de ver las posibilidades descolonizadoras de las tecnologías. Siguiendo a Hui: "El modo en que vemos la tecnología como mera fuerza productiva y mecanismo capitalista para incrementar la plusvalía nos impide vislumbrar en ella el potencial descolonizador y la necesidad de desarrollar y preservar una tecnodiversidad" (2020: 13).

Analizar las trayectorias de la tecnología en América Latina —en comunidades amerindias, clases populares, comunidades rurales o en proyectos nacionales— es relevante porque permite identificar narrativas, imaginarios y cosmologías tecnodiversas, las cuales obedecen a epistemologías diferentes a las occidentales, y que, a pesar de las formas de colonialidad del poder y del saber, sobrevivieron en prácticas culturales (apropiaciones, hackeos) y artísticas (literatura y otras formas de arte) que se apropiaron, crearon y resignificaron la tecnología. Por otro lado, analizar estas trayectorias de la tecnología en la región nos permitiría tematizar y abordar la relación humano-tecnología, que hoy constituye un imperativo para comprender nuestro lugar en el mundo desde una perspectiva descolonizadora. Esto implica analizar las relaciones entre agentes humanos y no humanos, donde las cosmovisiones amerindias pueden entregarnos algunas luces, "rechazando una interpretación unidireccional y modernista de la técnica que la toma como una esencia ontoantropológica que florece triunfal en la historia" (Danowski y Viveiros de Castro 2019: 180). Esto implica repensar la técnica y ampliarla, porque como señala Hui: "Sería sospechoso no tematizar la tecnología si se quiere sobrepasar la modernidad y la posmodernidad" (2020: 14).

Considero que la literatura digital latinoamericana constituye un terreno propicio para explorar las diversas trayectorias de la tecnología en la región, y su vínculo con la estética, la política y la diversidad de escrituras, humanas y no humanas. Las literaturas que experimentan con el código, es decir, aquellas que, a través de la interacción con los lenguajes de programación, dan origen o posibilitan lo que he llamado "estéticas digitales", permiten analizar las nuevas formas de organizar la creatividad, que avanza de forma paralela y se entremezcla con las que ya conocemos: escritura, tecnología libro, narraciones, temporalidad lineal. Estas últimas no fueron solo innovaciones tecnológicas, recordemos que la escritura y el libro no son solo técnicas, sino que se constituyeron en formas culturales que tuvieron un impacto histórico, en lo social, lo cultural y lo político.

El manejo de las técnicas de la escritura, la lectura y todo lo relacionado, posteriormente, con el sistema del libro (circulación, producción, recepción) se transformó en un campo de batalla cultural que se libró durante siglos, y que produjo exclusiones, dominaciones y formas de colonización, cuestión que Ángel Rama describe en *La ciudad Letrada* en relación con Latinoamérica.

La cultura digital, y en particular la literatura digital, como nueva forma de organizar la creatividad en nuestras sociedades contemporáneas no solo tiene que ver con "innovaciones técnicas" sino que asistimos al surgimiento de sistemas culturales que descansan sobre la lógica algorítmica. Cuando vemos una película en nuestro computador, jugamos un videojuego, navegamos en internet, lo que estamos haciendo es activar algoritmos, y descubriendo lo que estas operaciones generan. Asistimos a nuevas formas de percepción y experiencia, lo cual nos lleva a preguntarnos no solo sobre el funcionamiento de los algoritmos, sus dimensiones de eficacia y eficiencia, sino que también sobre sus estéticas y poéticas. Como señala Marcus du Satoy: "el arte generado por los ordenadores proporciona una herramienta sorprendentemente poderosa para entender cómo funciona la programación que los dirige" (2019: 13).

La interacción entre diversos lenguajes humanos y digitales permite generar una experiencia en la cual podemos "sentir" el código, es decir, un lenguaje que permite la manipulación, la extensión y la intervención, y que he llamado "hackeo cultural". En efecto, los algoritmos son lenguajes que moldean la experiencia humana contemporánea. Las literaturas digitales, al existir en estos lenguajes, posibles de manipular, generan en el lector/operador/jugador un "deseo" de intervenir, los caminos, las imágenes, y de esta forma, se abren posibilidades de apropiación. Los sujetos, entonces, no solo interpretan las obras, sino que deben actuar materialmente sobre ellas, activar sus códigos, lo que despliega diversas acciones en los dispositivos, que van desde la activación de códigos simples hasta formas de generación automática de escrituras. De esta forma, la experiencia estética digital que podemos observar en estas obras está marcada por formas de intervención e interacción con lenguajes digitales que son performados por los dispositivos que operamos.

Es así como emergen posibilidades. La literatura digital contiene una potencia que posibilita imaginar una descolonización de los algoritmos, descentrarlos de sus funciones y significados dominantes en el capitalismo actual, liberarlos de las amarras de la eficiencia y desautomatizarlos. Tomar el mando del lenguaje, no como "interactuados", es decir, sujetos pasivos ante la tecnología, sino que como "interactuantes", es decir, desde prácticas de apropiación y construcción de sentido respecto a nuestra relación con estas agencias no humanas digitales. Junto con esto, se abre la posibilidad de pensar el lugar y estatus de la tecnología de forma situada, más allá de las narrativas e imaginarios hegemónicos.

Bibliografía

Costa, Flavia (2012): "Tecnologías sociales". En: Kozak, Claudia (ed.): *Tecnopoéticas argentinas. Archivo blando de arte y tecnología*. Buenos Aires: Caja Negra, pp. 211–224.
Danowski, Déborah/Viveiros de Castro, Eduardo (2019): *¿Hay un mundo por venir? Ensayo sobre los miedos y los fines*. Buenos Aires: Editorial Caja Negra.
Du Sautoy, Marcus (2019): *Programados para crear. Cómo está aprendiendo a escribir, pintar y pensar la inteligencia artificial*. Barcelona: Acantilado.
Flores, Leonardo (2017): "La literatura electrónica latinoamericana, caribeña y global: generaciones, fases y tradiciones". En: *Artelogie*, 11. DOI:10.4000/artelogie.1590.
Hayles, Katherine (2017): *Unthought. The Power of the Cognitive Nonconscious*. Chicago: The University of Chicago Press.
—— (2008): *Electronic Literature. New Horizons for the Literary*. Indiana: University of Notre Dame Press.
—— (2004): "Print is flat: code is deep: the importance of media-specific análisis". *Poetics Today*, 25, 1, pp. 67–90.
Hui, Yuk (2020): *Fragmentar el futuro. Ensayos sobre tecnodiversidad*. Trad. Tadeo Lima. Buenos Aires: Editorial Caja Negra.
—— (2016): *On the Existence of Digital Objects*. Minneapolis: University of Minnesota Press.
Kozak, Claudia (2018): "Comunidades experimentales y literatura digital en Latinoamérica". En: *Virtualis*, vol. 9, No. 17, pp. 9–35. https://www.revistavirtualis.mx/index.php/virtualis/article/view/272 (última visita: 10/01/2022).
—— (ed.) (2012): *Tecnopoéticas argentinas. Archivo blando de arte y tecnología*. Buenos Aires: Editorial Caja Negra.
Lechtman, Heather (1981): "Introducción". En: Lechtman, Heather/Soldi, Ana María (eds.): *La tecnología en el mundo andino. Runakunap Kawsayninkupaq Rurasqankunaoa*. México: Universidad Autónoma de México, pp. 11–22.
Monsiváis, Carlos (2004): "*La ciudad letrada*: la lucidez crítica y las vicisitudes de un término". En: Rama, Angel [1984]: *La ciudad letrada*. Santiago: Tajamar Editores.
Pérez y Pérez, Rafael (2017): *Mexica*. Denver: Counterpath.
Quijano, Aníbal (2020 [2005]): "Colonialidad del poder, eurocentrismo y América Latina". En: Lander, Edgardo (ed.): *La colonialidad del saber: Eurocentrismo y ciencias sociales*. Buenos Aires: CLACSO, pp. 219–264.
Rama, Ángel (2004 [1984]): *La ciudad letrada*. Santiago: Tajamar Editores.
Rancière, Jacques (2014 [2000]): *El reparto de lo sensible. Estética y política*. Trad. Mónica Padró. Buenos Aires: Prometeo.
Simondon, Gilbert (2007): *El modo de existencia de los objetos técnicos*. Buenos Aires: Prometeo Libros.
Yeregui, Mariela (2020): "Tecnopoéticas subalternas (o algunos apuntes para desandar territorios)". En: *LiminaR. Estudios Sociales Y Humanísticos*, Vol. 18, No. 2, pp. 76–90. https://doi.org/10.29043/liminar.v18i2.759.

Carolina Ferrer
Convergencias y divergencias de la globalización y las humanidades digitales: constitución, circulación y desaparición de tendencias conceptuales

A comienzos del año 2020, basándose en el indicador *Elcano Global Presence Index*, Iliana Olivié y Manuel Gracia (2020) se preguntaban sobre la posibilidad de que la pandemia de COVID-19 signifique el fin de la globalización. Si bien estos investigadores consideran que es demasiado temprano para pronunciarse sobre ello, proponen tres escenarios posibles comparando el periodo postpandémico a las consecuencias de la crisis financiera de 2008. Análogamente, en el presente estudio nos proponemos analizar la evolución del concepto de globalización en el ámbito cultural, a través de la utilización de indicadores cienciométricos. De esta forma, actualizamos nuestra investigación anterior (Ferrer 2010) sobre el cambio de paradigma ocurrido a fines del siglo XX, momento en que la postmodernidad (Bertens/Natoli 2002; Hassan 2003) comienza a declinar al mismo tiempo que se observa la importancia creciente del concepto de globalización (Dirlik 1994, 2007; Lewellen 2002). Asimismo, en dicha época, los avances tecnológicos de la informática provocan el surgimiento de las humanidades digitales (Schreibman/Siemens/Unsworth 2004, 2016) y, un poco más adelante, observamos la irrupción de los datos masivos o *big data* (Boyd/Crawford 2012; Mayer-Schönberger/Cukier 2013). Sin embargo, dentro del contexto de la pandemia y del confinamiento que obliga a realizar actividades en modo virtual, cabe preguntarse si la epidemia de COVID-19 afecta de la misma manera la globalización que la evolución de las humanidades digitales.

Cabe destacar que el enfoque aquí utilizado difiere de las perspectivas tradicionales descendentes o *top-down* para desarrollar una perspectiva ascendente o *bottom-up*. De hecho, nuestro estudio se basa en millones de referencias contenidas en las bases bibliográficas que son el resultado de investigaciones realizadas por miles de académicos del mundo entero desde hace varias décadas. Por ello, podemos afirmar que este análisis se fundamenta en la ley de los grandes números y, al mismo tiempo, es tributario de las investigaciones efectuadas por la comunidad académica internacional.

Carolina Ferrer, Université du Québec à Montréal

Epidemiología de las ideas

Desde el punto de vista teórico, esta investigación se basa en la cienciometría, específicamente en modelos relativos a la constitución de paradigmas (Kuhn 1962), de surgimiento de especialidades científicas (Budd/Hurt 1991; Crane 1972; Price 1963; Tabah 1996) y de propagación de conceptos (Ackermann 2006; Goffman/Newill 1967; Tabah 1996).

A comienzos de los años sesenta, Derek de Solla Price (1963) estudia el comportamiento de diversas variables relativas al desarrollo de la ciencia. Específicamente, al observar la evolución de las publicaciones científicas, llega a la conclusión de que esta puede ser representada por la función logística: al comienzo, hay un incremento exponencial hasta un punto de inflexión, luego la tasa de crecimiento disminuye hasta llegar a un nivel de saturación.

Aproximadamente en esa misma época, Goffman/Newill (1964) proponen una generalización de la teoría epidemiológica y la utilizan para estudiar la transmisión de las ideas. En la presentación de su analogía, afirman: "People are susceptible to certain ideas and resistant to others. Once an individual is infected with an idea he may in turn, after some period of time, transmit it to others. Such a process can result in an intellectual 'epidemic'" (Goffman/Newill 1964: 225). Sin embargo, los autores señalan la existencia de varias diferencias entre estos dos procesos. La principal de ellas es que las epidemias culturales son esencialmente deseables, no así las enfermedades.

Con posterioridad a los trabajos de estos científicos, varios investigadores han utilizado los modelos epidemiológicos para analizar la difusión de las ideas. En los últimos años, algunos estudios han insistido en el aspecto intencional de las epidemias intelectuales. Por ejemplo, Bettencourt et al. afirman:

> First, people intentionally seek ways to extend the infectious period of an idea, usually by recording it and storing it in various documents. In this sense, the lifetime of an idea can largely transcend that of individuals. Second, short of vaccination the most effective strategy to stop a disease epidemic is through isolation, which reduces the contact rate. Ideas, unlike diseases, are usually beneficial and thus people's behavior tends to maximize effective contacts. (Bettencourt et al. 2006: 533)

Asimismo, una serie de publicaciones se dedican a analizar el papel desempeñado por las redes de investigadores en la difusión de las ideas. Paralelamente, otros estudios se proponen identificar el proceso de creación del conocimiento. Tal como lo señalan Lambiotte/Panzarasa:

> The juxtaposition of ideas in the mind of an individual may lead to syntheses and to the emergence of new ideas that can then diffuse and reach other individuals and cascade through the social network (Rogers, 2003; Valente, 1995). This propagation may in turn result

> in further syntheses and in the emergence of other new ideas which are then diffused and so on, thereby leading to a sequence of self-reproducing flows of new ideas. In principle, a good model for innovation and knowledge creation should therefore incorporate these two types of ingredients: synthesis and diffusion. (Lambiotte/Panzarasa 2009:186)

Como podemos constatar, en las últimas décadas, los modelos epidemiológicos se han vuelto cada vez más sofisticados con el propósito de estudiar la evolución de las ideas. Si bien estos han sido esencialmente utilizados en el análisis del crecimiento de las especialidades científicas, a nuestro parecer, podríamos obtener resultados interesantes si los empleamos para observar la evolución de conceptos más amplios. En este caso en particular, nuestro propósito es explorar la difusión de determinados conceptos relativos, por un lado, a la globalización —y otras tendencias culturales— y, por otro lado, las transformaciones provocadas por los cambios tecnológicos —especialmente el surgimiento de la ciencia de datos, las humanidades digitales y otras innovaciones afines— en diversas disciplinas.

Obviamente, para desarrollar el enfoque de la propagación de las ideas es necesario seguir el camino trazado por Derek de Solla Price e introducir la cienciometría. Inicialmente desarrollada por Price y Nalimov, la cienciometría —cuyo objeto es la medición de la actividad de investigación en ciencia y tecnología— se empezó a desarrollar en los años sesenta basándose, paralelamente, en la conceptualización de indicadores bibliométricos y en la construcción de un sistema de archivos de publicaciones académicas, hoy conocido como *Web of Knowledge*.

En el presente estudio, introducimos este enfoque para analizar los datos de otros bancos electrónicos: la *Modern Language Association International Bibliography*[1] y *Scopus*. Obviamente, la utilización de estas bases representa múltiples desafíos puesto que, a diferencia de *Web of Knowledge*, estas no fueron desarrolladas teniendo en cuenta la posibilidad de efectuar mediciones bibliométricas de su contenido. Sin embargo, dichas bases de datos nos parecen las más pertinentes para estudiar la evolución de los conceptos relacionados con determinadas tendencias culturales —globalización y otras—, así como los cambios relativos a las tecnologías de la información y las interrelaciones entre ellos.

Constitución de las muestras

En términos metodológicos, procedimos a la extracción de los metadatos de las publicaciones contenidas en *Scopus* y *MLA*. *Scopus* es una base bibliográfica

---
[1] De ahora en adelante, nos referiremos a esta base utilizando la sigla *MLA*.

que contiene más de 75 millones de referencias de diversas disciplinas, de los cuales 68 millones corresponden a publicaciones posteriores a 1970. Los tipos de documentos son artículos científicos, actas de congresos y libros.

MLA es la principal base de datos bibliográficos en literatura, contiene más de 3 millones de referencias y cubre 4 400 publicaciones periódicas. Esta base registra las referencias de 1850 al presente e incluye datos relativos a artículos, libros, capítulos de libros y tesis.

Para extraer la información, utilizamos el método de "palabra clave" (Callon/Courtial/Penan 1993), con el propósito de compilar las series de publicaciones relativas a los diferentes conceptos. Por un lado, obtuvimos los metadatos relativos a las grandes tendencias culturales: globalización, postcolonialismo, postmodernismo, decolonialidad, post-global, y, por otro lado, aquellos relacionados con los cambios tecnológicos: humanidades digitales, inteligencia artificial, ciencia de datos, *big data*. Por último, compilamos los metadatos relativos al concepto de pandemia. En todos los casos, utilizamos diferentes truncamientos de los términos en inglés. Las muestras obtenidas de *Scopus* totalizan más de 700.000 referencias y las de *MLA* aproximadamente 35.000 documentos. Para cada serie de documentos, elaboramos diversos indicadores.

Tendencias conceptuales contemporáneas

El Gráfico 1 corresponde a las muestras de publicaciones acumuladas desde el inicio de cada base bibliográfica, según los términos conceptuales indicados. Inmediatamente, constatamos la diferencia en el número de publicaciones, así como la importancia disciplinaria relativa. En el caso de *MLA*, la serie más importante corresponde a la del postcolonialismo, seguida por las del postmodernismo y de la globalización, mientras que aquellas relativas a los términos relacionados con las tecnologías de la información son bastante reducidas. La serie relativa a la pandemia es muy pequeña. Por el contrario, en *Scopus*, las series relacionadas con la informática son muy voluminosas, especialmente aquellas sobre inteligencia artificial y *big data*. Las publicaciones sobre la pandemia son también muy significativas en esta base de datos. Luego se sitúa la muestra sobre la globalización.

Al observar el Gráfico 2, que corresponde a las publicaciones en términos porcentuales, queda aún más en evidencia el sesgo hacia las humanidades de la base *MLA*, mientras que en *Scopus* constatamos la preponderancia de la informática y las ciencias biológicas.

Ahora bien, con el propósito de analizar las series temporales, obtuvimos las tendencias para los conceptos de 1970 a 2020. El Gráfico 3 corresponde a las referencias de *Scopus*. En particular, se destacan las publicaciones sobre inteligencia artificial, que superan las 350.000 referencias y crecen a tasas muy altas desde el comienzo. Si bien las series relativas a *big data*, humanidades digitales y ciencia de datos son mucho más recientes, éstas también experimentan grandes aumentos año tras año. La más importante de estas tres es aquella sobre *big data* con más de 86.000 publicaciones acumuladas en 20 años. Cabe destacar que las publicaciones sobre el concepto de pandemia, cuyo volumen acumulado asciende a más de 200.000 referencias, el año 2020 presentan un incremento de 65 veces con relación al año anterior, hecho evidentemente causado por el COVID-19. Las publicaciones contenidas en *Scopus* relativas a globalización, 49.000 referencias acumuladas, postcolonialismo, 13.000 referencias, y decolonialidad, 7.000 referencias, son de volúmenes mucho más reducidos que las anteriores, si bien estas tendencias muestran aumentos anuales sostenidos desde los años 1990. Al contrario, de 2013 en adelante, la serie sobre el postmodernismo, con un total de 12.000 referencias acumuladas, muestra incrementos muy reducidos y a veces disminuciones. La serie del término post-global, que se inicia a comienzos del siglo XXI, es muy reducida y no presenta grandes incrementos.

En el caso de las referencias contenidas en *MLA*, Gráfico 4, observamos una importancia relativa absolutamente opuesta: las series de publicaciones sobre el postcolonialismo y el postmodernismo son las más significativas, superando las 13.000 y 12.000 referencias acumuladas, respectivamente. Sin embargo, mientras las referencias del postcolonialismo aumentan sostenidamente desde comienzos de los 1990, aquellas sobre el postmodernismo disminuyen ostensiblemente desde el comienzo del siglo XXI. Ello viene a confirmar nuestra investigación de 2008 sobre el cambio de paradigma ocurrido a comienzos de los años 2000, que marca el fin de dicha matriz cultural y que coincide con la irrupción de la globalización. Aunque esta última tendencia muestra su apogeo en el 2010 con 454 publicaciones, el número de publicaciones anuales sobre la globalización supera desde entonces aquellas sobre el postmodernismo, y muestra más de 7.000 publicaciones acumuladas. En *MLA*, las referencias sobre decolonialidad no son muy significativas y aquellas sobre post-global son inexistentes. Las publicaciones relativas a humanidades digitales e inteligencia artificial no son muy importantes, con totales acumulados inferiores a 600 documentos. Las publicaciones sobre pandemia y *big data* son muy recientes y prácticamente insignificantes.

A su vez, el Gráfico 5 corresponde a la distribución lingüística de las publicaciones de *Scopus*. El inglés se impone claramente como idioma de publicación, superando el 84% de los documentos. Cabe destacar la presencia del mandarín o chino en las series relativas a inteligencia artificial, *big data* y pandemia. Luego viene el castellano que se destaca en las series sobre postmodernismo y decolonialidad. El resto de las publicaciones están distribuidas en otros 46 idiomas.

El Gráfico 6 representa la distribución lingüística de las series de *MLA*. En todas ellas, las publicaciones en inglés superan el 73% de las muestras. Luego vienen los documentos en castellano, francés y alemán. Finalmente, hay otros 38 idiomas que individualmente no superan el 1% de las publicaciones de la muestra.

En el Gráfico 7, presentamos las publicaciones de *Scopus* por disciplina. Desde luego, en las series relativas a inteligencia artificial y *big data* observamos la gran importancia de la informática, las matemáticas y la ingeniería, mientras que en aquella sobre pandemia constatamos la preponderancia de la medicina, la bioquímica y la inmunología. Obviamente, la presencia de las ciencias sociales, de las artes y las humanidades es mucho más significativa en las publicaciones sobre postcolonialismo, decolonialidad y postmodernismo, donde cada una acumula más del 30% de las referencias. En el caso de la serie de la globalización, las ciencias sociales representan el 39% de la muestra. Sin embargo, la participación de artes y humanidades es de sólo 11%, por cuanto administración de empresas y economía superan individualmente el 10% de las publicaciones. Confirmamos así que, como lo señaláramos el 2010, el fin del postmodernismo y el surgimiento de la globalización no sólo significa un cambio de paradigma cultural, sino además provoca una transformación disciplinaria, donde las humanidades pierden terreno con relación a las ciencias económicas y administrativas. Evidentemente, al analizar las series relativas a los cambios tecnológicos, la importancia de las ciencias sociales y las artes es mucho menor, excepto en la muestra sobre las humanidades digitales.

El Gráfico 8 representa las publicaciones por país. Salvo en el caso de la serie *big data*, donde el principal país es China, el lugar de publicación que acumula el más alto porcentaje corresponde a Estados Unidos. Como podemos observar, 20 países representan, individualmente, el 1% o más de la muestra total. Entre ellos, sólo encontramos 4 países pertenecientes al Sur Global: China, India, Brasil e Irán. Cabe destacar la importancia de la China, especialmente en las series sobre inteligencia artificial y ciencia de datos, además del caso de *big data* antes mencionado. La lista completa de países incluye cerca de 200 localidades o naciones, que conjuntamente representan el 21% de la muestra.

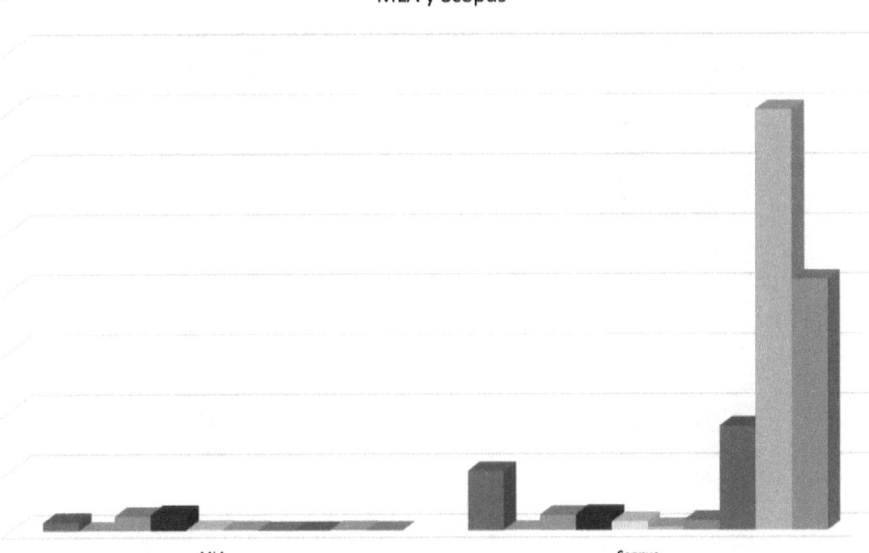

Gráfico 1: Publicaciones por concepto (MLA y Scopus).

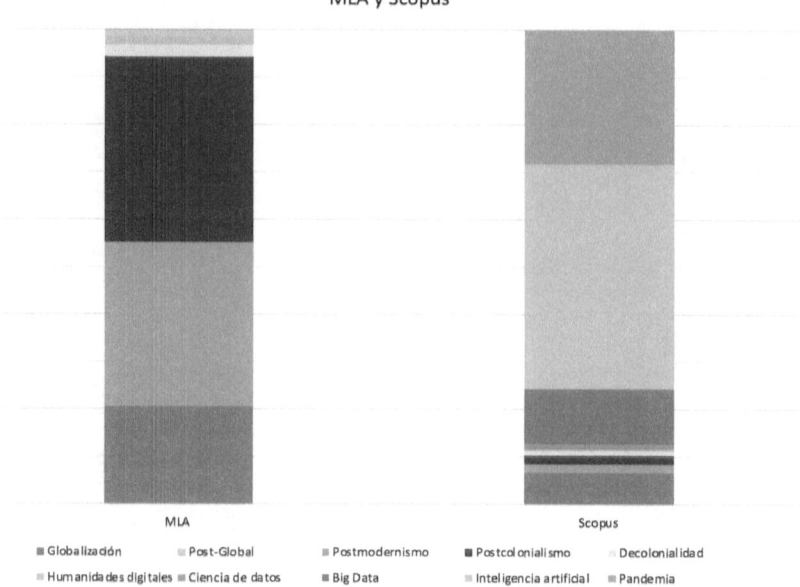

Gráfico 2: Publicaciones por concepto en términos porcentuales (MLA y Scopus).

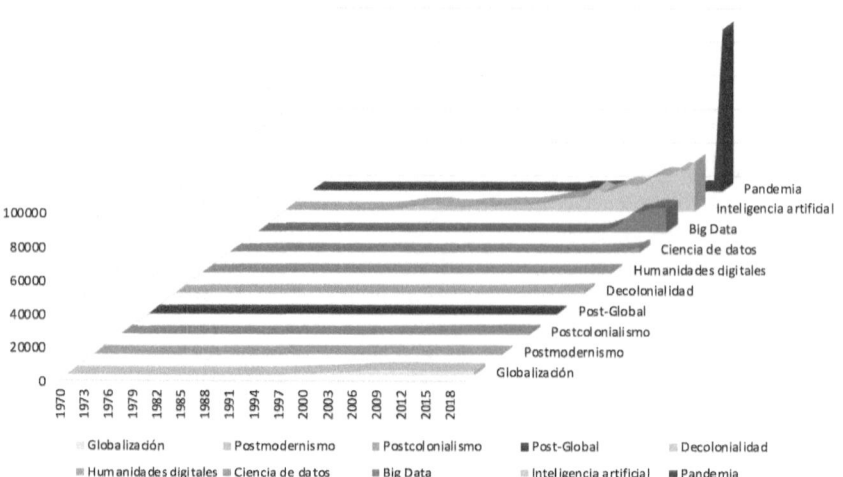

Gráfico 3: Cronologías de las publicaciones por concepto (Scopus 1970–2020).

Convergencias y divergencias —— 217

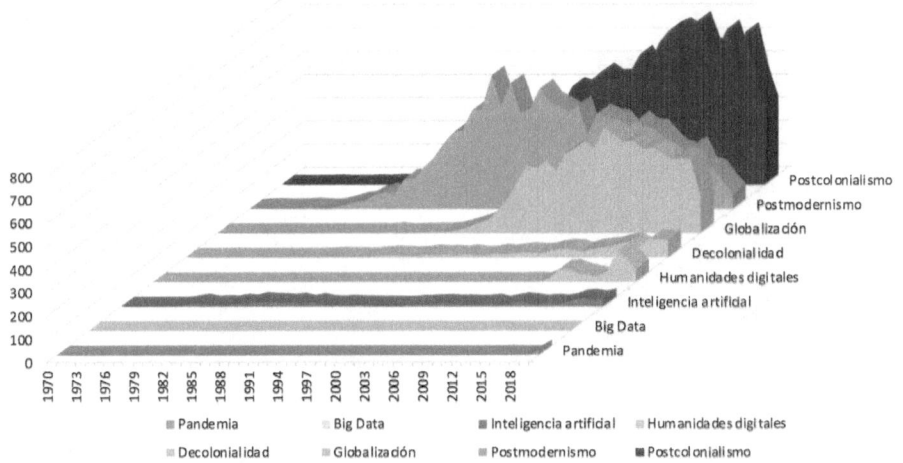

Gráfico 4: Cronologías de las publicaciones por concepto (MLA 1970–2020).

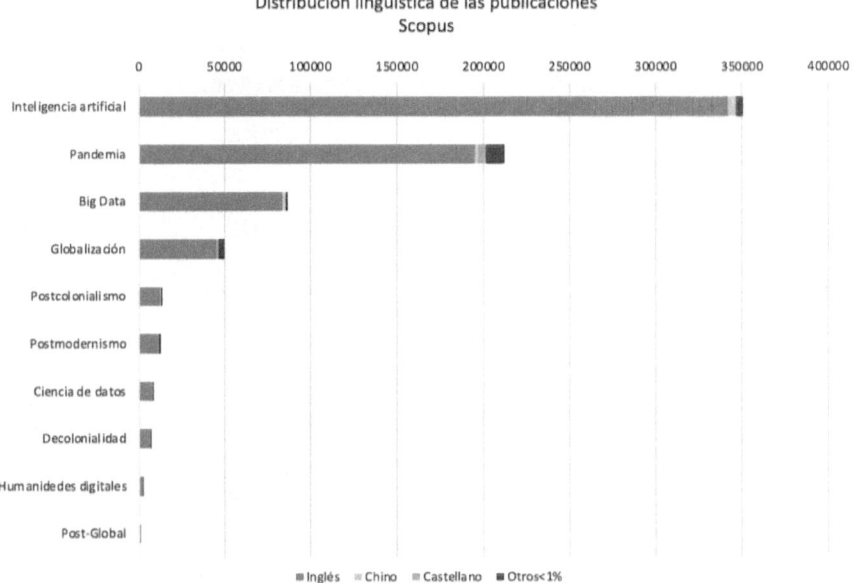

Gráfico 5: Distribución lingüística de las publicaciones (Scopus).

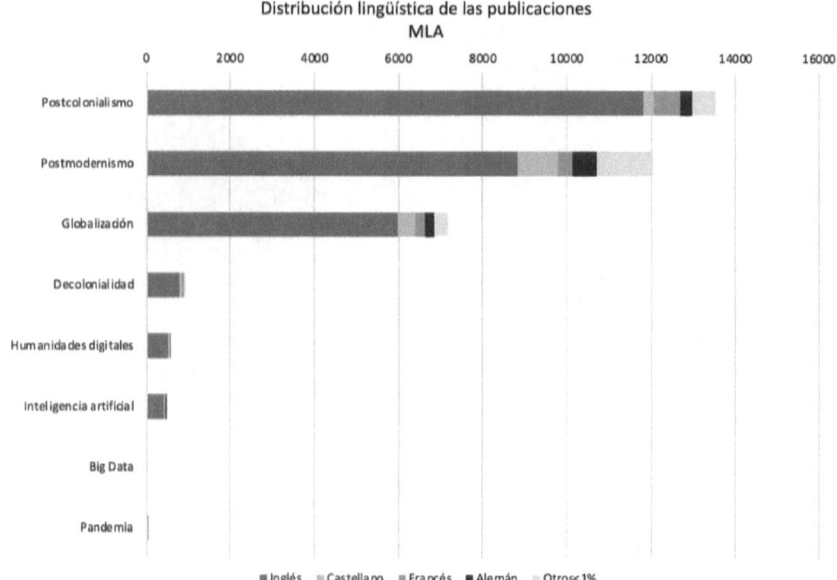

Gráfico 6: Distribución lingüística de las publicaciones (MLA).

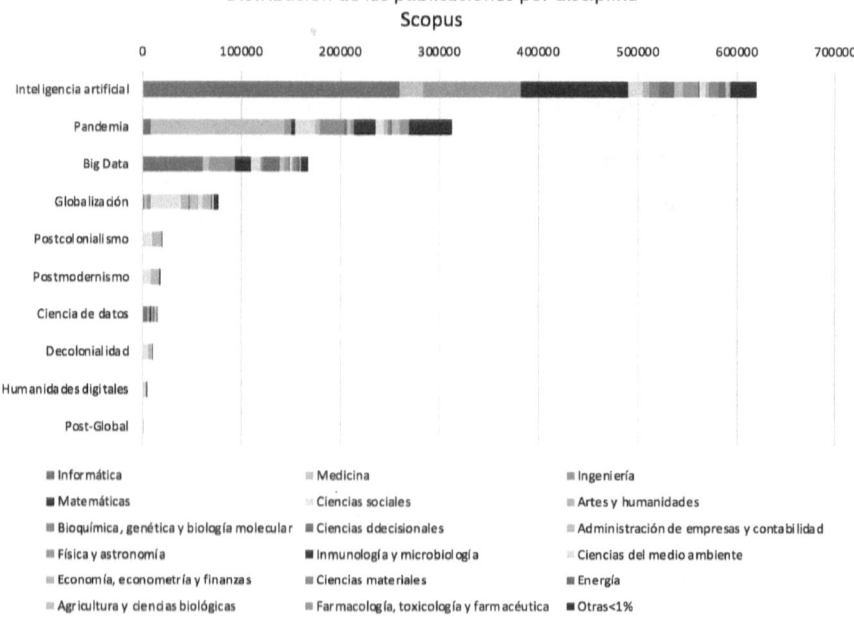

Gráfico 7: Distribución de las publicaciones por disciplina (Scopus).

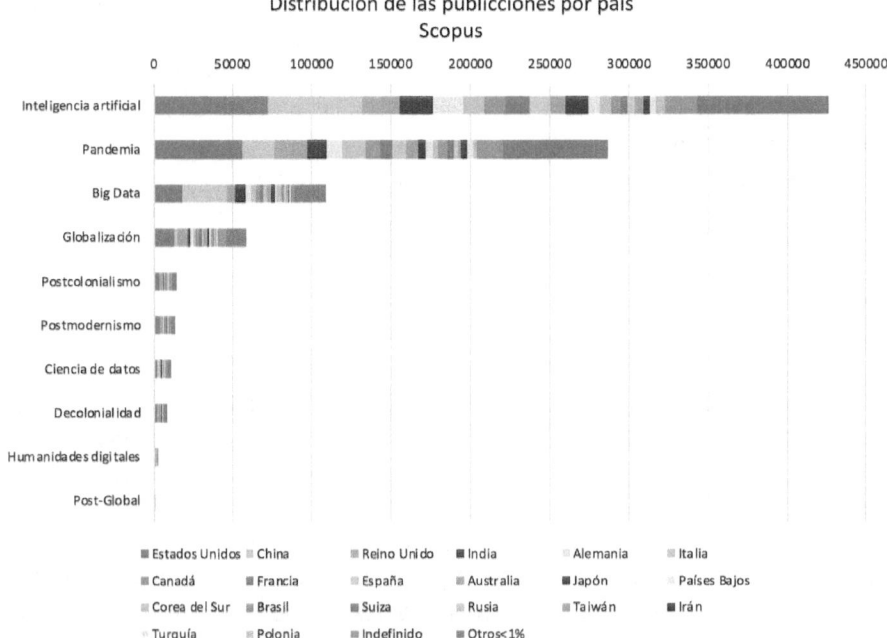

Gráfico 8: Distribución de las publicaciones por país (Scopus).

Análisis de resultados

A la luz de estos indicadores, podemos afirmar que los conceptos que se inscriben dentro de las ciencias llamadas exactas generan un volumen más importante de publicaciones, como lo demuestran las referencias de Scopus. Constatamos que la mayoría de los documentos son generados por los países del Norte Global y corresponden a documentos publicados principalmente en inglés. El análisis de las series de publicaciones relativas a los conceptos seleccionados nos ha permitido mostrar el contexto particular que atraviesa el mundo en una perspectiva temporal más amplia. En particular, con relación a las tendencias en el tiempo, constatamos que determinadas ideas pasan por procesos relativamente largos antes de establecerse como subespecialidad o de constituir una tendencia estable. Asimismo, observamos que un cambio de paradigma, tal como el fin del posmodernismo y el surgimiento de la globalización, puede traducirse, más allá de la transformación intelectual, en un reposicionamiento de las disciplinas.

Por lo demás, los acontecimientos importantes, tal como la pandemia de COVID-19, pueden provocar rápidamente una respuesta de parte de los investigadores, lo que conlleva un aumento muy significativo en el número de publicaciones sobre el tema en cuestión. Al contrario, observamos que determinados conceptos no logran imponerse, por cuanto sólo generan un número limitado de publicaciones. Tal pareciera ser el caso del término post-global. De ser así, esta última tendencia constituiría lo que Tabah (1996) y luego Ackermann (2006) han denominado epidemia de información fallida.

Conclusiones

La utilización de la perspectiva ascendente o *bottom-up* nos ha permitido estudiar la evolución de las tendencias conceptuales basándonos en miles de referencias que son el resultado de investigaciones realizadas por la comunidad académica mundial. De esta forma, los resultados obtenidos provienen de muestras significativas que hemos analizado gracias a la elaboración de indicadores temporales, lingüísticos, disciplinarios y geográficos. En este sentido, nos parece pertinente insistir en la gran riqueza de información contenida en las bases bibliográficas y en la importancia de desarrollar métodos cuantitativos que nos permitan explotar dicha riqueza, con el propósito de profundizar y hacer avanzar el conocimiento.

En particular, en lo que se refiere al estudio de la globalización y de otras tendencias culturales tales como la postmodernidad y el postcolonialismo, observamos que la evolución de las ideas corresponde a procesos largos, que cubren varias décadas, y que no responden de manera inmediata a eventos puntuales tales como la pandemia o la crisis financiera de 2008.

Por el contrario, el análisis de las innovaciones tecnológicas muestra crecimientos muy rápidos en cortos periodos de tiempo. Lo mismo ocurre en el caso de la pandemia, puesto que constatamos una rápida y voluminosa actividad científica como respuesta a la crisis sanitaria.

Todo ello indica diferencias importantes en cuanto a la rapidez de respuesta en las disciplinas científicas comparadas con las dinámicas culturales, mucho más lentas, subyacentes en las humanidades. Por ello, consideramos que, a pesar del gran impacto de la pandemia de COVID-19 y de las evidentes transformaciones que implican las nuevas ciencias de datos en las humanidades, es aún prematuro para afirmar que el mundo haya ingresado en una época post-global.

Bibliografía

Ackermann, Eric (2006): "Indicators of Failed Information Epidemics in the Scientific Journal Literature: A Publication Analysis of Polywater and Cold Nuclear Fusion". En: *Scientometrics*, 66, 3, pp. 451–466.
Bertens, Johannes/Natoli, Joseph (2002): *Postmodernism: The Key Figures*. Malden/Oxford: Blackwell.
Bettencourt, Luís/Cintrón-Arias, Ariel/Kaiser, David/Castillo-Chávez, Carlos (2006): "The Power of a Good Idea: Quantitative Modeling of the Spread of Ideas from Epidemiological Models". En: *Physica A: Statistical Mechanics and Its Applications*, 364, pp. 513–536.
Boyd, Danah/Crawford, Kate (2012): "Critical Questions for Big Data Provocations for a Cultural, Technological, and Scholarly Phenomenon". En: *Information Communication & Society*, 15.5, pp. 662–679.
Budd, John/Hurt, Charlie (1991): "Superstring Theory – Information-Transfer in an Emerging Field". En: *Scientometrics*, 21.1, pp. 87–98.
Callon, Michel/Courtial, Jean-Pierre/Penan, Hervé (1993): *La Scientométrie*. Paris: Presses Universitaires de France.
Crane, Diana (1972): *Invisible Colleges: Diffusion of Knowledge in Scientific Communities*. Chicago: University of Chicago Press.
Dirlik, Arif (2007): "Contemporary Challenges to Marxism: Postmodernism, Postcolonialism, Globalization". En: *Amerasia Journal*, 33, 3, pp. 1–17.
— (1994): "The Postcolonial Aura: Third World Criticism in the Age of Global Capitalism". En: *Critical Inquiry*, 20, 2, pp. 328–356.
Ferrer, Carolina (2010): "Postmodernité, postcolonialisme et globalisation: changement de paradigme, biais disciplinaire et virage idéologique". En: *Protée*, 38, 3, pp. 29–37.
Goffman, William/Newill, Vaun (1967): "Communication and Epidemic Processes". En: *Proceedings of the Royal Society of London Series a-Mathematical and Physical Sciences*, 298.1454, pp. 316–334.
— (1964): "Generalization of Epidemic Theory. An Application to the Transmission of Ideas". En: *Nature*, 204, pp. 225–228.
Hassan, Ihab (2003): "Beyond Postmodernism – toward an Aesthetic of Trust". En: *Angelaki: Journal of the Theoretical Humanities*, 8.1, pp. 3–11.
Kuhn, Thomas (1962): *The Structure of Scientific Revolutions*. Chicago: University of Chicago Press.
Lambiotte Renaud/Panzarasa, Pietro (2009): "Communities, Knowledge Creation, and Information Diffusion". En *Journal of Informetrics*, 3, pp. 180190.
Lewellen, Ted (2002): *The Anthropology of Globalization. Cultural Anthropology Enters the 21st Century*. Westport: Bergin and Garvey.
Mayer-Schönberger, Viktor/Cukier, Keneth (2013): *Big Data. A Revolution That Will Transform How We Live, Work, and Think*. Boston: Houghton Mifflin Harcourt.
Modern Language Association International Bibliography. www.mla.org.
Olivié, Iliana/Manuel Gracia (2020): "The End of Globalisation? A Reflection on the Effects of the COVID-19 Crisis Using the Elcano Global Presence Index". En: *ARI*, 60, pp. 1–16.
Price, Derek De Solla (1963): *Little Science, Big Science*. Nueva York: Columbia University Press.

Schreibman, Susan/Siemens, Raymond/Unsworth, John (eds.) (2016): *A New Companion to Digital Humanities*. Malden: Wiley and Sons.
—— (2004): *A Companion to Digital Humanities*. Malden: Blackwell.
Scopus. www.scopus.com.
Tabah, Albert (1996): *Information Epidemics and the Growth of Physics*. Ph. D. Thesis, Montreal: McGill University, Graduate School of Library and Information Studies.
Web of Knowledge. www.webofknowledge.com.

Benjamin Loy
La novela (post-)global como trampa
Kentukis (2018) de Samanta Schweblin

1 Atención selectiva y "literatura con atributos": formas de (no) leer la literatura (post-)global

El paradigma investigativo de la (nueva) literatura mundial ha ocupado un lugar dominante en el ámbito de los estudios literarios durante las tres décadas pasadas. Recientemente, sin embargo, se ha observado un cuestionamiento de este paradigma mundialista y de los presupuestos ideológicos acerca de 'lo global'. La noción de que esta fase de globalización acelerada ha llegado a su fin se está abriendo paso en los estudios de la literatura[1] como en las ciencias sociales y la economía[2]. Cabe destacar que una perspectiva crítica sobre dichos fenómenos de globalización no es algo nuevo dentro del campo de la literatura (y los estudios literarios), ya que en muchos casos han subrayado la profunda ambivalencia de los procesos globalizadores, particularmente desde la perspectiva del Sur Global[3]. Sin embargo, es en vistas de un escepticismo cada vez más generalizado hacia la globalización en su forma actual que se se deben buscar nuevas formas de abordar este panorama en transformación que, a falta de un mejor término, se podría denominar provisoriamente como *postglobal*.

Sin embargo, esta noción de lo postglobal no debe insinuar una ruptura absoluta con una época o una suplantación radical de un modelo socioeconómico. Se entiende más bien en el sentido de una percepción crítica del modelo imperante en el orden mundial después de 1989, así como el inicio de una transición hacia otras prácticas y, sobre todo, otros imaginarios de lo global. En un primer paso, lo postglobal apuntaría entonces hacia una forma de reflexividad en referencia a las consecuencias problemáticas surgidas a raíz de los procesos de integración y de interdependencia a escala mundial, sea en términos sociales, económicos, políticos, tecnológicos o ecológicos.

Para el caso de trabajos en el ámbito de *World Literature*, estas transformaciones plantean una serie de interrogantes relacionadas a los objetos de estudio

---

[1] Véanse las contribuciones en Müller/Siskind (2019).
[2] Véanse por ejemplo los estudios reunidos en Diamond (2018).
[3] Véase Müller et al. (2018).

Benjamin Loy, Universidad de Viena

y a las premisas metodológicas del campo de investigación. La más evidente sería la pregunta de qué manera este agotamiento de los discursos afirmativos de lo global se refleja a nivel temático de los textos. En cambio, un aspecto menos evidente concierne también la *forma de leer* la literatura que se podría derivar de esta transformación. Este punto no es evidente y requiere una puesta en perspectiva crítica de los paradigmas metodológicos que han dominado el campo de la literatura mundial en el último cuarto de siglo. Si bien es cierto que este campo se ha caracterizado por una heterogeneidad metodológica y temática, también es una obviedad que en la gran mayoría de trabajos acerca del tema han prevalecido dos paradigmas de abordar lo global en la literatura: me refiero, por un lado, a la acepción (proto-)sociológica de la literatura mundial en cuanto a sus condiciones de producción y circulación[4]; y, por el otro, a la tendencia de analizar textos literarios sobre todo en función de su 'relevancia' temática para dar cuenta de determinados fenómenos sociales, económicos, políticos y ecológicos relacionados a procesos de globalización contemporáneos y, en menor medida, históricos.

Esta reflexión sobre posibles consecuencias metodológicas me parece clave porque los paradigmas mencionados a su vez han respondido a la lógica imperante de los sistemas académicos contemporáneos. Estos no solamente han privilegiado 'lo global' por sobre otros tipos de textos (a nivel temático), sino también una determinada metodología para analizar esas formas de 'lo global en la literatura': en su afán por valorar lo 'relevante' de acuerdo a los parámetros de 'utilidad' y de 'mensurabilidad', dicha lógica sistémica ha afectado a los estudios literarios (globales) de manera significativa en el sentido de un nuevo giro hacia la dimensión material de la literatura (números de ventas, traducciones, archivos, 'redes', 'mapeos', 'gatekeepers'[5] etc.) o hacia una enfática inteligibilidad temática (al estilo 'el problema global x en los textos de z').

Como Robert Folger observó al respecto, la imposición del paradigma de *World Literature* contribuyó a aumentar la sujeción de los estudios literarios a las leyes del mercado, así como también reforzó una transformación radical en cuanto a la categoría de la atención como elemento de la recepción e interpretación del texto literario. La atención tradicionalmente conformaba el centro de las prácticas filológicas en el sentido de que "[a]ttention is one of the factors that produce individual and shared memory: memory of a specific text, and, through

---

4 Cabrían mencionar aquí – solamente para el caso de las literaturas latinoamericanas – los numerosos trabajos de autoras y autores como Ana Gallego Cuiñas, Gustavo Guerrero o Ignacio Sánchez Prado, al igual que los estudios realizados en el marco del proyecto *Reading Global. Constructions of World Literature and Latin America* (cf. Locane 2019, Müller 2022).
5 Véanse por ejemplo los estudios reunidos en Guerrero et al. (2021).

the workings of intertextuality, a whole universe of texts" (Folger 2013: 257). No es difícil reconocer que esa idea de una penetración profunda de los múltiples niveles y sentidos de un texto (y sus relaciones con otros textos y la tradición) ha sido sustituida paulatinamente por una nueva 'economía de la atención' orientada en las lógicas del mercado académico – y que el campo de *World Literature* ha hecho un aporte significante y problemático en ese sentido. Aparte de propuestas metodológicas como el "distance reading" de Franco Moretti, que ha radicalizado esta lógica de distanciarse de una lectura 'filológica' del texto, la tendencia más problemática del campo de *World Literature* actual consiste en su tendencia de leer textos literarios básicamente en función de su capacidad de responder a las lógicas de 'utilidad' y 'relevancia', es decir, a lo que prometa atención (y fondos) en el mercado académico. 'Literatura mundial', desde esa perspectiva, significa en primer lugar analizar textos con una orientación temática ostensible y 'relevante'. Deben ser textos capaces de ejemplificar un 'problema de orden global' (y en el mejor de los casos, ofrecer una forma y un mensaje ideológicos adecuados), por lo que la literatura dominante dentro del campo de la literatura mundial es una literatura con determinados atributos 'globalizables', aptos para ser explotados de acuerdo al paradigma[6]. Visto de esta manera, dichos enfoques metodológicos prevalecientes en los estudios de *World Literature* constituirían una forma de "onslaught on literature as a technology of attention" (Folger 2013: 259), es decir, reforzarían la tendencia hacia lecturas necesariamente 'superficiales' prefiriendo exponer la supuesta 'relevancia' temática del texto (en relación a determinadas etiquetas cotizando en el mercado académico global) ante una inmersión en las dimensiones textuales más profundas a nivel de la forma[7].

El presente estudio de la novela *Kentukis* (2018) de Samanta Schweblin pretende explorar las posibilidades de una lectura alternativa (*postglobal*) desde esta reflexión metodológica inicial. El objetivo de mi interpretación será demostrar de qué manera un cambio de 'atención' —en el sentido de un análisis enfocado en las microestructuras del texto— es capaz de modificar de manera

---

[6] No carece de cierta ironía que los estudios culturales y literarios en ese sentido han desarrollado una lógica académica en paralelo a uno de sus temas predilectos en cuanto a las representaciones negativas de lo global (y particularmente en América Latina): el extractivismo.

[7] Esta crítica de unas tendencias generales del campo de estudios no pretende ignorar el hecho, repito, de que importantes contribuciones han emprendido en términos metodológicos precisamente ese tipo de lecturas, ante todo el inminente estudio de Héctor Hoyos sobre la novela latinoamericana global que parte de un cuestionamiento explícito de "distant reading and sociologies of literature, since they miss crucial knowledge that comes from traditional, if critical and cultural theory-informed, close reading of a few key works" (Hoyos 2015: 204).

significativa los resultados de interpretación de una novela como *Kentukis*, que hasta el momento ha sido leída por la crítica como un ejemplo prototípico de la literatura mundial con referencia casi exclusiva a sus dimensiones temáticas. Mi argumento, por cierto, no es que la novela de Schweblin no sea, ante todo, una reflexión aguda sobre las dimensiones problemáticas de la comunicación digital y globalizada contemporánea; lo que quisiera demostrar es que —más allá de esta dimensión temática evidente del texto— *Kentukis* integra, a través de la forma de la novela y de una compleja argumentación metaliteraria basada en referencias intertextuales, una serie de elementos que se pueden leer como una crítica radical de ese tipo de 'lecturas globalizadoras' evidentes que el libro tiende a provocar a primera vista. Lo que el presente análisis propone, por lo tanto, es un cambio de enfoque hacia el texto en el sentido de una 'lectura postglobal'. Esta va más allá (o se queda más acá) de una interpretación centrada en las dimensiones 'obvias' y temáticas del texto para cuestionar la atribución (demasiado) evidente del lema 'global' a la novela de Schweblin.

Un argumento clave en ese contexto sería que *Kentukis* se caracteriza no simplemente por una problematización de un aspecto de la experiencia global —la comunicación digital y sus efectos— sino que integra, a través de su estructura, una crítica de nuestras formas superficiales de leer en el presente. La novela de Schweblin ofrece —y lo repito, menos por el contenido que por la complejidad formal subyacente del texto— una reflexión crítica en cuanto a las formas contemporáneas de percepción y de 'lectura' en el mundo digitalizado, ambas marcadas por un cambio tecnológico y medial radical que el libro refleja y subvierte. Desde una perspectiva que se puede llamar *postglobal* (en su demarcación de los paradigmas dominantes de la literatura mundial), mi análisis aspira entonces a mostrar cómo *Kentukis* en realidad es una especie de 'trampa' doble para sus diferentes públicos lectores: para la lectora 'común' porque decepciona, como se verá, todo tipo de deseo de coherencia o de identificación proyectadas hacia los personajes o los desenlaces de los múltiples relatos del libro; y para el lector 'profesional', equipado con las herramientas y perspectivas usuales de la crítica de la literatura mundial, porque le ofrece una serie de anzuelos interpretativos invitándolo a leer la novela de un modo evidente que, por el otro lado, lo obliga a dejar de lado otros elementos que cuestionarían radicalmente semejante lectura globalizadora (y que identificaré en su debida forma en lo que sigue).

2 La transparencia engañosa: el mundo como deseo y frustración en *Kentukis*

A primera vista, *Kentukis*, la segunda novela de Samanta Schweblin, reúne todas las características para clasificarla como un texto emblemático de la literatura mundial contemporánea: en un total de 35 fragmentos la novela narra las vidas de numerosas figuras en más de una docena de lugares en todo el mundo[8], todas conectadas en diferentes constelaciones a través de un aparato ficticio llamado "kentuki". El kentuki es un peluche con cámara manejado a distancia y de manera digital por personas desconocidas. La difusión global del kentuki es el punto de partida de la novela para discutir diferentes implicaciones tecnológicas, sociales, económicas, ético-jurídicas y estéticas de la integración global contemporánea. En ese sentido, la novela parece idónea para una lectura desde el paradigma de la literatura mundial, ya que cumple en muchos sentidos con los atributos elementales requeridos por ese tipo de lecturas 'sociológicas' mencionados arriba: se puede leer como una representación crítica del capitalismo digital (Staab 2019), como advertencia sobre la desaparición de la esfera de privacidad o, en la línea de los análisis del capitalismo emocional (Illouz 2007), como problematización de formas contemporáneas de alienación y de comodificación de los sentimientos. En ese sentido, *Kentukis* es un libro que encaja perfectamente con ese tipo de análisis enfocados en leer los personajes desde "las carencias afectivas de los sujetos neoliberales" (Jiménez Barrera 2020: 96) y los artefactos con forma de animales "como micromáquinas paranoicas que cifran la relación de lo humano con la técnica" (Feuillet 2020: 332) al ejercer una "presencia invasora y 'extractivista' de la intimidad" (Osorio-Restrepo 2021: 94).

A esos aspectos se les podrían añadir otras dimensiones afines a los debates contemporáneos sobre globalización, neoliberalismo, ecología y tecnología. Cuando en la novela se pregunta, después de la muerte de una mujer a raíz de un infarto en presencia de su kentuki, si "¿[h]ay parte de responsabilidad en el kentuki? [. . .] Y si la hubiera, ¿qué tipo de acciones legales podían aplicarse a estos nuevos ciudadanos anónimos?" (Schweblin 2018: 117), se trata de uno de numerosos ejemplos que se podrían situar en el amplio campo de las discusio-

---

[8] Los lugares que se mencionan son: South Bend, Hong Kong, Lima, Antigua (Guatemala), Honningsvåg (Noruega), Erfurt (Alemania), Oaxaca, Tel Aviv, Surumu (Venezuela), Buenos Aires, Sierra Leone, Taipéi, Lyon, Beijing, Umbertide (Italia), Zagreb, Barcelona y Vancouver.

nes trans- y posthumanistas del presente[9]. Asimismo, el funcionamiento de los kentukis se podría leer fácilmente —y algunos de los estudios mencionados tocan esos puntos— a partir de los escritos de un autor como Bruno Latour, sea mediante su teoría del actor-red (Latour 2008) o a raíz de sus reflexiones sobre los "cuasi-objetos" (Latour 2007)[10]. También sería perfectamente viable una interpretación del fenómeno de los kentukis como una parábola de las enormes desigualdades sociales y económicas persistentes en el mundo globalizado[11] o

---

[9] Ese aspecto se hace visible en la novela al insistir en el hecho de que un kentuki tiene una sola vida y que esa depende de la preocupación de su "amo" que lo tiene que cargar y velar por su bienestar, por lo que en el transcurso de la narración se discuten con creciente énfasis los derechos de los kentukis adquiriendo sucesivamente rasgos antropomórficos. Al mismo tiempo, los usuarios humanos de los kentukis reflexionan sobre condiciones post-humanas posibilitadas por esa tecnología, por ejemplo cuando el personaje de Marvin, un semi-huérfano guatemalteco, concibe su existencia desmaterializada y descorporizada como kentuki en Noruega como un modelo de vida utópico: "No era tan fácil ni rápido cruzar el pueblo, pero le gustaba pensar que, incluso ahora que en la cuenta de su madre no quedaba ni un euro, podría vivir como un kentuki un siglo sin preocuparse por el dinero. Podía comer y dormir en Antigua atendiendo cada tanto su cuerpo, mientras en Noruega los días pasarían tranquilamente, cargándose de base en base, sin añorar ni un pedazo de chocolate, ni una manta para pasar la noche. No necesitar nada de eso para vivir tenía algo de superhéroe, y si al fin lograba encontrar la nieve, podía vivir el resto de su vida en ella sin que siquiera le diera un poquito de frío" (Schweblin 2018: 158).

[10] En ese sentido se podrían leer, de acuerdo a los conceptos de Latour, las reflexiones continuas de la novela sobre la capacidad de los kentukis de cuestionar los límites entre realidad y ficción ("Sabía que la libertad en el mundo kentuki no era la misma que en el mundo real, aunque esto tampoco ordenaba las cosas si se caía en la cuenta de que el mundo kentuki también era real" (Schweblin 2018: 130)) y entre lo humano y lo no-humano, por ejemplo cuando los kentukis empiezan a contribuir a una mayor conciencia sobre posibles 'sentimientos' de una máquina (como cuando un personaje admite que "[n]unca se le hubiera ocurrido que ahora, además de todas las especificaciones que había que leer si se compraba un electrodoméstico nuevo, había que pensar también si se sería digno para ese objeto vivir o no con uno. ¿Quién pensaría, frente a la góndola de un supermercado, si el ventilador que está pensando en llevarse a casa estaría de acuerdo en ventilar a un padre en pañales mientras mira la televisión?" (Schweblin 2018: 46).

[11] La novela insiste repetidamente en el hecho de que la economía digital no supera de ninguna manera las asimetrías de la producción global sino que simplemente ofrece un dispositivo alternativo que se inserta en las estructuras de desigualdad ya existentes. Así, por ejemplo, un taxista en Oaxaca le paga cinco dólares por semana a un hacker-kentuki en Haití por advertirle los radares en la zona que conoce gracias a su hackeo de los sistemas municipales de seguridad vial; y Grigor, un vendedor de vivencias kentuki a la medida, describe cómo lucra con la desigualdad global al afirmar que "[h]abía gente dispuesta a soltar una fortuna por vivir en la pobreza unas horas al día, y estaban los que pagaban por hacer turismo sin moverse de sus casas, por pasear por la India sin una sola diarrea, o conocer el invierno polar descalzos y en pijama" (Schweblin 2018: 61).

como metáfora de la historia del internet entre las esperanzas libertarias iniciales y su comodificación y regularización actual[12]. Se podría, para nombrar un último ejemplo, profundizar también en las múltiples interrogantes legales planteadas por la novela, como el hecho de que el mundo esbozado por Schweblin es un mundo esencialmente post-estatal o post-institucional, ya que en casi ningún momento de la novela se encuentra la presencia de entidades del orden público (y en los pocos casos en que se hacen presentes son descritos en términos de una severa disfuncionalidad)[13].

Todos estos aspectos temáticos podrían servir como puntos de partida de un análisis más profundo de las condiciones de la comunicación y conectividad globales. Sin embargo, lo que me interesa discutir a continuación —siguiendo el enfoque metodológico esbozado arriba— es cómo la novela de Schweblin se sirve, en un primer paso, de una serie de estrategias formales para transformar la lectura de *Kentukis* en una experiencia análoga a la de la posesión y del uso de uno de los artefactos digitales en el texto. Esta experiencia se construye a partir de una determinada dinámica afectiva entre deseo y frustración que conecta la *user experience* de los dueños de los kentukis con la lectura de la novela. La atractividad de los kentukis se basa precisamente en la asimetría fundamental de la conexión entre amo y kentuki: ninguno de los dos partidos

---

[12] La historia de los kentukis funciona como una especie de metonimia de la historia o de las esperanzas proyectadas sobre el mundo digital y el internet desde sus inicios: la utopía de un espacio de intercambio y de comunicación global abierto —simbolizada por el principio del azar conectando kentukis y amos, así como la falta de regularización de la conectividad de los kentukis— es de corta duración. También ese aspecto se discute mediante el personaje de Grigor: el joven croata empieza a comprar grandes cantidades de códigos kentuki para averiguar lo básico sobre los amos (lugar de residencia, clase social, etc.) para luego armar un catálogo para usuarios que no están interesados en una constelación aleatoria sino en la compra de una vivencia "kentuki" hecha a medida – operación que, según el propio Grigor, solo anticipa la regularización definitiva del modelo: "Tarde o temprano aparecía alguien con más capital y mejores contactos. 'Regular' no era organizar, sino acomodar las reglas a favor de unos pocos. Las empresas se apoderarían pronto del negocio que había detrás de los kentukis, y la gente no tardaría en calcular que, si se tiene el dinero, mejor negocio que pagar setenta dólares por una tarjeta de conexión que se encendería al azar en cualquier rincón del mundo, era pagar ocho veces más para elegir en qué lugar estar" (Schweblin 2018: 61).

[13] La novela construye un episodio particular en el que se plantea el desfase radical entre las estructuras jurídico-policiales locales y las dinámicas transnacionales del crimen cuando el croata Grigor y su amiga Nikolina reciben una llamada de socorro de una niña secuestrada en la zona fronteriza entre Venezuela y Brazil. Ante la falta de reacción por parte de las instituciones los jóvenes finalmente optan por servirse de vías no-institucionales al "fotografiar la imagen de la chica y comunicarse con algún medio de comunicación no oficial para que las cosas realmente empezaran a moverse. [. . .] Nikolina llamó a varios medios y entregó todo el material" (Schweblin 2018: 183).

conectados a través del dispositivo puede escoger con quién y dónde se realiza su conexión, cosa que está sujeta al azar; además, existe una barrera de comunicación entre los dos, ya que el kentuki solo posee una cámara para ver y escuchar pero ninguna posibilidad de comunicarse, mientras que el amo solo le puede hablar al peluche sin saber quién lo mira y escucha por el otro lado[14]. El secreto del éxito de los kentukis, por lo tanto, reside precisamente en esa limitación autoimpuesta de su tecnología: "Al final, a la gente le encantaban las restricciones" (Schweblin 2018: 59).

La lectura del texto opera a su vez con esas mismas asimetrías y, en términos de la estética de la recepción, esos "espacios vacíos" en cuanto a la información y al saber de los lectores: la inexistencia de una instancia narradora auctorial y la preponderancia de una narración con focalización interna y de carácter escénico transpone la limitación tecnológica de los kentukis al nivel de la estructura narrativa de la novela. Sus lectores se hallan ante la misma dinámica de transparencia y opacidad que los amos y los kentukis, el acto de lectura —y en eso reside el carácter netamente 'realista' de la novela— es mimético en relación con la experiencia tecnológica y comunicacional de las figuras del texto.

La experiencia comunicacional —tanto de los usuarios del kentuki como de los lectores de la novela— es marcada por una profunda ambivalencia: por un lado, ambos artefactos estimulan la atención del espectador-lector al posibilitar un acceso ilimitado a esferas y vidas privadas y ajenas. Más allá de satisfacer un simple voyerismo, el kentuki y la novela se inscriben aquí en la lógica comunicacional de la época global basada en los principios de conectividad, simultaneidad y una superación de límites espaciotemporales y materiales pero también culturales, mentales y lingüísticos. A nivel del artefacto tecnológico del kentuki, este último punto se posibilita mediante un programa de traducción automática integrado con subtítulos creando una ilusión de transparencia de la comunicación. Este aspecto corresponde a nivel del lenguaje de la novela a una accesibilidad absoluta por parte de la lectora: el texto de Schweblin refuerza la ilusión de una inteligibilidad total mediante el hecho de que es redactado completamente en castellano y renuncia, con la excepción de unas pocas palabras como los rótulos de unas tiendas alemanas o unos caracteres chinos del manual del kentuki, a integrar elementos lingüísticos capaces

---

[14] "El kentuki podía no contestar, o podía mentirle. Decir que era una colegiala filipina y ser un petrolero iraní. Podía, en una casualidad insólita, ser alguien que ella conociera y no sincerarse nunca. En cambio ella debía mostrarle su vida entera y transparente, tan disponible como lo había estado para ese pobre canario de su adolescencia que se había muerto mirándola, colgando de su jaula en el centro de la habitación" (Schweblin 2018: 28).

de romper con esa ilusión. Se trata —igual que en el caso del kentuki como artefacto— de una novela 'fabricada' para un público global, por lo que bien podría clasificarse como parte de esa literatura "born translated" en el sentido de Walkowitz (2017)[15].

Dicha experiencia de una supuesta inteligibilidad universal es reforzada a nivel estructural de la novela por el hecho de que las diferentes historias mezclan géneros narrativos como el melodrama o el thriller, que a su vez forman parte imprescindible del repertorio narrativo global en literatura, cine y televisión[16]. Consecuentemente, las respectivas figuras y tramas parecen altamente intercambiables: las localizaciones de los personajes y sus identidades particulares aparentemente no poseen una importancia mayor. Son, para usar un término informático adecuado, meros *caracteres comodines* en la estructura básica de la novela de usar los kentukis como pretexto de una constelación narrativa experimental para reflexionar sobre los efectos de la conectividad global.

Por otro lado, la preponderancia de la transparencia y de lo visible es constantemente subvertida a nivel de la experiencia de los usuarios de los kentukis: esto no solamente vale para la mencionada asimetría entre ver y ser visto, sino que también afecta la dimensión de la comunicación entre los personajes. Muchos episodios del libro son marcados por los intentos de superar la barrera de comunicación impuesta por la imposibilidad del kentuki de comunicarse activamente con su amo. A raíz de la inconformidad con ese tipo de comunicación digital y unilateral, varios observadores buscan encontrar alternativas para comunicarse con los amos mediante sus kentukis. El hecho irónico de que recurren a las formas comunicacionales materiales más básicas, como la ouija o el código morse, remite no solamente a una la transparencia engañosa de la comunicación global sino también a un motivo que afecta la experiencia completa de los personajes de la novela y que podríamos describir, en un primer paso, como una forma de carencia de lo tangible y de lo material.

La presunta accesibilidad e inteligibilidad del mundo, tal como las experimentan los usuarios de los kentukis (y también los lectores de la novela), encubre en realidad una serie de carencias afectivas y corporales de las figuras. Un motivo recurrente de la novela es precisamente la búsqueda de emociones compartidas por los personajes que en su gran mayoría viven en constelaciones fami-

---

[15] La dimensión más visible en ese sentido es ya el título de la novela, *Kentukis*, como una palabra pronunciable universalmente que borra cada intento de localización concreta. No carece de cierta ironía, sin embargo, que algunas traducciones de la novela como la inglesa o la alemana renunciaron a mantener el título original.
[16] Acerca de esa globalización de géneros literarios véanse por ejemplo las contribuciones en Habjan/Imlinger 2016.

liares deficientes o en soledad[17]. El mundo de los kentukis posibilita para muchos de ellos la experiencia de emociones a primera vista 'auténticas' en el espacio de la comunicación digital: Marvin, el niño guatemalteco semi-huérfano, encuentra formas de reconocimiento inédito en su existencia como dragón kentuki en Noruega, la anciana peruana se transforma en una especie de madre putativa de una joven alemana, un padre italiano divorciado considera su kentuki como una especie de compañero co-paterno en la educación de su hijo etc. Sin embargo, todas esas relaciones terminan a la larga por decepcionar a los usuarios, ya que los kentukis a fin de cuentas solo posibilitan emociones fugaces e incapaces de satisfacer el deseo último de una materialidad tangible en las relaciones comunicacionales[18] e interpersonales: el niño guatemalteco nunca tocará con sus propias manos la nieve noruega que tanto anhela, la peruana tendrá que reconocer que solo fue objeto del fetiche sexual de la chica alemana y su novio y el padre italiano se da cuenta de que su kentuki co-paterno en realidad es un pedófilo. Todo tipo de comunicación y de relación virtual al final queda marcado por elementos de una profunda inseguridad: "Nunca quedaba demasiado claro cuál era la respuesta, ni si la respuesta era verdadera en su totalidad o marcaba solo su cercanía" (Schweblin 2018: 37).

En vistas de las analogías estructurales esbozadas entre la experiencia de los usuarios de los kentukis y el proceso de recepción de la novela se plantea entonces la pregunta de cómo esa experiencia de una carencia emocional de los personajes de la novela también afecta a los lectores reales del texto. Mi hipótesis es que Samanta Schweblin construye una decepción comparable para el lector de su novela, que al mismo tiempo funciona como una estrategia autocrítica de la presente y, por consecuencia, de las lógicas estéticas y comerciales de la literatura mundial descritas al inicio de este artículo. Este argumento complejo requiere mayor fundamentación. Y es que la novela no se limita a crear semejante efecto de desencanto mediante el hecho de que la mayoría de las historias terminan de manera abrupta; sino que se sirve de un episodio decididamente metaliterario, que ocupa en total casi un veinte por ciento de las páginas de la novela pero que ha sido ignorada básicamente por la mayoría de los análisis de *Kentu-*

---

[17] La causa de ello muchas veces es la globalización misma, como por ejemplo en el caso de Emilia, una anciana solitaria de Lima, que recibe su kentuki como regalo de su hijo que trabaja desde joven en Hong Kong.

[18] Véase por ejemplo el comentario sobre esa dimensión tangible de lo escrito y lo emocional en la figura de Emilia a quien "[l]e hubiera gustado tener el papel original, con la letra fina e inclinada de la chica para pegarlo en su heladera, porque a pesar del alemán, de la tinta fucsia y brillante, era una escritura sofisticada, algo que podría haber enviado un pariente lejano a alguna amiga desde el extranjero" (Schweblin 2018: 41–42).

kis. Me refiero a la historia en torno a un artista visual y su novia argentina en una residencia de artistas en Oaxaca que se sale visiblemente de los espacios y temas cotidianos de las demás historias encubriendo, como quisiera demostrar a continuación, la clave interpretativa que cambia fundamentalmente el sentido completo de la novela.

3 "¿Por qué esta historia no se trataba de otra cosa?" – la novela (post-)global como trampa y el fantasma de Juan José Saer

La similitud del 'funcionamiento' de los kentukis y de la novela misma en cuanto a la dialéctica entre transparencia comunicacional, por un lado, y los accesos limitados a informaciones, identidades y causas de numerosos sucesos[19], por el otro, afecta también en última instancia la (im-)posibilidad de satisfacer los deseos de una coherencia narrativa para los usuarios de los artefactos como para los lectores de la novela. Ninguna de las relaciones establecidas mediante los kentukis lleva a los involucrados a una experiencia de plenitud o de contacto duradero – un efecto que bien se podría generalizar también para el lector real de la novela. Las experiencias de defraudación y de desilusión llevan a numerosos personajes de la novela a renunciar voluntariamente a su participación en el mundo de los kentukis. Mientras que en algunas figuras prevalecen la rabia y hasta la violencia, como en el caso del padre italiano[20], otras, como Grigor, salen de los devastadores círculos comerciales y mentales del mundo de los kentukis por su cansancio y frustración:

> Y entonces lo entendió: no quería seguir viendo a desconocidos comer y roncar, no quería volver a ver ni un solo pollito gritando de terror mientras el resto lo desplumaba de los nervios, no quería mover a nadie más de un infierno a otro. No iba a esperar a que las benditas regulaciones internacionales llegaran para sacarlo del negocio, ya habían tardado demasiado. Iba a salirse solo. Vendería los dispositivos que le quedaban y se dedicaría a otra cosa. Accedió a la configuración general y, sin molestarse siquiera en sacar antes al kentuki de esa casa, cortó la conexión. (Schweblin 2018: 200–201)

---

19 Feuillet postula con razón la importancia de la figura del complot en la novela (2020: 322–332).
20 "Volvió a tomar la pala, la levantó en el aire y apaleó la tierra. Golpeó una y otra vez, compactándolo todo, hasta estar seguro de que, incluso si un ser vivo latiera en el fondo, ninguna grieta volvería a abrirse" (Schweblin 2018: 213).

Esa desconexión abrupta de las relaciones entre los personajes de la novela y la opacidad de numerosos sucesos se transponen, una vez más, también al nivel de la lectura del texto: a falta de una instancia narradora auctorial capaz de ordenar las tramas o de proveer informaciones más allá de lo que saben y experimentan los personajes, la sensación de desorientación y contingencia de las figuras corresponde a la noción dominante de la recepción por parte del lector real. El libro y sus tramas (en su mayoría) inconclusas se 'apaga' al igual que los artefactos tecnológicos. Sin embargo, la novela no se limita a ese efecto de lectura, sino que lo inserta en una reflexión más amplia sobre las modalidades de narrar 'lo global' tomando como punto de (auto-)crítica la propia forma y los contenidos de la novela. Esa autorreflexividad sería, a mi modo de ver, el eje central que permite situar a *Kentukis* en ese ámbito apenas delineado de lo postglobal, ya que supera de manera decisiva cualquier escenificación simple de un 'tema global' para cuestionar sus propios requisitos narrativos y sus condiciones de producción y de recepción en tanto 'novela global'.

El episodio de la novela que se hace cargo de esa autorreflexividad crítica es, como se ha señalado, la historia en torno a la pareja de Alina y Sven: ambos están pasando una temporada en el pueblo Vista Hermosa en Oaxaca donde Sven, un artista visual internacionalmente reconocido, trabaja en una nueva exposición en una residencia de artistas de todo el mundo. El espacio cerrado y autorreferencial de la residencia funciona como una metonimia del mercado del arte global sobre el que se comenta desde la perspectiva irónica de Alina: "Él era el que ganaba las becas, él que iba de acá para allá con sus grandes xilografías monocromáticas 'abriendo el arte al pueblo', 'llevando tinta al alma', 'un artista con raíces'. Ella no tenía un plan, nada que la sostuviera ni la protegiera. No tenía la certeza de conocerse a sí misma ni tampoco sabía para qué estaba en este mundo" (Schweblin 2018: 21)[21].

La presencia de Alina, una argentina sobre cuya biografía no se sabe nada pero de cuyas visitas regulares a la librería de Vista Hermosa se puede deducir que probablemente abriga algunas esperanzas artísticas (literarias) por su parte, se relaciona al principio de la novela con su ilusión de superar un estado

---

[21] La figura, cuyo nombre completo es Sven Greenfort, parece aludir al artista conceptual danés-alemán Tue Greenfort, conocido por sus instalaciones sobre temas del medio ambiente como algas o la historia del caviar. La novela se burla repetidas veces sobre la hipocresía del discurso supuestamente crítico del artista hacia el mercado y su evidente éxito en ese mismo mercado: "Exponía solo sus monocopias y sus xilografías —lo suficientemente grandes y grises para ocultar cualquier mediocridad—, mientras renegaba de su verdadero deseo, 'sacudir el mercado', que invocaba cada vez que tomaba demasiado" (Schweblin 2018: 115).

de enajenación: "Había bosques y montes, que empezaban a unos metros de esa gran habitación donde los habían hospedado, y la luz fuerte y blanca no le recordaba en nada a los colores ocres de Mendoza. Eso estaba bien. Eso era lo que había querido desde hacía unos años, mudarse de sitio, o de cuerpo, o de mundo, lo que fuera que pudiera virarse" (Schweblin 2018: 21). Sin embargo, la monotonía de la vida diaria en la residencia y el creciente desinterés de su novio pronto dejan defraudadas esas esperanzas: "Él avanzaba, ella oscilaba detrás de la estela que él iba dejando, intentando que no se le escapara de las manos. Correr, leer, el kentuki, todos sus planes eran de contingencia" (Schweblin 2018: 51). Es ante esa situación de enajenación y de frustración que se efectúa para Alina un momento de autoconocimiento que se puede considerar como una clave de lectura para la novela en su totalidad:

> Se sentía cerca de algún tipo de revelación, era un proceso que conocía, y la sola excitación por alcanzar una conclusión compensaba la somnolencia. Así que esa mañana, después de regresar de correr y tirarse en la cama con sus mandarinas, seguía dándole vueltas al asunto con el presentimiento de estar cada vez más cerca de algún tipo de revelación. Miró el techo fijamente y pensó que, si tuviera que poner las cosas en orden para inferir a qué tipo de descubrimiento estaba llegando, tendría que recordar un dato en el que hacía días que no pensaba. [. . .] una revelación mucho más profunda captó súbitamente su atención: nada le importaba tanto como para moverse en alguna dirección. En su cuerpo, cada impulso preguntaba para qué. No era cansancio, ni depresión, ni carencia de vitaminas. Era una sensación parecida al desinterés, pero mucho más expansiva. Acostada en la cama juntó las cáscaras en una sola mano y el movimiento la acercó a una nueva revelación. Si Sven todo lo sabía, si el *artista* era un peón abocado y cada segundo de su tiempo era un paso hacia un destino irrevocable, entonces ella era exactamente lo contrario. El último punto al otro extremo de los seres de este planeta. La *inartista*. Nadie, para nadie y nunca nada. La resistencia a cualquier tipo de concreción. Su cuerpo se interponía entre las cosas protegiéndola del riesgo de llegar, alguna vez, a alcanzar algo. (Schweblin 2018: 55–56)

El pasaje citado es sin dudas el que más se aleja de todo el resto de la novela y sus relatos sobre historias cotidianas siguiendo las lógicas narrativas de los géneros mencionados arriba. La interpretación de la reflexión de Alina, por lo tanto, exige aparentemente otro enfoque de lectura en el sentido de un *close reading* que los demás episodios del texto no precisan de la misma manera. Aparte de la incipiente revelación, que es mencionada tres veces pero que no se especifica, son sobre todo la reflexión sobre la pasividad y el concepto de la "inartista" que parecen, a primera vista, más bien herméticos. Sin embargo, la clave para la interpretación de este fragmento —y de la novela completa— se puede ubicar en una alusión intertextual no explotada por la crítica hasta el momento. La frase "Nadie, para nadie y nunca nada" remite, de manera visible, a la novela *Nadie nada nunca* (1980) de Juan José Saer[22], referencia que en su forma citada textual aquí no puede ser casual. Lo mismo vale para el concepto de la "inartista" que evoca un elemento clave de la (auto-)definición que el autor argentino, radicado en Francia desde 1968 y hasta su muerte en el 2005, dio en uno de sus ensayos intitulado "Gombrowicz en la Argentina":

> Ser polaco. Ser francés. Ser argentino. Aparte de la elección del idioma, ¿en qué otro sentido se le puede pedir semejante autodefinición a un escritor? Ser comunista. Ser liberal. Ser individualista. Para el que escribe, asumir estas etiquetas, no es más esencial, en lo referente a lo específico de su trabajo, que hacerse socio de un club de fútbol o miembro de una sociedad gastronómica. La posibilidad de ser perceptible como tal o cual cosa bien definida en el reparto de roles de la imaginación social es un privilegio del hombre, no del escritor. Del hombre – es decir de la primera ficción que debe abolir, como si fuera una estética ya perimida, el escritor de ficciones. La certeza de esa desnudez no sólo orienta o preside, sino que incluso es la justificación última del trabajo. A priori, el escritor no es nada, nadie, situación que, a decir verdad, metafísicamente hablando, comparte con los demás hombres, de los que lo diferencia, en tanto que escritor, un simple detalle, pero tan decisivo que es suficiente para cambiar su vida entera: si para los demás hombres la construcción de la existencia reside en rellenar esa ausencia de contenido con diversas imágenes sociales, para el escritor todo el asunto consiste en preservarla. La tensión de su trabajo se resume en lo siguiente: no es nadie ni nada, se aborda el mundo a partir de cero, y la estrategia de que se dispone prescribe, justamente, que el artista debe replantear día tras día su estrategia. (Saer 2014 [1990]: 17)

La referencia a Saer apunta entonces, en primer lugar, a un determinado concepto del artista y de autoría que, en el marco de la novela de Schweblin, cumple una doble función: es una crítica de la figura del artista encarnada por Sven, quien representa, como sugiere la novela en diferentes momentos, el modelo del artista plástico y visual contemporáneo vendiéndose como marca propia con sus etiquetas ya establecidas en el mercado internacional del arte; al mismo tiempo, el pasaje y la referencia intertextual revelan las aspiraciones artísticas (literarias) de Alina de una manera indirecta: "la inartista" le ofrece un modelo de autoría alternativo para pensar su (posible) obra de acuerdo a las posiciones de Saer.

La presencia de Saer, sin embargo, no deja de resultar sorpresiva en el marco de una novela como *Kentukis* considerando que la estética del autor argentino podría caracterizarse más bien como el opuesto radical de todos los principios predominantes del texto de Schweblin. La pregunta que habría que esclarecer, por lo tanto, sería la de la función de esa referencia inesperada más allá de la mencionada crítica del concepto de autor. Mi hipótesis aquí es que la

---

[22] Quisiera agradecer a Sebastián Paiva por una serie de conversaciones importantes sobre esta presencia fantasmal de Saer en Kentukis.

poética de Saer se erige no solamente como una crítica del concepto de autoría y de la estética del novio artista (representativas del mercado global del arte), sino de manera implícita también en contra de los propios principios narrativos de *Kentukis* como novela (y como 'novela global' en particular).

Este argumento se hace más transparente al considerar algunos rasgos generales de la obra del autor argentino y su posible significado en el contexto de su presencia en la novela de Schweblin. La figura de Alina (y el episodio completo en torno al artista Sven) se diferencia de los demás personajes e hilos narrativos de la novela por su carácter metaliterario y autorreflexivo – un aspecto que, teniendo en cuenta la alusión intertextual mencionada, remite directamente a lo que Julio Premat ha identificado también como base de la poética de Saer:

> El centro [. . .] de esos textos es, sin duda alguna, un interrogante acerca de la comunicación literaria, lo que se manifiesta en varios niveles distintos. Antes que nada, con una agudización de la *forma*, tanto en la exposición de mecanismos complejos de construcción, en la elección de estructuras sofisticadas de articulación narrativa, como en los metadiscursos del escritor que definen, repetidamente, el trabajo del autor en tanto que labor de resolución técnica: búsqueda de 'innovaciones' y de una forma verdaderamente expresiva. Además, las ficciones saerianas se caracterizan por un exuberante autotematismo, es decir que no sólo exponen sus modalidades de construcción, sino que acumulan imágenes de la propia creación, integran una distancia interrogativa frente a lo dicho, introducen personajes de escritores, citas y una amplia serie de mecanismos intertextuales y autorreferenciales que son, todos, una ficcionalización del acto de escritura y una estrategia que convierte cualquier elemento del relato en símbolo reflexivo de su propia génesis o existencia. (Premat 2002: 15–16)

Aparte de que los episodios de Alina comparten entonces la dimensión metaliteraria de la obra saeriana, la descripción de la enajenación del personaje femenino remite a otro elemento presente a lo largo de la narrativa de Saer: la existencia de Alina es marcada por una carencia de atención (mental y corporal) y una resultante búsqueda de momentos de contacto con dimensiones concretas y tangibles de su entorno y de una atención hacia la dimensión corporal y sensual de su existencia[23]. También ese aspecto se encuentra en numerosos textos de Saer, donde "la omnipresencia de lo perceptivo, el despliegue de sensaciones, el contacto con las substancias, también están sugiriendo otro núcleo

---

[23] Como leitmotiv de ese anhelo de lo concreto y tangible sirven las cáscaras de mandarinas que Alina acostumbra juntar y que luego empieza a depositar debajo de la almohada de Sven quien no la toma en cuenta: "¿Podía alguien estar tan enajenado como para dormir sobre cáscaras de mandarina una semana entera sin sentir el olor? Con qué tipo de hombre estaba viviendo?" (Schweblin 2018: 147).

de la obra [. . .] que es la importancia atribuida a lo pulsional en la construcción literaria" (Premat 2002: 16). Esa atención hacia lo visible y el detalle marcan también la percepción de Alina en *Kentukis*: su deseo de una existencia diferente a la permanente planificación, comodificación y (auto-)explotación de los artistas de la residencia la acerca a los modos de existir pasivos de muchos personajes saerianos (y en *Nadie nunca nada* en particular, si bien el contexto histórico de la novela es totalmente diferente). Al mismo tiempo, en la exploración del pueblo oaxaqueño por parte de Alina se puede leer un intento de una conexión con su entorno y con lo local que evoca —frente a los lugares y sitios intercambiables del resto de los episodios de *Kentukis*— lejanamente esa poética saeriana de una experiencia espacial concreta (Santa Fe y su emblemática construcción de "la zona" del delta fluvial)[24].

Habiendo establecido estos ecos saerianos en el personaje de Alina de manera aproximativa, habría que aclarecer la función concreta de la figura con respecto a las otras tramas de la novela. Mi hipótesis es, como se ha señalado anteriormente, que Alina (y su 'dimensión saeriana') sirve como figura reflexiva frente a los principios del resto de la novela y, en un sentido más amplio, del estatus de la literatura y de la lectura en el presente (post-)global. Para ambos aspectos los episodios protagonizados por Alina ofrecen una serie de argumentos plausibles. El primero consiste en una crítica formulada por la argentina hacia el final de la novela:

> ¿Por qué esta historia no se trataba de otra cosa? ¿Por qué nadie confabulaba con los kentukis tramas realmente brutales? ¿Por qué nadie metía un kentuki cargado de explosivos en una desbordada estación central y hacía volar todo en pedazos? Por qué ningún usuario de kentuki chantajeaba a un operador aéreo y lo obligaba a inmolar cinco aviones en Frankfurt a cambio de la vida de su hijo? [. . .] ¿Por qué las historias eran tan pequeñas, tan minuciosamente íntimas, mezquinas y previsibles? Tan desesperadamente humanas. (Schweblin 2018: 189–190)

El descontento de Alina se lee aquí no solamente como una crítica de las historias sobre los kentukis circulando en los medios de comunicación (a lo que se refiere Alina en primer lugar), sino igualmente al resto de la novela de Schweblin: tal como se había argumentado arriba, aparte de la trama metaliteraria en torno a Alina y Sven, el resto de las historias de Schweblin podrían clasificarse con las palabras de Alina como "tan pequeñas, tan minuciosamente íntimas, mezquinas y previsibles" — su reclamo sería entonces una autocrítica de la novela misma pero también de los modos narrativos del presente en general. Es decir que, por un lado, los episodios en *Kentukis* se pueden considerar como

---

[24] Acerca de esos espacios líquidos véase Dünne (2013).

representativas de los tipos de narraciones prevalecientes en la época digital con su preferencia por los microtextos y la escenificación constante de lo banal y cotidiano. Ante ella, la literatura y la capacidad de leer —entendiendo el acto de lectura como técnica cultural compleja— se encuentran en un proceso de devaluación y de desaparición constantes, un aspecto que se advierte igualmente en los episodios de Alina y su amistad con la bibliotecaria municipal, Carmen. Esta comenta en una de sus conversaciones sobre el creciente desinterés por los libros por culpa de los kentukis: "Así es la gente, manita, teniendo en el pueblo semejante biblioteca – y señaló sus cuatro pasillos vacíos" (Schweblin 2018: 53)[25].

La literatura o, mejor dicho, el libro como medio se encuentra en oposición absoluta a las tecnologías nuevas como los kentukis, lo que queda claro cuando se lee sobre la figura de Marvin: "Se aburría tanto que hasta había intentado dejar quieto al kentuki y estudiar. Al fin y al cabo, los libros estaban ahí, tan toscos y permanentes que a veces Marvin jugaba a abrirlos despacio, como reliquias de una civilización anterior. Pero siempre volvía al kentuki, a esa eterna noche oscura donde casi nunca pasaba nadie" (Schweblin 2018: 63–64). Su máxima expresión alcanza este discurso crítico de la multiplicación permanente de historias mundanas en el episodio final de la novela y la exposición que Sven había estado preparando durante la estadía en México y que se describe desde la perspectiva de Alina de la siguiente manera:

> Había kentukis por todos lados, tenía una lechuza a sus pies, de hecho, estudiándola. El piso estaba cubierto de círculos de plástico violetas y cada círculo contenía una palabra: 'tócame', 'sígueme', 'quiéreme', 'me gusta'. [. . .] Llevaba escrito en la frente un número de teléfono, de hecho casi todos los kentukis tenían algo escrito: números, correos, nombres. También tenían papeles pegados a la espalda. [. . .] Alina buscó un 'no' cerca, pero los dos que encontró ya estaban ocupados. Parecía haber tante gente como kentukis, y juntos componían una interminable secuencia de chillidos, conversaciones telefónicas y erráticos saltos de círculo en círculo. [. . .]. Alina [. . .] dio un salto en cuanto entendió que estaba parada en un 'te amo' y volvía a moverse para salir de un 'tócame' y un 'quiero'. Pero faltaba espacio para no decir nada, siempre se estaba pisando algo. (Schweblin 2018: 216)

La exposición funciona como una metáfora de la comunicación digital del presente en el que las opciones de la negación (el 'no' que Alina no encuentra) o del silencio ("faltaba espacio para no decir nada") no están previstas. La necesidad

---

[25] El motivo de la bibliotecaria municipal y el destino de los libros evocan igualmente el pasaje en *Nadie nunca nada* en el que la biblioteca municipal del lugar de los sucesos se quema ("No quedó lo que se dice nada de la biblioteca, que era una piecita llena de libros acomodados sobre estantes que cubrían dos paredes enteras", Saer 2014: 65).

de comunicarse —y de hacerlo de acuerdo con categorías expresivas siempre preconcebidas— va acompañada, además, de la imposibilidad de mantenerse al margen de esos procesos, aspecto que se hace evidente en la parte final de la novela. En la exposición de Sven, Alina se encuentra frente a una pantalla en la que se proyecta un video que la muestra a ella misma mediante la cámara del kentuki que Sven y ella tenían en casa durante su estadía en México. A raíz de su enajenación y su aburrimiento, Alina le había inferido una serie de daños y lesiones al kentuki – sin saber, como revela la exposición, que al otro lado de la cámara se encontraban Sven y también un niño pequeño observando todos sus actos violentos: "Sven la había exhibido en su propio pedestal, la había separado tan pulcramente en todas sus partes que ahora ella no sabía cómo moverse. Un hormigueo le pinchaba todo el cuerpo, incluso dentro, en el pecho, y se preguntó si no estaría dándole un ataque; de nervios, de pánico, de furia. De hartazgo" (Schweblin 2018: 219).

Lo que ese episodio final plantea no es solamente la dimensión abyecta de una existencia enajenada como la de Alina[26] y la amoralidad de un artista como Sven, sino también la imposibilidad de conservar espacios no-públicos y de experimentación, sea en la vida privada o artística. Si Alina en otro momento sostiene que el tratamiento de su kentuki forma parte de "un experimento con el Coronel Sanders, pero todavía estoy buscándole la forma" (Schweblin 2018: 151), entonces la exposición condensa la problemática señalada de un mundo contemporáneo que no conoce el anonimato. La ilusión de Alina de "no ser nadie [que] era otra forma de anonimato, una que la volvía tan poderosa como el [ser kentuki]" (Schweblin 2018: 110), queda radicalmente defraudada a raíz de su descubrimiento público en la exposición, o como se lee en las últimas frases de la novela sobre la reacción de Alina en el lugar de los sucesos:

> Las luces de Vista Hermosa se irían perdiendo poco a poco, hasta que solo pudiera adivinarse, en el punto más dorado de la cumbre, la luminosa galería del Olimpo. Se olvidaría de todos esos dioses y, sin ningún tipo de resistencia, se dejaría caer hacia la tierra. Se entregaría. Se lo decía, pero ya no podía volver a cerrar los ojos. Respiraba sobre los círculos, sobre cientos de verbos, órdenes y deseos, y la gente y los kentukis la rodeaban y empezaban a reconocerla. Estaba tan rígida que sentía su cuerpo crujir, y por primera vez se preguntó, con un miedo que casi podría quebrarla, si estaba de pie sobre un mundo del que realmente se pudiera escapar. (Schweblin 2018: 220–221)

---

[26] Véase también la observación de Feuillet al respecto de que "la tortura remite alegóricamente a un aspecto doblemente significativo: primero muestra el alcance de la perversión en una existencia alienada y, en segundo lugar, exhibe la potencia de infundir terror latente en lo humano" (Feuillet 2020: 326).

La imposibilidad de 'escapar del mundo' y de vivir en el anonimato, sin embargo, no se limitan a la existencia alienada de Alina, sino que se puede leer —en su dimensión metaliteraria— como una crítica hacia el sistema del arte y, por consecuencia, también del funcionamiento del mercado artístico y literario global contemporáneo de acuerdo con lo señalado arriba. En la literatura mundial y sus sistemas clasificatorios, basados en la categorización rápida en función de una comodificación inmediata del texto literario, los espacios para una literatura formalmente experimental cada vez son más escasos. Y es aquí donde se pareciera establecer la conexión más importante entre la figura de Alina en *Kentukis* y las posiciones de Juan José Saer con respecto a la literatura y la lectura. Advierte Saer en su ensayo "Una literatura sin atributos":

> Considero que actualmente, por razones económicas, políticas y sociales, el lector está condicionado de antemano y que los contenidos de tal o cual literatura le son impuestos a través de elementos extraliterarios. En la cubierta de los libros, en los artículos de los periódicos, en la publicidad, en el chantaje de la superioridad numérica de las obras más vendidas, se escamotea la realidad material del texto, cuyo valor objetivo pasa a segundo plano. El lector cree saber de antemano lo que debe encontrar en un libro – y que lo encuentre o no, no tiene finalmente ninguna importancia. Se podría decir, me parece, que se trata de una maquinación de carácter represivo destinada a abolir la experiencia estética que es un modo radical de libertad [. . .]. Es así como ciertas designaciones que deberían ser simplemente informativas y secundarias se convierten, por el solo hecho de existir, en categorías estéticas. Es lo que ocurre, por ejemplo, con la expresión 'literatura latinoamericana'. (Saer 2014: 265–266)

Lo que Saer en su texto de 1980 critica con respecto a la transformación de la literatura latinoamericana en un producto de exportación a raíz del boom para el mercado literario global[27] no ha perdido nada de su vigencia para las lógicas mercantiles y académicas de una *World Literature* del presente. El arte —al igual que las obras del artista danés en la novela, pero también el conjunto de historias 'banales' de Schweblin— siempre tienen que llevar ya un atributo para corresponder a las expectativas y necesidades clasificatorias del mercado. El hecho de que esa expectativa en el caso de *Kentukis* ya no se refiere a las dimensiones exotistas de la época del (post-)boom no significa que un texto como la novela de Schweblin pueda circular sin ese tipo de etiquetas o expectativas. Por el contrario, las lecturas de la crítica a lo largo del mundo son una prueba visible de que la dimensión temática 'global' de *Kentukis* ha transformado el texto literario complejo de Schweblin en lo que Saer critica en otro ensayo intitulado "La novela y la crítica sociológica" como una forma reductora y

---

[27] Véase acerca del concepto de "literatura latinoamericana" también las reflexiones en Guerrero et al. (2020).

autoritaria de las lecturas sociológicas de la literatura a raíz de su "tendencia a considerar los procesos más generales de la sociedad como el contenido que debe hacerse visible en las obras narrativas" (Saer 2014: 229).

4 Conclusión

Tal como se ha señalado al principio de este estudio, un patrón de lectura dominante dentro del campo de la llamada "literatura mundial" contemporánea sería precisamente esa tendencia a leer obras literarias, en primer lugar, en función de su valor explicativo de esos "procesos más generales de la sociedad" que menciona Saer. *Kentukis* como novela y su recepción global serían un ejemplo claro de esa tendencia. Sin embargo, ese tipo de lectura e interpretación solamente funciona si el enfoque de análisis se limita exclusivamente al gran conjunto de esas "pequeñas historias" que conforman la mayor parte del libro de Schweblin. Son ellas que se prestan precisamente para ese tipo 'lecturas sociológicas' discutiendo la novela en función de los fenómenos de la comunicación digital planetaria. En cambio, si se toman en serio las preguntas que plantean los episodios en torno a la pareja de artistas y si se cambia el enfoque de lectura hacia las micro-dimensiones del texto, como en el caso de la referencia intertextual a Saer, la dimensión compleja y (auto-)crítica de la novela se hace visible: en su centro —y en eso consiste la ingeniosa trampa que Schweblin inserta en el texto— se articula una burla de esas lecturas demasiado evidentes y, quizás también, un anhelo por otras formas de escribir y de ser leída de una manera diferente, formas que no corresponden a la superficialidad temática y reduccionista del presente en el marco de la literatura global. La figura de Alina representaría una tendencia crítica de ese modelo (que, si se quiere, podría llamarse postglobal): el sentido de los episodios en torno a la pareja de (in-)artistas conforman dentro de la novela 'banal' de Schweblin lo que Saer identificó como

> los núcleos poéticos de la narración [que] no están en el saber expuesto sino en los momentos en que la consciencia del personaje se hace autoconciencia y conciencia del mundo. Sin la fluidez de los nexos estructurales, marcados por el desarrollo de la conciencia de Hans Castorp, la variedad de los temas expuestos [en *La montaña mágica*] no constituiría más que un catálogo de conocimientos ya verificados (Saer 2014: 226).

En su diseño formal del choque de ese 'catálogo' de las tramas 'globales', diseñadas como anzuelos para las lecturas superficiales de la crítica, y ese 'núcleo poético' en torno a la figura de la "inartista", *Kentukis* entraría precisamente en esa categoría de ficción que Saer clasifica como una antropología especulativa[28]: "Quizás [. . .] esta manera de concebirla podría neutralizar tantos reduccionismos que [. . .] se obstinan a asediarla. Entendida así, la ficción sería capaz no de ignorarlos, sino de asimilarlos, incorporándolos a su propia esencia y despojándolos de sus pretensiones de absoluto" (Saer 2014: 16). Desde esta perspectiva también se revela el misterio del título de la novela. A primera vista, *Kentukis* se presenta como una novela 'global': consumible a la rápida, al estilo de un pollo de la cadena estadounidense, con sus figuras planas y sus tramas fácilmente digeribles que dejan sabor a poco o nada, es decir, el menú ideal para los críticos siempre voraces y formados de acuerdo con la lógica de la literatura mundial. El genio de Samanta Schweblin consiste en haber escondido al interior de este pedazo de *fast food* literario unas pistas apenas visibles permitiendo, como diría otro maestro constructor de ficciones, "a unos pocos

---

[28] La idea de la ficción como "especulación" bien podría reforzarse para el caso de Kentukis mediante otra referencia intertextual, que sería la obra de la autora de ciencia-ficción norteamericana Ursula K. Le Guin. La novela de Schweblin lleva un epígrafe tomado de un relato de Le Guin, *The Left Hand of Darkness* (1969) ("Nos contará usted de los otros mundos / allá entre las estrellas, / de los otros hombres / de las otras vidas?", en el original: "Will you tell us about the other worlds out among the stars— the other kinds of men, the other lives?"). En el prefacio de su novela, Le Guin a su vez critica la tendencia de leer libros de ciencia-ficción de una manera reduccionista como predicciones del futuro concebidas según un esquema más o menos simplista y previsible: "Science fiction is often described, and even defined, as extrapolative. The science fiction writer is supposed to take a trend or phenomenon of the here-and-now, purify and intensify it for dramatic effect, and extend it into the future. 'If this goes on, this is what will happen.' A prediction is made. Method and results much resemble those of a scientist who feeds large doses of a purified and concentrated food additive to mice, in order to predict what may happen to people who eat it in small quantities for a long time. The outcome seems almost inevitably to be cancer. So does the outcome of extrapolation. Strictly extrapolative works of science fiction generally arrive about where the Club of Rome arrives: somewhere between the gradual extinction of human liberty and the total extinction of terrestrial life" (Le Guin 1976: 26). Ante ese tipo de lecturas reduccionistas, Le Guin resalta precisamente la capacidad especulativa de la literatura y su carácter metafórico como medio de esa especulación —algo que bien podría aplicarse también a *Kentukis* donde los dispositivos y la novela en su funcionamiento análogo adquieren ese mismo carácter especulativo y metafórico (cf. Le Guin: "All fiction is metaphor. Science fiction is metaphor. What sets it apart from older forms of fiction seems to be its use of new metaphors, drawn from certain great dominants of our contemporary life—science, all the sciences, and technology, and the relativistic and the historical outlook, among them. Space travel is one of these metaphors; so is an alternative society, an alternative biology; the future is another. The future, in fiction, is a metaphor. A metaphor for what? If I could have said it non-metaphorically, I would not have written all these words, this novel functions as a crippling censorship over high art, and to allow the 'paraliterary' forrn thereby to inherit the vocation of giving us alternate versions of a world that has elsewhere seemed to resist even *imagined* change" (26–27)).

lectores —a muy pocos lectores— la adivinación de una realidad atroz o banal" (Borges 1987 [1956]: 13).

Bibliografía

Borges, Jorge Luis (1987 [1956]): *Ficciones*. Madrid: Alianza.
Diamond, Patrick (ed.) (2018): *The Crisis of Globalization: Democracy, Capitalism and Inequality in the Twenty-First Century*. London: I.B. Tauris.
Dünne, Jörg (2013): "Vom Fluss ohne Ufer zum Swimmingpool. Flüssige Räume bei Juan José Saer". En: *Romanische Forschungen*, 125, pp. 226–238.
Feuillet, Lucía (2020): "Los dispositivos del complot en *Kentukis*, de Samanta Schweblin". En: *Mitologías hoy*, vol. 22, pp. 317–335.
Folger, Robert (2013): "The Absent Cause of World Literature." En: *European Review*, Vol.21, no. 2, pp. 252–262.
Guerrero, Gustavo/Locane, Jorge J./Loy, Benjamin/Müller, Gesine (2020): "A modo de introducción. Literatura latinoamericana: inflexiones de un término". En: Guerrero, Gustavo et al. (eds.): *Literatura latinoamericana mundial. Dispositivos y disidencias*. Berlin/Boston: De Gruyter 2020, pp. 1–16.
Guerrero Gustavo/Loy, Benjamin/Müller, Gesine (eds.) (2021): *World Editors. Dynamics of Global Publishing and the Latin American Case between the Archive and the Digital Age*. Berlin/Boston: De Gruyter.
Habjan, Jernej/Fabienne Imlinger (eds.) (2016): *Globalizing Literary Genres*. London: Routledge.
Hoyos, Héctor (2015): *Beyond Bolaño. The Global Latin American Novel*. New York: Columbia University Press.
Illouz, Eva (2007): *Cold Intimacies: The Making of Emotional Capitalism*. Cambridge: Polity Press.
Jiménez Barrera, Joaquín Lucas (2020): "Del capitalismo de lo somático a la tecnología de la afectividad. Representación de las subjetividades neoliberales en *Los cuerpos del verano* (2012) y *Kentukis* (2018)". En: *Mitologías hoy*, vol. 22, pp. 87–101.
Latour, Bruno (2008): *Reensamblar lo social: Una introducción a la teoría del actor-red*. Buenos Aires: Ediciones Manantial.
— (2007): *Nunca fuimos modernos. Ensayo de antropología simétrica*. Buenos Aires: Siglo XIX.
Le Guin, Ursula K. (1976 [1969]): *The Left Hand of Darkness*. New York: Ace.
Locane, Jorge (2019): *De la literatura latinoamericana a la literatura (latinoamericana) mundial. Condiciones materiales, procesos y actores*. Berlin/Boston: De Gruyter.
Müller, Gesine (2022): *How Is World Literature Made? The Global Circulations of Latin American Literatures*. Berlin/Boston: De Gruyter.
Müller, Gesine/Locane, Jorge/Loy, Benjamin (eds.) (2018): *Re-Mapping World Literature. Estéticas, mercados y epistemologías entre América Latina y el Sur Global*. Berlin/Boston: De Gruyter.
Müller, Gesine/Siskind, Mariano (eds.) (2019): *World Literature, Cosmopolitanism, Globality: Beyond, Against, Post, Otherwise*. Berlin/Boston: De Gruyter.

Osorio-Restrepo, Valerie (2021): "Intimidades en red: exhibición y vigilancia en *Kentukis* de Samanta Schweblin". En: *Perífrasis. Revista de Literatura, Teoría y Crítica*, vol. 12, no. 24, pp. 87–104.
Premat, Julio (2002): *La dicha de Saturno. Escritura y melancolía en la obra de Juan José Saer*. Rosario: Beatriz Viterbo.
Saer, Juan José (2014): *El concepto de ficción*. Buenos Aires: Seix Barral.
— (2004 [1980]): *Nadie nada nunca*. Buenos Aires: Seix Barral.
Schweblin, Samanta (2018): *Kentukis*. Barcelona: Random House.
Staab, Philipp (2019): *Digitaler Kapitalismus. Markt und Herrschaft in der Ökonomie der Unknappheit*. Berlin: Suhrkamp.
Walkowitz, Rebecca (2015): *Born Translated. The Contemporary Novel in an Age of World Literature*. New York: Columbia University Press.

5 **New Narratives of Migration and Displacement**

Gustavo Guerrero
Perder el mundo
la poesía venezolana ante la experiencia de la migración

Durante sus primeros años de exilio en Nueva York, Hannah Arendt acuñó un término para describir la condición de aquellos que habían sido privados del mundo donde sus palabras y sus gestos contaban y tenían un significado: *Worldlessness* (Arendt 2004 [1951]: 612–615). Junto a otras dos nociones claves —*Homelessness* y *Statelessness*—, esta constituye, como es sabido, un capítulo central de su reflexión sobre el totalitarismo en la inmediata postguerra. Sin embargo, lejos de circunscribirse a aquel momento, su fuerza interpretativa ha adquirido en las últimas décadas una nueva actualidad ante la crisis climática planetaria, el fenómeno de los estados fallidos y las vastas migraciones y desplazamientos de población a los que estamos asistiendo (Fistetti 2008: 110). Todos reconfigurarían un entorno inestable, quizás uno de los últimos paisajes de la modernidad, donde el término de Arendt, reciclado, califica formas particulares e inéditas de dominación y exclusión.

Valga recordar que *mundo* no es, para la filósofa, una extensión física ni geográfica; no es un lugar natural sino el fruto de la labor humana: es aquello que los hombres construyen y comparten *entre ellos* a través del tiempo, interactuando e intercambiando responsablemente lenguajes, acciones y objetos. Digamos que es la fábrica de lo social vista como un espacio intermedio, colectivo, plural y público. Por eso, desde el punto de vista de Arendt, no estamos en el mundo, sino que lo erigimos y a la vez formamos parte de él. Sin embargo, también podemos perderlo cuando experiencias como las persecuciones, la deportación, el exilio o el *insilio* nos aíslan de los otros, privándonos de nuestros interlocutores y de nuestras referencias familiares, arrancándonos del tejido comunitario que reconocía plenamente nuestros fueros y arrojándonos a un territorio ajeno donde, al igual que los refugiados y los apátridas, ya no contamos como individuos o personas en una esfera pública, ni disponemos de derechos políticos que avalen la significación de nuestras palabras y nuestros actos (Gottsegen 1993: 57). Formulada originalmente como uno de los resortes del totalitarismo, esta desposesión, que es la que sufren tantos y tantos migrantes en la actualidad, conlleva una reducción radical de lo humano a la vida desnuda y a la más rigurosa intemperie, como diría Agamben.

Gustavo Guerrero, CY Cergy Paris Université

∂ Open Access. © 2023 the author(s), published by De Gruyter. This work is licensed under the Creative Commons Attribution-NonCommercial-NoDerivatives 4.0 International License.
https://doi.org/10.1515/9783110762143-015

Ahora bien, por extrema que parezca, no se trata de la única forma de alienación que Arendt imagina. Existe en su pensamiento posterior otra no menos crítica y determinante: la desaparición no ya del sujeto sino de la tarea interhumana, del *entre* en sí mismo, que resulta del rápido proceso de atomización en nuestras sociedades de masas y desemboca en este oscuro presente que nos ha vuelto incapaces de hacernos responsables de la construcción de un futuro y, por ende, de la concepción de un mundo en común (Straehel 2017: 369–373). Lo uno no va evidentemente sin lo otro y ambos apuntan por igual a la crisis del cosmopolitismo y el humanismo ilustrados que, durante dos siglos, de Kant a Derrida, hicieron de nuestra idea del mundo un horizonte colectivo y universal de justicia y reconciliación. Hoy, el regreso de los nacionalismos más autoritarios y el miedo al otro parecieran haber sepultado las ilusiones que albergamos cuando pensamos el planeta como una tarea compartida.

Si la dramática descomposición de la sociedad venezolana en las primeras décadas del siglo XXI confronta a nuestra joven poesía con una recia experiencia de la catástrofe, la multitudinaria diáspora de más de 5 millones de personas —una crisis solo comparable hoy con la Siria (ACNUR, 2021)— no ha hecho más que redimensionar dicha experiencia llevándola a un nivel más vasto, variado e intenso, a otra escala de realidad. Tal como lo muestran los títulos de los libros de Santiago Acosta (*1983), Adalber Salas Hernández (*1987) y Jesús Montoya (*1993) a los que se han otorgado recientemente importantes premios internacionales —me refiero a *El próximo desierto* (2019), *Salvoconducto* (2015) y *Hay un sitio más allá de los incendios* (2017)— escribir poesía es dar una respuesta a la excepcional circunstancia que los marca, elaborando una poética catastrófica y/o post-catastrófica, cuyo reto es decir, sucesiva o simultáneamente, el colapso de Venezuela y las calamitosas condiciones de supervivencia de la población, la larga agonía de una nación en ruinas y la diáspora de cinco millones de sus gentes, el duelo de un sueño moderno y de una idea de comunidad mundial. Junto a Natasha Tiniacos (*1981) y Alejandro Castro (*1986), con quienes comparten la experiencia de la emigración, los tres forman hoy un compacto grupo que toma la palabra con una clara conciencia del momento terminal que les ha tocado vivir y de la fractura civilizatoria que los sitúa en una posición insólita y paradójica: entre un pasado del que acaso no haya mucho que rescatar y un porvenir que parece cerrarse inexorablemente.

En sus libros, cada cual explica las causas y razones que lo llevaron a dejar el país: "¿Motivo del viaje? Porque yo ya no soy / yo ni mi casa es ya mi casa. . .", avanza Salas Hernández en el último poema de *La ciencia de las despedidas* (Salas Hernández 2018: 50). "Los hijos del desarraigo / nacimos / con lágrimas en los pies. . .", agrega Tiniacos en su *Historia privada de un etcétera* (Tiniacos 2011: 47).

Y Castro, como si concluyera y para definir su migración, escribe con ironía en su libro más reciente, *Parasitarias* (2019):

> Es soñar que se vuelve a empezar de cero,
> otra lengua, otro rostro que devolverle al cemento,
> otra voz, hormigón y herrumbre,
> donde no crecen los mangos,
> donde nada crece. Y es soñar
> que se está perdido para bien
> (Castro 2019: 47)

Marcharse de Venezuela no supone, para ellos, escapar de un infierno para llegar a una suerte de paraíso abierto y cosmopolita donde estaría asentado positivamente el mundo verdadero. Por el contrario, insisto en que hay un continuum entre las dos experiencias, pues también el orbe de afuera experimenta su pérdida como construcción y horizonte común —su *Worldlessness*— ante la situación a que nos ha conducido un sistema internacional desigual y globalizado, cuyo poder de devastación es tal que ha hecho imposible imaginar un porvenir para el planeta. "Nuestras crisis son las mismas / y todas las ciudades se caen a pedazos", escribe Acosta en un poema que intitula elocuentemente "Irse". Y agrega unos versos después, como para confirmar que no hay reino prometido:

> Bendícenos, Señor, a los que te hemos traicionado.
> Sálvanos de la pobreza, sálvanos de la desesperanza.
> Sálvanos, Padre, de Barcelona, sálvanos de Madrid,
> sálvanos de San Francisco, de Nueva York, sálvanos
> de Buenos Aires. La beatitud no es más que un sueño violento,
> pero tu salvación es puro misterio,
> un gueto abandonado que hemos venido a poblar
> (Acosta 2018: 11)

Ese gueto pareciera que es lo poco que queda del *mundo* como proyecto colectivo de la humanidad, como ese final feliz de la historia al que debía conducirnos la globalización. En su último libro, *El próximo desierto* (2019), que recibió en México el premio José Emilio Pacheco, Acosta parte de un epígrafe de Fredric Jameson —"We need to develop an anxiety about losing the future"— para pintarnos un paisaje planetario distópico, incierto y devastado, "una geografía de la catástrofe", según señalan los jurados (Acosta 2019: 12). Lluvias ácidas, ciudades colapsadas, pandemias, agricultura intensiva, extractivismo, tráfico y explotación de la mano de obra migrante, hambrunas, protestas, represión, estados de sitio. . . el poeta recorre los distintos escenarios de nuestra crisis civilizatoria a la manera de un testigo de su época y elabora una narrativa del hoy como callejón sin salida: "Este es el único eslogan que todavía tiene alguna validez: / 'Vienen tiempos feroces. / Nada de lo que suponemos es cierto'" (Acosta 2019: 31).

La tradicional doble retórica del sujeto migrante que, o bien construye su nostalgia idealizando el lugar que ha dejado, o bien celebra las bondades del lugar al que llega, idealizándolo igualmente, no opera aquí en el cruce entre pasado y presente. No hay memoria infeliz por lo que quedó atrás, ni encomio hacia lo que se está viviendo. Las dos instancias forman parte de una misma experiencia de pérdida del mundo sobre un continuum temporal que hace a nuestros poetas unos contemporáneos de sus contemporáneos y participes del mismo desastre. Salas Hernández escribe así en su libro ya mencionado, *La ciencia de las despedidas*, un conjunto de poemas entre los cuales destacan distintos discursos sobre el viaje, la extranjería, la memoria, la exclusión y la lengua. Sin embargo, al recuerdo de una Caracas signada por la miseria, las desigualdades y la violencia, y sobre todo por la omnipresencia obsesiva de la muerte, corresponde una suerte de prosaica y discreta historia universal de la infamia donde crímenes, ejecuciones, vejámenes y atropellos se suceden a todo lo largo del planeta y de sus diferentes edades, desde Kansas City hasta Auschwitz-Birkenau, o desde el neolítico hasta nuestro siglo XXI. Sirva de ejemplo el poema XVII, que da título al volumen y lleva un epígrafe de Ossip Mandelstam: "Estudié la ciencia de la despedida / en los calvos lamentos de la noche".

> En Nataruk, al norte de Kenia, arqueólogos
> hallaron los restos de 27 seres humanos
> amontonados en la palma seca de lo que
> solía ser un lago. La datación por radiocarbono
> de conchas y sedimentos minerales permitió
> estimar que los cadáveres tenían entre 9.500
> y 10.500 años de antigüedad. Se trataba de
> un grupo diverso: hombres y mujeres adultos
> –una de ellas embarazada–, ancianos, niños.
> Varios tenían las manos atadas. Todos
> presentaban traumatismos graves, señales
> de golpes realizados con objetos
> contundentes, como mazos, así como
> heridas producto de armas punzopenetrantes.
> Los expertos creen que los 27 sujetos fueron
> reducidos, ejecutados sistemáticamente y
> lanzados al lago, donde el limo se ocupó
> de conservarlos. Es así como los cuerpos
> aprenden a hablar, a decir la vida sin
> elocuencia, en kilos de carne, bilis,
> flema y saliva, polvo y brillo inclemente.
> La vida labios abiertos, dientes cariados,

> osamenta de plomo. Cuero extendido
> bajo la furia del mediodía, su ojo tosco y
> cóncavo. Desaparición, despedida,
> miembro fantasma, ciencia trunca.
> (Salas Hernández 2018: 27)

Salas Hernández arma su poemario a través de este contrapunto entre la referencia a los migrantes de Venezuela y la referencia a las geografías y los tiempos más diversos y aciagos, poniendo en escena, dentro del proceso mismo de composición, la naturaleza descentrada del discurso migrante con esas constantes idas y venidas que miman y reproducen el movimiento del viaje. Y es que, como bien supo observar Antonio Cornejo Polar hace ya muchos años a propósito del problema de la desterritorialización discursiva, "el desplazamiento migratorio duplica (o más) el territorio del sujeto y le ofrece o lo condena a hablar desde más de un lugar; es un discurso doble o múltiplemente situado" (Cornejo Polar 1996: 841). Tal inestabilidad politópica y politrópica pide a su vez una lectura que, en lugar de reducir el texto poético a una sola matriz homogénea, sea capaz de seguir la circulación del sentido entre territorios, tiempos, culturas y lenguas distintas, asumiendo sus contradicciones, incongruencias e incompatibilidades como parte de proceso de construcción de una voz y una escucha nuevas.

Natasha Tianiacos se mueve con soltura por estos espacios liminares e intermedios donde sus crónicas de lo íntimo se proyectan en una experiencia del exilio y crean un singular punto de encuentro entre lo interior y exterior. "No podrías haber nacido en otra época mejor que esta, / en la que todo se ha perdido", escribe provocadoramente en el manuscrito inédito de su nuevo libro, *Mignumi o el cuerpo del deseo*. Hace ya algunos años, en una reseña de *Historia privada de un etcétera* (2011), Luis Enrique Belmonte señalaba con buen tino que, en los versos de Tiniacos, "el sujeto se desplaza por zonas de la existencia que suelen pasar inadvertidas, reconociéndose en aquello que va quedando del tránsito", y agregaba de seguido que "el carácter excéntrico de esta poesía nos impele a indagar en lo ajeno y plural para encontrar las huellas de lo cercano y propio" (Belmonte 2012). Hay sin lugar a duda una fuerte tensión dialéctica en la sensibilidad de la poeta, que genera universos compuestos, heterogéneos y complejos, emocional y conceptualmente. "Hablar es llevar una vida doble", afirma en uno de los poemas del manuscrito ya citado. Pero acaso los versos que nos den la mejor medida de la alta densidad de su escritura estén unas páginas después, en una poesía bilingüe y politópica. No es fácil describir exactamente lo que hace en ella con las palabras, pero digamos que, buscando en la repetición de una frase hecha una cierta familiaridad con la lengua inglesa, la yuxtapone, hemistiquio con hemistiquio, con una secuencia caótica en español que *desfamiliariza,* si se me permite el neologismo, su lengua materna. Tiniacos crea así un vivo efecto de contraste entre los dos idiomas e inventa un inusitado ritmo común que circula entre ellos, como si tratara de resumir, encabalgándolos, los múltiples lugares de su enunciación:

Animal de afuera, animal de adentro:

Los olores de las estaciones salen por la boca.
Cuando mi madre se despide es una petición de tiempo
y "que la luz nos guíe como un par de zapatos".
From where I stand la línea del horizonte
es menos paisaje y más arriba.
From where I stand o aproximaciones,
como números en la planilla de la aduana.
From where I stand mi perro es una cifra redonda
que ladra en vocales fuertes.
From where I stand con cada roncha seca,
cada jeringa que dejé queriendo más mi tacto,
cada acera ambarina donde la libertad ha sido un entreacto,
el tránsito de una vida a otra.
From where I stand la gente camina y agradece.
Gracias pues aquí sigo,
aquí proclamo mi presencia y nadie la arrebata.
Anclado, diría,
From where I stand, el jardín
si la podadora pasa por alto.
From where I stand nada sucede,
pongo la alarma y el teléfono me priva.
From where I stand el zumbar de mis oídos me gobierna.
From where I stand, garrapata a la deriva.
¿Te has preguntado alguna vez cómo concibe el mundo,
equilibrándose en una rama a punto de saltar, comer y morir?
From where I stand aprendo a esperar de sombra al árbol
que cuenta hasta tres y se rehúsa.
Seré paciente, amor, si te haces laguna
y me dejas seca *From where I stand* con todo y eso,
tiendo a enamorarme, mi charquito, mi república.
From where I stand ser el peor requiere también una destreza.
From where I stand ningún metal es frío,
ningún metal es frío en la nuca,
lo prometo con la nuca en la mano.
From where I stand la tanqueta militar retrocede.
From where I stand el sonido de los niños,

el sonido de los niños

curándose solos,
puestos al sol para que ayude el viento

que solo quiere estar más cerca de la tierra.
(Tiniacos, *Mignumi*)

Haciendo gala de un oído capaz de trabar una singularísima relación entre sus dos espacios y sus dos lenguas, en su *in-betweenness*, Tiniacos las trabaja desde adentro, sin ocultar las diferencias ni buscar necesariamente una síntesis conciliadora ni un posible hogar: "No soy el campesino que ha migrado / sino la extranjera en el mundo / y me protege Hermes, el dios de los umbrales, / en mi constante viaje ante-morada" (Tiniacos, *Mignumi*). Sus experimentos con los idiomas son acaso la faz más visible de la problematización de los vínculos con la lengua materna que se ha vuelto un tema recurrente en la última poesía de Castro, de Salas Hernández y de Montoya. Este último, por ejemplo, incorpora recientemente a sus propios poemas traducciones de poesía brasileña y nos ofrece incluso una elocuente personificación en la sección "Lingua" (*sic*) de su *Rua São Paulo* (2019):

Mudo nudo

Con escalofrío, la lengua se levanta a barrer la casa.
Cepilla su desganado cuerpo, pintarrajea su músculo
ausente de vértebras.

Hoy es lunes clarividente, y hay que barrer la casa,
    piensa ella.
 La casa de la lengua no es robusta,
  sus paredes son blancas y verdosas,
  su sala cristiana nos mira, nos mira girar
pasillos delgados como sombras.
  Simbólica no es, herbívora de luz, ¿*é*?
La lengua, ¿una máscara vaciada?,
 ¿una cáscara neurótica?

La lengua tiñe cosmética su atareo,
¿ustedes le dijeron algo? Díganle la verdad,
porque estoy tan solo, quiero decir, tan sola la lengua está
 que inventa una deshabitada acentuación,
un oportuno corte. . .
(Montoya 2019: 80)

Al igual que Tiniacos, Montoya se mueve en las fronteras encabalgadas de una imaginación dialógica, jugando con la prosodia del portugués en este libro donde además da cuenta de su viaje por tierra hasta el Brasil y de sus aprendizajes en la ruda escuela del extranjero. Su poesía heteroglósica y traductora, como la de tantos otros poetas contemporáneos, busca alguna forma de concierto en medio del desconcierto y acaso resguarda la semilla de esperanza que sembró el cosmopolitismo moderno y que aún perdura en nuestra visión del mundo como una instancia emancipadora. Digamos que es una manera de recordarnos que seguimos viviendo y escribiendo en presencia de los otros. O mejor, que dicha presencia arroja algo de la escasa luz fraterna que el quehacer poético todavía puede brindarnos a principios del siglo XXI, pero que no es visible sino desde la oscuridad que constituye el momento contemporáneo como experiencia de la pérdida del mundo.

A mi modo de ver, si la más joven poesía venezolana ha logrado hacerse en estos años recientes un lugar destacado dentro y fuera de Venezuela es porque, dolorosa y lúcidamente, ha entendido cuál es la condición de lo poético en las circunstancias actuales y, sin ceder a la tradición, ha conseguido apoderarse del lenguaje necesario para describirla. Estamos hablando de una experiencia de la desilusión, el despojamiento, la orfandad y la desesperanza. Y acaso también del duelo y la melancolía, como trata de redefinirlas Mariano Siskind en uno de sus últimos ensayos (Siskind 2018). Solo que aquí el acto mismo de seguir escribiendo poesía, como bien lo sabía Roberto Bolaño, es una tácita y contundente manera de seguir vivo, de resistir y de escapar del nihilismo. Por eso quisiera dejarle la última palabra a Salas Hernández y citar, para concluir, el poema final de *Salvaconducto*. Su representación de los métodos de la policía política, de la violencia, el atropello y la humillación que privan a un hombre de un lugar entre los hombres bien podría tener evidentemente un título o un epígrafe sacado de la obra de Hannah Arendt: *Worldlessness*. Lo esencial, sin embargo, es que el poeta sabe que no es positivamente otro el lenguaje con que hoy tiene que escribir nuestra pérdida del mundo, si quiere preservar el poder de lo poético para imaginar una alternativa y para sugerir, con alguna veracidad, que aún existe una casa común más allá de este presente.

Salvoconducto

Una madrugada de estas, las palabras van a forzar
la puerta de tu casa. Caminando sin hacer ruido, irán a
buscarte a tu cuarto; te encandilarán con linternas, te cerrarán
la boca de un golpe, arrancarán las sábanas para entregarte
a los perros del frío. No podrás hacer nada, tendrás una
capucha sobre la cabeza y el peso de un hierro en la frente.
No podrás hacer nada. Cuando te saquen así, cuando te insulten
las palabras, cuando te aten de manos y pies y sientas su hedor
a aguardiente y sus temblores de bazuco, cuando te dejen en
la garganta su crujido, su pólvora y su herrumbre –entonces
por fin sabrás que el miedo es tu pan, tu alfabeto. Ya no podrás
poner piedras sobre los párpados de los poemas para que no
despierten, piedras en sus bocas a montones, piedras en los

oídos para romperles el tímpano con ese silencio.
Tendrás que dejar sonar las palabras en la entraña intacta de
esa sordera. Permitirles sacudirse como animales de hojalata, ir y
venir con su respiración arrítmica, de motor que rasga la noche.
Las mismas palabras que te pusieron contra la pared y te
rompieron la nariz. Las que no tienen arrepentimientos
ni penitencias. Las que suenan a tiro, ambulancia, patrulla,
padrenuestro. Las que te brindan a veces un cigarro para
espantar el hambre. Las que no están en ningún pasaporte,
en ninguna cédula, partida de nacimiento o defunción, las que
te roban el nombre para venderlo de contrabando.
Ellas serán tu salvoconducto.
(Salas Hernández 2015: 90–91)

Bibliografía

ACNUR (2021): "Situación en Venezuela". En: La Agencia de la ONU para los Refugiados, https://www.acnur.org/situacion-en-venezuela.html (última visita: 08/01/2022).
Acosta, Santiago (2019): *El próximo desierto*. Guadalajara: Universidad de Guadalajara.
— (2018): *Cuaderno de otra parte*. Caracas: Libros del Fuego.
Arendt, Hannah (2004 [1951]): *The Origins of Totalitarianism*. New York: Schocken.
Belmonte, Luis Enrique (2012): "Ninguna realidad es insignificante". En: *Prodavinci*, http://historico.prodavinci.com/2012/12/04/artes/ninguna-realidad-es-insignificante-por-luis-enrique-belmonte/ (última visita: 08/01/2022).
Castro, Alejandro (2019): *Parasitarias*. Caracas: Libros del Fuego.
Cornejo Polar, Antonio (1996): "Una heterogeneidad no dialéctica: sujeto y discurso migrante en el Perú moderno". En: *Revista Iberoamericana*, LXII, n° 17, pp. 837–844
Fistetti, Francesco (2008): "Hannah Arendt à l'âge de la globalisation". En: *Tumultes*, n° 30, pp. 109–124.
Gottsegen, Michael G. (1993): *The Political Thought of Hannah Arendt*. New York: State University of New York Press.
Montoya, Jesús (2019): *Rua Saõ Paulo*. Caracas: Fundavag Ediciones.
Salas Hernández, Adalber (2018): *La ciencia de las despedidas*. Valencia: Editorial Pre-textos.
— (2015): *Salvoconducto*. Valencia: Editorial Pre-textos.
Siskind, Mariano (2018): "Towards a Cosmopolitanism of Loss: Essay about the End of the World". En: Müller, Gesine/Sisikind, Mariano (eds.): *Beyond, Against, Post, Otherwise*. Berlin/Boston: De Gruyter, pp. 203–235.
Straehle, Edgard (2017): "Sobre la barbarie: reflexiones de Arendt sobre *la pérdida del mundo*". En: *Bajo Palabra. Revista de Filosofía*, II época, nº 17, pp. 359–376.
Tiniacos, Natasha (en preparación): *Mignumi o el cuerpo del deseo* (manuscrito).
— (2011): *Historia privada de un etcétera*. Caracas: Cámara Escrita.

Ignacio M. Sánchez Prado
México, Estados Unidos y la era post-global
De la cultura fronteriza a la nueva cuestión binacional

I

Entre los textos que capturan las paradojas de la relación entre México y Estados Unidos, *On the Plain of Snakes* (2019) de Paul Theroux ofrece una de las visiones más completas y complejas. Theroux, quizá el mayor cronista de viajes en la literatura anglosajona, estructura su itinerario en dos etapas. Primero, recorre la frontera entre ambos países desde el Océano Pacífico hasta el Golfo de México, cruzando de un lado a otro en los distintos pares de ciudades vecinas (Juárez-El Paso, Laredo-Nuevo Laredo, etc.), para después viajar en carretera por México desde la frontera norte hasta el estado de Chiapas en el sur. En el cruce que conecta Yuma, Arizona, con San Luis Río Colorado, Sonora, Theroux apunta la enorme facilidad del cruce hacia México: "Just a walkway, no formalities, no one on either side looking at my passport or asking my name. It was the simplest crossing I'd ever made in a long career of crossing borders, and it happened to be a lovely day, so the idea of strolling so easily into another country lifter my spirits" (2019: 41). Tras recorrer la zona turística —una combinación de pintoresquismo con la emergencia de establecimientos médicos y dentales dirigidos a estadounidenses que buscan evadir los costos de su sistema privado de salud—, Theroux llega al parque industrial, donde los trabajadores de compañías como Daewoo y Bose Flextronics laboran tan cerca del muro fronterizo "to hear the radios crackling in Border Patrol vehicles and see the metal barbecues in the backyard of bungalows in Arizona's Las Villas division" (2019: 41). Sin embargo, esa facilidad de cruce no es recíproca y la hipervisibilidad de los Estados Unidos desde el lado mexicano es un recordatorio de que el ejército de trabajadores manufactura la mercancía de lujo adquirida por aquellos que habitan los suburbios visibles desde la fábrica carecen del derecho de caminar unos pasos hacia el país del norte. Theroux invita a sus lectores: "The next time you clap on your expensive Bose headphones or fire up your car stereo, you had to consider that they were put together a hundred yards from Arizona by someone living in a hut in the Sonoran Desert, and longing (because the US was easily visible) for something better" (2019: 41).

Ignacio M. Sánchez Prado, Washington University in St. Louis

On the Plain of Snakes provee a sus lectores una de las visiones más claras de la paradoja binacional de México y Estados Unidos, aquella que ha emergido en la tensión entre la creciente integración económica entre ambos países, y la intensa securitización del territorio estadounidense resultante en gran medida de la paranoia económica y política que resiste dicha integración. Aunque mucha de la securitización reciente tiene sus orígenes en la presidencia de Bill Clinton. Greg Grandin observa que la integración económica de México a los Estados Unidos a través del Tratado de Libre Comercio de América del Norte (TLCAN o NAFTA en sus siglas más reconocidas) atraía hacia el modelo capitalista de la post-guerra fría al país que constituía "the birthplace of the twentieth century's first great social revolt against U.S. capital" y que, tras el éxito de la línea dura reaganista en contra de las economías alternativas del Tercer Mundo, figuras como Henry Kissinger veían en México una vanguardia que, tras las reformas de Carlos Salinas de Gortari, creaban un modelo global en contra del estatismo de izquierda (2019: 237). A la vez, continúa Grandin, "the Clinton administration knew that NAFTA would lead to a spike in undocumented migration and planned accordingly", suscitando el crecimiento del aparato físico y biométrico de seguridad fronteriza y alimentando en alianza con los nativistas del Partido Republicano la xenofobia dirigida en contra de la población mexicana (2019: 244–245). En estos términos, *On the Plain of Snakes* da cuenta de la materialización física de esta paradoja, una continuación del régimen necropolítico moderno que simultáneamente extrae valor económico de México a los Estados Unidos a la vez que restringe la integración política y territorial que se anuncia en la vida cotidiana de las ciudades fronterizos y los cruces que se dan cada día.

II

Las fronteras, observa Manlio Graziano (2018), son simultáneamente obsoletas y reales. Por un lado, los flujos del capital y de la migración, del comercio y la información digital, han ejercido una potente fuerza desterritorializadora que ha socavado los regímenes modernos de soberanía y ha desvanecido en el aire, para usar la familiar metáfora de Marx, mucha de la solidez del estado-nación pre-neoliberal. Por otra parte, las fronteras son reales en la medida en que vivimos una radical intensificación de los regímenes militarizados de control y de la movilización política del etnonacionalismo como respuestas a las desestabilizaciones en los ámbitos de la subjetividad y la economía resultantes de dicha desterritorialización. Por esta razón, concluye Graziano, la gradual disolución de las fronteras refleja la crisis del estado-nacional moderno y su soberanía, alimentando, a su vez, un deseo político de refortalecimiento de la seguridad fronteriza, particularmente alimentada por las ansiedades económicas generadas por la migración y la globalización (2018: 80). Ante esta realidad, en un enciclopédico estudio sobre lo que llama "fronteras líquidas", Mabel Moraña argumenta que

> de la misma manera en que el concepto de ciudadano/ciudadanía constituyó una de las plataformas principales para organizar y pensar la modernidad, la noción de sujeto migrante (la figura que nombra esa expresión, la posición que marca ese concepto, los procesos de producción de significados que articula, constituye el lugar (al menos uno de los principales lugares) desde donde evaluar el capitalismo globalizado, sobre todo en cuanto a su costo extra-social (2021a: 22).

En clave deleuziana, Moraña enfatiza "las líneas de fuga a través de las cuales se disgrega el centralismo de lo nacional y se lanza a la exterioridad una fuerza política y social multitudinaria" que emerge como una "energía política que no puede ser desarticulada por efectos de la codificación securitaria" (2021a: 24).

La frontera México-Estados Unidos es indudablemente uno de los ejemplos paradigmáticos de esta situación. En datos recabados en 2021, se observa una enorme intensificación de los cruces de migrantes y su encuentro con la policía migratoria en los Estados Unidos. Según el análisis de John Gramlich y Alyssa Scheler (2021), los encuentros de migrantes con autoridades migratorias en 2021, arriba de 1.6 millones, rompen los récords de migración masiva establecidos tanto en la ola resultante de la crisis económica mexicana de 1982 como aquella que acompañó la crisis de 1994. Sin embargo, los números nos dicen también que México ya no es sólo, ni predominantemente, el lugar de origen de los migrantes, convirtiéndose en país de paso para concentraciones cada vez mayores de inmigrantes centroamericanos, haitianos, cubanos, venezolanos, colombianos y hasta africanos, que recorren el territorio del hemisferio en busca de los Estados Unidos. La multiplicación de orígenes nacionales en el cruce fronterizo ha resultado en un cambio paradigmático de la frontera, que implica cada vez menos una línea física, y cada vez más un aparato securitario descentralizado.

Como demuestra el periodista Todd Miller en *Empire of Borders* (2019), la frontera México-Estados Unidos ya no está definida solamente por el espacio territorial. Más bien, consiste en mecanismos físicos y digitales extraterritoriales diseñados para alcanzar un campo de visión total respecto al movimiento de objetos y cuerpos en el hemisferio y los océanos, con un aparato de rastreo que cubre las fronteras internacionales de todos los países del continente y varios satélites en Europa, Asia y Africa. De esta manera Miller documenta la forma en la cual la Border Patrol y ICE, los dos organismos de control migratorio, entrenan a sus contrapartes hemisféricas desde la frontera México-Guatemala hasta Brasil, así como la participación de varios territorios de ultramar en la protección del régimen fronterizo estadounidense. Miller muestra de manera consistente un esfuerzo de soberanización absoluta del movimiento territorial de parte de los Estados Unidos, y con la participación de los gobiernos nacionales de todas las extracciones políticas, con el fin de administrar de manera eficiente la versión real de la frontera —aquella diseñada para restringir la circulación de cuerpos y mercancías exteriores al gobierno del neoliberalismo tardío— y su versión obsoleta, creando mecanismos tecnológicos y militares de libre circulación del comercio y el capital económico y simbólico, así como de los actores y agentes de esos flujos.

Este proceso político y cultural se ha materializado en las estéticas literarias, mediáticas y culturales dentro de un marco geocultural que se ha denominado "Greater Mexico", término que ha desarrollado creciente popularidad a partir del énfasis en la articulación binacional entre México mismo y las culturas mexicanoamericana y chicana. El término fue originalmente acuñado por Américo Paredes (1993) para designar el área común entre lo que llamaba el "México de adentro", la nación mexicana" y el "México de afuera", las comunidades que viven en los Estados Unidos. Autores como José E. Limón (1999), Alan Eladio Gómez (2016) o Cara Kinnally (2019) han demostrado la importancia de dar cuenta de la cultura mexicana en ambos lados de la frontera como parte de un sistema sociohistórico de *longue durée* que da cuenta de las distintas manifestaciones ideológicas y estéticas de la producción cultural de la región. Las obras literarias de años recientes, legibles desde este marco, nos permiten pensar conceptualmente las tensiones y fantasmagorías que definen la tensión entre la soberanía inmaterial del flujo del capital y la soberanía material de la infraestructura de administración de los territorios. Al discutir la cuestión de post-globalidad que convoca a los textos de este volumen, se enfatiza el paso hacia la categoría de lo planetario, una articulación entre el mundo como cartografía simbólica y las dimensiones antropocénicas del cambio climático—en particular diálogo con la formulación de este concepto en el trabajo de Ursula K. Heise (2008) y Dipesh Chakrabarty (2021). La literatura post-global es, para mí, aquella que se enfrenta al colapso de la imaginación totalizante de la globalización, y de formas que la acompañan como la llamada "novela global" (Hoyos 2015; Kirsch 2016; DeLoughry 2020), para enfrentarse a un presente paradójico que simultáneamente reterritorializa las identidades y mecanismos soberanos de la nación, y prolifera los espacios liminales, como los cuadrantes binacionales, las fronteras y los espacios en estado de excepción.

III

En el caso específico de México, se trata de un giro que va más allá de los debates durante el cambio de siglo entre la novelística de cariz global que encarnó, entre otros, el grupo del Crack, y las novelísticas transculturales, particularmente aquella identificadas con la producción del norte de México y la frontera, que eran dos caras de la misma moneda pero aparentaban ser irreconciliables (Sánchez Prado 2020). También pertenece a un régimen que deriva del momento de consolidación corporativa de la edición en México y lo que llamé en uno de mis libros "occidentalismo estratégico", que buscaba una estética literaria alineada a la nueva transnacionalización pero resistía la demanda por formas derivativas del realismo mágico (Sánchez Prado 2018). Como discute Mabel Moraña en su detallado estudio de la obra de Yuri Herrera, Fernanda Melchor y Valeria Luiselli, titulado significativamente *Nosotros los bárbaros*, la literatura más reciente se define por formas distintas de "una producción simbólica que revela, mediatizadamente, la tensión entre el particular momento de desarrollo que atraviesa la cultura nacional y los procesos de transnacionalización cultural del capitalismo tardío" (2021b: 24). Moraña proporciona en su libro una valoración diferenciada que aprecia más la técnica literaria de Herrera por encima del exceso de Melchor y, con mayor énfasis, de la escritura de Luiselli, a la que considera una autora de estilo artificial y afectado. Una crítica más radical de la literatura mexicana que ha alcanzado visibilidad transnacional, particularmente en su representación de la violencia, es la de Oswaldo Zavala, quien arguye en *Los cárteles no existen* (2016) la idea de la narcoliteratura como implícitamente cómplice en la difusión de las narrativas sobre el narcotráfico del discurso securitario mexicano, y, en un artículo más reciente (2022), considera la literatura mundial mexicana como producto de un campo literario neoliberal interesado en la distinción social y cultural en el campo literario transnacional.

Las continuidades del debate entre transculturación y cosmopolitismo, y los efectos del campo literario neoliberal, pertenecen a una red de producción cultural que se puede caracterizar de manera más compleja desde una perspectiva binacional. Estrictamente hablando existe un campo binacional de producción literaria mexicana, si consideramos la presencia de varios escritores mexicanos en los Estados Unidos, incluyendo a figuras de gran visibilidad como Valeria Luiselli, Álvaro Enrigue, Pedro Ángel Palou, Cristina Rivera Garza o Yuri Herrera. Igualmente se podría mencionar el rol que los doctorados en literatura y los programas de escritura creativa han tenido en la formación de un grupo aún más sustancial de autores, incluyendo a poetas como Román Luján o Manuel Iris, ambos graduados con doctorados estadounidense, o a aquellos que han pasado por las maestrías de escritura creativa en lugares como New York University

(Jazmina Barrera y Brenda Lozano son dos ejemplos) o la University of Texas in El Paso (cuyos graduados incluyen a Herrera y al poeta Mijail Lamas). También existen escritores como Carmen Boullosa, Dolores Dorantes of Naief Yehya, que viven en los Estados Unidos sin participar directamente en estas estructuras. Y, en años recientes, la traducción constante de autores mexicanos al inglés ha contribuido de manera clara a su participación en una estructura cultural binacional, aunque descentralizada. Esta lista, que caracteriza sobre todo a autores del campo que podría llamarse "literatura mexicana" no abarca necesariamente a autores mexicano-americanos y chicanos, y que tienen distintos grados de conexión (y en algunos casos una desconexión total) con el campo literario mexicano. Ni tampoco abarca el creciente número de autores estadounidenses que, como Theroux, contribuye intermitente a la construcción de una cultura binacional.

No es de sorprenderse entonces que el término Greater Mexico comienza a ser traducido y redefinido desde la perspectiva de los estudios mexicanos. El ejemplo más claro de esta nueva apropiación es el volumen colectivo *El gran México. Las culturas mexicanas más allá de las fronteras* editado por José Manuel Valenzuela Arce. En su introducción, siguiendo la pista de Paredes, Valenzuela Arce define a El Gran México como "una (re)construcción sociocultural, simbólica e identitaria que alude a comunidades mexicanas-chicanas, imaginadas, transfronterizas y transnacionales. El Gran México refiere a imaginarios sociales anclados en reconocimientos compartidos que incluyen historias y tradiciones socioculturales comunes" (2020:14). El libro contiene un valioso mosaico de perspectivas, de lo cual destaca sin duda la posibilidad de discutir la cuestión mexicano-americana en español, en un libro de circulación en México, donde las comunidades diaspóricas han sido ignoradas y hasta rechazadas por mucho tiempo en los campos de producción cultural. Sin embargo, pese a enfatizar el concepto de Paredes, el libro captura, salvo contadas excepciones, una caracterización del gran México aún anclada en la idea de una comunidad diaspórica, ya que la mayor parte de los capítulos se enfocan en la producción mexicana en los Estados Unidos, sea la de los productores culturales nacidos en México y radicados del otro lado de la frontera, o, en la gran mayoría de los ensayos, la cultura chicana y mexicoamericana.

Resulta imaginable ampliar la cartografía del concepto del Gran México para pensar de manera más extensa los flujos de producción cultural en el circuito binacional México-Estados Unidos sin restringirse a la identidad o ciudadanía de los productores culturales, o la descripción de un campo literario unificado. Para este fin, me parece productivo desplegar una serie de categorías críticas que permitan dar cuenta de la naturaleza política y estética de los flujos que definen la relación entre los dos países, incorporando los modelos de los estudios chicanos y mexicano americanos, el campo académico mexicanista y los estudios fronterizos con el estudio de nuevas dimensiones críticas y sociales resultantes de la integración entre México y Estados Unidos resultante del TLCAN y otros procesos. Es claro que estas lógicas comienzan a manifestarse de maneras cada vez más intensa. El considerable incremento en la traducción y publicación de autores mexicanos en Estados Unidos es un fenómeno. Igualmente significativo es el creciente reconocimiento de la cultura mexicanoamericana como parte integral de la cultura mexicana, que se observa en el libro de Valenzuela Arce, y como mis coeditores y yo buscamos lograr al incluir un capítulo sobre el Gran México en nuestra *A History of Mexican Literature* (Sánchez Prado, Nogar y Ruisánchez Serra 2016). A esto también habría que agregarse libros como el de Theroux, o en el ciclo de novelas de Don Winslow (2005; 2015; 2019) sobre el agente de la DEA Art Keller y el desarrollo de la Guerra contra las Drogas en México. O casos como la reciente controversia en torno a la novela *American Dirt* de Jeanine Cummins (2021), que, como he discutido en otra parte (Sánchez Prado 2021), levantan preguntas importantes sobre la forma en que se imagina a México desde los Estados Unidos. Lo que se observa desde esta visión de conjunto es una red cultural en la cual la simbolización, representación y visibilización de los puntos de encuentro de los dos países funciona en el contexto de una matriz de nodos culturales irreductible a un campo de producción cultural único, pero que representa un territorio cultural pensable desde la idea de frontera, pero con extensiones y dimensiones binacionales que nuestras estrategias de territorialización crítica no acaban de capturar.

IV

Una exposición exhaustiva de la idea de la evolución en la idea de frontera en el siglo XXI requeriría de un espacio más extenso que el de este artículo. Sin embargo, conviene traer a colación algunas ideas de esta evolución para dar cuenta de la manera en que las tensiones inherentes a las definiciones teóricas de la frontera permiten ensayar ideas sobre la cultura binacional. En el erudito recorrido de Mabel Moraña (2021a: 435–517) en torno al concepto de frontera, se observa una particular evolución del término de la idea de delimitación, a la idea de entre-lugar o espacios híbrido, y la emergencia de producciones y teorizaciones que consideran a las fronteras tanto espacios de capital simbólico como paradigmas y metodologías que exceden al espacio físico. Paralelamente a su estudio sobre el tema, Moraña compiló el volumen *Liquid Borders*, donde un grupo de estudiosos dedicados a la zona mediterránea y el hemisferio americano dejan patente lo que la compiladora define como "the pervasive encounters between the massive fluxes of transnational migrants and the material and intangible obstacles imposed as proliferating *dispositifs* of border governmentality in the globalized world" (2021c: 1). En el caso de Moraña, el desarrollo teórico lleva a la discusión sobre el migrante como una de las cuestiones centrales del 2021.

En paralelo a esta discusión, hay que decir que en el caso particular de la frontera México-Estados Unidos opera hoy en día un debate entre teorías políticas que buscan dar cuenta de la paradoja que subyace el encuentro entre flujos y securitización descrito por Moraña. El problema territorial que aqueja la integración norteamericana es radicalmente distinto al que se ha constituido al norte del otro lado del Atlántico, donde la Unión Europea, aún con la crisis que ha significado el Brexit, ha permitido imaginar y atestiguar la existencia paralela de la integración económica con la política. Aunque no está de ninguna manera libre de fricciones, Europa ha creado, como discute Étienne Balibar, una dialéctica crítica en la cual se pueden pensar escalas de ciudadanía que pueden ir desde formas exclusionarias de la comunidad, hasta la posibilidad de una ciudadanía transnacional a nivel global (2002: 126). En el caso de la frontera México-Estados Unidos, la característica definitoria es precisamente el quiebre de esa simetría, donde el flujo libre de mercancías y capital es acompañado de un régimen acceso diferenciado a la ciudadanía—que va desde la imposibilidad de entrada o la condición indocumentada hasta membresías en sistemas de pre-monitoreo que facilitan el tránsito, como Global Entry (Emmelhainz 2016). En estos términos, Sandro Mezzadra y Brett Neilson aciertan al observar que la idea de frontera como muro y límite no facilita "an understanding of the diffusion of practices and techniques of border control within territorially bound spaces of citizenship and their associated labor markets. We claim that borders are equally devices of inclusion that select and filter people and different forms of circulation in ways no less violent than those deployed in exclusionary measures" (Mezzadra/Nielson 2013: 7). En el caso de la frontera México-Estados Unidos, lo crucial es la multiplicidad de culturas, subjetividades y violencias que suscita la relación diferenciada entre distintas personas, así como la diferenciación entre personas y mercancías.

En el programa televisivo *La frontera*, un documental de 2021 conducido por la chef mexicana Pati Jinich y transmitido por la televisión pública estadounidense, se observa esta lógica de una manera brutalmente simple y palpable. Al inicio del segundo episodio, observamos ganado que cruza libremente la frontera, ya que es criado en México y posteriormente comercializado en Estados Unidos. Uno no puede perderse la violenta ironía de que el ganado tiene un cruce sancionado que no le es permitido a millones de seres humanos, tanto los ciudadanos mexicanos que históricamente han sido violentados por la seguridad fronteriza, como a los migrantes de diversas nacionalidades varados en el lado mexicano de la frontera como consecuencia de la política *Remain in Mexico* del gobierno estadounidense. Es una manifestación viva de la circulación de mercancías y la restricción de personas. Esta paradoja ha fomentado gradualmente el avance de una cultura de la frontera que captura ese espacio sugerido en el título de un libro de ~~Heriberto Yépez~~, *Transnational Battle Field* (2017), un híbrido entre poemario y ensayo que presenta sin piedad la relación binacional posterior al 11 de septiembre y a la firma del TLCAN como un espacio de violencia y colonialidad, del cual es cómplice la poesía norteamericana desde Walt Whitman hasta figuras contraculturales contemporáneas como Charles Olson y Amiri Baraka.

V

El paradigma de cultura fronteriza como entre-lugar y espacio, popularizado en los años ochenta tras el éxito académico del libro *Borderlands/La Frontera* de Gloria Anzaldúa (1987), potenciando en el pensamiento de las décadas subsecuentes una idea de la frontera México-Estados Unidos "como espacio generador de sentido y productor de prácticas innovadoras", así como "el ámbito en que nuevas formas identitarias y post-identitarias emergen en relación con las formas de conciencia que ese espacio social promueve, y en base a las experiencias específicas que tienen lugar en torno a las vivencias de transitoriedad, rechazo, persecución, resistencia, combinación de culturas, lenguas, costumbres y creencias" (Moraña 2021a: 454). Estas ideas, a su vez, contribuyeron a la teorización de matrices culturales que interpretan esos intercambios transculturales como generativos, pese a la enorme violencia que los subyace. Es el caso de Walter Mignolo (2000), para quien el pensamiento de Anzaldúa es parte del ensamblaje crítico que define conceptos de "border thinking" y "languaging", o de escritoras como Stephanie Elizondo Griest, quien concluye su colección de crónicas *All Agents and Saints* con una visión utópica de las fronteras: "Spend enough time straddling one, and you can't help but wonder what bliss might follow if we all just embraced the spaces in between" (2017: 274).

Una versión contemporánea de esta línea de pensamiento es la encarnada en la obra del escritor Santiago Vaquera-Vásquez, un escritor autodefinido como fronterizo cuya obra se escribe en distintos registros del Spanglish, fluyendo de manera casi única entre México, Estados Unidos y sus espacios intermedios. En "The Unbearable Lightness of Being Fronterizo", Vaquera-Vásquez claramente delinea su pertenencia tanto a la línea que bien de Anzaldúa como a la idea del espacio fronterizo como utopía de encuentro político y cultural.

Vaquera hace eco de la obra del escritor sudafricano Breyten Breytenbach y su concepto del *Middle World* como "a world between nations and populated by migrants" (2019: 138; Breytenbach 2009). Así, Vaquera-Vásquez refiere a la frontera México-Estados Unidos, pero la engarza a una epistemología del viaje, en su caso a Turquía, para plantear una estética de la "unbearable lightness" o "insoportable levedad" —término tomado de Milan Kundera (1984)— definido tanto por los fantasmas y espectros que se acarrean en el cruce como por su capacidad de desmantelar narrativas reificantes de nación.

A pesar de la enorme productividad cultural que esta forma de fronterizo continúa teniendo —particularmente su urgencia con relación a la creciente xenofobia y violencia anti-mexicana materializada en la presidencia de Donald Trump y en el asesinato masivo de mexicanos en un Walmart de El Paso, Texas en 2019—, no es de sorprender que la obra de autores como Yépez manifieste una noción mucho más crítica y escéptica de las posibilidades de este intercambio. También publicada por Commune Editions en Oakland, la poeta Wendy Trevino, originaria del Valle del Río Grande, cuestiona en su libro *Cruel Fiction* el legado de Anzaldúa y la potencialidad política de su obra tanto en la dimensión epistemológica de la frontera como en el carácter utópico del mestizaje. El poema donde hace referencia directa a Anzaldúa lo deja clarísimo:

> Gloria Anzaldúa was also
> From the Valle. Her Wikipedia
> Page says she was born in Harlingen like
> Me. I read *Borderlands/La Frontera:*
> *The New Mestiza* in college, after
> One of my Philosophy professors
> Recommended it to me. At the time
> I was more than anything excited
> To be from the same place as this published
> Writer, but to be honest, I didn't
> Understand how "living between cultures"
> Made us special. I didn't even see
> How the "cultures" were distinct. I still don't
> Her approach didn't resonate with me.
> (2018: 82)

Este poema opera en dos gestos que revelan los desafíos generados por un entendimiento post-fronterizo de la cultura binacional. Primero, enfatiza las continuidades entre los dos países, sobre todo sus historias de violencia y exclusión; el poemario en particular ataca la idea de mestizaje y denota la existencia de estamentación racial en ambos lados de la frontera. Segundo, resiste la idea del espacio fronterizo como espacios de productividad debido a su encuentro entre dos culturas. A cambio, Trevino invita a sus lectores a pensar a la frontera en su historia de violencias y exclusiones:

> No one remembers the Alamo or
> Vicente Guerrero or the ban on
> Communication between Mexicans
> & slaves in parts of Texas. I don't know
> How much it matters, but I imagine
> A Valley where you learn about the Plan
> Growing up & the "Buffalo Soldiers"
> Of the 24th infantry, who marched
> On Jim Crow Houston's predominantly
> Black San Felipe district & opened
> Fire on the police —I imagine
> Life in that Valley & how it would be
> Harder not to hear these stories in that
> Place. It's hard to imagine but I try.

El deseo de imaginar una historia definida por las violencias soberanas y las resistencias igualmente violentas ante ella, una frontera que no es sólo punto de encuentro entre mexicanos y estadounidenses pero da cuenta de las poblaciones negras e indígenas, apunta hacia una forma de concebir y estetizar el Rio grande en un devenir de frontera a historia binacional y multirracial.

VI

La *longue durée* de la frontera México-Estados Unidos como mitología del excepcionalismo estadounidense (Grandin 2019) ha derivado así en formas culturales, ideológicas y políticas que plantean la binacionalidad más allá de la transculturación fronteriza y sus configuraciones utópicas. Aquí me parece necesario sugerir que el paso del paradigma fronterizo a la idea de la integración desigual de la cultura binacional México-Estados Unidos está posibilitada por el hecho de que la formulación de mucho del pensamiento fronterizo suscitado de Anzaldúa en adelante es en parte una configuración residual de lógicas culturales precisas de los años ochenta y noventa, incluyendo la amnistía de un gran número de mexicanos indocumentados bajo la ley de inmigración de 1986, la ley de doble nacionalidad aprobada en México en 1998 y, por supuesto, las posibilidades inscritas en la promesa de integración norteamericana con la firma del TLCAN en 1994. En el siglo XXI, la condición binacional ha sido redefinida por iniciativas securitarias como el muro fronterizo, la Iniciativa Mérida y la Guerra contra el Narco, así como el énfasis en el des-encuentro fronterizo inscrito en la obra de autores como ~~Yépez~~ y Trevino, parte de una tendencia, identificada por Ignacio Ballester Pardo (2020), de una poesía mexicana fronteriza sincronizada con las violencias políticas del espacio binacional. Y, como estudia Mikkel Nørregaard Jørgensen (2019), la obra de Trevino plantea una oposición radical a la idea misma de frontera en la medida en que es impensable sin violencia, prefiriendo un horizonte utópico de organización comunal.

Estos desplazamientos culturales encuentran paralelos en debates muy recientes sobre la viabilidad de las fronteras. Por un lado, ha emergido una perspectiva abolicionista, representada de manera particular por el pensador y activista Justin Akers Chacón. En su libro *The Border Crossed Us*, Chacón parte del régimen económico de la frontera a partir de parámetros similares a los que he venido discutiendo, describiendo un "North American Model of Bordered Capitalism" fundado en "new constitutions of capitalism that sanctify transnational rights for multinational capital that supersede the rights of people. In essence, so-called free trade and free markets have eliminated all borders to its movement and barriers to its circulation, creating a supra-economy for capital that operates in opposite manner to the bordered and restricted world of labor" (2021: 9). Informado por el pensamiento anarquista y sindicalista, Chacón entiende que la separación fronteriza no es tanto una separación de culturas o ciudadanías, sino parte de "an unmasked form of class warfare, in which a new transnational architecture has been forged out of the intensification of imperialist extraction and labor exploitation in order to augment and extend methods of capital accumulation" (2021: 9). En consecuencia, Chacón propone un modelo de solidaridad socialista y lucha de clases orientado hacia la abolición fronteriza: "The growth of a new and generational socialist and anticapitalist left, rooted in working-class struggle and broad support for the necessity to replace capitalism with socialism, shows the possibility for envisioning and realizing a world without borders in our lifetimes" (2021: 235). El horizonte utópico de Chacón corresponde al de Trevino, imaginando el espacio binacional como punto de partida de una abolición de fronteras que pueda dar lugar a un futuro que termine con la violencia y la explotación laboral necesaria para sustentar la frontera. Por esta razón, la noción de hibridez cultural y de zona intermedia que avanzan los estudios fronterizos tradicionales es interpretada desde esta perspectiva como un elemento superestructural que limita la imaginación emancipatoria de un mundo sin fronteras.

Un modelo alternativo es el que propone Paulina Ochoa Espejo en *On Borders* (2020). Más que sumarse a la presuposición de la frontera como inherentemente violenta, la politóloga mexicana radicada en Estados Unidos propone un modelo de soberanía territorial que sustituye el modelo de "Desert Island" basado en la identificación de territorio con identidad, a un modelo que llama "Watershed", que garantiza los derechos y la administración del territorio como lugar, sin importar la identidad de sus ocupantes. Ochoa Espejo argumenta que las fronteras son necesarias por que la delimitación territorial es la base de cualquier orden político liberal que garantiza las libertades individuales y el estado de derecho (2020: 168), pero argumenta que dichos derechos pueden concederse igualmente independientemente de la identidad nacional o étnica de los ocupantes. Este modelo imagina una suerte de institucionalización binacional, y global, de un régimen de soberanías plurales entre las cuales cualquier persona pueda viajar en libertad, pero debe participar también de los deberes cívicos de su lugar de ubicación (2020: 248). Si, como propone el filósofo Thomas Nail, la migración suscita una kinopolítica entendida como un orden social definido por sus "regimes of motion" (2015: 24), los modelos políticos propuestos por Chacón y por Ochoa Espejo pueden leerse básicamente como formas (distintas y hasta opuestas entre sí) de organizar órdenes sociales donde el movimiento sea parte integral del orden social y no un elemento desterritorializante al que hay que limitar por medio del aparato securitario.

La estética que se manifiesta dentro de estos cuadrantes en torno a la libertad y la política del movimiento permite vislumbrar las posibilidades literarias de un espacio binacional cuyo centro no es la frontera, sino una imaginación cada vez más integrada y difuminada en los territorios de ambos países. No es casual que en las últimas dos décadas hayan emergido textos literarios en ambos lados de la frontera que reactivan la *road narrative* estadounidense, un género ostensiblemente de formación atado en particular al *Bildung* de subjetividades masculinas blancas. Indudablemente, *On the Plain of Snakes*, donde Theroux viaja con el privilegio del pasaporte norteamericano y la inmunidad que le garantiza su raza y ciudadanía a lo largo de México y lo ancho de la línea fronteriza cae allí. Sin embargo, Theroux es mucho más inteligente que sus precursores. Consciente de su punto de partida invoca a Jack Kerouac y su declaración de haber encontrado "the magic land at the end of the road" al cruzar a México (2019: 4; Kerouac 2003 [1957]: 276). Theroux contrasta esta perspectiva describiéndose como un sujeto invisible y disminuido: "But leaving home for Mexico when I feel peculiarly ignored and weakened in status is not sad and lamentable. It is the way of the world" (2019: 4). Desde esta perspectiva, Theroux describe México con gran sofisticación y sabiduría, en buena medida porque su libro está construido como una polémica en contra de dos tradiciones literarias: la anglófona (Waugh, Lawrence, Greene, Kerouac) incapaz de capturar a México por su presuposición de supremacía cultural frente al país y su perspectiva exoticista y racista, y la mexicana (Carlos Fuentes, Octavio Paz), que nunca le parece a la altura del país. El libro logra capturar mucho de México en este nuevo contexto binacional precisamente porque busca escribirse a contrapelo de las tradiciones de representación simbólica que han constituido la división y diferencia entre Estados Unidos y México.

VII

Por supuesto, uno debe anotar aquí que el libro más exitoso en esta vertiente es *Lost Children Archive* (2019), de Valeria Luiselli, escrito originalmente en inglés y beneficiario de una atención mediática y crítica sin precedentes para una novela mexicana en el campo estadounidense. No me voy a detener en particular en la novela, en interés de concluir este ensayo reflexionando sobre textos menos conocidos y estudiados. Pero conviene mencionar que las lecturas más sustanciales de la novela presentan un cierto grado de escepticismo al juego central de la novela: un texto altamente autoficcional (y en ello alineado tanto a la prosa literaria dominante en las editoriales independientes de la literatura estadounidense como a un boom del género en Latinoamérica, influido sin duda por la escritura en inglés) que opta por narrar no la experiencia migrante directa, sino la posición de la autora como figura incapaz de dar cuenta de su posición como migrante legal en un país donde se encarcela y desaparece a los migrantes indocumentados. La clave de la novela es su recurso a la erudición, lleno de copiosas citas de la alta literatura que filtran y evaden el trauma de confrontación directa con la violencia así como la posibilidad del modo testimonial que suele ser más común en la prosa política latinoamericana.

Es fácil entender porque opta Luiselli por esta vía. Si Luiselli hubiese impostado la voz de una migrante centroamericana, hubiera sido acusada con mucha facilidad de impostación y de explotación del tema—que por otra parte ya había explorado en un libro testimonial en el que se constituye como entrevistadora de niños en los centros de detención de migrantes (Luiselli 2017). Por otro lado, la autoficción y el diálogo con la tradición literaria sin duda demuestra una alineación de Luiselli con varios proyectos de escritura en la prosa literaria norteamericana (al lado de autores como Tao Lin o Maggie Nelson) y en la literatura mundial (W.G. Sebald, Emmanuel Carrère, etc.), lo cual explica en parte la amplia resonancia de su libro. Moraña, apreciando más el estilo transcultural de Yuri Herrera y Fernanda Melchor, expresa una fuerte crítica a esta apuesta literaria, mostrando irritación ante su "discursividad escrituraria" basada en la reiteración de recursos literarios del modernismo anglosajón y el uso de una autoficción que "es demasiado intensa e inclina el balance de la narración hacia la centralidad autorial, supeditando a ésta la cuestión temática" (2021b: 427–428). Moraña concluye con fuerza:

seducidos por el *pathos* elegiaco que atraviesa la historia americana, los intelectuales registran y acumulan esos eventos traduciéndolos en discurso y archivo, guiados por una propensión historicista que sea justa en la recuperación y el ordenamiento del dato, en sus repercusiones estéticas y en su valor como materia prima pasible de ser elaborada como literatura o como discurso auditivo. Escritura y oralidad convergen en el archivo que la clase media intelectual venera como monumentalización de la pérdida y, quizá, de la culpa. (2021b: 428–429)

Para Moraña, el carácter calculado y distante de la ficción de Luiselli termina entonces por disolver las cuestiones políticas y críticas en la autoficción.

En la crítica académica estadounidense, estos mismos mecanismos son leídos desde una perspectiva que los valora de manera más positiva. Valentina Montero Román, por ejemplo, argumenta que el archivo en Luiselli permite desplegar "its fragmentation, recombinant and recursive organization, and narrative multiplicity as a way to demonstrate the complexity and irreducibility of the refugee crisis and the constructions of Latinx difference that develop alongside it" (2021: 168). Esto, continúa Román, permite a Luiselli desarrollar un "thematic focus on archival exploration as a means for exploring the relationship between racialization and archival precarity" lo cual, a su vez, convierte la evocación formal del archiva en "a tool for confronting the challenges of telling a knotty, unending story of racialized removals" (2021: 169–170). Patricia Stuelke por su parte identifica en la novela el problema de que la violencia a la que se enfrentan los niños migrantes "seems to exceed the narrative capacity of any of the forms at Luiselli's disposal: the road novel, but also the legal intake form, the essay and autoficción, all forms Luiselli experimented with over the course of writing the novel" (2021: 44). Así, Stuelke sugiere interpretar a la novela como "a response to the creeping intimacy of literary life with settler colonial surveillance capitalism in the 'age of Amazon'" fundada en el "reenactment" tanto de la *road novel* masculina como de la fantasía infantil de la cultura indígena ("playing Indian"). Esto, concluye Stuelke, resulta "in exploring the degree to which child play across sovereign difference might oppose the brutal bureaucratic violence of the xenophobic carceral settler state, the novel builds a critique of the frontier road novel fantasy that it cannot quite sustain" (2021: 45).

Tanto Montero Morán como Stuelke, más allá de sus diferencias en la valoración del libro, reconocen en *Los Children Archive* una suerte de mirada disruptiva posibilitada por la mirada construida que a Moraña le parece excesivamente artificial. Así, identifican en ella no tanto una autoficción que supera el tema representado, sino una escritura consciente de los límites de los marcos representacionales y genéricos que ella misma despliega, en un momento donde la gran tragedia migratoria no puede narrarse directamente, en parte por la precariedad simbólica de las subjetividades desposeídas por el aparato securitario (la postura de Montero

Morán) y en parte por el vaciamiento mismo de la política de la imaginación literaria en la era de la tecnologización (como plantea Stuelke en diálogo con la sociología de la era de Amazon de Mark McGurl [2021]). Esto hace eco de un fenómeno que ha definido la obra de Luiselli desde que comenzó su circulación en inglés, una muy notable diferencia entre lecturas generalmente negativas en México y en el medio de habla hispana, y una valoración mucho más positiva en inglés.

Reflexionando sobre esto, Cheyla Rose Samuelson lee en la divergencia crítica de Luiselli la necesidad de constituir una crítica literaria transnacional que rompa con las idiosincrasias nacionales y regionales que surgen de tradiciones específicas para satisfacer "the necessity of a critical approach that incorporates an understanding to the multiple points of origin that converge in her texts" (2021: 192). Esta diferencia plantea bien las irregularidades del terreno literario binacional, donde la estética de Luiselli encuentra mejor acomodo en el ámbito de la lengua inglesa representando una perspectiva mexicana que es mucho más disruptiva en los Estados Unidos que en su tradición de origen. Claramente, lecturas como la de Stuelke muestran que la posición de exterioridad de Luiselli vis-á-vis las tradiciones nucleares de la literatura del excepcionalismo estadounidense acarrean gran parte de su poder crítico. Esto también es reconocido, de manera distinta por Moraña: "La tensión muy notoria entre exterioridad y cultura nacional no está resuelta en Luiselli, y éste es, a mi juicio, uno de sus puntos de interés" (2021b: 15). Luiselli permite vislumbrar, aún en su tranquilidad dentro de ciertos registros del campo literario neoliberal, una literatura operativamente binacional, pero no fronteriza, definida no por la síntesis entre dos imaginarios nacionales, sino por la consistente incomodidad que los imaginarios de la región ejercen entre sí.

VIII

Otro libro de interés, pero mucho menos visitado por la crítica, es *Ahora me rindo y eso es todo* (2018) de Álvaro Enrigue. La crítica de *Lost Children Archive* ha omitido la discusión del texto de Enrigue a pesar de que están conectados abiertamente: el viaje que Luiselli ficcionaliza forma también parte, con menos ficcionalización de la novela de Enrigue, y las referencias a los Apaches en Luiselli son el tema central de Enrigue. De hecho, ninguno de los textos sobre Luiselli aquí citados hace referencia a ella. *Ahora me rindo y eso es todo* narra la historia de la captura de Gerónimo y la derrota de la Apachería frente a las tropas mexicanas y estadounidenses en la frontera del siglo XIX, con paréntesis refiriendo el viaje de investigación que Enrigue realizó con su familia. Esta omisión tiene dos posibles razones. Por un lado, puede ser mero desconocimiento de la novela de Enrigue, que no se publicó en inglés, y ha tenido una circulación relativamente modesta. También es enteramente posible que al explotar el éxito de Luiselli, algunos críticos hayan razonablemente decidido no opacar el triunfo de una autora con la referencia a su excompañero. De cualquier modo, las conexiones personales pueden ser dejadas de lado, para dar lugar al hecho de que Enrigue, un autor con una trayectoria importante en la literatura mexicana, ha también participado en la configuración de una estética binacional.

Literariamente, *Ahora me rindo y eso es todo* activa a contrapelo otro género literario del excepcionalismo estadounidense, el Western. Claro conocedor de la literatura del siglo XIX, Enrigue despliega su novela entremezclando el discurso de la ley y el orden del Western, encarnado en el teniente coronel José María Zuloaga, encargado de la persecución de Gerónimo, y el tropo latinoamericano de la cautiva, que, como estudió Susana Rotker (1999), juega un rol central en las narrativas fundantes del conflicto entre los estados-nación y los pueblos indígenas. La intervención de Enrigue opera no tanto en un archivo consciente de su insuficiencia, como en Luiselli, sino, de una manera quizá más clásica, en la articulación totalizante de la novela que excede formalmente los recursos genéricos que la constituyen. Dicho de otro modo, si Luiselli, como sugiere Stuelke, pone en escena los límites del *road novel* y la autoficción al dar cuenta del excedente de la historia que busca narrar, Enrigue da cuenta de la insuficiencia del Western como mecanismo fundante ofreciendo una narrativa mucho más vasta y compleja que finca en la novelización una capacidad imaginativa que reemplaza los huecos del archivo. Estos huecos se manifiestan en los paréntesis autorreflexivos (no estrictamente autoficcionales) en los que Enrigue guía al lector sobre los límites de su propia investigación. Podría decirse que es una novela que opera más en la fe en la ficción como mecanismo de memoria crítica que caracterizó el boom de novelas históricas latinoamericanas de los años sesenta a ochenta del siglo XX que la narrativa precarizada y autoficcional del siglo XXI.

IX

Recorriendo de sur a norte, *Yerba americana* (2008) de Pablo Soler Frost plantea una alternativa distinta al *road novel* binacional. Soler Frost es un autor respetado de libros eruditos, y esta novela es anómala en su producción, aunque escrita con la sofisticación y oficio literario de sus otros, muy distintos, libros. La novela tiene un origen peculiar, ya que la historia fue originalmente escrita para el guión del filme *40 días* (Juan Carlos Martín 2008). En otra parte he discutido ese filme como parte de un nuevo grupo de *road movies* relacionadas con el capitalismo avanzado en México (Sánchez Prado 2016). Soler Frost decide novelizar el guión, lo cual lleva al libro. Los protagonistas son dos hombres, Andrés y Pato, y una mujer llamada Ecuador, quienes negocian sus relaciones de amistad y deseo en el contexto de un viaje por carretera, que inicia de la Ciudad de México hacia Real de Catorce, cruza la frontera, recorre las zonas post-industriales hasta llegar a Nueva York, para después ir hacia el Oeste y concluir en la tierra del pueblo Navajo.

En una lectura muy detenida de la novela, Paul Goldberg (2013) la conecta tanto con una larga tradición de narrativas de viaje de mexicanos a los Estados Unidos, así como con su clara filiación a Kerouac y con José Agustín. Proponiendo una reelaboración del *ethos* de la contracultura de los años sesenta actualizado a un presente definido, podría decirse, por su derrota, Soler Frost opta por una narrativa fragmentaria, en estampas, con discontinuidades, enmarcada por referencialidades culturales contradictorias. Por ejemplo, las secciones del libro se titula "Soul," "Country," y "Blues," pero los capítulos de cada sección están extraídos, respectivamente, de la poesía de Gustavo Adolfo Bécquer, Rubén Darío y Amado Nervo. Contraposición de Latinoamérica con Estados Unidos, de dos modernidades en temporalidades distintas, pero ambas presentes y anacrónicas, *40 días* es quizá una de las formalizaciones más inteligentes y acertadas de la estética kinopolítica que permite vislumbrar la binacionalidad en su carácter precario, en su extensión territorial, en los fantasmas y fragmentos que la definen. Notablemente, es una narrativa del cruce fronterizo que evade la centralización de la migración documentada, permitiendo, en esa elección estratégica, la centralización de la mirada narrativa en el espacio de los Estados Unidos como imperio en decadencia.

Yerba americana tiene diferencias estilísticas y estructurales considerables con *Lost Children Archive* y *Ahora me rindo y eso es todo*. No mantiene el recurso al archivo ni la experimentación modernista de Luiselli, y está en las antípodas de la ambición expansiva y totalizante de Enrigue. Pero es, a la vez, un texto precursor de estas novelas en ambos aspectos, algo que se ha omitido por la escasa atención que se le ha prestado al trabajo de Soler Frost. Sin embargo, el patrón trazado por el viaje de sus personajes, de Nueva York a la zona Navajo (es decir, del centro urbano del imperio a la cultura indígena) se encuentra ya formulado en esa novela. Asimismo, Soler Frost apela, como hace Luiselli unos años después, a su propio archivo cultural —una mezcla de cultura del rock y del jazz con referencias a la alta literatura y otras artes— como marco de lectura e interpretación de un corazón de las tinieblas norteamericano. En la geografía de Soler Frost, quizá más amplia en su recorrido que las otras novelas, aunque su descripción sea más parca, Estados Unidos aparece en las ruinas de la catástrofe de Katrina, la desolación de la industria del Sur, las marcas de su historia de violencia. *Yerba americana* traza así una mirada donde las subjetividad y perspectiva de sus personajes, en tránsito temporal y no en migración, crea distintos subrayados y énfasis de la intermitente relación entre ambos países.

X

Para concluir este ensayo, quiero traer a colación un último libro de recorrido binacional, que presenta una perspectiva distinta de la mirada estadounidense sobre México, para cerrar el círculo abierto al principio con Paul Theroux. Como mencioné anteriormente, Theroux es parte de una tradición de autores anglosajones que han buscado representar a México en su escritura literaria, pero su libro *On the Plain of Snakes* se funda en el rechazo de esa tradición. Incluso un muestrario básico sobre el tema, como el que se encuentra en la antología *Gringos in Mexico* de Edward Simmen (1988), denota una complicada mezcla de fascinación, exotización y rechazo de la que Theroux busca separarse. La lucidez y los límites de Theroux en sus interpretaciones de un México de enorme complejidad cultural y marcado por la relación con los Estados Unidos se posibilitan claramente por la manera en que ser un estadounidense blanco le abre puertas y le concede un cierto grado de inmunidad en su viaje, algo que él reconoce, pero que es sin duda patente para cualquiera que vea la facilidad con la que circula incluso en territorios que han sido acechados por el conflicto y la violencia. La experiencia de Theroux se contrasta con la de la antes mencionada Stephanie Elizondo Griest.

Griest es una escritora nacida en Corpus Christi, Texas, de origen mixto—hija de un estadounidense y una mexicana. Tras buscar una experiencia cosmopolita que la llevó a los países del bloque comunista, y a escribir su libro *Around the Bloc* (2004), Griest viaja a México a explorar sus raíces mexicanas. Mostrando claramente el oficio periodístico de Griest, el libro mantiene un equilibrio entre el género norteamericano de la *memoir* y la crónica, lo cual le permite, entre otras cosas, atestiguar los levantamientos de maestros en Oaxaca, conversar con activistas políticos y enfrentar a la policía fronteriza. Las lecturas más a profundidad del libro han enfatizado, correctamente a mi parecer, la definición en el proceso del viaje, de una identidad chicana y mexicana. María Antonia Oliver-Rotger (2016) apunta que la experiencia bicultural de Griest no le permite escapar algunos tropos que limitan la perspectiva estadounidense sobre México, como la fascinación turística con ciertos detalles o las marcas de blanquitud en su interacción con el contexto mexicano. Sin embargo, Oliver-Rotger también valora el hecho de que

Griest no tiene la mirada de superioridad cultural característica de otros viajeros anglos, debido a su "self-consciousness as a doubly marginal subject ('Mexican' in the U.S.; 'American' in Mexico)", lo cual "leads her to approach multiple discursive formations and the diasporic history/ies behind them to her position as an 'ethnic' subject in the United States, as well as to her position as an American tourist, reporter, or ethnographer in Mexico (2016: 125–126).

Por su parte, la crítica Melissa Castillo Planas (2020a), también de identidad birracial blanca-mexicana, debate con la birracialidad de Griest en un ensayo autoetnográfico, argumentando la importancia de adoptar una identidad atada a la idea de "Latinidad" que Griest nunca reivindica. Más allá de las políticas que subyacen las distintas opciones de identificación étnica, Planas, hija de la distinguida profesora de literatura mexicana Debra Castillo y autora de un excelente estudio sobre la cultura mexicana en Nueva York (2020b), traza en dialéctica con Griest vías paralelas de recorrer una binacionalidad definida por el carácter diaspórico y expandido de la idea de ser mexicana en ambos países.

La preponderancia de ficciones y crónicas de recorrido carretero, sumado a los debates intensos sobre la naturaleza política y cultural de la frontera México y Estados Unidos permiten, como he intentado trazar aquí, plantear formas de pensamiento de la cultura post-global, en la cual ese sueño de planetarización por el capital y por la desterritorialización tiende hacia una reterritorrialización que ya no es del todo la del estado nación. La integración mexicana ha difuminado lógicas que se habían pensado como fronterizas por mucho tiempo. Así, la cartografía geocultural del espacio México-Estados Unidos, producto de una integración desigual y tensa, ha expandido tanto las lógicas de hibridez y creatividad del pensamiento del Gran México, como el espacio de batalla transnacional del que habla Yépez en una forma de existir, pensar, escribir e imaginar que define cada vez más la vida de los habitantes de Norteamérica. En ese espacio, quizá ya no seamos fronterizos como Vaquera Vásquez ni tengamos que preguntarnos si somos suficientemente mexicanos o estadounidenses. Es posible que la imaginación anarquista de Trevino o Chacón o, al menos, la utopía liberal de libertad de tránsito pensada por Ochoa Espejo y practicada precariamente por las narrativas kinopolíticas de la región, sean los primeros mapas de un futuro más regional que nacional.

Bibliografía

Anzaldúa, Gloria (1987): *Borderlands/La Frontera*. San Francisco: Aunt Lute.
Balibar, Etienne (2002): *Politics and the Other Scene*. Trads. Christine Jones, James Swenson and Chris Turner. Londres: Verso.

Ballester Pardo, Ignacio (2020): "Poetas en la frontera de México-Estados Unidos de América. Heriberto Yépez y Esther M. García". *Literatura mexicana*, 31, 1, pp. 99–131.
Breytenbach, Breyten (2009): *Notes from the Middle World*. Chicago: Haymarket Books.
Chakrabarty, Dipesh (2021): *The Climate of History in a Planetary Age*. Chicago: University of Chicago Press.
Chacón, Justin Akers (2021): *The Border Crossed US. The Case for Opening the US-Mexico Border*. Chicago: Haymarket.
Cummins, Jeanine (2020): *American Dirt*. Nueva York: Flatiron.
DeLoughry, Teresa (2020): *The Global Novel and Capitalism in Crisis. Contemporary Literary Narratives*. Nueva York: Palgrave MacMillan.
Emmelhainz, Irmgard (2016): "Decolonization as the Horizon of Political Action". En: *E-flux Journal*, 77, http://worker01.e-flux.com/pdf/article_76637.pdf (última visita: 30/11/2021).
Enrigue, Álvaro (2018): *Ahora me rindo y eso es todo*. Barcelona: Anagrama.
Goldberg, Paul (2013): "Reading the Road Trip in the Age of Globalization. Travel and Place in Pablo Soler Frost's *Yerba americana*". En: *Confluencia*, 28, 2, pp. 19–36.
Gómez, Alan Eladio (2016): *The Revolutionary Imaginations of Greater Mexico. Chicano/a Radicalism, Solidarity Politics and Latin American Social Movements*. Austin: University of Texas Press.
Gramlich, John/Scheller, Alissa (2021): "What's Happening at the U.S.-Mexico Border in 7 Charts". En: *Pew Research Center*. Noviembre 9, 2021, https://www.pewresearch.org/fact-tank/2021/11/09/whats-happening-at-the-u-s-mexico-border-in-7-charts/ (última visita: 27/11/2021).
Grandin, Greg (2019): *The End of the Myth. From the Frontier to the Border Wall in the Mind of America*. Nueva York: Metropolitan Books.
Graziano, Manlio (2018): *What is a Border?* Trad. Marina Korobko. Stanford: Stanford University Press.
Griest, Stephanie Elizondo (2017): *All the Agents and Saints. Dispatches from the U.S. Borderlands*. Chapel Hill: University of North Carolina Press.
—— (2008): *Mexican Enough. My Life Between the Borderlines*. Nueva York: Washington Square Press.
—— (2004): *Around the Bloc. My Life in Moscow, Beijing and Havana*. Nueva York: Villard.
Heise, Ursula K. (2008): *Sense of Place, Sense of the Planet. The Environmental Imagination of the Global*. Oxford: Oxford University Press.
Hoyos, Héctor (2015): *Beyond Bolaño. The Global Latin American Novel*. New York: Columbia University Press.
Jørgensen, Mikkel Nørregaard (2019): "Horizons Without Borders. Wendy Trevino's *Cruel Fiction* and the Utopian Poetry of the Commune". En: *Studies in Arts and Humanities*, 5, 1, pp. 49–66.
Luiselli, Valeria (2019): *Lost Children Archive*. Nueva York: Alfred A. Knopf.
—— (2016): *Los niños perdidos. Un ensayo en cuarenta preguntas*. México: Sexto Piso.
Kerouac, Jack (2003 [1957]): *On the Road*. Nueva York: Penguin.
Kinnally, Cara A. (2019): *Forgotten Futures, Colonized Pasts. Transnational Collaboration in Nineteenth-Century Greater Mexico*. Lewisburg: Bucknell University Press.
Kirsch, Adam (2016): *The Global Novel. Writing the World in the 21st Century*. Nueva York: Columbia Global Reports.

Kundera, Milan (1984): *La insoportable levedad del ser*. Trad. Fernando Valenzuela. Barcelona: Tusquets.
Limón, José E. (1999): *American Encounters. Greater Mexico, the United States and the Erotics of Culture*. Boston: Beacon Press.
Nail, Thomas (2015): *The Figure of the Migrant*. Oxford: Oxford University Press.
Mezzadra, Sandro/Nielson, Brett (2013): *Border as Method, Or, The Multiplication of Labor*. Durham: Duke University Press.
McGurl, Mark (2021): *Everything and Less. The Novel in the Age of Amazon*. Londres: Verso.
Mignolo, Walter (2000): *Local Histories/Global Designs. Coloniality, Subaltern Knowledges and Border Thinking*. Princeton: Princeton University Press.
Miller, Todd (2019): *Empire of Borders. The Expansion of the U.S. Border Around the World*. Londres: Verso.
Montero Román, Valentina (2021): "Telling Stories that Never End. Valeria Luiselli, the Refugee Crisis at the Border and the Big, Ambitious Archival Novel". En: *Genre*, 54, 2, pp. 167–192.
Moraña, Mabel (2021a): *Líneas de fuga. Ciudadanía, frontera y sujeto migrante*. Madrid: Iberoamericana Vervuert.
—— (2021b): *Nosotros los bárbaros. Tres narradores mexicanos en el siglo XXI*. México: Bonilla Artigas.
—— (ed.) (2021c): *Liquid Borders. Migration as Resistance*. Londres: Routledge.
Ochoa Espejo, Paulina (2020): *On Borders. Territories, Legitimacy & The Rights of Place*. Oxford: Oxford University Press.
Olivier-Rotger, Maria Antonia (2016): "Travel, Autoethnography and 'Cultural Schizophrenia' in Stephanie Elizondo Griest's *Mexican Enough*". En: *Interdisciplinary Literary Studies*, 18, 1, pp. 112–129.
Planas, Melissa Castillo (2020a): "Latinx Enough? Whiteness, Latinidad and Identity in Memoirs of Finding Home". En: *Prose Studies*, 41, 2, pp. 179–192.
Planas, Melissa Castillo (2020b): *A Mexican State of Mind. New York City and the Borderlands of Culture*. New Brunswick: Rutgers University Press.
Rotker, Susana (1999): *Cautivas*. Buenos Aires: Ariel.
Samuelson, Cheyla Rose (2021): "Towards a Transnational Criticism. Bridging the Mexico-US Divide on Valeria Luiselli". En: *Chasqui*, 49, 2, pp. 176–194.
Sánchez Prado, Ignacio M. (2021): "Commodifying Mexico. On *American Dirt* and the Cultural Politics of a Manufactured Bestseller". En: *American Literary History*, 33, 2, pp. 371–393.
—— (2020): "The Persistence of the Transcultural. A Latin American Theory of the Novel from the National-Popular to the Global." En: *New Literary History* 51, 2, pp. 347–374.
—— (2018): *Strategic Occidentalism. On Mexican Fiction, the Neoliberal Book Market and the Question of World Literature*. Northwestern: Northwestern University Press.
—— (2016): "Journey to the Ruins of Modernity. *Euforia* and *40 Días*". En: Garibotto, Verónica/Pérez, Jorge (eds.): *The Latin American Road Movie*. Nueva York: Palgrave, pp. 53–72.
Simmen, Edward (ed.) (1988): *Gringos in Mexico. An Anthology*. Forth Worth: Texas Christian University Press.
Stuelke, Patricia (2021): "Writing Refugee Crisis in the Age of Amazon. *Lost Children Archive*'s Reenactment Play". En: *Genre*, 54, 1, pp. 43–66.
Theroux, Paul (2019): *On the Plain of Snakes. A Mexican Journey*. Boston: Houghton Mifflin Harcourt.
Trevino, Wendy (2018): *Cruel Fiction*. Oakland: Commune Editions.

Valenzuela Arce, José Manuel (ed.) (2020): *El Gran México. Las culturas mexicanas más allá de las fronteras*. México: Universidad Autónoma Metropolitana/Gedisa.
Vaquera-Vásquez, Santiago (2019): "The Unbearable Lightness of Being Fronterizo. Reflections on Border Crossing". En: *Ex-Centric Narratives. Journal of Anglophone Literature, Culture and Media*, 3, pp. 136–50.
Winslow, Don (2019): *The Border*. Nueva York: William Morrow.
— (2015): *The Cartel*. Nueva York: Alfred A. Knopf.
— (2005): *The Power of the Dog*. Nueva York: Knopf.
~~Yépez, Heriberto~~ (2017): *Transnational Battle Field*. Oakland: Commune Editions.
Zavala, Oswaldo (2022): "Neoliberalism, Distinction and World Literature in the Twenty-First Century". En: Sánchez Prado, Ignacio M. (ed.): *Mexican Literature as World Literature*. Nueva York: Bloomsbury.
— (2018): *Los cárteles no existen. Narcotráfico y literatura en México*. Mexico: Malpaso.

www.ingramcontent.com/pod-product-compliance
Lightning Source LLC
Chambersburg PA
CBHW020224170426
43201CB00007B/308